WAR IN THE RUINS

Edward G. Longacre

WAR
IN THE
RUINS

The American Army's
Final Battle Against
Nazi Germany

WESTHOLME
Yardley

Frontispiece: GIs of the 100th Infantry Division running through the bombed-out streets of Heilbronn, Germany, in April 1945. Germany would surrender three weeks after the end of the unexpectedly fierce battle for this city. (*National Archives*)

Westholme Publishing, LLC
904 Edgewood Road
Yardley, Pennsylvania 19067

ISBN: 978-1-59416-117-9

Printed in the United States of America.

In memory of my cousin
S1c Raymond Mehlbaum, USNR,
lost in the sinking of the USS *Indianapolis*, July 1945

And dedicated to the soldiers of the
100th Infantry Division, living and dead, who fought to
make the world a safer place for generations to come.

"In combat you saw life and death, youth and old age, and you had the feeling that you knew all there was to be learned in the world, and you knew it instinctively, and no matter what you read in books from here on out, it could never do more than confirm what you already knew."

—*Frank L. Gurley, A Company, 399th Infantry Regiment*

CONTENTS

List of Maps

FOREWORD

WHEN you view their photographs from France and Germany, the first thing that strikes you is how impossibly young they look. Although they wear the unit patch of the 100th Infantry ("Century") Division on their shoulder, you cannot believe they are soldiers—these are kids, eighteen- and nineteen-year-olds fresh from their senior proms or with, at most, a year of college under their belt. In fact, they were kids, but soldiers as well. Thrown into the cauldron during the last six months of the fighting in the European theater of operations, they were forced to grow up with violent suddenness. By the time they were twenty— if they made it that far—they had gone through an aging process that can best be described as shattering.

Beginning the first week in November 1944, these GIs of the 100th Division—not only the beardless draftees but their West Point-trained officers and Regular Army noncoms as well—experienced hell on earth for hours, days, and weeks at a time. To sustain life on a battlefield abounding in horrors, they burrowed deep into the earth, huddling in holes barely large enough to hold them and their equipment. There they remained for interminable stretches, braving not only the rigors of combat but weather almost as likely to inflict bodily harm: bone-numbing cold, icy rains, and day-long snow showers. When conditions permitted, they gulped down rations that nourished the body but all too often caused diarrhea and constipation. They lived not only without basic comforts but in shockingly unsanitary conditions, unable to cleanse hands and feet, going weeks without a shower or a change of clothing, at times forced to relieve themselves within a few yards of their subterranean habitations—if not in them. Results included frequent bouts of hepatitis (sometimes called "yellow jaundice"), trench foot, and dysentery.

Every day the division was on the line, death lurked and often beckoned. The boys-turned-men endured sniper rounds, the strafing of Luftwaffe fighters, 88-mm howitzer barrages, blasts of *panzerfaust* (bazookas) and *nebelwerfer* (rocket-propelled artillery), and Mauser rifle and semiautomatic Schmeisser "burp gun" fire. When able to leave their holes, they sloshed through an especially sticky species of mud and passed through woods so dense they blotted out the sky, hoping that artillery-induced "tree bursts" did not bring trunks, limbs, or razor-like splinters crashing down on them. Ordered out on patrol, they crossed terrain infested with barbed wire, tripwire-activated hand grenades, and a variety of unseen weapons, including the omnipresent Schu mine, which, when trod upon even gingerly, could blow off a man's foot or part of his leg.

That anyone managed to survive this rich assortment of terrors—and many more survived than succumbed to them—is a tribute not only to the shepherding skills of their officers, especially those of their division commander, Maj. Gen. Withers A. Burress, but also to the survival skills they had acquired during an extended period of training in the United States. For months after being activated at Fort Jackson, South Carolina, in November 1942, the Century Division was known, rather derisively, as a show unit, its people regularly put through combat simulations for the benefit of War Department dignitaries, visiting Allied leaders, manufacturers whom the army wished to court, and ROTC cadets. In June 1944, dozens of Centurymen joined a one-thousand-man contingent that marched through the streets of New York City to publicize a war-loan drive.

By the time the GIs paraded up Broadway, America's involvement in the war was already two and a half years old. Widely circulating rumors had it that the 100th Division would never go overseas. But events on the other side of the world dictated otherwise:

only days before the war-loan exhibition, U.S., British, Canadian, and Free French troops had brought the war to Europe by invading northern France on D-Day. Three months later, the Centurymen received their long-overdue deployment orders. Days later they were crossing the Atlantic in troopships bound for a second invasion site on the Continent, this along the French Riviera.

The division should have been ready for what followed, for by October 1944, it had undergone three separate training periods. The first had taken place at Fort Jackson and other Southern installations. The second, which ran from November 1943 to January 1944, involved maneuvers in the Cumberland Mountains of eastern Tennessee that would stand the command in good stead when it began maneuvering through the High Vosges mountain chain of northeastern France. The third regimen commenced soon afterward at Fort Bragg, North Carolina, and extended until the unit's shipment overseas. The extra training had been made necessary by the wholesale departure of troops originally assigned to the Century but now needed overseas as replacements for units that had seen debilitating combat in North Africa, in Sicily, and on the Italian mainland. By March 1944, the division had lost several thousand recruits by transfer to combat-ready units, 20 percent of the command's original strength.

The losses were made good, in large measure, by an influx of recruits fresh from college-based training courses as part of the recently terminated Army Specialized Training Program (ASTP). This program, begun two years earlier, had been designed to teach recruits and draftees who had scored high on IQ and general aptitude tests how to become engineers, foreign language experts, and medical personnel. Other replacements came to the division after being forcibly washed out of fighter-pilot and antiaircraft-artillery training. The need for riflemen in the critical months of fighting that lay ahead was undeniable. Even so, the erstwhile ASTPs were understandably upset at having their military education unceremoniously ended in the apparent interest of stockpiling cannon fodder. Nor were they happy to be handed over to regulars, espe-

cially drill sergeants, who treated them with undisguised con-
tempt. Convinced that their new charges were pampered elitists,
the regulars determined to demolish their sense of superiority
through training of the harshest, most demanding stripe. In the
end, however, those who observed their progress with an objective
eye came to view the whiz kids as worthy additions to the division.
As befit their high intelligence, they learned, with commendable
speed, not only the basics of service life but the crucial nuances
that went far toward ensuring survival in combat.

Though heavily represented by recruits from the Eastern
Seaboard, the Century Division drew its personnel from every state
of the Union. Undaunted by the magnitude of the task confronting
them, their officers and noncoms slowly and carefully molded this
heterogeneous mass of would-be warriors—kids from the big cities,
the suburbs, the small towns, and the farms of America—into a
remarkably effective fighting force. Within a month of reaching the
front, these newcomers to the European theater had pierced the
Germans' Winter Line, a venerable defensive position that had
been the unattained objective of attackers since the first century
BC. After muscling its way through the High Vosges, the division
attacked and nearly breached the vaunted Maginot Line that even
the Germans, when conquering France in the summer of 1940, had
been unable to overrun. In mid-December 1944, the Century was
suddenly ordered on the defensive in response to German dictator
Adolf Hitler's surprise attack in the Ardennes region of eastern
France, Belgium, and Luxembourg. When the Wehrmacht struck
farther south the following month in a second counteroffensive,
Operation Nordwind, the division became the only component of
the U.S. Seventh Army to hold its original position, although many
of its units were surrounded, cut off, and nearly annihilated. Finally
returned to an offensive posture in mid-March, the 100th captured
the French citadel of Bitche, another objective assaulted by many
armies over the centuries but never carried. Then it was full speed
ahead through the French province of Alsace, driving the rapidly
retreating enemy to and across the Rhine River into the German
heartland.

By this point, the vaunted Siegfried Line having been broken, the war in Europe appeared to be in its final stage. But then resistance to the Century's push stiffened along the east bank of the Neckar River in bomb-shattered Heilbronn. In that seven-hundred-year-old city, a major industrial and communications center still operating for the benefit of the German war machine, Hitler's subordinates had battened down for a last-ditch stand that for sheer ferocity would exceed anything the now-battle-hardened "Sons of Bitche" had thus far experienced. Here at Heilbronn, the stage was set for a showdown on which hinged the success of the Allied effort in a critical sector of the European theater. And here, too, the skill, strength, and tenacity these Centurymen had acquired during five months of almost continuous combat would be put to the ultimate test.

The sometimes-tortuous road that had brought the 100th Infantry Division to this critical juncture, and the fiery completion of that journey, have never received historical attention commensurate with the value of the division's contributions to the Allies' triumph in Europe. This book is an attempt to redress that oversight.

(Editorial Note: All quoted material has been rendered verbatim. In some instances, however, essential punctuation has been added and grammatical lapses have been corrected in the interest of promoting clarity.)

The 100th Infantry Division in Europe, 1944–45.

TABLE OF ORGANIZATION

100TH INFANTRY DIVISION
(November 1942–January 1946)

397th Infantry Regiment

1st Battalion	2nd Battalion	3rd Battalion
A, B, C, D	E, F, G, H	I, K, L, M companies

398th Infantry Regiment

1st Battalion	2nd Battalion	3rd Battalion
A, B, C, D	E, F, G, H	I, K, L, M companies

399th Infantry Regiment

1st Battalion	2nd Battalion	3rd Battalion
A, B, C, D	E, F, G, H	I, K, L M companies

(Divisional Artillery)

373rd Field Artillery Battalion (155 mm howitzers)

374th Field Artillery Battalion (105 mm)

375th Field Artillery Battalion (105 mm)

925th Field Artillery Battalion (105 mm)

325th Engineer Battalion

325th Medical Battalion

Special Troops Battalion

100th Cavalry Reconnaissance Troop

100th Quartermaster Company

100th Signal Company

800th Ordnance Company

100th Military Police Platoon

The town of Wingen-sur-Moder in Alsace, France, was retaken by German forces during Operation Nordwind. Here, artillery bursts mark the beginning of an American counterattack in early January 1945. (*National Archives*)

ONE

NORTH WIND

As midnight approached on December 31, 1944, snow began to fall on the American soldiers of the 100th Infantry Division hunkered down around the medieval town of Bitche in northeastern France. In the eyes of some of the GIs, the weather evoked nostalgia, a real white Christmas like the popular Bing Crosby song played constantly on Armed Forces radio. "At home, the setting would have been perfect," one soldier recalled. "There was a greeting-card touch in the dancing snowflakes, the icicle burdened trees, the red-tiled farm buildings cloaked in holiday coats of white."[1]

Those who could avoid direct exposure to the weather—the fortunate few who were able to sleep under a roof rather than in one of the hastily dug foxholes or slit trenches that pocked the countryside—maintained a frame of mind in keeping with the season. Nineteen-year-old Pvt. Bernard S. Miller Jr. of G Company, 399th Infantry Regiment, stationed near Hottviller, four miles northwest of Bitche, saw nothing that would interfere with his outfit's celebration of the approaching new year. The headquarters of Miller's platoon had been set up in a barn in which the native of Nameoki, Illinois, enjoyed warmth, food, and a feather bed (which he shared, however, with three buddies). Yet these were temporary comforts; in a day or so, Miller and his comrades would rotate back into the one- and two-man holes that topped a windswept ridge whose forward slope supported an outpost. But for the moment, the war was outside.[2]

Others in the division, exposed to the elements, did not share Miller's rosy view. Twenty-year-old John M. Khoury, whose L Company of the 399th was posted outside Lemberg, four miles southwest of Bitche, entertained gloomy thoughts as the old year moved to a close. The Brooklyn-born private, son of Syrian immigrants, had been through two months of near-constant combat under the most trying conditions, "and I felt like a very old man. I had thought for some time that the war was never going to end. Thanksgiving and Christmas . . . had come and gone, and there was no end in sight. What was the use of fighting? We had been living in the rain and snow during one of the coldest winters in recent European history. We shivered as we trudged out on patrols, and we never felt warm. Death would not have been a bad alternative. I did not tell my thoughts to any of my buddies. Besides, we had to move out to our next battle, and I had to forget such a stupid idea."[3]

The 100th Division, nicknamed the "Century," was composed of three infantry regiments, the 397th, 398th, and 399th, four artillery battalions, and several support units. The division had been in near-constant combat in the Vosges Mountains and on the plains of Alsace-Lorraine for two months, and now, on this freezing cold New Year's Eve, found itself in an elongated, exposed position astride the Maginot Line, the vaunted, fortified barrier that had failed to stop the German invasion four years earlier. The 399th, with Lt. Col. Elery M. Zehner commanding, held the right flank of the division's position along a line running south and west of Bitche. In the division's center and rear was the 398th Infantry (Col. Robert M. Williams commanding), spread out to cover Enchenberg, Sierstal, Holbach, and Goetsenbruck; its extreme front extended from the outskirts of Bitche northwest to just beyond the village of Urbach. The division's left flank, which stretched as far west as the hamlet of Rimling, eight miles from Bitche, and which encompassed such towns as Bettviller,

Holbach, Petit Rederching, Rohrbach, and Guising, was guarded by Lt. Col. John M. King's 397th Infantry. The regiments' areas of operations overlapped to a certain extent, as elements of both the 397th and 399th occupied Hottviller and Holbach.[4]

Pvt. Thomas O. Jelks of Baltimore, Maryland, a machine gunner in M Company, the heavy-weapons unit of the 397th's 3rd Battalion, recalled the last night of 1944 as the worst of his military career: "It was cold and snowing and the temperature was way below freezing. . . . The ammo belts on my [heavy, water-cooled] machinegun had gotten wet and frozen stiff and with that the gun would not function." Jelks had to pry the frozen belt out of the gun and replace it with a fresh can of ammunition. The weapon's supply of coolant threatened to freeze as well, but it was far too cold to resort to a popular expedient when fluid was scarce or ineffective: pissing into the gun's coolant jacket.

Forced to remain in a foxhole just west of Rimling, Jelks had to summon every survival skill he had learned during three years in the Maryland National Guard and two months of combat in Europe. To endure the falling snow and biting winds he had wrapped himself in layers of clothing: long johns, a wool shirt, a sweater, field jacket and pants, heavy gloves. A white parka with a fur liner covered his helmet, while two pairs of heavy woolen ski stockings were tucked into his combat boots. Most of his comrades encased their feet in rubber-soled, leather-topped, felt-lined boots known as "shoepacks," which permitted greater room for one's toes and promoted mobility across frozen earth, but Jelks's feet were too small to fit comfortably into them. Going without shoepacks may have saved him from frozen feet or trench foot, each of which had claimed dozens of victims within his battalion. The cramped fit of socks and boots forced Jelks to remove his footwear quite often, "and when I did I changed socks each time and pinned the wet socks inside my jacket where they would dry out and warm up for the next change."

But the weather had taken a toll: Jelks was fighting a fever and a persistent cough—the onset of walking pneumonia. Ordinarily his condition would have sent him to the battalion aid station, but every man who was able was needed at the front. Another reason Jelks remained on the line was the loyalty he felt toward his company's commanding officer, who was known for looking after his men. For the past several days, the captain had visited the front carrying a bottle of whiskey, "giving everyone who wanted it a small shot in our canteen cups. I sure wanted it," Jelks recalled. "I don't know where he got the whiskey, but he was great for sharing it with us."5

Jelks's superior might have been expected to make the same gesture this evening, New Year's Eve, but when he made his rounds at 6 p.m., he came empty-handed. He delivered instead the first news Jelks had heard of the enemy offensive to the north. On December 16, Adolf Hitler had sent three German armies, two of them armored, to attack Allied forces in the heavily wooded Ardennes region of northeastern France, Belgium, and Luxembourg. The fierce assault fell heavily on advance units of the U.S. First Army, part of Lt. Gen. Omar N. Bradley's 12th Army Group.

The offensive had come as a rude surprise to Bradley's superior, Gen. Dwight D. Eisenhower, the supreme Allied commander, especially since it had followed a series of enemy reverses that seemed likely to permit a rapid advance across the Rhine River into the heart of the Fatherland. Several First Army units were overwhelmed and surrounded, including the green 106th Infantry Division, most of which was forced to surrender. But the attackers lost ground to spirited counterattacks as well as to an acute shortage of fuel for the Panther and Tiger tanks that had spearheaded the drive. Although the penetration created a gigantic bulge in the 12th Army Group's line, it failed to endanger critical objectives west of the Meuse River. Word had come down from higher headquarters that a secondary attack in the Seventh Army's sector was expected at any time: "It was not known when—but it *would* happen."6

After the captain left, Jelks made sure the new gun belt and ammo can were in workable condition. Then he hunkered down behind his weapon, which pointed east across a draw that bisected an open field—a potential avenue of enemy advance—and kept his eyes glued on the dark, snow-veiled horizon.[7]

The Ardennes offensive may have struck home far to the north of the Maginot forts, but it had repercussions for the 100th Division, part of Lt. Gen. Alexander "Sandy" Patch's U.S. Seventh Army. Soon after the offensive began, Lt. Gen. George S. Patton Jr.'s Third Army, deployed on Patch's upper flank, had hastened north to reinforce beleaguered comrades and relieve besieged garrisons such as that at Bastogne, Belgium. In the wake of Patton's redeployment, Lt. Gen. Jacob L. Devers, commanding 6th Army Group at the southern end of the Allied front, had been forced to spread his resources—not only Patch's Americans but also the French First Army of Gen. Jean de Lattre de Tassigny— alarmingly thin in order to cover the ground Patton's Third Army had vacated.

The dogfaces of the Century, who held the center of the Seventh Army's line, were supported more or less closely on their left (west) flank by the 44th Infantry Division. But a gap of ten miles separated the Century from the 45th Division on its right, southeast of Bitche. To help bridge the gap, General Patch had positioned an *ad hoc* unit, Task Force Hudelson, consisting of two cavalry (light armored) squadrons, an armored infantry battalion, and supporting detachments. Made up largely of units designed to reconnoiter, not to seize or hold ground, Task Force Hudelson left the right flank of the 100th Division vulnerable. The Century Division's commander, Maj. Gen. Withers A. Burress, a graduate of the Virginia Military Institute and a veteran of three decades of army service, was troubled by the intelligence reports of pending enemy operations in his sector, which threatened to target the most vulnerable points on the Allies' southern flank.[8]

The soldiers of the 100th were alert to the rumors of increased activity opposite their front, but most were preoccupied with more immediate threats to men and weapons from the cold, and with the pending new year. "The front was quiet and the Germans were retreating from the Bulge. The word was out that the artillery would unleash a barrage to celebrate the New Year," recalled

Private Miller. Ordinarily, a shelling was sure to attract counterbattery fire, but Miller was not especially concerned. "From our outposts we had gotten a few reports of noises like motors and tanks, but it was assumed that the Germans were probably using trucks to move their troops back—if that is really what was heard. There had been some rumors of activity on the flanks of the Division but nothing official. And it was New Year's Eve and we were winning the war and all was well and we were somewhat relaxed."[9]

Regardless of how near and active the enemy might be, the 100th Division was prepared to celebrate. Near midnight, four 105-mm howitzers of Battery B, 374th Field Artillery Battalion near Rimling lobbed shells at a selected target, a warehouse inside German lines known to have been used as a barracks. Lt. Eli Fishpaw, commanding Battery B, recalled that "the rounds were no sooner on the way than we received an urgent request for Nan-Baker [normal barrage]" fire. The call was worrisome, for the object of normal barrage—directed at a preestablished target between the lines—was to cover the division's infantry units in the event of enemy attack. As Fishpaw later noted, "at 2359 on 31 December 1944, that is exactly what happened."[10]

Lieutenant Fishpaw's reference was to the first sustained thrust of a major counteroffensive that Hitler and his generals had been planning for more than a week. Designated Operation Nordwind (North Wind), the attack was designed to exploit the weaknesses in the Seventh Army's sector, which, upon Third Army's northward shift, had expanded from about 80 miles in length to more than 120. The German high command sensed an opportunity to envelop the western flank of the Seventh Army while also striking farther south toward the connecting point between the two major components of General Patch's command, the VI and XV Army corps. If driven home with force and blessed with the advantage of surprise, this thrust might do more than create a bulge in the Allied lines—it might clear northern Alsace and Lorraine of the Americans and further disrupt and divert Allied operations.

The tactical element of Nordwind—a rough compromise between competing plans drawn up by Hitler and his ranking subordinate, Field Marshal Gerd von Rundstedt, architect of the Ardennes offensive—encompassed an assault on the Saar River Valley defenses west of Rimling by a Panzer-Grenadier division and an infantry division of *Kampfgruppe* (Army Group) G, as well as an assault southwest of Bitche toward the Vosges chain by four infantry divisions from *Kampfgruppe* Oberrhein.[11]

The main effort, the Saar Valley assault, had been entrusted to Gen. Johannes von Blaskowitz, who would not, however, control the supporting operations farther east and south. This unwieldy arrangement threatened to complicate the offensive, one already burdened by the quality and quantity of the troops involved. Having waged war on the Continent for the past five years and on two fronts since Hitler's June 1941 offensive against the Soviet Union, the Wehrmacht, Germany's military establishment, was no longer the potent weapon it had been in the early days of the war when conquering Poland, Denmark, Norway, the Low Countries, and France through application of overwhelming ground and air superiority. Slow but steady attrition had ravaged virtually every German infantry formation, necessitating widespread reorganization, consolidation, and refitting.

By the close of 1944, most of the infantry units opposing the Allies in eastern France were built around the remnants of divisions that had been decimated on the western front. These somewhat-motley organizations were compromised by limited mobility. The blitzkrieg tactics of the early war period had been weakened by an insufficiency of armored units and mechanized transport—most German artillery was horse-drawn, just as during World War I. Thus the Volks-Grenadier divisions that opposed the invaders of Europe in 1944 had been designed to fight mainly on the defensive, a mission that had taken on a special urgency as the Allies neared the Rhine River and, beyond, the German homeland. Moreover, the Volks-Grenadier divisions were top-heavy with recruits who had received barely enough training to grasp the basics of soldiering.

Perhaps even more detrimental to unit efficiency, the organizational concept behind the Volks-Grenadiers and the tactics that underlay it were seriously flawed. Each of the three regiments that made up a Volks-Grenadier division consisted of two battalions, compared to the three that made up every American infantry regiment, one of which was usually held in reserve during combat operations. Thus, to cover the same frontage as a U.S. division, a Volks-Grenadier division would have to place all of its soldiers on the firing line, allowing for no reserves at all. Modern weaponry that could deliver fire at greater rate than the standard American shoulder arm (the M1 Garand semiautomatic rifle) theoretically compensated for these organizational and personnel deficiencies. However, although two out of every three German platoons were supposed to be armed with state-of-the-art assault rifles (MP-43s and MP-44s), most units had to rely on bolt-action Mausers of older pattern, which were more difficult to load and only accurate at shorter ranges. Therefore, the Volks-Grenadier concept was unable to overcome the unfavorable odds under which the Wehrmacht of 1944 labored.[12]

The only way German infantry could hope to overwhelm opposing forces of equal or greater size was by massed assault, such as the human-wave tactics they had encountered on the Russian front and those used as a last resort by their Japanese allies fighting half a world away. The German high command did not normally favor this style of warfare, but on New Year's Eve 1944, it would give it a try.

The first assaults of Operation Nordwind, launched in the fading light of late afternoon, gave no indication of what was to come. The Germans targeted A and B companies of the 399th, entrenched on the hills south of Bitche. The effort, too limited to hold any gains, was turned back by small-arms fire. Just after dark, the Germans struck again in the same area, outside the village of Reyersviller, this time in greater numbers. Heavy machine-gun fire eventually broke up the assault, but the scale of the action was ominous.[13]

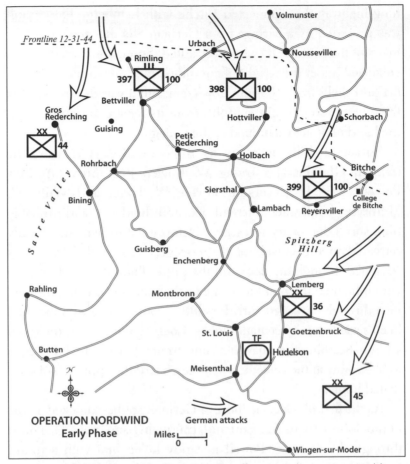

Operation Nordwind was the final German offensive in the west in World War II. The Germans attempted to exploit weaknesses in the Allied lines in eastern France following their earlier attack through the Ardennes—the "Battle of the Buldge"—which caused the Allies to move significant portions of their strength to Belgium and points further north.

At about 10 p.m., more than four hours after the initial assault, another wave of attackers swept toward the 399th's sector. This time they struck at outposts all along the regiment's front, including a detachment of six men of B Company holed up in the College de Bitche, an abandoned classical academy on the outskirts of town. Other Germans overran listening posts set up atop hills and inside farmhouses on either side of the southwest-running highway that connected Bitche with Lemberg. The assault was preceded by a barrage from German 88s that accounted for many of the twenty GIs who were killed. Soon, however, the drive collapsed under the weight of combined machine-gun and mortar fire and shells from 105-mm howitzers. But it was discovered that the enemy had cut off the 399th from its most exposed outpost, the handful of men stationed at the college.

Surrounded by as many as three hundred Germans, the trapped GIs—Privates Irving W. Bower, Juan Meza, Andrew Powell, Carl L. Eyyerson, Porter W. Lane, and Willis C. McIntyre—confronted a fateful decision: hold out (and probably die), surrender, or try to escape. Determined to live, they hastily retreated to the bowels of the college, even as their attackers streamed through the doors on the upper floor. A French civilian who inhabited the building came to their aid, leading the trapped men through darkened corridors into a room where windows had been sealed shut by cement blocks. Locking the door to the room and unsheathing their bayonets and trench knives, the GIs began to hack away at the cement, when they heard the approach of hob-nailed boots.

As the first block came loose, a German soldier knocked a hole in the door with his rifle butt and, candle in hand, poked his head through the opening. Powell instantly killed him with a round from his M1. A full-blooded Paiute from Nevada's Walker River Reservation, Powell had been guarding the door. While his buddies chiseled away at the blocks, Powell continued to fire through the door at other approaching Germans, keeping them back long enough for a passage to be carved through the concrete. The hole was just large enough for each man to wriggle through in turn; Powell, guarding the rear, was the last to climb through. Probably for lack of ammunition, the group took only one weapon, the light-weight M3A1 45-caliber submachine gun Meza carried.

Once through the hole, the men found their escape far from assured. They had entered another room that led to a basement corridor about to be occupied by approaching Germans. One German attempted to bar their path, but Meza cut him down with

The College de Bitche, an abandoned school used as an advance outpost by the 399th Infantry Regiment. Overrun during Operation Nordwind, the men stationed at the college were trapped and had a harrowing escape back to American lines. (*National Archives*)

a burst from his "grease gun" (so called because the weapon closely resembled a standard mechanic's tool). Before other Germans could appear, the squad located the college's furnace room, which promised at least a temporary hiding place. Through the daylight hours of January 1, the men huddled behind heavy machinery, escaping detection, although a seemingly endless succession of Germans occupied the building and began searching for them.

After darkness fell and the hunt appeared to have subsided, the men made a break for it, fleeing the sooty room and hastening up an unguarded stairway to a corridor with an outside door at its end. At first glance the corridor appeared empty, but as the Americans moved down it they discovered three German soldiers fast asleep, their backs to the wall. Praying that the door at the end of the hallway would not squeak, the GIs stepped over the recumbent enemy, carefully turned the knob, and slipped out into the snow just as a sentry making his rounds disappeared around the corner of the building.

Aided by the weather, especially the winds that muffled the sounds of their movement, they covered a three-hundred-yard field at the dead run, disappeared into the woods beyond, and headed up a slope toward their own lines. A half-hour later they were halted by an American voice demanding they give the password. Throwing up his hands, Bower explained, "We're just looking for Baker Company. We've been lost for 16 hours." The division historian commented: "The six men could have kissed that sentry. . . . At the front, one can never tell what will happen in such a situation. But, fortunately, the soldier believed them. By midnight, they had been taken to an artillery headquarters to be identified."[14]

While Powell and his buddies were scrambling out of the college, comrades posted between Rimling and Bitche were fighting to extricate themselves from a situation just as desperate but on a grander scale. The two prongs of the enemy pincers bit almost simultaneously into the American lines in the Saar Valley and toward the Vosges. A few minutes past midnight, the main body of the 399th came under massed attack, the extent and ferocity of which they had never experienced. Until this hour, Pvt. Henry T. "Tom" Bourne Jr., a rifleman in G Company of the 399th, had found his platoon's position near Hottviller veiled in silence, or something close to it. However, the nineteen-year-old native of Woodstock, Vermont, had not been lulled into a state of complacency. Looking back on this night years later, he mused that "quiet in war isn't real silence, you never cease hearing the crump of artillery near or distant, and small arms fire never really seems to stop either, but sometimes there's relative quiet," as on this deceptive occasion.

Then the division guns started in, and everything changed: "Suddenly there is an enormous crash of noise as our artillery shells go screaming over our heads, salvo after salvo. Next we hear the sounds of a firefight: mortars, machine guns, rifles. The Battalion on our right is under heavy attack!" Beneath the expanding racket, Bourne could hear the high-pitched voices of the attackers, wave after wave of them, as they cut diagonally across his unit's line. Bourne was dumbstruck: "The Germans are acting crazy; they must be drunk or drugged. They're running straight at our neighbors' positions, screaming and firing as they come." In heavily accented English, they called their enemy every derogatory name they knew. The preferred greeting appeared to be, "You dirty American bastards!"[15]

As Private Bourne indicated, *Kampfgruppe* Oberrhein's attack fell heavily on the far right of the 399th's 3rd Battalion as well as on Task Force Hudelson, farther to the east and south. This task force, the reconnaissance unit that had been pressed into service to help hold the division line, was not equipped to resist the wailing hordes that swarmed over it; within minutes, the Century found itself without support in that sector. An early indication of the division's predicament was a frantic call on the field telephone at 399th regimental headquarters. The caller refused to give his name but identified himself as an officer in the 117th Reconnaissance Squadron. This unit, a part of Task Force Hudelson, now under assault by elements of four Volks-Grenadier divisions, was "falling back a little," as the caller put it. "How far is a little?" asked Maj. Lawrence A. Conrey, the 399th's director of plans and operations. "About two thousand yards" was the answer. Blurting out an oath, Conrey asked, "Do you have to fall back so far all at once?" Believing a further reply unnecessary, the caller hung up.

Two thousand yards was bad enough; in fact, the 117th retreated at least eight miles southwest, as far as Wingen-sur-Moder. When its commander discovered that the Germans had recaptured that town, he pulled up stakes again. By late afternoon, the 117th was rumbling west out of the combat zone. Farther east, elements of the 45th and 79th Infantry divisions also came under attack. Cut off from the balance of VI Corps, soon they, too, appeared on the verge of heading for the rear.[16]

With Task Force Hudelson gone on their right, the men of the 399th's 3rd Battalion held their positions grimly, determined to sell their lives as dearly as possible, if it came to that. Private Khoury, whose L Company was struck by the same offensive that scattered Task Force Hudelson, doubted that the attackers expected such stiff resistance as they received:

Immediately, without any order to open fire, they were met with a tremendous fusillade of machine gun and rifle fire. From my position in a foxhole, I got out and crouched behind a tree to be able to see better and move easily. I fired at the gray shadows in front of me with my M-1 without taking time to slowly aim and squeeze off each round. There were so many of them coming toward us that it was more important to fire as rapidly as possible. . . . The firing from our line was furious and harrowing. We kept shooting and shooting and shooting. It seemed to last for hours.

Khoury echoed the belief of many comrades that the enemy had been fortified with booze or opiates that stupefied rather than energized them:

Drunk with schnapps, [they] gave us very little return fire. It was hard for them to yell curses at us and fire their bolt-action Mauser rifles or their machine pistols accurately while running at us. I do not know how many enemy soldiers were hit in front of us, but I know that their attack was broken. They stopped their charge at us and moved off to our right flank. We had held fast on our line, and it became quiet after a few hours.[17]

Dozens of defenders sacrificed their lives to keep that line intact. One of Khoury's buddies in L Company, Pvt. Maurice E. Lloyd, had remained at his heavily wooded outpost along a railroad track east of Lemberg throughout the initial phase of the attack, firing his Browning Automatic Rifle (BAR) at shadowy figures approaching from every direction. Because he refused to withdraw, his fate was preordained: at some point, a Mauser bullet spun him about and knocked him down. The enemy rushed past, leaving him for dead. Desperately wounded, "Mo" Lloyd dragged himself across the frozen earth into a dense thicket, where he found refuge in a log-covered foxhole. The battle passed him by; his buddies never heard from him again, never learned what had become of him. Thirty years later, a hiker from Lemberg stumbled upon Lloyd's well-sheltered remains, an aged Browning clutched in his skeletal hands.[18]

South of L Company's position, C Company of the 399th, stationed on Reyersviller Ridge along the Bitch-Lemberg highway, came under heavy assault and was forced to relinquish ground. The unit did so grudgingly and only after giving a strong account of itself. Minutes after midnight, one of C Company's platoons found itself surrounded on a hill along the highway by "an overwhelming force of crazy" Germans. Under the relentless pounding, sections of the line buckled and came apart. GIs in groups large and small streamed toward the rear, turning and firing as they topped hills and ridges and raced across snow-frosted fields. Several outposts were cut off, including one occupied by Pvt. Thomas Richards and three comrades. Later Richards described his predicament: "I was lying there right along the Bitche highway with my rifle cradled when two heads pop up not 15 yards away on the other side of the road. One of 'em says, in perfect English 'Stick 'em up, Joe.' I didn't have time to tell 'em my name isn't Joe, so I just plug 'em both between the eyes. Then I turned to ask my buddies if maybe we should pull back but they've already parted."[19]

Not every member of the 399th, even those temporarily isolated by the assault on the right, gave ground. When "five hundred dope-happy Germans" flooded the area around Schoenberg where B Company had set up a farmhouse command post, its thirty occupants feared the worst. But because the attack in this sector was helter-skelter and the enemy formations were strung out, there seemed no cause for panic. Because the house also served as the company's supply store, there was enough ammunition to support a stand—an exceptionally effective one. Over the next few hours, a single machine gun operated by Sgt. Clifford La Belle poured twelve thousand rounds into the attackers, who began to pile up on the whitened earth like cordwood. One participant observed that "riflemen in the windows got four krauts for every five shots, it was that easy." Mortars from the company's heavy-weapons platoon added their weight, blowing jagged holes in the attack columns. When armored units came up in rear of the infantry, Capt. Altus Prince fired off three cases of antitank grenades with good results.[20]

Nearby units, even those confronted by better-aligned attackers, provided dramatic support. Sgt. Rudolph Steinman of D Company, a native of Switzerland who had served a hitch in the French Foreign Legion before emigrating to Chicago, set up another machine gun on the right flank of B Company. He did not have to wait long for targets; soon at least a company of "insanely charging Germans" rushed toward his position from the area of the college. When an ammo bearer, Pvt. Thomas W. "Rip" Farish, suggested that he and Steinman "get the hell out of here" before being overrun, the fortyish Steinman, who had enlisted in 1942 and had won a Distinguished Service Cross, the nation's second highest award for military valor, for the Vosges campaign, snorted his disapproval: "Take off? Look at 'em come! I've been waiting two years for this." Steinman began firing when the nearest attackers were fifty yards off. By some accounts, he felled one hundred Germans before survivors broke and scrambled to the rear. Farish later remarked that he had "never heard a machine gun sing the way that one did."[21]

Whether drunk or sober, despite the deadly resistance they met at almost every turn, the Germans kept coming. Their persistence forced the artillery observer at B Company headquarters, Sgt. William Bartscher, to call in fire from every battery in the 925th Field Artillery Battalion. The grid coordinates he gave over the telephone endangered everyone in the command post, but there was no way to avoid it. "Got that?" yelled Bartscher. "That's right, the target is the farmhouse where we are right now. Blast away!" Within minutes, shells were hurtling overhead to burst on all sides of the house. Almost immediately "the krauts stopped shooting [and] started screaming."

As the enemy fell back, four groups of GIs rushed out of the farmhouse and began to make their way back to their own lines. One group headed north toward the Maginot Line, half of whose fortifications were in American hands; following some hair-raising

A 100th Infantry Division machine gun crew waits warily for a renewed German assault. (*National Archives*)

adventures, they made it to safety. The other groups retreated up the hill to Reyersviller, where they were pursued and overtaken. Those taken prisoner included the grenade-firing Captain Prince and Sergeants La Belle and Bartscher.[22]

The first group found sanctuary because the Maginot forts were so formidable as to be impervious to direct assault. Their current occupants, which included E Company of the 399th, threw back every assault made on their position during January 1. The Germans should have appreciated the futility of attacking these works. When invading France in May 1940, they realized that laying siege to these defenses, encased as they were in layer upon layer of concrete and steel, was impossible and bypassed them instead. The forts had fallen only after Paris was occupied and the French government sued for peace.

Sgt. John C. Angier III, whose F Company of the 399th had taken part in the earlier assault on the Maginot emplacements in December, described the position as a series of pillboxes and artillery casemates, each fronted by long, wide fields of fire. Angier was especially impressed with one work in the center of the line— the Citadel de Bitche—which he described as "an unconquerable fortress. It was like those you read about in books, built of high gray stone, with a fifty-foot moat and draw bridges, but modern weapons. The entire network of pillboxes in the Maginot Line was connected to this great citadel by underground tunnels. These tunnels were seven to fourteen stories under the surface. They were large enough to house their own railway system, roads for trucks and bicycles, garrison troops, kitchen, warehouses and storage space for equipment and ammo. I never dreamed of such a thing being possible. The Krauts could have locked themselves in there and stayed for years before coming out."[23]

Even so, American firepower, including tons of explosive charges and hundreds of five-hundred-pound bombs delivered from above, had caused the Germans to abandon perhaps half the forts and pillboxes in the defense chain. Hundreds of defenders, many of them still alive, had been entombed inside, their escape hatches sealed off by the detonations.[24]

While the 399th Infantry Regiment held on for dear life under the pounding of *Kampfgruppe* Oberrhein, its comrades on the left were fighting just as desperately, if not more so, in and near Rimling, where a road network that gave access to extended points on the American line came together. In this sector, too, the German assault achieved strategic surprise, largely because no artillery barrage preceded it. The troops who attacked here, led by fanatical members of the Waffen-SS, richly endowed with tanks and tank destroyers, knew how to exploit such an advantage.

The route of advance of General Blaskowitz's Army Group G ensured that first contact would occur west of Rimling, where elements of the U.S. 44th Division occupied low, open ground that left them even more exposed than the Century Division units in and around the village. The 3rd Battalion of the 397th Infantry covered most of Rimling, with the 1st Platoon of K Company holding the northwest side, including the commanding crest of Schlietzen Hill. The remainder of K Company was dug in east of the 1st Platoon, covering the northern edge of town. The east side of Rimling was held by L Company, while I and M companies populated its lower environs. The 397th's 1st Battalion had assumed a defensive position on the regiment's right flank, extending some two kilometers east of the 3rd Battalion. The 2nd Battalion was in regimental reserve south of Rimling, occupying the villages of Rohrbach, Petit Rederching, and Guising.[25]

Word of a pending attack kept the foxhole dwellers in each battalion of the 397th on high alert, especially the members of the most exposed component, the 3rd Battalion. Throughout the day of the thirty-first, the battalion sent out patrols north and northeast of Rimling but discerned no enemy activity. Nevertheless—and despite the fact that the battalion's front was covered by seven hundred freshly laid land mines—the battalion's commander, Maj. William Esbitt, put his people on an around-the-clock watch. That meant every man on the line, including the feverish Tom Jelks, whose machine gun had been set up on the reverse slope of Schlietzen Hill, about four hundred yards behind K Company's front line. Even the seriously ill were manning the front. Pvt. John L. Sheets, the youngest member of I Company's 2nd Platoon, recalled a buddy, a rifleman hastily converted into a machine gunner, who cowered behind a log emplacement south of Rimling, the lower half of his clothing, and the sleeping bag he had crawled into, soaked in excrement. The unfortunate GI later recalled that "I was suffering miserably from dysentery. . . . I crouched over a machinegun I did not know how to fire and prayed for death" that would not come.[26]

When the advance elements of Blaskowitz's army group approached Rimling just shy of midnight, they struck along the entire front of the 3rd Battalion. K Company, especially its 1st and 2nd platoons, was first to absorb the assault, which, as Jelks noted, "came in waves all the rest of the night." Having somehow evaded the minefield, a group of two hundred or more SS troops, shouting the typical obscenities as well as more fanciful epithets ("American gangsters!"), rushed up Schlietzen Hill and into the midst of both platoons.

Jelks realized that the absence of artillery preparation was intended to enhance surprise, "but the enemy were the ones surprised by the reception they received." The rifles and machine guns of 3rd Battalion opened immediately. "The rate of fire," the Marylander reported, "was terrific, it was rhythmic and sustained, and lasted for over an hour." On the battalion's right flank, a machine gun manned by one of Jelks's buddies, Pvt. Leon Outlaw, ripped gaping holes in the attack column. Gunners in the rear of Outlaw's position joined in, with impressive results. "We had those guys in the neatest cross fire I had ever seen," recalled Pvt. Wilfred B. Howsmon Jr. of B Company. "They tried to fire back but they were completely at our mercy."[27]

The battle might have been going well on the far left, but toward the east a squad-size body of Germans infiltrated the 1st Platoon and, gaining the unit's rear, scorched it with machine-gun fire. The attackers were routed only after a couple of Sherman tanks trundled up from the outskirts of town and shelled them mercilessly. Meanwhile, German patrols were targeting the position of K Company's 3rd Platoon and that of L Company along the road to Urbach, northeast of Rimling. This assault was turned back, too, but a handful of Germans penetrated to within rifle range of L Company's command post. These and other attackers displayed a suicidal fanaticism alien to their opponents, firing from upright positions instead of hugging the ground or taking cover behind ridges and trees. Hundreds toppled onto the frozen ground, although many of the wounded continued to fire from where they lay.

Late in the morning, the first wave finally receded, as the Germans withdrew and regrouped. During the ensuing lull, the men of the 397th heard sounds of combat toward the west—an unsettling experience. Shortly before Rimling came under assault, elements of the 44th Division had sent word they were under assault by a Volks-Grenadier division and a separate Volks-Grenadier regiment. It had become increasingly evident that the Century Division's link to the 103rd Division, still farther west, was coming undone. But when, late on New Year's Day, one of the

44th's regiments fell back, exposing the rear of the 397th and endangering the left flank of the entire division, no one in Rimling got the word. The source of the communications breakdown was never identified.[28]

Although increasingly vulnerable on the left, the 397th kept reconsolidating its position and strengthening its lines. During the early hours of New Year's Day, it endured a second heavy assault, this preceded by a barrage, the enemy now aware that it had lost the advantage of surprise. This effort was met not only by rifle, machine-gun, and mortar fire all along the regimental line, it was also answered by the 105-mm howitzers of the regiment's cannon company, as well as by the 155-mm "Long Tom" howitzers of the 373rd Field Artillery Battalion. This "foolhardy assault" by several hundred "screaming and shouting fanatics," came from the north and northwest and again targeted K Company. Resistance, however, was overwhelming; the fire unleashed along the length of the company's position "maimed or killed whole groups of the attackers."[29]

Once the bloodletting ceased, there came another lull, which lasted for most of the night. Even in the dark, small-unit attacks were reported in various sectors. Shortly after 2 a.m. on January 2, General Blaskowitz unleashed a third major attack, this also preceded by artillery and strengthened by armored units. Detecting the one-thousand-yard gap that had opened between the 397th and the now-precipitately withdrawing 44th Division, the Germans began to loop around K Company south of Schlietzen Hill. Flooding into Rimling, they were met by riflemen rushing up from below and by others previously positioned to cover the rear.

One of the reinforcements was Private Jelks's machine-gun crew, dug in atop a ridge that ran south from Schlietzen, where it was amply supported on both flanks: "To my left were two riflemen and two men with a bazooka, then two men with [Browning automatic rifles]. To my right were two more riflemen, then another bazooka, and another rifleman, then two men with a light machine gun. Behind me were [my first] sergeant and one rifle-

man. All together, we made up a 15-man strongpoint of the left
rear of 'K' Company."

Having taken position in the dead of night, Jelks and his comrades had spent nervous hours squinting into the darkness, watching for the first sign of the enemy. As dawn neared, someone
yelled, "Here they come!" Jelks peered over the ridge to see
Germans "pouring over the top in a long column. Their dark uniforms against the white snow made them perfect silhouettes in the
bright moonlight. Their column was going right across my front
from right to left. At a range of 500 yards, I . . . waited until the
front of their troops were directly to my front. I laid on my trigger
and fired a long continuous burst while traversing to the right as
fast as I could. When I got to the top of the ridge with my initial
burst of fire, I traversed left and started all over again. They were
all on the ground by that time, and I could see my tracers and bullets kicking up snow and dirt, where they were hugging the
ground."

When he returned his attention to the front of the enemy column, Jelks's first can of ammunition was empty. Working in feverish tandem with his ammo carrier, he was ready to fire again within seconds. By then, however, everything was quiet, and Jelks held
his fire: "I could not tell if they were dead or wounded or just lying
still, playing possum. I estimated there were about 70 or 80 men
in the bunch that came over the ridge and some of them got back
over the top, when I started to shoot, and escaped."[30]

Casualties piled up on other sectors of the 397th's main line of
resistance. Panther and Tiger tanks had accompanied each wave
of attack. While waiting to go into action, two Tigers had parked
in front of a farmhouse below Rimling, close to the position of the
2nd Battalion, 397th Infantry. Unbeknown to the tankers and the
SS infantrymen accompanying them, the house had been turned
into a forward observation post for Lieutenant Fishpaw's battery.
The post occupied the second floor in company with its escort, a
squad of riflemen. When German infantry began to enter the
house from the rear, the GIs hesitated to fire for fear of alerting the

tankers to their presence. They soon realized, however, that the din of battle prevented any sounds from escaping the house.

Taking position at the top of the stairs, the escort shot down a dozen Germans as they climbed, one by one, to the second floor. "Our guys," Fishpaw wrote, "would push the bodies out the window and into the alley in the back yard where the other Germans couldn't see them. Their bodies were soon covered by deep snow." The riflemen kept up their carefully crafted slaughter until the Tigers finally rumbled off to fight elsewhere.[31]

Although the 397th was taking a heavy toll of their opponents, not every observer was impressed. During the January 2 fighting below Schlietzen Hill, an SS general, "perhaps with a snoot full of schnapps," stumbled inside the 3rd Battalion's lines and was taken prisoner. According to Private Sheets, "he was a real character, telling his captors, 'you Amis [Americans] are lousy infantry, you shoot at anything that moves.' Needless to say he made the day for the American privates he was haranguing." Sheets added that at Rimling, "Jerry paid dearly and did not gain ground no matter what the Kraut generals' opinion of American infantry."[32]

Although his pride in his regiment's ability to stand and defend was understandable, Sheets misspoke. What was later called "the most vicious and determined German assault" that the 397th had ever experienced resulted in a slow but continual withdrawal from the outfit's forwardmost positions. The K Company troops who had held Schlietzen Hill slowly abandoned the crest, only to find themselves continuing to attract artillery, mortar, and sniper fire in heavy volume. With the assent of Major Esbitt, K Company's 2nd Platoon prepared to retake the heights, only to be stymied by another wave of attackers—SS infantry bolstered by a few Panzers. An artillery barrage finally drove back the Germans and held the tanks at bay. Around noon on January 2, K Company's 2nd Platoon counterattacked and reoccupied the crest. But the position was soon on the verge of proving untenable once again.[33]

The picturesque little village of Rimling suffered heavily at the attackers' hands, as did the GIs who occupied it. As the historian of the 397th noted, throughout the entire operation, each enemy drive was made by numerically superior forces, with tanks, with self-propelled weapons, and limitless amounts of artillery and mortar barrages which eventually reduced the entire town to ruin, forcing us into the deep damp cellars. These cellars, which became the homes of [those of] us fortunate enough to be in the town and not on one of the hills or in the fox-holes, were also peopled with civilians taking refuge from the deadly shells.[34]

Because the offensive was almost entirely directed at the left and front of the 397th Infantry, the regiment's 1st Battalion and other units to the east of the town, including most of the 398th, endured only sporadic, small-scale attacks. Even so, the assault did not let up throughout January 2: "The enemy seemed to come and come." The machine guns and mortars manned by Jelks, Outlaw, and other heavy weaponeers had dispatched hundreds of attackers, but "there were always new men to take the places of the fallen. . . . Large groups made suicidal frontal attacks, while others kept the flanks busy and tried all manner of infiltration tactics to destroy our supply lines and communication wires."[35]

Given the near-continuous pressure felt by the 397th, and the equally formidable assault that continued to batter the lines of the 399th to the east, it appeared a matter of time before the division must relinquish its doggedly defended positions.

Preliminary efforts to reestablish a defensive line south of the division's original positions began late on New Year's Day when elements of the 399th fell back southwest from the Bitche vicinity to Reyersviller and then several miles farther, to Enchenberg.

At the outset of the withdrawal, divisional morale also wavered. Pvt. Franklin L. Gurley of A Company, 399th Infantry, who would become the scribe of his regiment, recalled the frigid, frantic night of January 1 as "the low point of the war" for his outfit. D

Company's Pvt. Arthur Knight observed that by dawn of the second, with the 1st Battalion's fall-back well under way, "the morale of the troops was at rock bottom and there was a feeling of great insecurity."[36]

Morale sank further when, upon reaching Enchenberg, Gurley's and Knight's battalion was ordered to countermarch to Lambach and Sierstal, there to cover the withdrawal of other elements of the regiment. Pvt. Robert Richard Fair, also of D Company, considered the retrograde "the worst march of my life. The night was freezing cold, the road icy, and we were all exhausted." Thanks to the around-the-clock vigilance demanded of his unit in recent days, "this was the third night with practically no sleep. But march we did down to Lambach, Sierstal, and out on the Reyersviller road where we set up our guns in a little valley to the left of the highway."

Digging foxholes was always a laborious exercise, but on January 2 "it was almost impossible. We found a pickaxe and our entrenching tools, but it was extremely difficult breaking through the snow and ice. . . . We spent all day digging, logging over, and firing our guns. We got some return fire for our trouble but none of us paid any attention to it." That night "was another killer. It was again cold, in the teens, and we had no blankets or sleeping bags. . . It was a wonder that any of us were alive by the next day."[37]

Private Knight, who was taking a turn as a regimental jeep driver, observed that "there was some doubt whether or not we could hold these new positions. During the retreat nearly everyone had lost equipment. . . . We could not fire our mortars since we had no base plates so the whole Battalion was in a pretty critical situation." When shuttling his comrades in D Company back to Lambach and Sierstal, the young Montanan observed that "they did not say much, just sat quietly in my jeep and shivered. They did not complain about not having bedrolls nor that they had hardly anything to eat but a ration or two. They did not know if they would be joining their buddies stretched out like logs in the snow or live to suffer from the cold and fear a little longer."[38]

While most withdrawing units left no one behind to occupy what they had vacated, some companies and platoons were relieved by fresh troops rushed up from the rear or the far flanks. By late on January 2, L Company of the 399th, having thrown back a half-hearted attack near Lemberg, was suddenly spelled by troops from Task Force Harris, an *ad hoc* grouping of units from the 63rd Infantry Division, a XV Corps component newly arrived in the theater. John Khoury, who like most of those in L Company wore a gnarly beard, noted that the newcomers "appeared clean-shaven with spotless uniforms and weapons. . . . We placed them in our foxholes and told them: 'Good luck!'"

Khoury realized all too well what the newcomers were in for; soon enough, they got an inkling: "One of them, who was probably 18 and just out of high school turned to me, trembling, and asked, 'Where are they?' I pointed toward the enemy line and said, 'They are over there about 200 yards in front.' He trembled as he looked at me and sobbed quietly. Then there was nothing more I could say."

While en route to the rear, Khoury reflected on the exchange of positions. He had been struck by the glaring contrast between "these green, young boys sent to the front to relieve us grimy, tough, veteran dogfaces. We were all about the same age. What could I say to them? Don't worry. You'll be alright. It's only a war. Nobody gets wounded or killed. That's just noise you hear. In a little while you'll go home to your mother. Perhaps, I should have told them the philosophy of the old dogfaces, like me: You've got to kill or be killed!"[39]

John Sheets, fighting on and near Schlietzen Hill, entertained similar thoughts when his platoon was relieved a few nights later by another "clean and green" unit. The old-beyond-his-years Ohioan was especially troubled when he learned that, unable to resist German infiltration, forty or fifty of the replacements surrendered before morning. One of the newcomers had been killed just before I Company fell back. The greenhorn's death tapped a source of disgust and sorrow in Sheets: "Here was another of the thousands of scared, helpless kids, yanked from their mothers' nest and sent to the slaughter. Why didn't company management keep this kid in the company [command post] for a few days? The GIs, doing nothing, hanging around there, could have consoled him. . . . Did he know his time had come?" Eventually, Sheets quit looking for answers, but he never rid himself of the urge to rationalize the fluctuating fortunes of combat, especially those that victimized innocent youngsters and spared others, mostly older but no wiser and with no greater claim to survival.[40]

Thoughts just as troubling and every bit as unfathomable gnawed at the thousands of other members of the Century Division as they hustled to the rear, their breath coming in frigid bursts. Many of the displaced GIs had more questions than answers. Pvt. Samuel L. Resnick, a mortar man in D Company of the 399th, was dazed by his company's abrupt departure. In retreat, the company had left behind everything that could not be carried off, "all the comforts we had set up during our brief stay, our mortars as well." At first the Brooklyn-born Resnick assumed that his unit alone had been dislodged, but on the road back he saw that "hundreds were retreating, confused, lost, and unbelieving."

Not everyone seemed committed to getting beyond range of those drunken, cursing Nazis as quickly as humanly possible. When the commander of Resnick's platoon ("young and inspired by duty") ordered the mortar crew to retrieve the weapons it had abandoned, the men at first refused, "but then at his insistence, and with his hand on his pistol, we all turned around and headed back." Other members of D Company, streaming past, gave Resnick and his buddies a disbelieving look. By the time the platoon reached its abandoned bivouac and began to carry off their weapons, the enemy was only yards away. "We managed somehow to evade them," Resnick recalled, "and safely joined up with the rest of our company walking toward the rear. I walked dejectedly, glancing behind me." Miraculously, the Germans made no attempt to cut off D Company in midflight.[41]

For some of the retreating men, the worst part was having to abandon the French farming villages they had been occupying for days or weeks, leaving the civilians to the mercy of the invaders.

Pvt. Donald A. Waxman of the 399th's C Company never forgot the anguished faces of the people of Reyersviller: "The men and women and children were all standing outside their barns, staring—bewildered, stunned, terror-stricken with the thought of the returning *Boche*." So ended, it appeared, the liberation of a much-oppressed populace.[42]

The fears and regrets that troubled the GIs streaming south from the Maginot Line in the dead of night were many and disturbing. With each passing kilometer, they began to coalesce around a central core of concern. With a seemingly inexhaustible supply of German soldiers flooding over every sector of the Seventh Army's positions, and absent any indication that the offensive would recede in the new year, was it just possible that the war was not, after all, close to the end? For that matter, was it being won?

TWO

THE 100TH INFANTRY
DIVISION

It began quietly enough, a little more than eight months after Japan's surprise attack on the U.S. fleet at Pearl Harbor had forced America into a world war. In mid-August 1942, a number of War Department officials—the commanders of the Army Ground Forces, the Service of Supply, and the Second and Third armies—began assigning officers to a cadre around which a new infantry division would be built. Command of the division went to Maj. Gen. Withers Alexander Burress, who, although not a West Pointer, had established a distinguished pedigree in the prewar service.[1]

Born in Richmond, Virginia, in 1894, Burress had graduated from his state's military institute—the alma mater of Army Chief of Staff George C. Marshall and at which George S. Patton Jr. had spent a year before going on to West Point. At the Virginia Military Institute (VMI), Burress excelled not only in the classroom and on the drill plain but also, despite a rather unprepossessing physique (five feet nine and less than 170 pounds), on the gridiron. He impressed his instructors and teammates with his brains, energy, and competitiveness. He made lifelong friends, forged important

connections, and gained the enduring nickname "Pinky" in reference to his reddish hair, alabaster complexion, and many freckles.
Soft-spoken and dignified, he allowed deeds to speak for him, and
they did so eloquently. By 1914, his graduation year, his superiors
had marked him as an officer of merit and ability.[2]

Three years later, Burress went to France with the American
Expeditionary Forces as a second lieutenant in the 23rd
Regiment, 2nd Infantry Division. As his outfit's assistant operations officer, he saw action at Chateau Thierry, along the Marne,
and in the St. Mihiel offensive. After the armistice was signed, he
served as commandant of cadets and professor of military science
at VMI, whose superintendent, retired Marine Corps Maj. Gen.
John A. Lejeune, pronounced Burress "a very successful leader of
young men." A cadet whose father had played with Burress on the
football team considered him "a stern disciplinarian but very fair,
which could be a tough assignment in dealing with a group of
high-spirited college men."

When his assignment at VMI ended, Burress attended, succes-
sively, the Infantry School at Fort Benning, Georgia, the
Command and General Staff School at Fort Leavenworth, Kansas,
and the Army War College in Washington, DC. In 1935, he
returned to VMI for a five-year stint as its commandant. The year
after Hitler invaded Poland, Burress gained a prestigious position
on the War Department General Staff in Washington. Soon after
America entered the war, he was back at Fort Benning as assistant
commandant of the Infantry School. Early in 1942, he was
assigned to duty in the Puerto Rican Department, from which he
was recalled, at the behest of General Marshall, to lead the 100th
Division as a two-star general. Marshall's faith in his fellow VMI
alumnus would prove well-placed.[3]

From his first days in command, Burress showed himself to be
mindful of the well-being of his troops and desirous that they
receive full credit for what they achieved. Even before the Century
was officially activated, he instructed its public relations officer:
"Remember that this division is going to be made of more than
15,000 officers and men. It does not consist of just a commanding

general and a few other high-ranking officers. . . . I want you to see that the officers and men who do the work and the fighting get recognition for what they are doing."[4]

Burress would win the unalloyed support of those men, many of whom came to regard him as a father figure. Others, impressed by his quiet dignity and Southern mannerisms, saw him as a latter-day Robert E. Lee. Superiors and colleagues alike learned to depend on his steady-going leadership. The respect and confidence he inspired would result in an unusually lengthy tenure with the Century. Although turnover among division commanders was extremely high, many being relieved for failure to perform to superiors' standards, Burress

Maj. Gen. Withers A. Burress was commanding officer of the 100th Division from its inception to the end of combat in World War II. (National Archives)

would finish the war as one of only three officers to have led the same division from basic training through the close of its combat service.[5]

Burress was typically low-key when participating in the ceremony that marked the 100th Division's activation. This took place on November 15, 1942, at Fort Jackson, a World War I-era installation in a corner of South Carolina that abounded in sandy soil, scrubby trees, and second-growth vegetation. On Jackson's dusty parade ground, Maj. Gen. William H. Simpson, commander of XII Army Corps, to which the 100th would be assigned, delivered a brief address before a gathering of local civilians that included state officials and business leaders. Simpson—future commander of the U.S. Ninth Army under Eisenhower—stressed "the severe trials which lay in the path of the Century Division." The unit's historian noted that the speaker "clairvoyantly predicted the important role" it would play in helping gain victory in Europe. After Simpson spoke, state Sen. Edgar A. Brown, representing

South Carolina Gov. Richard M. Jeffries, delivered an oration filled with patriotic slogans and appeals to national pride. He urged the embryonic unit to get to work at "annihilating Hitler and the yellow men across the Pacific" and declared that "you men of the 100th can decide the course of civilization for a thousand years to come."

During the proceedings, the new division's flag was ceremoniously handed to its leader. Although lacking the glibness of an orator, Burress rendered a response worthy of the occasion. He cited the duty he felt toward the nation that had bred him and to the young men he would lead in combat. He accepted the command

> with a full realization of the responsibility it entails, and all it symbolizes: the responsibility that we have to our high cause and our country, the responsibility to mothers and fathers, to give their sons the best in preparation for battle. To these ends and to the accomplishment of our immediate task, which is success in battle, we do hereby dedicate, without reservation, all that is in us.

Burress added the obligatory appeal to divine support: "With God's help and guidance we shall succeed." Spectators cheered and clapped, a military band thumped and tooted, and salutes were exchanged all around. Thus a worthy enterprise was launched and a small but not insignificant step taken toward a goal that an earlier war had failed to attain: making the world safe for democracy.[6]

Shortly before the activation ceremony, the War Department had completed assigning Burress's ranking subordinates. These included Col. Maurice L. Miller, assistant division commander; Col. Theodore E. Buechler, commander of the division artillery; and the leaders of the regiments that would furnish the bulk of the command's manpower, Colonels William A. Ellis (397th Infantry), Robinson E. Duff (398th Infantry), and Andrew C.

Tychsen (399th Infantry). All were professional soldiers with years of service in the regular army or the reserves, and all but Ellis would attain the rank of general officer.

The forty-eight-year-old Miller, a native of Minnesota, was a 1916 graduate of the U.S. Military Academy. During World War I, he had commanded a battalion of the 34th Division in France, where he was wounded. In the peacetime army, he had been an instructor at West Point and a staff member at the Infantry School. At Fort Benning, he forged a close friendship with Burress, who upon activation of the 100th Division selected him as his executive officer. Miller was, like his superior, steady-going and reliable, but a heart condition would deprive him of a long association with the Century.[7]

Buechler, a Nebraska native, West Pointer, and 1933 graduate of the Command and General Staff School, would serve as the division's artillery chief through its critical activation and training period before being replaced in October 1943 by Brig. Gen. John B. Murphy, a member of the West Point Class of 1918 who had graduated too late to see action in World War I. In the interwar army, Murphy had drawn a succession of field artillery command, staff, and instructor assignments that took him as far away as Hawaii. Before joining the 100th Division, he had commanded a brigade in the 7th Armored Division during its stateside training period.[8]

Of the regimental commanders, only the forty-nine-year-old Tychsen—like Burress a veteran of thirty years' army service— would leave a lasting mark on the division. A native of New Jersey, in boyhood he had relocated with his family to the northern plains. At twenty he dropped out of college to enlist as a private in the Minnesota National Guard, quickly rising to first sergeant. After serving on the Mexican border during the army's fruitless pursuit of Pancho Villa, Tychsen entered the Reserve Officers Training Corps (ROTC). A high score on an aptitude test gained him a direct commission to captain. In 1917, he went overseas as a member of the 88th Infantry Division. In France he commanded a machine-gun unit that fought in the Vosges Mountains sector as well as at Verdun and in the Meuse-Argonne campaign. In 1919, Tychsen joined the regular service, where he spent the next twenty-three years as an ROTC instructor, a staff officer under then-Col. George C. Marshall and other superiors, and a student at various service schools, including Leavenworth. Somehow he found time to coauthor a celebrated manual on cadence marching.

When America entered the European war, Tychsen was in command of a unit of the Organized Reserves in Camden, New Jersey. Assigned to lead the 399th Infantry, he would prove to be a martinet, a severe disciplinarian, and a commander hard to please. According to Private Gurley, who became chief scribe of the 399th, Tychsen's men referred to him (behind his back, of course) as "Old Spit and Polish," as well as by several other nicknames— "not all complimentary." In time, however, Tychsen won their grudging respect for the thoroughness with which he trained the regiment for battle and the utterly fearless way he led it in the field.[9]

Ellis's, Duff's, and Tychsen's outfits traced their lineage to National Army units activated during World War I. Each was disbanded at the close of that conflict, only to be reconstituted in the early 1920s and assigned to an Organized Reserve unit. The coat of arms of each outfit displayed colors and insignia that symbolized its state attachment. For the 397th, blue and black connoted the infantry and the coal-mining region between the Monongahela and Ohio rivers of West Virginia; the unit's motto was "Death Before Dishonor." Blue waves and a diamondback rattler adorned the heraldic shield of the 398th Infantry, previously headquartered at Charleston, West Virginia; the regimental shield carried the motto "On the Alert." A similar sentiment, "I Am Ready," was emblazoned on the coat of arms of the 399th Infantry, whose origins dated to Lexington, Kentucky. The regimental shield displayed a Kentucky long rifle and a powder horn. The latter design greatly impressed its new colonel. "The Regiment had a very handsome coat of arms," Tychsen later recalled. "I grew to be very proud of that insignia. We were known at once as the Powderhorn Regiment."[10]

The patch of the division into which these units would be integrated was less colorful and perhaps less evocative. Worn on the left shoulder of every Centuryman's uniform, it consisted of the numeral "100" in white and gold on an infantry-blue background. The simplicity of the insignia would not prevent it from becoming a potent symbol of unit pride.

The editor of the 100th Division's official history, *Story of the Century*, saw a far-reaching significance in that ceremonial passing of the command flag to General Burress. On that occasion, "something more than speeches or bands or latrine duty had happened. The Century Division was no longer an embryo. It was no longer anything as impersonal as an 'It' or a 'They.' The 100th had been born. A living, breathing, pulsating entity had been created out of the heart and will of a united nation. From now on, 'It' or 'They' would not suffice. From 15 November 1942, it was 'We.' *We* fighting men of the Century."

Some of these men had already arrived. Cadre officers had been in place since mid-October; in later weeks, they were augmented by four hundred "filler" officer personnel who came to the division principally from Officer Candidate School (OCS). By mid-October, one thousand five hundred noncommissioned officers, most of them from the 76th Division, others from replacement training centers mostly in New England and the Middle Atlantic states, "added brain, bone, and sinew to the fighting machine struggling to crack its shell." The greater part of this machine—the recruits—began to trickle into Fort Jackson within days of the activation ceremony; within weeks they became a veritable flood. By year's close, some thirteen thousand enlistees and draftees were clogging the twenty-five-year-old installation outside Columbia, the state capital.[11]

The initial contingent included eighteen-year-old John Angier. At first, the armed services did not consider the native North Carolinian to be soldier material; severely myopic, he had failed his navy physical. Despondent over his situation, Angier dropped out of college and headed north to take a defense job in the shipyards of Baltimore. He considered himself to be marking time before the army, which had lower physical standards than the sea service, snatched him up, and he was right. Through some miscommunication, however, he would not learn until he was overseas that his local draft board had classified him 4-F, "with a notation that I would never be called into the Army." By then Angier, drawing on four years' experience in a military prep school, had won an Expert Infantryman's Badge and promotion to platoon sergeant. He would finish his military career as a battle-hardened lieutenant.

Angier had begun his army service by enlisting in a paratroop battalion and was sent to Fort Bragg, North Carolina, for training. He spent a few weeks drilling on muddy practice fields before the War Department decreed that all recruits who wore glasses would be shipped out to regular infantry units. Happenstance sent him to the 100th Division as a member of the first contingent of recruits at Fort Jackson. Upon his arrival, Angier's feelings probably mirrored those of the thousands of youngsters who followed him: "As I stepped off the train my first impression was a complete blank. To think that I had left all of that good rain and mud for acres and acres and acres of sand, scrub oak, and more sand! . . . Well, I was in the Army, and what more could I expect? Anything any better than this would have surprised me so much that I would have fainted."[12]

Few of Angier's fellow recruits fainted upon reaching Fort Jackson. However, the training regimen they were introduced to took a toll on those who lacked the physical skills, the stamina, and the fortitude to transition from happy-go-lucky teenagers to accomplished fighting men. Their cadre staff went to great lengths to knock the civilian mentality out of them and, as one of Angier's superiors put it, make them "the best damn soldiers in this man's Army."[13]

The instructors strove to teach their new charges not only the basics of soldiering but the nuances of the profession to which they had bound themselves through their own volition or at the urging of their draft boards. More than a few recruits insisted that their noncoms were motivated by a sadistic desire to inflict as much pain and misery as possible during the time these idealistic, innocent youngsters were at their mercy.

That time was relatively brief, yet lengthy enough for its purpose. Basic training, which consumed twelve to seventeen weeks depending on circumstances, commenced at Fort Jackson three days after Christmas 1942, to be followed by three months of unit training. The recruits' day began at 5:30 a.m., when reveille was blown. By 7 a.m. they had eaten breakfast, made sure their quarters were orderly enough to pass inspection, then underwent various forms of physical training, including calisthenics and a turn on the post obstacle course. Beginning in mid-January, they were introduced to the weapons training range, "where we waited for the tardy winter dawn to permit firing." Becoming conversant with the care and handling of small arms such as the M1 sometimes proved a painful process, especially for those recruits—especially kids from the cities and suburbs of the East—who lacked experience with firearms.[14]

Given enough time and practice, most novices became sufficiently adept at handling the tools of war—including 45-caliber Colt automatic (actually semiautomatic) pistols, air- and water-cooled 30-caliber machine guns, 60- and 81-mm mortars, and other specialty weapons—so that they knew how to protect themselves and their comrades in a variety of hostile situations. Later they would learn how to wield bayonets, grenades, and even bazookas; how to protect themselves against a poison gas attack; and how to succeed at hand-to-hand combat. Some recruits were schooled in Asian defensive arts, though few enjoyed the experience. According to a member of the 375th Field Artillery Battalion, "judo classes were among the more unpopular features of training. Some men took their judo training [too] seriously," with the result that the classes had to be disbanded "before the law of 'the survival of the fittest' could take its toll."[15]

Every feature of basic training was an arduous test of the recruit's ability to endure and overcome. One of the most memorable was the infiltration course, which simulated an invasion of hostile territory. Sometimes known by the sarcastic name "mental conditioning course," this exercise required the would-be soldier to maneuver under full pack across open ground almost the length of a football field, to surmount obstacles including ditches and barbed wire, and evade dynamite charges planted in the ground. The recruit had to accomplish this mainly from the prone position and to the accompaniment of small-arms and machine-gun fire. At first he was subjected to "dry fire"—blank rounds—but at some point he found live ammunition whizzing barely three feet above his head. A veteran of the 397th never forgot "being one with the worms, burrowing for the entire 75 yards as if our life depended on it"—which it did.[16]

Other demanding exercises, never fondly remembered, were the three-, six-, and nine-mile hikes required of each recruit every week during basic training. At some point, he was subjected to a twenty-five-mile hike on which he lugged a full pack of equipment in addition to his M1, which weighed nine pounds, or a nineteen-pound Browning Automatic Rifle. Virtually every recruit complained of the frequency and severity of these and other exercises ("God, did we march!" exclaimed one veteran), although those who took a mature view of this training admitted its value. Pennsylvanian Thomas J. Tillett of H Company, 398th Infantry, declared that "twelve weeks of Basic Infantry Training . . . [made] me a man. Long hikes and then Hikes with a full 40[-pound] pack would gradually get those muscles to another level. I started at 135 Pounds and changed all that to muscle."

Despite his continuous progress, Private Tillett, a machine gunner, sometimes felt intimidated by his newly acquired comrades: "It still seemed to me that everyone else was older and about twice my size." They differed from him in other ways, too, including their choice of words and how they uttered them: "Most spoke a language that I had never heard before. Swearing was something I had never used before and soon it seemed as natural as if I had always talked that way. Life experiences were so differ-

100th Division soldiers marching through a forest in southern France soon after their arrival in Europe. These GIs are carrying a variety of equipment and armament, including bed rolls, shovels, ammunition boxes, and a .30 caliber machine gun and its tripod. Before long, most soldiers in combat discarded all but the most important field tools and personal equipment. (*National Archives*)

ent on the farm, in the big cities and on the bayous of Louisiana that it seemed every night I heard another strange story."[17]

Tillett's eye-opening exposure to young men from distant corners of the country, with their unique mannerisms, attitudes, and dialects, was the result of a large and socially diverse nation at war. By early 1943, the melting-pot process was in full swing at Fort Jackson and dozens of other training installations throughout the land. Through close confinement and enforced teamwork, basic training helped create a cohesive, integrated team from the disparate elements of American youth: scions of old New England families and the less fortunate offspring of South Boston and East Hartford; cocky, jive-talking zoot-suiters from "New Yawk" and "New Joisey"; sons of the New South, fulfilling family military tra-

ditions; kids from the farms, towns, and cities of the weather-rav-
aged plains and the solid-stolid Midwest; youngsters from the villages, ranches, and oil fields of the Southwest, including sizable
contingents of American Indians and Hispanic-Americans; mel-
low Angelenos and urbane San Franciscans; and descendants of
the hardy pioneers of the Pacific Northwest. This gathering of the
disparate and far-flung—an "amalgam of Runyonesque and
Faulkner like characters," in the words of one college-educated
recruit—came together on the flat, dusty fields of the Carolina
Piedmont.

As soon as its manpower began to arrive, the Century Division
assumed shape and organization. In quick time the command
expanded from its primary components—the 397th, 398th, and
399th Infantry regiments, the 373rd, 374th, 375th, and 925th
Field Artillery battalions, and their associated headquarters elements—to include a variety of combat support units: the Division
Headquarters Company, the 325th Engineer Combat Battalion,
the 325th Medical Battalion, a Special Troops battalion, the 100th
Cavalry Reconnaissance Troop, the 100th Quartermaster
Company, the 100th Signal Company, the 800th Ordnance Light
Maintenance Company, and the 100th Military Police Platoon.

The next phase of divisional training, involving combined
arms, began in mid-July when the recruits left Fort Jackson for a
two-week round of field exercises. During this period, the various
units of the Century came together to form regimental combat
teams—ad hoc combined-arms units—and operate for the first
time as a cohesive entity. The men "sweated on long marches,
deployed through thick woods, and learned to make one canteen
of water last for a day's drinking and washing." The division's historian added that "with the temperature in the 90's, however, we
didn't do much washing."

By the end of August, having solved six regimental combat-
team problems, the Century began training as a division. In stifling
heat, the troops maneuvered through chigger-infested stands of

cypress trees and loblolly pines and across fields abounding in saw grass, sand fleas, and a ubiquitous climbing vine known as kudzu. Directed personally by General Burress and his ranking subordinates, the "Battle of South Carolina" attracted visits from top brass, including General Simpson and Lt. Gen. Lloyd R. Fredendall, commanding general of the Second Army. Fought mainly across a twenty-five mile stretch of "battlefield" between the towns of Winnsboro and Chester, the exercise ended in victory for the Century and with the sound defeat of its numerically inferior opponent, the 6th Cavalry Regiment (Mechanized). By late October, the division had returned to Fort Jackson, where the liberal issuance of passes enabled the recruits to celebrate their triumph and homecoming with wine (or at least beer), women (those able to elude the long arm of their families), and song (much of it rendered in boisterous but slurred tones).[18]

The Battle of South Carolina formed a prelude to an even larger and more strenuous round of campaigning in the wild. In mid-November, most of the division was trucked to the Tennessee Maneuver Area, a fifteen-thousand-square-mile tract atop the steep and rugged Cumberland Plateau. In this forbidding environment, the recruits, who were slowly but surely rounding into some semblance of combat troops, spent two months maneuvering as part of a corps-size force. That force included elements of the 35th and 87th Infantry divisions, the 14th Armored Division, and the 3rd Cavalry Group, units that the Century sometimes joined and sometimes opposed in simulated but quite realistic combat.

At first, bad weather—which included several days of near-freezing rain—the treacherous terrain, and inadequate clothing caused unit morale to plummet. It revived once the men were permitted to build fires and spend a sufficient time resting in the rear of the fighting lines. Objectives were more easily attained, and exercise scores improved across the division. This trend lent further encouragement to the troops, who began to appreciate the benefits of roughing it. The scribe of the 925th Field Artillery Battalion noted that with passing time "we knew that our training was paying off. The officers were becoming more efficient in handling the mass movement of troops and in combat-team coordination. We were learning to work under adverse conditions. We were being hardened to the cold, the rain, and the mud, and learning to get along with the makeshift instead of the prepared."[19]

Only later did the division learn that this phase of its training, which had helped whip it into fighting trim, might have been dispensed with had events played out differently. During the summer of 1943, the command stood a good chance of being shipped directly from Fort Jackson to England to take part in the cross-channel invasion of the Continent. When that operation was postponed to the spring of 1944, the War Department decided the Century was not yet needed in Europe. Frank Gurley, among others, theorized that the division had been sent to Tennessee for winter maneuvers "more or less to keep busy and kill time while awaiting the order to pack for overseas."[20]

The beneficial effects of the maneuvers were nearly squandered once the exercise ended in January 1944 and the participants were transported to their new duty station, Fort Bragg, North Carolina. Initially Bragg was thought to be the stepping-stone to deployment overseas, but in a matter of weeks the division had grown too small to go into action anywhere.

By early spring, some three thousand five hundred recruits, all from the lower ranks, had departed Bragg, but not as Centurymen. They were bound for the replacement depots ("repple depples," in army parlance), whose mission was to supply infantry units already in combat with reinforcements. Most of the departing men would be assigned to the U.S. Fifth Army, then struggling to break out of a beachhead on the Italian mainland near Anzio and Nettuno against heavy German opposition, and the Sixth Army, which had just made an amphibious landing at Saidor on the coast of Japanese-held Papua New Guinea as part of Gen. Douglas MacArthur's Huon Peninsula campaign. The loss of so many combat-ready troops severely compromised divisional readiness.

It became clear that the Century was not about to go into the field any time soon.

Over the next eight months, replacements were funneled to Fort Bragg from an array of units, including airborne, military police, and barrage balloon trainees; Special Services members; and Army Air Forces and antiaircraft recruits whose classes had been washed out in order to feed the army's constant hunger for riflemen, machine gunners, and mortar men. The largest source of replacement manpower was the Army Specialized Training Program (ASTP), whose members found themselves ejected from the hallowed halls of learning and deposited on the practice fields of Bragg and other training installations. This program, implemented in December 1942, was designed to "provide the continuous and accelerated flow of high grade technicians and specialists needed by the Army." Applicants for these positions, most of whom were already on active duty, were required to have a high school diploma (or, if older than twenty-two, to have completed at least one year of college), and to have scored a minimum of 115 (later raised to 120) on a standardized IQ test. A qualifying ASTP candidate would be sent to one of 227 land-grant universities around the country that had contracted with the army to provide instruction in such areas as engineering, foreign languages, personnel psychology, and medicine. Secretary of War Henry L. Stimson and Army Chief of Staff Marshall had begun to heed the concerns of ASTP critics, including Lt. Gen. Lesley J. McNair, commander of U.S. Ground Forces, who complained that "with 300,000 men short, we are sending men to college." Early in 1944, the War Department began shutting down the program, although elements of it would remain in operation throughout the war. It was estimated that between three thousand and four thousand of the washouts found their way into the 100th Division at some point in 1944–45.[21]

The newcomers, many of whom seemed to regard themselves as students instead of soldiers, did not like their altered status one bit (the program's demise was "one big rip-off," a veteran of the 398th recalled many years later, with more than a trace of bitterness). When they reached Bragg, ex-ASTPs were especially both-ered by the "difference in intellect" between themselves and their instructors, many of whom appeared functionally illiterate. "We were a bunch of youngsters, scarcely out of high school," wrote Private Miller of the 399th, another ASTP, "but quite confident of our intellectual abilities." Not only did the college men consider themselves superior intellectually to their noncoms, they believed, as J. P. Smith put it, that "we were smarter than our officers—which in some cases was true." Private Smith admitted, however, that "there is nothing worse than an eighteen-year-old kid who thinks he knows everything!"[22]

But not every recruit harbored a grudge against his instructors. Private Bourne of the 399th, who before joining the ASTP had spent a year at Yale University (where he admitted to "not learning much except how to ingest alcohol"), changed his early, quite unfavorable opinion of his instructors, but it took time:

> We of the ASTP were very young, had been quite privileged for the most part, in and out of the Army, and it was very easy at first for us to think of these guys as mindless cowboys and sadists. They were experienced professional soldiers, a few years older for the most part, who knew a great deal more about what we were supposed to be doing than we did and scorned us in turn as smart-assed kids. That had to change and it did. Most of us turned out to be good soldiers when the time came to prove it, and most of us realized that the cadre was one of the major reasons for this.

That said, a balanced perspective on his training period "didn't percolate down into my brain until many years later. How do you rationalize that some guy whom you really hated and feared saved your life over and over again, even though he may have at first despised you as well? It's a tough thing to process, but it's better after you do."[23]

As befit recruits whom their instructors thought of as playing at war, while at Bragg elements of the Century became performers. VIPs, including newspaper publishers who could furnish the army with favorable publicity and businessmen courted by the War Department were invited to observe the division conduct infantry-artillery attack exercises using live ammunition. Other simulations edified manufacturers who wished to observe how the war goods they produced were used in action. Secretary Stimson, Undersecretary of War Robert Patterson, visiting Allied commanders, and General McNair reviewed the division at different points. Members of the division even traveled to New York City in June 1944, and marched down Fifth Avenue as part of a War Loan drive.[24]

While the 100th Division had proven itself adept at military showmanship, its ability as a combat command remained untested, and the timing of that test remained uncertain. The Century appeared to be stigmatized by its frequent participation in parades and exhibitions, which had given it, in some circles, a reputation as a show division. This image was strengthened by its acceptance of numerous Special Services personnel, including a five-hundred-man contingent from the recently disbanded Army War Show Task Force, a group that had traveled around the country putting on demonstrations of military hardware as part of the war bond effort.[25]

Some openly referred to their command as a "4-F outfit" that would never go overseas. The big brass appeared to agree. Late in July, Gen. Ben Lear, the new commander of U.S. Ground Forces (General McNair had been killed during an inspection tour of Europe), spent two days at Fort Bragg reviewing the division from top to bottom. The division's historian stated that Lear "was publicly non-committal as to his impressions." Rumor had it, however, that upon departing the installation he told a group of officers, "If the war is over when this outfit goes overseas, then, God bless you; however, if the war is still on, may God help you!" According to another rumor, General Marshall, who continued to consider

Withers Burress "a top notch general," had had to talk Lear out of giving the division an unsatisfactory rating.[26]

Other, more welcome rumors indicated that the division would ship out before the end of the summer. As early as mid-July, the recruits were being trained in jungle warfare, suggesting an imminent transfer to the Pacific. Still other rumors had the division bound for such remote climes as Alaska and Norway. With passing weeks, however, it became increasingly likely that its destination would be the European theater. While the division's composite battalion was en route to New York for the war-bond parade, America had learned of Operation Overlord, the invasion of the European continent by U.S., British, Canadian, and Free French troops under the overall command of General Eisenhower. The opening of a new front suggested an imminent need for troops on the ground in northern France.

Then, ten weeks after D-Day, elements of the U.S. Seventh Army—principally the 3rd, 36th, and 45th Infantry divisions of General Devers's 6th Army Group, followed by forces from the French First Army—launched an amphibious assault, known as Operation Dragoon, on the coast of southern France. A complement to Overlord, this second invasion secured for the Allies additional port facilities on the French Riviera while also supporting the recent Allied breakout from Normandy. By mid-September, supervision of Dragoon had passed from the commander of the Mediterranean theater to Eisenhower's Supreme Headquarters Allied Expeditionary Force.[27]

On August 29, two weeks after the first landings near Marseille and St. Tropez, General Burress assembled the thousands of officers and men under his command and announced that the division had received orders to deploy overseas. It would leave North Carolina as soon as it passed final qualifications and inspections and packed up. He did not disclose the destination, but the division had been alerted to stand by for shipment to some point in Europe.

Frank Gurley noted that Burress, addressing the troops in an exaggerated Virginia drawl, likened the division's immediate future to final conditioning before a prize fight. The general reported having heard "some fellows complainin' we been trainin' too long here at Fort Bragg. But Ah'll tell you this, when you're gonna take on Jack Dempsey, the Big Champ, you need all the trainin' you kin git!" According to Gurley, these words drew "wild applause." An only slightly less enthusiastic reaction greeted Colonel Tychsen's speech to the 399th. Tychsen assured his men that, contrary to the well-publicized opinions of some high officials that "the war in Europe is all over but the shouting . . . I'm here to tell you we'll need less shouting and more *shooting* if we hope to win. I can promise you that this Regiment will see plenty of combat before it's finally over."[28]

Eager to shed the label of permanent training unit, the men of the Century were ready to ship out, but they had few illusions about what lay ahead. "Most were tired of training," Private Fair observed, "but were not anxious to go into combat." Private Howsmon agreed that the division was eager to remove the "repple depple image" it had acquired, "and most of us, I think, felt that it was time we got into the war. This is not to say that we didn't have fear about what lay ahead. No one looks forward to being shot at and maybe killed, but I believe, as a unit, our state of readiness and general morale overwhelmed the fear."[29]

The exodus from Bragg began on September 25, when a contingent of the division entrained for New York City, the port of embarkation. Over the next several days, this vanguard was followed in increments by the balance of the command: 762 commissioned officers, 44 warrant officers, and 13,189 enlisted men. Within twenty-four hours, the multitude began arriving at Camp Kilmer, New Jersey, across the Hudson River from Manhattan. Accommodations at that two-year-old embarkation center were Spartan at best, but the duty demanded of the soldiers there was light. It consisted largely of clothing and equipment inspections and lectures on various subjects such as the importance of safeguarding military information (to enhance deployment secrecy the men were ordered to remove the division patches from their uniforms). Another lecture informed the soldiers of their rights under the Geneva Convention if taken prisoner.

On October 5, everyone was readied to move out. Late that afternoon, the men of the division, clad in full-dress uniforms and woolen overcoats, carrying their rifles and lugging not only full field packs but also duffel bags crammed with their belongings, left Camp Kilmer for the thirty-minute ferry ride across the Hudson to New York. Debarking at the ferry slip, they passed up a steel stairway to a pier where several transports were berthed. In the darkness of early evening, the GIs filed across the main decks of the ships and down into their holds, which had been converted into sleeping quarters. Almost one thousand nine hundred troops were crowded into one of the vessels, the U.S. Army Transport (USAT) *J. W. McAndrew*. One of them, a private in the 399th, identified the ship as one that his father, an employee of the Brooklyn Navy Yard, had helped convert years before into a military vessel: it had originally been a banana boat operated by the United Fruit Company.[30]

Six thousand three hundred forty-one officers and men of the 397th and 399th infantries inhabited the USAT *George Washington*, whose 23,788-ton displacement made it the largest troop carrier in the army. Built in Germany in 1908 as a passenger liner, it had been interned in New York at the outset of World War I; in 1917, it had carried thousands of doughboys, including then-Capt. Andrew Tychsen, to the fighting front in Europe. After the war, it had borne President Woodrow Wilson and his staff to the peace conference at Versailles. Other members of the Century's fleet included USAT *Henry Gibbins*, the USS *Monticello*, the USS *General Gordon*, the USS *General J. R. Brooke*, and the SS *Santa Maria*; each carried nearly two thousand troops. Convoy vessels included an escort carrier, the USS *Solomons*; a destroyer, the USS *Dewey*; and three destroyer escorts. One GI aboard the *George Washington* thought that the escort vessels "did not look very formidable because they were so much smaller than our ship, but they were floating arsenals."[31]

The first ships to sail cast off from Pier 19 on the morning of October 6, 1944. Then and there began an adventure most of the soldiers would never forget—for good and for ill. Landlubbers with weak stomachs and inner ear problems quickly became seasick, some before their ship cleared the harbor. Khoury recalled that when belowdecks "the smell of vomit from sick men was overpowering. It was great to be topside where hardly anyone got sick, but if a man did get seasick he just heaved over the side."[32]

Those who could not keep food down gave their meal tickets to those with hardier constitutions. The men were fed two meals per day, consumed while standing in the ships' galley and wearing life jackets. Pvt. Paul S. Mosher of I Company of the 397th, whose stomach revolted with every roll and pitch of the *Washington*, could keep down only fruit cocktail, provided by a friend working in the ship's galley. Mosher consumed so much of it on the voyage that in later years he could not stand the sight of it. Other GIs developed lifetime aversions to the smells of diesel fuel and exhaust, and even such common scents as cooking grease and boiled eggs. Wilfred Howsmon recalled a greater variety of smells: "a mixture of every body odor known to man."[33]

Throughout the voyage, men's ears were assailed by the noise of the ship's engines and other heavy machinery. Storage space was at a premium and maneuvering room so limited that "two men passing had to right angle and squeeze by." Most of the men had to bathe and shave in saltwater, which left a residue on the skin and a sensation of being unclean. Only those who made friends with their ships' naval, coast guard, and merchant marine crews got to shower in fresh water, as the crews themselves did.[34]

The situation worsened for everyone when, four days out of New York, the winds changed, the seas grew frighteningly rough, and a full-fledged hurricane—the worst in almost two decades, according to older crew members—struck the flotilla. Ships were tossed about like driftwood; at one point the *Washington* nearly collided with the *McAndrew*, an event that would have sent hundreds of young men to a watery grave. John Courter recalled that when lying on his bunk he would find himself "practically standing on my head and then standing on my feet with my stomach doing a flip-flop up to my throat and then to the other end. . . . I later learned that we were within five degrees of capsizing." By order of the ships' captains, the soldiers were kept belowdecks for forty-eight hours, all hatches closed, until the storm abated. By then even the hardiest seagoer had been laid low by sickness or terror, or both.[35]

On October 17, after twelve days at sea, the coast of Africa became visible off the starboard bow. Passing Morocco, the transports entered the Straits of Gibraltar. At their mouth they witnessed a sobering sight: the burning hulks of two U.S. merchant ships that had been torpedoed by German U-boats.

The voyage continued along the coast of North Africa. The ships passed Algiers and then turned north toward the Balearic Islands. Here they encountered another storm—tame by comparison with the hurricane—that continued until, on the twentieth, they entered the harbor of Marseille. That night, because the landing facilities had been virtually destroyed by the retreating enemy, the men scaled the sides of their ships via rope nets, a harrowing experience for troops under such heavy weight as they carried: one misstep and they might drown. At least one man lost his footing and was crushed between the hulls of two ships berthed side by side. Most of the GIs were conveyed to shore by landing craft; others crossed the harbor on foot via the decks of partially submerged ships, sunk by the Germans in a futile effort to make the harbor unusable by their enemy.[36]

Climbing ashore in the dark, the Centurymen had a limited opportunity to inspect their new surroundings. Few Frenchmen beyond local stevedores were on hand to greet them as they set foot on the shore of the country where, after frustratingly long delays, they would be introduced to a shooting war. In fact, the only truly memorable welcome they received upon landing came courtesy of a German radio broadcast by "Axis Sally"—a.k.a. Mildred Gillars of Portland, Maine, a would-be actress who had emigrated to Germany in the 1930s and had become a leading Nazi propagandist. Even as the Centurymen were touching dry land in southern France, Sally gave out this cheerful greeting: "Welcome, 100th Infantry Show Division! We have 20 divisions just waiting to welcome you." Lieutenant Fishpaw of the 374th Field Artillery Battalion recalled that the balance of the broadcast featured American dance tunes. "We enjoyed the music," he recalled, "but her statement about twenty divisions waiting for us took the joy out of it." Also troubling was the evident fact that the precautions taken by the division to prevent the enemy from learning of its arrival had failed. Accordingly, 100th Division patches were quickly reattached to the men's shoulders.[37]

Punctuating Sally's greeting, the enemy provided sound effects on cue. John Angier recalled that "as we continued to grope our way in the darkness to the outskirts of the city, we could hear in the distance the rumble and roar of heavy artillery firing round after round into the southern sector along the Mediterranean coast. Little did we know that the fighting was that close."[38]

THREE

TO THE FRONT

The Centurymen had not expected the people of Marseille to turn out in mass to greet them, children strewing petals in their path, women (and perhaps men as well) planting kisses on freshly shaven cheeks. Yet they had anticipated a welcome of some sort, a gesture of thanks for the coming of American troops like those who had helped liberate Paris two months ago. In fact, the only locals who seemed excited were street urchins who extended upturned hands in hopes of cadging chewing gum and candy, or luxuries for their families (*"Cigarette pour papa?" "Chocolat pour mama?"*). Older inhabitants who made an effort to communicate with the newcomers displayed a studied apathy as well as a sense of defeatism. Having surrendered to Hitler in 1940, they professed to believe this was no longer France's war—it was now America's to win or lose.[1]

Axis Sally may have sounded pleased by the division's arrival, but her words gave many GIs a sense of unease. Her prior knowledge of the Century's movements was troubling, especially in light of the precautions taken to mask details of its deployment. She knew enough about the Century to deride its frequent employment in public exhibitions and simulations. She even knew something no one in the division knew—General Burress's favorite song, the Ethyl Waters-Sophie Tucker standard "There'll Be Some Changes Made," which she played during a subsequent broadcast. Her evident familiarity with the Century, and especially her reference to multitudes of Germans prepared to oppose the division (Private Gurley learned that the nearest enemy air bases were only thirty minutes away in northern Italy) had an unnerving effect on young men spending their first night in a strange land.[2]

Sam Resnick of the 399th recalled that he and many of his buddies, whether willing to admit it or not, "were frightened by those words [of Sally's]. . . . With all of our security, with the protection and precautions of the US Army, we had fooled everyone including ourselves, but not the lady on the radio." Over time "we were to hear from her quite often and each time, it demoralized us a bit more, although at times she did let us know where we were and where we were going and against whom we would be fighting—some solace after all, something to diminish the dreadful, unknowing fear."

Along with thousands of comrades, on the night the division landed, Private Resnick trudged out of the port city in near-total darkness and under a persistent rain toward a staging area twelve miles to the north. "We marched tired, weary, hungry," he wrote, "with our fully equipped backpacks, our ever-present burdens, into the void, trusting only the one in front whom we could not see. We moved along, trying to imagine the road we were on from the sound of our feet on the ground, reaching for and touching the pack of the one in front for assurances, sometimes forming a chain, a linking of humanity, by holding onto our handkerchiefs. Every hour or so, we stopped for a break, dropping to the ground, feeling on either side for the [re]assuring bodies of our buddies."

Soon after the march resumed, a horrid scream rent the night, followed by "painful moaning." Resnick wondered, "had we encountered the enemy and was one of our guys knifed or strangled?" When it became known that a soldier from his own company had fallen from a small bridge into a dry creek bed, the New Yorker was both relieved and fearful: "This was our first war casualty, a portent of many more to come."[3]

Resnick was not the only newcomer to express fear of what lay ahead. On its first night in France, Sergeant Angier's platoon marched from the docks to the 399th's assembly area "tired and wet . . . not giving a damn for anything but sleep." But over the next few days, as the unit prepared to move to the front, "the tension grew greater and greater. The men were getting jittery and began to gather in small groups to talk in whispers and sometimes pray" when they ought to have been cleaning their rifles and checking their ammunition supply. The platoon's newly acquired commander was not on hand just then, so a concerned Angier called everyone together and gave a little pep talk: "What's wrong with you guys? . . . You act like a bunch of recruits. Let's get right before it's too late. We have been like brothers for the past two years. We are like a team and I have the greatest confidence in all of you. I know you are afraid, but don't kid yourself, I'm afraid too. You have got to forget it 'cause we have a job to do."

These and other words of wisdom and encouragement appeared to have the desired effect. Angier was satisfied that his men would comport themselves ably and confidently, if he provided them with a good example of leadership. "I had never been in combat before," he mused, "nor had the lieutenant, but the men knew me, believed [in] me, trusted me as I did them, and they weren't too sure of him. We ate together, slept together, trained together, drank together, and became one." Thanks to the arduous training everyone had received back in the States, the same could have been said of virtually every squad, platoon, and company in the 100th Infantry Division.[4]

The men remained in their assembly area until October 28. They camped in woods, on open ground, in plowed fields, "which, after several days of continuous rain and the pressure of thousands of GI boots, soon turned into shin-deep mud." Private Miller recalled that his company had "shelter halves pieced together into pup tents . . . lined up in rows—a real army bivouac." Miller noted that he and his buddies did not mind the rain so much, but "cold Winter winds were starting to blow in." They did mind the lack of privacy available at the open-air latrines that had been dug on the outskirts of the assembly area. Most lacked walls or tent flies to preserve their users' modesty; some were located adjacent to roads heavily traveled by the locals. "We were embarrassed as we sat there in the open," reported John Courter of D Company of the 399th, "but the French did not even glance our way. They had more important things to think about!"[5]

At first the men were assigned the standard duties common to a stationary force: physical training exercises, rifle inspections, tactical instruction. Then, as if they were not sufficiently occupied, hundreds of GIs were pressed into service unloading equipment and ammunition from the ships, piling them onto the docks, then carting them to the assembly area where they could be stockpiled. The troops worked side by side with German and Italian POWs under guard, but they received little assistance from the local stevedores, who were staging a work slowdown and threatening to strike—another indication that the people of southern France were less than enthusiastic about American troops establishing a foothold on their soil. Those who remained on the job treated the GIs pressed into working beside them rather rudely. When they learned that one member of L Company, 399th, was from Chicago and that a buddy of his hailed from small-town Iowa, the Frenchmen began imitating, respectively, machine guns and pigs.[6]

The work helped the soldiers pass the time while they awaited shipment to the front, but it was laborious and sometimes dangerous. Private Frank Hancock, who had been trained to man a heavy machine gun in M Company of the 399th, was detailed to unload 155-mm artillery rounds from shipborne pallets onto railroad cars. To his horror, one of the shells slipped out of his hands: "It bounces on the cobblestones and falls on my toe. Painful, but no explosion!" Another novice longshoreman, Bernie Miller, dropped a cargo container that broke open "to reveal khaki colored ladies underpants. We couldn't figure out where all those lady soldiers were—we sure didn't have any with us."[7]

Those not detailed as dock hands spent much of their time setting up heavy weapons, having an occasional drill, and awaiting orders. To break the monotony, many availed themselves of passes to visit a city that connoted Continental charm, although some, heeding rumors that Marseille crawled with thieves, pickpockets, and black marketers, armed themselves with concealed trench knives. For the most part, Marseille disappointed: France's oldest city had been scarred and parts of it flattened by bombs from German and Allied aircraft. Many quaint-looking shops were closed or without electrical power. Those restaurants that remained open had limited menus, although even if short on food they appeared to be well-stocked with wine and spirits, bottles of which the men carried back to camp and secreted there.

Other establishments were doing a thriving business. Pvt. Richard P. Drury of the 397th Infantry's E Company observed that "the houses of ill repute were easily identified by the long lines of soldiers outside waiting their turn." The nineteen-year-old from Worcester, Massachusetts, did not join the queues: "Memories of the training film we were subjected to at Fort McClellan, Alabama, were still too strong for me to take any such risks." Less restrained comrades caused problems for their units, such as when the entire kitchen crew of the Anti-Tank Company of the 397th was detained overnight after being caught in a brothel in a section of the city off-limits to GIs. All in all, thought a fellow member of the unit, "the delights of a foreign metropolis in wartime are greatly exaggerated."[8]

Yet there were colorful sights to behold, and some of the sight-seers were just as colorful. Private William C. Watson, a South Carolinian in A Company of the 398th, found Marseille a city of "bizarre excesses . . . filled with people from all over the world. There were Senegalese in their colorful military and civilian dress, people from the sub-Saharan French colonies, and Moroccans, Arabs, and Orientals"—even bearded, turban-wearing Sikhs from India. Frank Gurley was amazed by the daring and agility of the Senegalese, who would stand in the path of the city's antique, fast-moving trolley cars "until the very last moment, when they leaped aside to escape death by an inch or two." Gurley and some bud-dies spent most of their time in the city "ogling girls . . . and buy-ing perfume for the women back home (in my case, my mother). . .

.. At the outdoor market, we bought bread and grapes and drank wine from paper cups on a park bench."9

At least one GI lost his life while visiting Marseille. Going the risk-taking Senegalese one better, the unidentified soldier jumped from one of the city's nonstop trolley cars and suffered fatal injuries when he hit the cobblestone street. A bystander from I Company of the 397th waited with the corpse until members of the division's graves registration detail came to haul it away, along with the man's belongings, which they stowed in the mattress cover that he and every other soldier had brought from Fort Bragg. It occurred to the bystander that the dead man would be buried in that cover: "Then it hit home. Everyone had carried his own burial shroud to the war."10

The Century had reached the European theater at a turning-point in the campaign to evict the Nazi army from France and send it streaming across the Rhine River into the German heartland. While the officers and enlisted men marked time in camp or took in the fleshpots of the Riviera, their commanders were planning how the division would contribute to attaining this objective. A few days before General Devers visited division headquarters on October 23 to deliver marching orders, General Burress had his regimental commanders report to him and now-Brig. Gen. Maurice Miller, the assistant division commander, at Marseille's Hotel Grande.

In a postwar conversation with Frank Gurley, Colonel Tychsen revealed what transpired at the conference. With a grave expression, Burress informed his subordinates that "the front lines are beyond the Moselle River in the foothills of the Vosges Mountains. Our advance has slowed to a snail's pace. This has its good side in giving us what is called an old lady's sector of the front while our boys get used to the weather and the feel of combat." He went on to say that Maj. Gen. Lucian Truscott, commander of the Seventh Army's VI Corps, "plans to work our regiments in one at a time between his veteran divisions. This will allow our boys to break in alongside units who know all the enemy's tricks." Then Burress ordered his subordinates to assemble their supply vehicles as quickly as possible for the 450-mile movement to the Vosges front. He wanted them to cram their regiments' trucks with as much ammunition as they could hold—"twice the load we all had strictly adhered to in our training back home." They had been built to carry the load, Burress declared, adding that "this was war and [they should] get on with it."

His words provoked some discussion among the regimental commanders. Colonel Ellis of the 397th—who had taught military science at VMI when Burress was commandant there in the 1930s—openly doubted that the division had the "necessary know-how" to increase the capacity of its vehicles on short notice: "That's a specialized task for Ordnance," he opined. Ellis's view did not sit well with his superior, but it was shared by Col. Nelson Fooks, Colonel Duff's successor as commander of the 398th, who reported having "no trained specialists available" to handle such a chore.[11]

Only Tychsen was willing to predict his ability to meet Burress's timetable. As he explained in his memoirs, "I felt very glad that I had been willing to send a group of our officers and men to a specialty school [that taught how to break down and reassemble vehicles] during our training period and so we were ready and able to assemble everything ourselves, while unfortunately, the other regiments had to wait for ordnance personnel to come and do the job before they could proceed north." This expertise would put Tychsen's outfit "ten days ahead of the others" in terms of its readiness to depart for the front.

Burress was delighted with Tychsen's response. "As soon as you get your vehicles in shape," he said, the 399th would leave the Riviera. "Yours will be the first regiment to meet the enemy." With that, the conference broke up and the colonels returned to their units to prepare for an imminent movement.[12]

Burress's insistence on rapid deployment sprang from his knowledge that the division was expected to occupy, as quickly as possible, a critical sector of Seventh Army's position. During the past two months, while the Century had been completing its training, the forces that had broken out of Normandy—Bradley's 12th Army Group and the 21 Army Group of Field Marshal Bernard Law Montgomery—had made rapid progress eastward in furtherance of the "broad front" strategy favored by General Eisenhower, the supreme commander. By mid-September the Allies had reached the German border within sight of the Siegfried Line—the vaunted defense cordon that the enemy called the West Wall. Then logistical problems created by the great distances the Allies covered caused the offensive to shudder to a halt along a front that ran from the Rhine south to the Meuse River.

Increasing enemy resistance was another factor in the decelerating drive. Although it was backed up nearly to the Siegfried Line, the German army had regained much of the strength it had lost during its retreat across France. By the close of September, it had amassed well over two hundred thousand troops—though many were poorly armed, trained, and equipped—and about five hundred tanks. The numbers were many times higher than they had been only a month earlier.[13]

The Allies had made several attempts to recapture momentum, but resistance continued to mount; the Germans were fighting with a sense of desperation and a fanatical urgency. Bradley's army group made only slight progress, while Eisenhower's plan to open the Belgian port of Antwerp and cross the Lower Rhine (Operation Market-Garden) ended in disaster. Eisenhower then switched objectives to the Ruhr River Valley, center of Germany's industrial base, a mission he assigned to Bradley's army group. The U.S. First Army captured fortified Aachen, Germany, on October 21, but only after suffering heavily; subsequently, it lost more than thirty thousand men while attacking through the Huertgen Forest, along the German-Belgian border. Strong resistance and continuing supply problems combined to stall the offensive once again, causing battlefield and home-front morale to suffer. Post-Normandy predictions by Allied officials that the war would be carried deep inside Germany and won by Christmas were now seen as symptomatic of overconfidence, shortsightedness, and hubris.[14]

Weeks before the 100th Division reached Marseille, most of the elements of the 6th Army Group—the U.S. Seventh Army of "Sandy" Patch, and General de Lattre's French First Army—had added their weight to the southern flank of the Allied drive. On September 14, Patch's command joined hands with Patton's Third Army, operating on the right of Eisenhower's forces, at Chaumont, France. As General Devers wrote, "this junction completely sealed the fate of several hundred thousand Germans cut off in south and southwest France. . . . [O]ne great German column estimated as high as 40,000 men was moving east when the gap was closed at Chaumont. The commander found his escape route definitely sealed, halted and opened negotiations with the 12th Army Group to the north for immediate surrender."[15]

Following the linkup with Patton, the infantrymen of VI Corps, consisting of the 3rd, 36th, and 45th divisions, drove northeast toward high ground along the Meurthe River (a tributary of the Moselle) between St. Dié and Raon-l'Etape This action, known rather whimsically as Operation Dogface, petered out short of its objective because Patch's vanguard, the 45th Division, which had been fighting continually since invading Sicily and the Italian mainland, had exhausted itself against inspired enemy resistance. As the compiler of the Seventh Army's postwar *Report of Operations* put it, "for the first time since D-day the Allied advance met an organized foe, entrenched in prepared defensive positions, forming an established line." Still, Dogface was a necessary prelude to an even larger offensive planned for mid-November, intended to chase the enemy out of the Vosges and onto the lowlands of Alsace.[16]

German resistance had a prevail-or-die quality to it. In mid-October, Hitler ordered Army Group G "under all circumstances" to deny the western slopes of the Vosges to the enemy at least until the spring of 1945. A successful holding action of such duration would permit the Siegfried Line—whose defenses had atrophied over the past several months but were now being strengthened by thousands of slave laborers—to attain, or at least approach, impregnability. The First and Nineteenth armies of *Kampfgruppe* G were to hold their positions in the mountains to the last man, preventing U.S. forces from carrying the Vosges passes and reaching Alsace, where the Americans could make better use of tanks and artillery. The effectiveness of those weapons would be limited amid the steep, tree-lined peaks of the Vosges, while the low fog ceilings and visibility common to the ninety-mile-long chain would hinder, and perhaps prevent, air support.[17]

Despite its name, the Hautes Vosges, where the 100th Division would spend the first weeks of its field service, consists of peaks whose elevations are considered moderate by Continental standards. Abounding in beds of rose-colored sandstone, these craggy heights are heavily forested on their lower slopes. The evergreens thin out toward the mountains' rounded summits, which abound in open spaces adaptable to pastureland. The slopes on the south and west of the chain feature steeper inclines than those found farther east, toward the Rhine River. These and other facts of geography and geology suggested that maintaining steady progress toward the German border would be a challenge for the Century.

The challenge had a historical component that was daunting to say the least. Through twenty centuries of warfare, no attacking army had penetrated a line of defense established in the Vosges. Those who had failed included Romans, Huns, Burundians, Swedes, Austrians, Bavarians, Germans (during the Franco-Prussian War of 1870–71), and the French themselves (in 1915–16). Presumably having learned from history, the Germans were in a position to extend this record of futility by exploiting the many defensive capabilities of their so-called Winter Line.[18]

If the task ahead of it gave the Century Division pause, one factor worked in its favor, although no one knew it at the time. The enemy units the division would encounter in the mountains were every bit as inexperienced in combat as it was. The opposition would consist primarily of the 708th Volks-Grenadier Division, which had been formed only ten days before the Century left Fort Bragg for its port of embarkation. The 708th, built around the remnants of a division decimated during the fighting in western France, had received less than two months of training before being committed to the defense of the High Vosges. The division had relieved a Panzer unit that had been guarding the Meurthe River east of Baccarat and the northward approaches to the strategic Saverne Gap.

Keith E. Bonn, a leading historian of the Vosges campaign, points out that "like so many men of the 100th Infantry Division, who were 'retread' antiaircraft gunners, Air Corps crewmen, and ASTP 'whiz kids,' many of the NCOs of the *708th Volks-Grenadiers* were reclassified *Luftwaffe* and Navy crewmen; most of the *Landsers*, or infantry soldiers, were inexperienced replacements between the ages of 18 and 45." And yet the division had entered upon the fall campaign at full strength—three battalions per regiment instead of the standard two—and its men wielded the new MP44 assault rifle and MG42 machine gun. "Thus," writes Bonn, "not numbers, not equipment, but training and leadership would make the main difference between the two units."[19]

As the only element of the Century ready to move, the 399th Infantry Regiment left the assembly area outside Marseille by motorized transport early on Saturday, October 28. The vanguard of the first large formation of reinforcements to reach southern France trundled north aboard two-and-a-half-ton trucks filled with men, equipment, weapons, and ammunition. It ascended the Rhone River Valley, an important inland trade and transportation route since the times of the ancient Greeks and Romans. In virtually every town and village the convoy passed, Frenchmen came out to bestow the boisterous welcome denied the GIs by the blasé cosmopolites of Marseille. According to Frank Hancock, "every town slows our trucks, for on both sides of the road the population stands elbow to elbow, shouting, and waving French and American flags. We hear again and again: 'Viva Le Americans! Welcome!' Schools empty, the children watch and wave, shout and

The 100th Division was moved quickly to the frontline in November 1944 where they relieved the 45th Division near St. Remy, France.

laugh! We float in a carnival atmosphere, a once in a lifetime experience for them—and for us."[20]

The roads the 399th traveled led to the village of Valance, site of a famous cavalry school that Colonel Tychsen remembered from his World War I service. Although shuttered by the decline of the horse cavalry, the school was manned by a caretaker detachment of elderly soldiers who acted as if the place was still a flourishing institution. "I was much amused," Tychsen recalled, "by the men meticulously accounting for every detail. . . . I thought how useless it was to be so careful about something that was absolutely obsolete in modern warfare."

The next day, Tychsen's men moved on to Dijon, where he stopped not to sample the town's world-famous mustard but to meet at a girls' college with Maj. Gen. William W. Eagles, commander of the 45th Division, which the Century was to support once it reached the front. Old acquaintances from their days at Fort Benning and also the Command and General Staff School, the two officers had a pleasant talk during which Eagles confirmed General Burress's understanding that the 100th Division "would gradually be integrated into the line." In a matter of minutes, however, everything changed. Suddenly called to the telephone, Tychsen's host returned to relay an order from his immediate superior, Maj. Gen. Edward H. Brooks, the newly assigned successor to General Truscott as commander of the VI Corps, that the 399th was to rush to the front, where it would immediately relieve the 179th Infantry Regiment of Eagles's command. The rest of the Century, as soon as it arrived, would likewise go into line at once instead of gradually.[21]

Thus far, the trip north had been remarkably swift and smooth, especially considering the weight under which many of the trucks were groaning. In later years, Private Khoury learned that the move from Marseille was "the fastest deployment in U. S. military history of an entire infantry division." Frank Gurley noted that as the convoy began the final leg of its trip to the front early on the thirty-first, it made unusually quiet progress. "Though the trucks were normally driven in a noisy and undisciplined manner," he noted, "tonight the drivers kept their vehicles under strict control, shifting gears quietly under their weighty human cargoes, and idling the truck motors as softly as cats purring in the gathering gloom." Their passengers, too, had fallen silent: "Most of us were lost in thought, asking ourselves questions for which we had no answers." Three questions were uppermost in their minds: "What will it be like? How will I act under fire? Will I still be around tomorrow night?"[22]

The atmosphere of introspection was deepened by scenes of carnage, a harbinger of what lay ahead. En route from Dijon, the men in the trucks viewed the results of the enemy's futile attempt to escape from the trap set for it in southern France. Both sides of the road were lined with the smoldering wreckage of vehicles and weapons that had fallen prey to American air attacks. Pvt. Jack Pointer of G Company found the fields on either side covered "bumper to bumper with everything from tanks to bicycles, all burned and knocked out. Foxholes along the road were numerous and [there] were many other signs that war had been in this area not too long before we arrived."[23]

The historian of the 397th Infantry, whose regiment took this same road a few days later, commented that "we were intrigued by the sights and despite the smell of decomposed bodies could not help but keep our eyes riveted on the sides of the roads." As unsettling as the sights might seem to troops about to enter combat for the first time, they offered a reassuring sign of the offensive might of Seventh Army: in the entire column "there was not one vehicle worth even scrap. A good job had been done."[24]

At midday on October 31 ("what a Halloween night," recalled Pointer, "with scares for us new boys, fresh from the States"), the trucks halted at a designated assembly area on the outskirts of Fremifontaine, a sleepy farming village among the Vosges foothills. The men alighted and set up pup tents on the side of a trail that ran through a woodlot. They had been told they would remain there in bivouac for three days before moving up to the front. That destination, only a few miles away, pulsed with the dull but constant thunder of artillery, which threatened to prevent a sound night's sleep. A more disturbing report, although one hardly unexpected, was received late in the afternoon: the regiment would move up the next morning, relieving elements of the fought-out 45th Division. In the assembly area, the men were directed to turn in their duffel bags, which they were assured would be returned to them as soon as they took up a semipermanent position. In fact, they would not see their belongings again for six months.[25]

The weather added to the difficulty of getting adequate sack time. Twenty-two-year-old Sgt. George F. Tyson Jr. and his twelve-man L Company rifle squad crowded around a fire barely large enough to warm them all. The winds were so fierce that some men shielded their faces with their rarely used gas masks. "There were occasional rains that kept the area muddy and the morale down," Tyson remembered. "Then we retired for the night. Little did we know about the many nights in our future and how we should have enjoyed what little comfort we had at that time."

In the dark hours of early morning, one of Tyson's men heard a noise in the bushes and fired off several rounds from his M1. Going forward at dawn, he discovered his victim, the Century's Division's first confirmed kill in the combat zone—a cow that had wandered away from a local farm.[26]

Before dawn on November 1, the men of the 399th awoke stiff, sodden, and chilled to the bone. They packed up their tents, wolfed down a breakfast of K-rations, then began to trudge north in a column of ducks—a line of troops on either side of the road, the men spaced five yards apart. At eight o'clock they reached an open area southwest of the village of La Salle. This was the position that had been held for thirty days straight by the 179th Infantry Regiment, an outfit well-known for the fighting it had done on Sicily, in Italy, and in southern France, as well as for a talented enlisted man, soldier-cartoonist Bill Mauldin, creator of the long-suffering GIs Willie and Joe.

In later years, several elements of the 399th would claim to have been first to go into line. John Khoury forever insisted the honor belonged to his L Company ("the last for roll call, last in a parade, last to board the ship, but first to disembark and first to enter combat"). Frank Gurley, who made a careful study of the various claims, concluded that at least one scout from each of several companies of the 1st and 3rd battalions reached the front virtually simultaneously to begin exchanging positions with the corresponding battalions of the 179th.

It was possible, however, that a few of the 399th's combat engineers, wishing to confer as soon as possible with their colleagues in the 45th, got there first. It was also possible that forward observers from the 925th Field Artillery Battalion were first on the scene in order to coordinate fire plans and familiarize themselves with target reference points established by the 45th's divisional artillery. Regardless of the order of arrival, Gurley wrote, "the relief of the 179th by the 399th was carried out flawlessly." Regimental records indicate that the movement was completed just after noon, although the men of the 179th did not depart until evening. By 7 p.m., most of the 179th having gone to the rear, command of the sector was passed to Colonel Tychsen.[27]

The new arrivals were struck by the appearance of the troops whose foxholes they were about to occupy. Frank Gurley found them to be "friendly, rugged looking guys, with beards and camouflage netting on their helmets. . . . The rain seemed to run off their helmets onto their raincoats and onto the ground without getting them the least bit wet. It was our first look at combat men and we were duly impressed." Other observers, including Private Bourne, were startled by the "hollow-eyed, half-dead look" on the veterans' faces, a sight "we'd never seen before, but were soon to know well."

Though tired beyond measure, many of the veterans greeted the new arrivals with hard-edged humor. Sergeant Tyson recalled that some of the old soldiers "were making fun of us with all of our equipment, full field packs, ammo packs, gas masks, and bayonets. All any of them had was a rifle, bandoliers, and a raincoat." Some took the time to orient their replacements to the local situation and even suggested which weapons were more effective in dealing with the enemy. Others were less generous with their time and advice. "The enemy is that way," one GI told Private Pointer, "there is the hill you are supposed to capture, go get it, good-bye."[28]

The 179th had a right to be curt and even surly. In northeastern France and in Italy, it had seen heavy fighting and suffered accordingly. When Lt. James P. Shields, a platoon commander in C Company of the 399th, met his bearded, rumpled counterpart in the 179th, the latter inquired about the size of his unit. Forty men, said Shields. "We got eighteen," his acquaintance remarked. "Guess you'll have to dig some more holes." In answer to another question, Shields replied that L Company had 187 men. "We got about ninety," he was told. "That's all you'll have soon."[29]

The bearded officer was correct about the lack of accommodations. As soon as the exchange of positions was complete, the men in the 1st and 3rd battalions of the 399th began to dig foxholes for the first time in a combat zone. They found that their compact entrenching tools made little dent in the hard ground surrounding La Salle. A few men were fortunate to borrow round-point D-handle shovels and full-size picks from the men of the 179th. With these "man-size" tools, Frank Hancock "dug furiously. . . . It wasn't five minutes later and I had a hole six feet across and four feet deep."[30]

Not every digger made uninterrupted progress. "No sooner had we started digging," wrote John Angier, "when the Krauts opened up with their 88's. Brother, that was it. Everyone jumped for their holes and prayed that they wouldn't be joined later by an 88." Angier believed the enemy "must have known we had arrived in that sector that night, because they really poured it on. After the first barrage we had become somewhat seasoned to the Jerry artillery, but we had yet to fight them face-to-face. That was coming later and we all knew it. Fortunately, no one was hit, and with pencil in shaky hand, most of us settled down to write what we thought was our last letter home."[31]

Some of Angier's buddies took up weapons rather than shovels and launched the division's first advance in the direction of its enemy. Private Fair and his machine-gun platoon were ordered out along a road that ran through an open field to pour a harassing fire into enemy troops believed to be occupying a nearby woods. The mission made Fair realize that, with the veterans of the 179th gone to the rear, "we were on our own. It was an unsettling feeling."

It was so dark when his squad started that the men could hear but not see each other, even the man directly in front. The sense of isolation left everyone "as scared as I was," Fair believed. Then a rifle shot rang out, and everyone hit the ground, only to learn that a GI had shot himself while climbing in or out of a foxhole. The advance cautiously resumed until Fair was certain they were about to walk right into the German lines.

Finally the column turned off the road and into a clearing, where Fair set up his gun. He was ordered to fire a few rounds at the woods: "The gun made so much noise and there was so much light coming out of the barrel every time we fired that I was sure a German patrol would seek us out and kill us all!" But the woods proved to be vacant, and the squad spent the night cold and tired—without tents or even blankets—but uninjured. The next morning, the men returned to their original position. Despite their failure to locate the enemy, Fair and his comrades "felt pretty good about ourselves. We had fired the first shots in the war for the 399th Regiment." No one had heard about the cow-killer of L Company.[32]

Fair's belief to the contrary, the noisy fusillade he had unleashed against the empty woods was not the first shot fired by the Century Division. A few hours earlier, members of M Company's mortar platoon, taking up positions vacated by the mortar men of the 45th Division, had loosed some rounds toward the enemy lines, apparently without taking a careful sighting. Even earlier, a howitzer of the 925th Field Artillery had dropped some shells in the direction of enemy-occupied St. Remy, two miles north of La Salle. The division's historian duly commemorated the occasion: "That shot, hurled through the dimness of the late afternoon, was fired for registration [to fix target coordinates] of one of the battery's pieces. It was a sound which in the months to come was to be heard in a terrifying crescendo by the enemy."[33]

The 399th's position placed the outfit on the left, or north flank, of the VI Corps line west of the Meurthe River. On its left, the regiment connected with those troops of the 45th Division who had yet to be relieved by the rest of the Century. On the right, the 399th linked with the 3rd Division—one of the most celebrated formations in the army, home to Sgt. Audie Murphy, fated to become the most decorated American soldier of the war—as well as with the veteran 36th Division. Later the newly arrived 103rd Division would also go into position south of the 399th.

As soon as the 103rd and the balance of the 100th had gone into line, the 6th Army Group would attempt to complete Operation Dogface, prior to launching a major offensive in cooperation with a movement by Patton's Third Army toward the occupied city of Metz. To gain the final objectives of Dogface, the VI Corps was to operate against the center of the enemy's position by forcing a crossing of the swift-flowing Meurthe near Baccarat, a town whose capture had been assigned to elements of Maj. Gen. Wade Haislip's XV Corps, which operated on the left of VI Corps. Once over the river, General Brooks's corps was to drive southeast through the rail and road center of Raon-l'Etape and capture the high ground beyond, known as "the gates of the Vosges." South of VI Corps, Free French forces would make demonstrations to keep the Germans in place until they could be surprised and routed.[34]

Preliminary operations got under way on the 399th's front on November 3, one day after yet-to-be-relieved elements of the 45th Division advanced to St. Benoit, midway between Rambervillers and Raon-l'Etape, about twelve miles short of the Meurthe. Since the shelling of the 925th Field Artillery had failed to drive the enemy out of St. Remy, early that morning a platoon of L Company of the 399th under Lt. Thomas Plante moved cautiously toward that village. The element of surprise was lost, however, when the platoon's inexperienced scouts scaled Hill 416.9 (so designated because of its height in meters) one mile east of the village and stumbled upon a squad-size force of Germans—riflemen and machine gunners—dug in less than fifty yards away. The surprise encounter resulted in the wounding of Pvt. Estil G. Crittenden of Louisville, Kentucky, the division's first battle casualty. Because Crittenden was quickly surrounded, he also became the first Centuryman to be taken prisoner.[35]

The casualty balance was soon evened. John Khoury, armed with a 1903-model Springfield rifle, the weapon of choice for snipers, was in the thick of the fighting near St. Remy, his unit opposed by enemy troops dug in behind good cover and firing machine guns "that spewed bullets at twice the rate of ours." This day, for the first time, the youngster from Brooklyn got the full sensory experience of war: "All around us, the smell of gunsmoke filled the air and the noise of gunfire was deafening. I lay behind a tree with my 1903 sniper's rifle trying to see something to aim at. Nearby I could hear an M1 rifle going full blast, as if fired blindly." Whirling about, he called to his buddy, Pvt. Al Lapa, "What are you firing at?" Lapa shouted back, "I don't know, but I'm going to scare the hell out of them!" A moment later, a round whined past Khoury's skull. Meant for him, the bullet struck another target. He heard someone, perhaps Private Crittenden, cry out in pain and terror: "Medic! Medic! I'm hit!"

Hoping to take down the unseen assailant, Khoury quickly fired off all five rounds in his cartridge. In the smoke and tumult, he could not tell if he had hit anything, but he felt a stinging blow to his shoulder each time he pulled the trigger of his bolt-action rifle. He had stopped to reload when a whisper-thin voice spoke to him from close by: "*Nicht schiessen!*" Whirling about, Khoury found a German soldier, not six feet away, staring him in the face. "My rifle was not even loaded! He could have easily shot me or bayoneted me before I could have defended myself!" But the man had no weapon, and Khoury decided that he had said, "Don't shoot!" More surprised than frightened, he searched the German and found nothing except a piece of bread, apparently his only rations.

After an hour's standoff, the fighting came to an inconclusive end. Having found it impossible to gain ground against what appeared to be a larger and better-positioned force, Lieutenant Plante withdrew the platoon, minus Crittenden, to its starting point. Khoury fell back with the rest, his prisoner—the first enemy soldier captured by the Century Division—in tow.

When Khoury reached L Company's bivouac, a soldier of the 179th Infantry who had lingered with the 399th pointed to Khoury's prisoner and suggested, "Let's see how big a hole you can put in his back." Khoury was shocked: "That struck me as insane, because I could have been dead just a few minutes before. Besides, if we shot every enemy soldier who wanted to surrender, none ever would. . . . Nevertheless, the war was over for that German, but not for me. From that moment on, I knew I had received a gift of time that I prayed would last until the end of the war."[36]

This would not be the only time that GIs, including members of the Century, urged captors to shoot their prisoners. Usually it was an impulse driven by the heat of battle, and quite often the result of an urge to avenge the killing or wounding of a buddy. Some members of the division admitted mistreating POWs, and at least one prisoner was shot down. Tom Bourne was present when, during the Vosges campaign, an enemy position was overrun and its defenders surrendered as a group. "Just before I reached the position," he recalled, "there was a burst of gunfire . . . [and] a German soldier lay face down in the dirt in a flowing pool of brilliant red blood. After surrendering, he had not been able to resist taunting our men, in fluent English. The war was over for him, he had said, and no doubt he'd be sent to the States as a pampered prisoner of war, while we had to stay there in the wet and filth and probably die. This snapped something in the mind of one of my fellow [rifle]men who was standing a few feet away. . . . I was horrified and revulsed, but our friend showed no sign of remorse, or that he necessarily considered himself finished shooting, so no one said anything." Bourne concluded that "this was, in a sense, cold-blooded murder, though probably mitigated by something like temporary insanity, and certainly, given the circumstances, provoked." More than anything else, the incident "simply underline[d] the dehumanizing nature of war."[37]

Concurrent with the operations of L Company, a patrol from B Company under Lt. Jack Reid advanced from the bivouac and occupied La Salle. Early in the evening, Reid and his men probed toward the scene of their comrades' fight without encountering any opposition. Near midnight, however, a German patrol strayed to within rifle range of La Salle's occupants. Alert to any movements in the area, Reid's men opened fire, killing the officer in charge as well as two of his men—the first human casualties inflicted by the division—and scattering the others.[38]

The news that Germans were in the vicinity vied with the miserable weather to deny the men of the 399th much sleep that

night. John Angier, whose unit had just reached the bivouac outside La Salle, reported that as he and his buddies bedded down,
the cold rain turned frigid. Moreover, the night was pitch dark:
"You could not see your hand before your face, but somehow or
other I managed to get the platoon spread out and digging in for
the night. Every time your shovel would hit the dirt, those damned
Krauts would lob in a few mortar shells to let you know that they
were still up and awake. It was miserable, wet, muddy, and cold,
trying to dig a hole to protect yourself."

Angier managed to carve out about three feet of earth before the
hole filled up with water. "I gave up in disgust," he wrote. "I sat
down in the water, threw my raincoat over my head, and proceeded to light up one cigarette after another . . . those that I could find
that were dry enough to smoke." Private Pointer of G Company
also spent a "miserable night. . . . We were supposed to move out
on trucks [to a new bivouac, presumably under canvas] that afternoon, but they didn't come. . . . It was raining and we had no tents
or anything so we curled up on the ground in groups of five or six
men and tried to keep warm under our rain coats."

Pointer believed that "I was more afraid that nite than at any
other time. . . . The waiting made me so nervous that I was shaking all over. I tried to hide it but most all the other fellows were
doing the same thing."[39]

It was still coming down the next morning when Colonel Tychsen
ordered a large force to revisit St. Remy and drive out its occupants. The mission was assigned to the 1st Battalion, the "Red
Raiders" of Colonel Zehner's. Like his superior, Zehner was a
West Pointer, a strict disciplinarian, and a stickler for military eti-
quette. Frank Gurley recalled that "he never smiled and struck us
all as a sourpuss." He was also as brave as they came—"Audie
Murphy stuff" minus the Texas drawl.[40]

With Zehner at its head, B Company again took the advance,
with C Company assuming a defensive position in its rear. The
other Red Raider companies tagged along behind, as did L

Company of the 3rd Battalion, making a return visit to the village. Word had come down that St. Remy was no longer heavily held—perhaps the enemy had already left—but the report was incorrect. As B Company advanced through a woods and across a deeply furrowed pasture on the edge of town, all hell broke loose: the Germans opened up with rifles, Schmeisser burp guns, and machine guns. B Company immediately went to earth in the middle of the woods, as did the units farther to the rear. "That was a scary moment in my life," Sergeant Tyson remembered. "Being inexperienced in fire fighting, the whole company was pinned down." For several minutes the battalion was unable to move, even to shift its position slightly. Then, unexpectedly, the Germans who had resisted from the outskirts pulled back into the village. The GIs cautiously resumed the advance, but then mortar shells began to rain down, splintering trees and inflicting casualties. "If I'd had false teeth," wrote Tyson, "I probably would have swallowed them."

As the troops approached the town, with the spire of its church clearly visible in the distance, snipers began to target them from the steeple; other, unseen defenders opened up as well. Again the column slowed to a halt, this time pinned down on open ground, a dangerous position to be in. Colonel Zehner, one of the few in the column who had never left his feet, turned to the prone GIs and signaled for them to follow. With steady tread, he walked toward the church, firing his Colt pistol, seemingly oblivious to the torrent of missiles flying toward him. Highly impressed, his men bobbed up and trailed after him. Their show of strength had the desired effect: gradually but firmly they evicted the Germans, who took refuge on high ground beyond the village. "We cleared the houses one at a time," said Tyson, "going inside and searching each one while several men covered us from the outside."

The battalion occupied St. Remy throughout the night despite the intermittent shelling of artillery and mortars. Most of the men slept in barns and in haystacks ("they were not Beautyrest mattresses, but it was better than nothing"). In the morning reinforcements came up to secure the Century's first captured town.[41]

The taking of St. Remy affected the 399th in two ways: Zehner became the first member of the Century to receive the Distinguished Service Cross, and the Red Raiders gained an enviable reputation. As Lt. Robert M. Stegmaier (later a colonel and G-4, or chief logistics officer, of the division) put it, "the 1st Battalion 399th was marked thereafter as a unit upon which in the direst of conditions, you would get a spirited and . . . effective response."[42]

By November 6, the balance of the Century Division—the 397th and 398th infantries, along with their associated artillery battalions and support units—had finally arrived to relieve those portions of the 45th Division that had not gone to the rear. The Johnny-come-latelys at once experienced the misery of life at the front and the fear that life engendered.

Pvt. (later Sgt.) Lester O. Gluesenkamp, a member of C Company of the 397th who had grown up in an Illinois farming village with a large German-American population, recalled his days in basic training, which he had considered some of the most trying and difficult of his life, filled as they had been with endless routine, exhausting marches, and tedious drills. Here in the Vosges, he began to revise his estimate of what constituted an undesirable situation:

> Instead of perspiration, it was now rain, snow and sleet which penetrated our clothes as the cold penetrated our bodies. The mountains were covered with dense pines, interspersed with a few open fields and with endless hills and valleys. The woods were dark and eerie in the sunless daylight. The darkness gripped you with the fear of an unknown enemy who was imagined to be hiding among the snow covered trees.[43]

Bedding down outside St. Remy, from which the last enemy sniper had been driven, the newcomers found living conditions nearly unbearable. The earth remained almost impervious to foxhole construction. Private Caldon R. Norman of A Company of the 398th spent his first night on the line in a slit trench that someone else had dug and that he shared with two buddies. He recalled "water streaming down the sides of the trench and collecting in pools where we sat and more water dripping from the attempt at a roof. . . . [I] was as cold and wet and miserable [as] I ever was up to that point. I thought longingly of a warm bed, of home, of even the barracks at Fort Bragg!"[44]

Other GIs of the 398th suffered just as much, if not more so. Pvt. John Costello of C Company spent his first night in weather so raw and blustery that hypothermia had begun to set in by the time he found shelter and communal warmth. Somehow he managed to squeeze into a "large-size pit" that held six other GIs; Costello could hardly breathe, let alone move, throughout the night.

Another member of the 398th, nineteen-year-old Pvt. John A. "Dick" Good of H Company, bedded down on top of a hill, exposed to even higher winds than many of his comrades endured. His unit had not been equipped to withstand this kind of weather—the men lacked heavy coats and shoepacks—and the elevation Good inhabited "was steep enough that they had a [rope] line that you would almost have to pull yourself along" to get to the top. Hoping to dig a hole deep enough to shelter his six-foot-six-inch frame, he succeeded in burrowing down only a foot and a half. He stretched out in this poor imitation of a foxhole all night under the steady, bone-numbing rain. He fell asleep from sheer fatigue, only to be awakened by a hail of "screaming meemies"—rounds of *nebelwerfer*. The shells did not fall near enough to produce casualties, but Good never forgot his first exposure to their fearful shriek.

Having somehow survived the night, Good was sent down the rise in the dim light of morning, where he had to detour around an open field sewn with Schu mines. Along its edge he found the mangled body of a German soldier, killed not by a mine but by an artillery round. It was as frightening an introduction to combat as any neophyte soldier could have experienced. And yet Good had gotten some sleep, much-interrupted though it had been. A buddy,

Private Tillett, stayed awake through the night kicking a tree to stave off freezing.[45]

For three days after going into line, the 397th and 398th—stationed in and near Baccarat and northwest of St. Remy, respectively—tried to gain information on enemy positions and movements. Having taken few prisoners, the regiments sought this intelligence through reconnaissance and the interrogation of local civilians. The 398th expected to see its first sustained action on the sixth, when its 1st Battalion advanced toward a suspected enemy strongpoint about three thousand yards northeast of its bivouac area. The movement stirred up no enemy troops, however, and after leaving one company to hold the reconnoitered ground, the other three returned to their former positions, unbloodied but feeling somewhat more like veterans than before. That same day the regiment's 3rd Battalion, operating on the left of the 1st, took position near the village of Ste. Barbe.

GIs take cover in a shallow trench in a French forest. The leaves have already fallen; soon, these soldiers would experience one of the coldest winters of the war. (*National Archives*)

On the eighth, Colonel Fooks sent all three battalions, supported by the 398th's cannon company, to a point just southwest of Raon-l'Etape along the highway from Rambervillers. The 397th saw only slightly more activity this day; two patrols launched by K Company resulted in one German killed, one wounded, and one captured. As late as the tenth, the 397th had no other physical contact with the enemy in and around Raon-l'Etape. Still, every man in the regiment realized that a major push toward that occupied town was coming.[46]

The soldiers never forgot what it felt like to go out on their first patrol, a mission that a member of the 397th came to describe as "the distilled essence of terror." Years later, Pvt. Thaddeus Samorajski of the 398th not only recalled the experience but claimed, "I can see, and feel and taste it." The vivid way he describes it, and his use of the present tense, bear him out:

Before being ordered out on patrol, Samorajski and several other members of A Company sprawl about on the ground inside their bivouac area, each with "an eye on the nearest foxhole in the event of an incoming shell." After only a few days on the line, they are anything but models of soldierly decorum. As Samorajski describes them, "they are a motley group; tired, and already weary of war. There is little effort at hygiene. Same old clothes day after day. Same dirty unshaven faces with blood shot eyes. No brushing of teeth. No toothpaste. No brush. Just gag down a can of C-rations if you can, followed by a trip to the nearest tree. Not much in at the oral end; not much out on the anal, but lots of urination for some strange reason."

The men's attempt at relaxation ends as the platoon sergeant, Ardilio Malavasi, approaches, having just come from a conference with the company's commander. Malavasi points from man to man, recruiting "volunteers" to reconnoiter a hill across an open field from the unit's position. Samorajski, a Polish kid from rural Massachusetts, is among the selectees: "Aw shit, Sarge," he exclaims, "why me?" The sergeant is irritated by the pleading tone: "Grab your rifle and get your ass over here. . . . The Captain wants to know if there are any Krauts up there. Lock and load!"

Samorajski is "genuinely pissed. My friend Paul and I spent most of the night on outpost duty behind a machine gun. It was tough duty because the Germans often moved around at night and we were positioned to be the first point of contact should they decide to probe our perimeter. It was bitterly cold and no chance for sleep. That night finally passed and no Germans but by early dawn, the tension and cold finally got to us. I began to shake real bad. . . . Now it was several hours later and the sergeant looked like he meant business. Nobody screwed around with our Sergeant—not even the officers."

Off they go. Led by the noncom no one dares to screw with, a party of half a dozen wide-eyed youngsters utterly new to this sort of thing begins to cross a frozen field flanked by woods. They advance to the accompaniment of artillery fire from front and rear—most of it distant, some of it too close for comfort. As they move, they scan the horizon for the unseen enemy and the ground in front for unseen mines. Samorajski, not wishing to move ahead of the sergeant or fall behind the rest, studiously keeps pace with his buddies: "Movement is cautious now and ears work at fever pitch. God how the heart pounds. I wonder how far the sound of it carries."

Suddenly a "strange, sweet smell" wafts up on the frigid air, a scent he experienced for the first time on the truck ride from Marseille: "The smell of something once living but now dead. A dense pallor of smoke from the artillery fire blends with the gray snow-laden sky. Exploding shells and the occasional burst of machine gun fire in the distance reaches the ears. There is something for the eyes too. The spoils of war litter the forest floor"—combat packs and cans of C-rations, probably left behind by members of the 45th Division. Suddenly "a shell whistles through the air and explodes a scant hundred yards to our front. There is instant communication with Mother Earth. Another shell bursts off to the left but farther away. . . . Still that sweet nauseating smell of something dead. We are up again and moving, desperately searching the terrain ahead."

As they near the presumed location of the enemy, every man goes low once again, then begins to crawl, "careful, cautious, rifles forward. The ridge line is up ahead. Real damn careful now. There may be some Germans waiting on the other side. Christ that damn smell again! I feel like throwing up but can't. We continue moving. At last—just a yard or two from the top of the ridge. The Sergeant crawls up and hunkers down beside me. Rifle at the ready, both of us edge up to the top. A quick glance and nothing. Then another look and I spot a body about twenty feet in front of me, slightly to the left. The Sergeant points to another body on the right. Farther away there are more brown clumps scattered about on the forest floor. Looks like about twelve in all. I look more closely. Americans. Damn! Must have been ambushed while out on patrol. Probably from the Forty-fifth Division that we just relieved."

Samorajski works his way on his stomach until he reaches the body on his left: "He's lying on his back with one leg bent over the other. Christ, just a kid. Seventeen maybe. Round babyfaced. Poor Bastard. Probably never shaved. . . . Strangely, I feel compelled to make a decision about his hometown. For some reason, I pick Cleveland, Ohio." He crawls to the next corpse: "Sort of a delicate body, one leg askew and rifle still clutched in both hands. The face I see is older than the first, thirtyish maybe. A face with an impeccably trimmed little mustache, clean shaven. I wonder how the hell he managed that while in combat. The eyes were open and staring up. I think there is a smile on his face. Maybe he caught a glimpse of Heaven during his last moments of life."

Because this man lies close by the first, Samorajski wonders if the two might have been buddies, perhaps "from the same home-town . . . one possibly motivated by the perversity of youth and passion for adventure. The other, a patriot perhaps, who could have sat out the war because of his age or a fancy job but gambled it all for his country and lost." The next body in the grouping lies face down, too close to the enemy line for Samorajski to inspect.

He is suddenly aware that the other patrolmen are looking anxiously about, especially toward the rear: "Dead Americans mean live Germans. Where the hell are they?" The answer comes moments later in a burst of machine-gun fire from a wooded hill, directed at the right flank of the patrol. The enemy having been located, it is time to clear out—"no need to wait for an order from the sergeant. Another machine gun cuts in on our left. Bullets claw the air. Go legs go. The thunk! thunk! thunk! of bursting mortar shells sounds behind us. . . . Oh Christ! One of our guys is down. No! He's getting up. Dumb bastard must have stumbled over something." With speed and agility born of the will to survive, everyone scrambles to the rear, and makes it home alive.

Back at the company bivouac, "freezing and exhausted," Samorajski is depressed and gloomy: "Dead or alive—what the hell's the difference. Another tomorrow just meant one more chance to catch a bullet or piece of shrapnel in some precious place." When the captain makes his rounds, he inquires if everyone got back. Assured that they did, he interrogates two members of the patrol—Samorajski and Malavasi. They study the captain's map board "to see if we can figure out where those damn machine guns and mortars are located." The position is to be attacked the following day.

Samorajski finds the denouement anticlimactic and strangely unsatisfying: "Next morning artillery fire plastered the hell out of the German positions. Even before the smoke cleared, two rifle platoons including the Captain charged up the hill and shot the hell out of a few stunned Krauts. My platoon was back in reserve during the entire operation. I never even got to fire a single stinking shot."[47]

On the morning of November 9, final efforts to relieve the 45th Division having been completed, General Burress officially assumed command of the Century's sector of the line west of the Meurthe. Patrolling and long-range skirmishing wound down as Burress prepared to execute the plans that Generals Devers, Patch, and Brooks had formulated for crossing the river, taking Raon-l'Etape and other strategic objectives, breaking the Winter Line, clearing the High Vosges, and pursuing the enemy across the German border. The great offensive designed to rid France of the forces that had occupied its cities and countryside for the past four and a half years was set to begin.[48]

FOUR

THE VOSGES

Snow had been in the air since the day the division reached the combat zone, but it did not fall until November 9. Private Gurley cheerfully described "flurries of white crystals cascading down through the filtered air below the pine roofs, fusing a little life into the soggy air." The widespread mantle of white gave the bivouac area of the 399th Infantry Regiment a serene, almost holy, appearance. It seemed fitting that the regiment's Catholic chaplain, Father Thaddeus J. Koszarek, should come up in his jeep to say Mass below quietly dripping pine boughs. A K-ration carton was transformed into an altar; the chaplain donned his vestments over his field jacket; and as he began the service, the "silently descending snow added appropriate atmosphere."

Gurley, who had visited the shrines of Paris and Marseille, admitted that "it wasn't Notre Dame, but perhaps proved that the Mass didn't need lavish properties or calculated pomp to be meaningful." Soldiers of various religious affiliations, and some with none at all, "knelt down in the wet pine needles even though they knew their pants were wet enough already." The chaplain preached an interfaith sermon, Communion was distributed to all believers, and the congregation departed with a sense that the mind had been relieved and the soul cleansed, or at least spit-shined.[1]

The snowfall may have been picturesque, but it threatened to complicate execution of the coming offensive, which already promised to be a complex undertaking. Both corps of the Seventh Army would be heavily involved, and close coordination would be imperative. General Haislip's command would jump off first, on or about the twelfth or thirteenth. Moving to the north of General Brooks's troops, XV Corps would cross the Meurthe at Baccarat, a city known for its fine crystal, and the namesake of a high-stakes card game. Then it would head east, seizing Sarrebourg, driving through the Saverne Gap, enveloping its defenders, and heading for Strasbourg, the historic capital of Alsace. The offensive was designed to drive a wedge between the German Nineteenth Army and, farther north, the German First Army.

No later than two days after XV Corps jumped off, VI Corps's zone would come alive. The plan called for Brooks's troops to cross the Meurthe between Raon-l'Etape and St. Dié, uproot the enemy on the other bank and drive them east through Hantz Pass and, farther south, the Saales Pass, with the ultimate objective of linking with XV Corps near Strasbourg. When General Patch determined that Haislip should start out on the thirteenth, Brooks was ordered to move on the fifteenth. However, the VI Corps leader realized that his command, which had barely assimilated the Century Division and was still adding the 103rd, would not be ready to move on the assigned date. The western bank of the Meurthe had been secured only around Baccarat and neighboring St. Michel; the enemy still controlled both sides of the river around Raon-l'Etape and from St. Dié south. Before he could undertake his role in the offensive, Brooks believed that the entire west bank of the river had to be in Allied hands. Not until the twentieth did he expect to begin his push, attacking toward St. Michel with the veteran 3rd Division in the lead.

Because of unit placement and the need for fresh troops to shoulder much of the burden, Brooks assigned the clearing of the east side of the stream to the 100th and 103rd divisions. The 103rd would move first, attacking toward St. Dié, the key to the road network that ran through the Vosges. As conditions dictated, the Century Division would support the 103rd by rolling up the left flank of the German line via a southeastern attack, or by driving to the northeast in the direction of Bionville and Allarmont (as it turned out, the former maneuver was the one put into execution). Much was being asked of the newcomers, especially the men of the 100th. Because the division would operate on the corps's northern flank, should it fail to attain its objectives, the 3rd ("Rock of the Marne") Division, which held the line between the Century and the 103rd farther south, would be imperiled, and a dangerous gap might open between XV and VI corps as they advanced east.

To enhance the prospects of success, General Brooks ordered the Century to begin its work at the earliest possible date. On the twelfth, he directed General Burress to cross the Meurthe without further delay and move north to Raon-l'Etape, which Seventh Army headquarters considered "the nerve center of supply and communications in the German system of defense." As soon as they secured that medium-size city and some neighboring venues, Burress's troops were to head east along Route N-424, the highway to both the Hantz Pass and the road center of St. Blaise-la-Roche. If the Century began its operations by the fifteenth, five days before the 3rd Division jumped off, Brooks was certain that his main effort would succeed. He realized, however, that he was asking a lot of an inexperienced command, especially in light of the fact that before the Century reached the front, the veterans of the 45th Division, who had been assigned to take Raon-l'Etape, had been stopped four miles from the city and held there by the local defenders.[2]

Why had Brooks assigned a new and untried unit such a critical role in the coming campaign? Perhaps he had begun to see that the Century was already proving itself steady-going, determined, and reliable. Not only had the division received favorable publicity for its attack on St. Remy, in subsequent days several members had comported themselves bravely enough to win awards. On the sixth, after a day of clearing roadblocks and mines northeast of St. Remy, elements of the 399th pushed out the highway toward the Meurthe in the vicinity of St. Odile and encountered a strongly held German position near Woods Six, an area of "rectangular pine groves teeming with dugouts and camouflaged machine guns." Compelled to cross seven hundred yards of open pasture-land, the men of A and C companies were suddenly pinned down by intense mortar and machine-gun fire. They did not remain immobile for long. Covered by well-placed shells from the regiment's cannon company, the troops surged forward in a driving rain and overran the position. Lt. Paul "Dutch" Loes of C Company charged a machine-gun nest and wiped it out with his tommy gun. Scout Charles Hoak of the same company played dead in front of another machine-gun emplacement; when the Germans took their attention from him, he rose up and destroyed the nest with rifle fire and grenades. Loes and Hoak received the Distinguished Service Cross for their achievements.[3]

So too did Cpl. Robert L. Ethridge, whose motorized section of Battery C, 375th Field Artillery, was ambushed two days later at a roadblock on the heavily wooded outskirts of Thiaville. Although pounded by rifle, mortar, and machine-gun fire from many directions—and despite the unit's total lack of combat experience—Ethridge and his comrades stood firm against the onslaught, refusing to abandon the howitzer they had been pulling. Struck by a mortar fragment, Ethridge shrugged off the wound, climbed to the top of the truck that had towed the howitzer, and manned the machine gun mounted on its roof. He created bloody havoc among the enemy until cut down by small-arms fire. Outnumbered and nearly surrounded, most of the members of the section escaped through the woods, but not before rendering their weapon inoperable. Ethridge was posthumously awarded the Distinguished Service Cross, while two of his comrades, one of whom had also been killed, received the Silver Star. By war's end, an additional thirty-two members of the Century would win the DSC for valor in combat, while Silver Stars would go to more than five hundred others.[4]

Yet although it was becoming clear that the division had its share—perhaps more than its share—of heroes, it was also composed of men who failed to meet the demands of war and the expectations of their leaders and comrades. Even this early in the division's combat life, more than a few Centurymen had shown they lacked the mental and physical strength that front-line service demanded. One of Pvt. Don Hildenbrand's comrades in E Company of the 397th, while on nighttime outpost duty across from a suspected enemy position, suddenly broke down, writhing at the bottom of a machine-gun emplacement and "moaning and groaning about how he just had to get out of there, he couldn't stand it anymore." Afraid the man would give away their position, Hildenbrand did all he could to quiet him short of strangulation before he was able to hand him off to someone going to the rear. Fortunately for Hildenbrand's peace of mind, he never saw the man again.[5]

Not everyone whose rank and outward demeanor indicated an ability to shoulder responsibility and perform effectively in any situation proved able to withstand the rigors of combat. Private Khoury had a vivid recollection of a man widely considered to be one of the toughest platoon sergeants in his company. The sergeant had ridden his men hard throughout basic training, claiming that only harsh discipline would make soldiers of them and warning that no matter how severe life at Fort Bragg seemed, "it would be hell and ten times worse when [we] went into combat. No non com was more highly regarded than he was." But when the sergeant led the platoon on its first night patrol, the same thoughts that disturbed lowly privates such as Khoury—the fear of stumbling into the arms of an unseen and well-armed enemy, of making any unwanted noise while on patrol ("the snapping of a twig underfoot sounds like the falling of a tree in the cold, crisp night air")—caused the sergeant to freeze up shortly after leaving the company bivouac, and he fell "to sobbing and trembling."

The patrol successfully performed its mission, and although fired upon returned to its own lines intact, but it was forced to drag along the wailing sergeant. Shortly afterward, the man was sent back to a medical facility, where he remained for nearly a month. Later he returned to his outfit, but his nerves were shot. Being of no further use to his unit, he was reduced to the ranks and assigned to a permanent position in the rear.

Such behavior, because it imperiled the lives of others, could not be tolerated. It also had a psychological component: it served to break the bond that united comrades in combat, what Khoury called the "cement that binds infantry dogfaces together." And yet, perhaps because they could easily see themselves, under certain pressures, acting in a similar manner, some GIs entertained a certain amount of sympathy for those among them who showed human weakness. The Nazi element in the German ranks may have thought of themselves as supermen, but few GIs made that mistake when evaluating themselves or their comrades. For his part, Khoury "could not find it in my heart to condemn" his sergeant, who had been "given a responsibility greater than his ability to handle it. His bravado had been an act to bolster his courage, but fear shattered his façade."[6]

Another member of the 399th, Private Bourne, took a more expansive view of the issue. He recalled "almost always being afraid" during his time at the front, "but for some reason, though I was never even remotely heroic, I always stayed where I was supposed to be and went where I was told. Why, in the face of such raw fear?" The great majority of his buddies did the same, though Bourne was never sure whether they were as scared as he was. From his earliest days on the line, there were those in his squad, his platoon, his company who could not cut it when danger beckoned and lives were on the line. As Bourne put it, "a few broke down completely and were taken away, a few others were adamant in their refusal to face the danger and were given rear echelon assignments guarding baggage, or whatever else they did." And yet

> there was no disbelief in the sincerity of the dropouts, no scorn, no bitterness that I can recall. There was rather [a] feeling [of being] sorry for them and maybe some fleeting envy. This was an advance taste of the enormous tolerance of

the combat man for the non-combatant. Life is too fragile, too temporary, to waste any of it on anger or recrimination, and the combat life is too awful to wish it upon anyone who doesn't have to be there, for any reason. As I reflect on it I can't recall any feelings manifested of elitism or martyrdom, either one of which would have seemed well justified, given the conditions we endured during the next five or six months.[7]

From the hour the Century assumed its role in the mid-November offensive, the skill and savvy of General Burress and his determination to avoid casualties whenever possible characterized his tactics. One of his specialties, which he had developed during his stint at the General Staff School, was the art of crossing rivers under fire. He used that know-how to persuade General Brooks to revise his plan of attack in a way that saved time, trouble, and, by avoiding a frontal assault, men's lives. Burress was aware that the enemy held a heavily fortified line that ran from around Neufmaisons, northeast of Raon-l'Etape, down the east side of the Meurthe and then across the river toward St. Dié. Instead of adopting Brooks's idea that the Century should fight its way across the Meurthe in assault boats above or below Raon-l'Etape, Burress favored crossing two of his regiments farther upstream via a bridgehead that had been secured at Baccarat. Such a tactic would enable the Century to gain the rear of the Germans on the hills north and west of Raon-l'Etape. Before the attack got under way, Burress's third regiment, along with the division artillery and other support elements, would mount a limited assault along the west bank of the stream to hold the enemy in place long enough for it to be taken by surprise from another direction. After some consideration, Brooks approved the change of tactics.[8]

The movement got off to a successful start. Before dawn on the tenth, the 397th and 399th Regiments boarded trucks that carried them across the bridgehead at Baccarat. The next day, Armistice

Members of E Company, 397th Infantry, marching along a road near Raon-l'Etape, France. (*National Archives*)

Day, saw little activity beyond brief advances in the continuing rain and snow to secure jumping-off points for the attack scheduled to begin on the twelfth. Precisely at 11 a.m., the hour at which the fighting had ceased twenty-seven years earlier, Burress moved the divisional command post from Rambervillers to Ste. Barbe, closer to the front. The new headquarters occupied ground quite close to the place where Burress had campaigned as a young officer in the American Expeditionary Force.

Germans POWs interrogated at the command post enabled Burress's G-2 (Intelligence Section) staff to evaluate the strength of the enemy opposing the division. The figure settled upon was three thousand two hundred troops, committed piecemeal along the river and in the mountains to the east and north. It was learned that in addition to the 708th Volks-Grenadiers (estimated at two thousand strong), the Century was facing other elements of General Friedrich Wiese's Nineteenth Army, including infantry and armored units.[9]

At 7:30 a.m. on the twelfth, the Century went into action at division strength for the first time. The army's official history of the Vosges campaign states that the troops "were both nervous and excited, anxious about what the future attack would bring, yet

more eager than the veteran soldiers to show what they could do."
That description held true for some men, such as Tom Jelks, the
newly assigned leader of a machine-gun squad in M Company of
the 397th. One week earlier, shortly after taking up his position
following the relief of the 45th Division, the Marylander had fired
forty rounds into a woods sheltering a German mortar unit that
had been shelling Jelks's squad. Moments later, his lieutenant
came running up, demanding to know what Jelks had fired at. Jelks
explained, and his superior replied: "You don't shoot at them like
that. It will make them mad and they will shoot back at us some
more." Jelks was dumbfounded: "I said that I was sent over there
to shoot Krauts and that was what I was doing!"[10]

More typical of the GIs about to go into combat for the first
time were those who felt tired, confused, and fearful. Jelks's comrade in the 397th, Private Gluesenkamp, spoke for many of these
men: "We were at the line of departure at 7:30 A.M. and everybody was so, so tired and yet we had not even started to fight.
Nobody knew what it was to fight and everyone was scared." He
recalled that during most of the fighting they did this day, "we did
not know where we were, where we had been, or what was in store
for us over the next hill or valley."[11]

Ready or not, they were hours or minutes away from the experience of combat. The 399th, which had the lead on the left flank,
moved into position on the hills of the Bois de Bingotte (Bingotte
Woods) beyond Baccarat. Almost immediately, the Powderhorn
Regiment stirred up resistance. Frank Gurley heard "a Jerry
machine gun let rip with a long, panicky burst of fire, like a watch-
dog that suddenly awakens at a noise and starts yapping." Against
this initial opposition, the 399th established a line of outposts on
the high ground. Its next objective was the far right flank of the
enemy line near Neufmaisons. If that position could be taken and
held, the Century would control the strategic highway from Raon-
l'Etape up the Plaine River Valley.

Farther to the right, the 397th had deployed to fill in the
ground between the 399th and the river. The 397th's objectives

were the hamlet of Bertrichamps, two and a half miles northwest of Raon-l'Etape, and then the latter town, a critical hinge in the Winter Line. The 397th's historian noted that "as we crossed the line of departure at 0900 gripping our rifles tensely, everything was quiet. Company A crossed a stretch of open terrain about 100 yards deep and started up a steep hill. Now came the baptism! The 'wumpff' and 'crunch' that were enemy mortars and the whistling of the 88s soon came to be as familiar a sound as the motor of a car." Yet the first barrage was the most memorable. As a rifleman in I Company recalled, "there are many 'firsts' in our lives—the first kiss, the first drink, the first sexual adventure, the first cigarette. Many you remember. Some you forget. But hardly anyone forgets the scream and whine of the first German 88 that you know is headed your way."[12]

While their enemy was dug in on favorable terrain, the 397th and 399th had to struggle foot by foot across ground soggy from rain and coated almost everywhere in mud. A member of the 398th, who occupied the same ground a few days later, described the forbidding environment: "Hills were not gradually sloped but instead were steep and the men constantly exposed themselves in scaling the tough scrub bushes. There were many such hills which seemed to stretch in a never-ending range, [with] Jerry constantly looking down our throats and spraying our advance up the tortuous hillsides."[13]

On the 397th's front, the Germans, who were found dug in along a wooded ridge, had withstood a heavy artillery barrage. They gave as good as they got, replying with artillery and mortars that inflicted several casualties. Even hard-bitten officers like Lt. John Bacos of C Company found the fire "too hot at this spot" to be endured. The Centurymen were forced to go to earth early and often, but good cover was scarce. One of the 397th's heavy machine gunners joined the last survivor of a mortar crew that had been wiped out early in the action. Both men huddled behind

　　a long, thin log. I heard a lot of shouting and when I looked
　　up I saw a lot of Jerries running around and shooting at us

only 30 or 40 yards away. The log wasn't enough to protect us and every time we raised up a little we drew fire so we just lay there sweating it out. I had a grenade in my pocket and was trying to work it out. I looked over to the other guy just in time to see him shot through the head and die. I planned to give the grenade a heave and try high-tailing it back through the woods. I just about worked it out when I saw a Jerry about 10 yards away with his rifle pointed at me. It wouldn't have taken much to pull the trigger so I got up with my hands high.[14]

The fighting this day shattered the bodies and minds of many a youngster immersed in the cauldron of combat for the first time. C Company of the 397th suffered sixty casualties in less than thirty minutes, victims of a mortar and artillery attack from hidden positions that confounded the GIs ("You can't fight artillery with rifles," recalled Les Gluesenkamp, "when we did not know where the guns were located"). The medics of the company were overwhelmed by the carnage. One broke down completely. "The last we saw of him," wrote Pvt. Kenneth Bonte, "he was beating his head against a tree before they took him away."[15]

As the 397th and 399th strode—or inched—forward, the 398th and the 100th Reconnaissance Troop, which had remained on the west bank, began to spread out to hold a twelve-mile line between Baccarat and a point south of Etival, a town that the 1st Battalion of the 398th had captured on the ninth. As it did so, the 105-mm howitzers and the 155-mm Long Toms of the division artillery pounded away at the enemy across the river, while 50-caliber machine-gun rounds ripped through the streets of Raon-l'Etape in hopes of making its occupants believe the main attack would come from that direction.

General Burress was determined that quick and steady progress would be made toward every objective. Late in the day, he informed Colonel Ellis by field telephone that the 397th was to "move fast before nightfall. . . . Keep the men moving." He had similar instructions for the commander of the 399th. Both outfits responded splendidly. The 399th's 1st Battalion captured the vil-

lage of Veney and advanced to the foot of the high ground southwest of Neufmaisons. Meanwhile, the regiment's 2nd Battalion
slogged through mud and up wooded heights to seize high ground
south of the 1st's position. Starting out at the same time as the
399th, the 1st and 2nd battalions of the 397th attacked southeast
along the river against Germans holding the lower end of the woods
known as the Fôret de Petit Reclos. Against fierce opposition coming from atop heavily wooded ridges as high as one thousand five
hundred feet, the 397th occupied Bertrichamps and then pushed
on, killing many Germans and taking dozens of prisoners.[16]

By now the day's action was winding down. In some places the
German dead lay in piles, but they were not the only casualties
found in the woods around Bertrichamps. Private Bonte and the
rest of C Company advanced across a meadow on the edge of
town, then through a dense forest. Moving up a slight incline,
Bonte, in advance of his buddies, spotted three helmets attached
to "tattered, weather-worn overcoats." The garments, identifiable
as World War I-issue, covered the skeletons of three French soldiers who had lain in the spot where they had fallen more than a
quarter-century ago.[17]

In return for the casualties it inflicted, the 397th suffered twelve
killed, including Sgt. Marion C. Fordham, a squad leader in A
Company, who, though felled by a wound, sprang to his feet and
rushed a machine-gun emplacement, firing his M1, and, when his
rifle clip was exhausted, heaving grenades at the enemy. When his
last grenade was gone, Fordham, with fixed bayonet, plunged into
the midst of the enemy and fought them hand-to-hand before
finally being killed.[18]

The thirteenth was a frustrating and costly day for the division,
although it ended on a note of hope and heroism. Shortly after
dawn, the 1st Battalion of the 397th was supposed to renew its
advance to Raon-l'Etape, but the wretched weather—snow and
severe cold—prevented it from starting on time. Before it could

move out, shortly before 9 a.m. the regiment was attacked by infantry covered by a barrage of 88s. The attack was driven back by artillery and mortars, but it had temporarily disrupted the 397th's communications system. The attack had also overturned some of the regiment's expectations about combat. Indirect fire, especially tree bursts that brought deadly splinters down on men's heads, had counted for many casualties in the 397th. Now-Sergeant Howsmon of B Company was confused: "The mortars and artillery shells at Fort Bragg all seemed to explode in open fields." Those hit by razorlike shards of wood included Howsmon's buddy Toby Reich. Howsmon never forgot the sound of Reich crying for his mother as he died.[19]

Early this day, the 399th's 2nd Battalion attacked through the Fôret de Petit Reclos and into a clearing west of a steep elevation two miles below Neufmaisons. Tom Bourne of G Company advanced into a clearing paralleling a road thickly wooded on both sides: "The enemy was out there we'd been told, but we advanced several hundred yards in eerie silence." Then he saw a group of German soldiers flee a house at a crossroads just up ahead. "Oh, God," he told himself, "maybe they've pulled out, we've scared them off. There was nothing—and then suddenly there was everything: rifle and machine gun fire, mortars, artillery everything. We had walked into a rather obvious trap." In the confused melee, Bourne's superior, Capt. Melvin D. Clark, was wounded along with three other officers; twenty-five men were killed or wounded. (One casualty, the company's executive officer, hastened to the rear with a superficial wound that cost him the confidence of his superiors, to say nothing of his men. Bourne noted that he spent the "rest of his time with us back at Battalion headquarters with the cooks and company clerks, frightening replacements with horror stories about life at the front.")[20]

Somehow the ambushed troops—which included elements of the 399th's 1st and 3rd battalions as well as the 2nd—managed to hold their position against multidirectional fire until late in the day, when opposition suddenly slackened. After dark the regiment was able to fall back from what it now called "Purple Heart Lane"

100th Division GIs returning German fire during the division's advance through the woods toward Raon-l'Etape. (*National Archives*)

and regroup. Some of its men continued to press forward, however, hoping to find and bring off wounded comrades, many of whom had been disabled close to the enemy line. Time and again, the would-be rescuers failed in their mission. Frustrated beyond measure, they unknowingly gave way to Chaplain Koszarek, who, without revealing his intentions to anyone, started out alone to locate the wounded, guided only by a telephone wire that had been strung into the area where G Company was ambushed. The mission was risky indeed, since the ground over which the chaplain walked and crawled was alive with Schu mines—four-inch-square wooden boxes filled with a quarter-pound of dynamite—and "Bouncing Betties," mines that, once triggered, would launch themselves into the air and explode with a devastating spray of steel pellets and fragments.

Several hours after beginning his unauthorized mission, the chaplain appeared at company headquarters to inform an astonished Capt. Millard B. Hayes that he had found and spoken to several of the wounded. For a second time, Koszarek risked his life to lead a team of litter bearers to the fallen men. After helping administer first aid, he led the rescued and the rescuers back to the 399th's lines. For his nonclerical heroics, Captain Koszarek would be decorated with the Silver Star.[21]

Many elements of the division suffered on the thirteenth, but the casualty count appears not to have been substantial enough to convince General Burress's immediate superior that the division had been seriously engaged. In the early hours of the fourteenth, Burress was routed out of a three-hour sleep by a phone call from corps headquarters. General Brooks wanted an update on the previous day's report of operations, claiming that "there is no way you could have encountered as much opposition as you report. Your casualties aren't high enough." His superior's complaint rankled Burress, who did not believe that a low casualty rate necessarily indicated light fighting. He kept a prudent hand on his temper, however. He patiently explained that the division had made progress that day—scant though it might appear at corps headquarters—through "skillful maneuver" rather than frontal assaults guaranteed to increase the body count. Slowly but surely his soldiers were gaining their assigned objectives, and he was proud of the way they were doing it. Impressed by his subordinate's rationale, Brooks ("a nasty hard-driver," in the words of Burress's military secretary) hung up without another word.[22]

The fourteenth was another day of little progress on the division's front. Its opponents no longer seemed interested in delaying tactics; apparently, they had decided to put their might into holding a multilayered line of defense. This line, a series of ever steeper hills, rugged ridges, and clotted woods, skirted and sometimes crossed the road between Neufmaisons and Raon-l'Etape, barring the path of both of the advancing regiments. In hopes of surmounting these natural obstacles as well as the continuing snow and rain, the 397th resumed its southeastward attack, this time in regimental strength and with a three-company front. Its 1st Battalion attacked Clairupt, a river town on the road between Baccarat and Raon-l'Etape. Though the battalion was pinned down on Hill 316 on the outskirts of the village, a bazooka-wielding member of C Company, supported by squads of riflemen, knocked out a key enemy position, enabling the 1st to seize and occupy Clairupt.[23]

The 3rd Battalion of the 397th, holding the right flank of the outfit, had a much more difficult time of it this day. Ordered to assault a line of hills west of the Neufmaisons-Raon-l'Etape road, the battalion was savaged by an enfilading, or flank, fire that made casualties of dozens of men. Caught on open ground crisscrossed by wire fencing and commanded by heavy guns in the woods beyond, the battalion found itself in a trap similar to that in which the 399th had been caught the previous day. "Mortar rounds were hitting the trees above, spraying shrapnel down on us," recalled nineteen-year-old Sgt. Robert G. Tessmer of Dearborn, Michigan, a member of I Company. "Then the German machine guns and rifles opened on us from the hill in front." Tessmer could find no targets at which to aim his Browning Automatic Rifle: "The Germans were dug into trenches and had strung barbed wire and mines in front of us. They started picking us off one by one as we tried vainly to hide behind trees. We couldn't see a thing to shoot at as they were so camouflaged. I felt like we were pinned down for hours."[24]

Two of Tessmer's comrades lay side by side, unable to move forward or backward under the continuing barrage. Private Mosher of Delaware, Ohio, turned to his close friend, Norman Nisick of Benton City, Washington, and shouted: "Norm, you and I are not going to live." Mosher was wrong—by some miracle he and his buddy survived the battle, as they would the war—but many others were not so fortunate. Another member of I Company, Private B. Lowry Bowman of Atlanta, Georgia, estimated that within a few minutes of the first shelling, forty men of his company alone lay dead or wounded. Some were paralyzed by shrapnel wounds to the head, while one of the company's medics died from a bullet "through the Red Cross on his helmet."

When the shelling finally slackened, I Company picked itself up and tried to go forward. "Panting, sweating and even crying," Bowman wrote, "the company struggled on up and over the mountain." Once on the other side, however, it was again on open ground within range of German artillery and small arms. For hours the men lay face down on the snowy earth, stunned into immobility. "Instead of pulling back, mounting an attack or attempting a flanking movement," John Sheets wrote, "we were left in place to be pounded by enemy artillery all day long."[25]

Finally, the order came to withdraw. GIs able to do so scrambled for the rear. "I jumped up," Tessmer admitted, "and ran as fast as I could, stumbling over bodies and wounded men. The shells kept coming and the bullets were whizzing all around. I don't know why I didn't get hit because our situation was so desperate and the Germans had every advantage." I Company continued to fall back until its officers told it to dig in, whereupon the men frantically hacked at the frozen ground to escape a sporadic rain of artillery fire. "Total confusion reigned," wrote Tessmer. "We expected a counterattack but thank God, it did not materialize or we would have all died in our first day of combat." Afterward, no one could say how far the company retreated. Years later, Bowman studied the regimental records: "The morning report says 1,000 yards. That's more than a half-mile. Probably it was farther."[26]

For the 3rd Battalion, it had been a horrific day, but, as Sheets noted, what followed was, in many ways, worse: "The night of the slaughter was long, cold and wet. The sleep, if any, was fitful and the nightmares were awful." He learned from comrades detailed to remove the fallen that "the dead were piled up like cordwood."[27]

Clearly, ineffective leadership was to blame for the ambush, and so heads rolled. The lieutenant colonel commanding the 3rd Battalion, who had neglected to send out scouts to provide warning of trouble, was relieved. Private Sheets never got over the high-level bungling on the fourteenth: "This horrible day brought out the green, inexperienced, inept leadership in the 3rd battalion, 397th Infantry, from top to bottom." Fortunately, battle experience and personnel turnover would rectify the problem in relatively quick time. With the exception of a similar occurrence two days later, units of the Century would not again be cut off beyond range of quick support, except in response to hasty or ill-conceived orders from above division level.[28]

The 399th Regiment, on the division's left flank, also had a rough time on the fourteenth. Attacking north and west of the ground on which G Company had suffered the day before, the regiment spent five hours hammering away at heavily defended Hill 431.3. In the end the regiment was forced to withdraw six hundred yards beyond the Neufmaisons road while tanks lumbered forward in support and guns positioned well to the rear softened up the objective preliminary to another attempt to take it the following day. Before calling it a night, however, a platoon of G Company regained the position it had yielded under pressure, ensuring that the road remained in the division's hands.

According to the Century's official historian,

> the inspiring thing about this attack of the division on 14 November is not that we made a little progress, but that the assault could be attempted at all. An entire week of rain and snow had turned the earth into a mass of mud. The foot soldier could move only with greatest difficulty, and his slowness increased the danger to his life. It was almost impossible to move heavy artillery pieces forward. The supply situation threatened to bog down inextricably. The infantry had been living on a diet of K-rations since the beginning of the attack and were suffering from diarrhea and trench foot. Most of us, knowing these things, would have smiled a bit wryly at the suggestion that the Century was on the eve of an immensely successful attack.[29]

But it was, and the fact became evident on the fifteenth, the second anniversary of the division's activation. The day began and ended as a holding operation for the 397th west of the Neufmaisons road. Most of the work was shouldered by the regiment's support units. Its cannon company and field artillery battalion directed a combined total of 334 rounds at those enemy positions in the infantry's front. The 83rd Chemical Battalion laid down a smoke screen to blind a German observation post across the river from Clairupt, while attached armored and tank destroyer outfits shelled the defenders of Raon-l'Etape.[30]

That same day, a historic breakthrough occurred on the 399th's front. The regiment attacked northwestward against a barbed wire-enclosed blockhouse, du Rouge Vetu, along the Neufmaisons-Raon-l'Etape road as well as two strategic elevations: Hills 431.3 and 409.9. The regiment's 3rd Battalion, spearheaded by I and K companies and fighting with extraordinary power, wrested each of these heavily defended positions from the enemy. Frank Gurley was especially impressed by the maneuver his comrades employed to carry the first of the hills: "Using the roadway itself as a 'parapet,' World War I style, they had fired up the slope at the German entrenchments on Hill 431 from the defilade [that is, off the Americans' flanks] offered by the road. Finally, they stormed across the road and drove the Germans out of their positions." In fact, they penetrated five hundred yards beyond the Neufmaisons-Raon-l'Etape road, a breach so wide that not even desperate counterattacks could repair it.[31]

This critical accomplishment owed not only to the unflagging persistence displayed by the two companies in reaching and gaining the hill mass but also to a supporting assault by L Company against the same position from the north. Both hills had been softened up by a combined barrage by the 373rd and 925th Field Artillery Battalions augmented by the heavy guns attached to VI Corps headquarters. To exploit the breakthrough, the 397th's 1st Battalion passed through the 3rd Battalion and continued the attack toward the main line of enemy defense. By noon, both of the strategic hills as well as adjacent ridges were firmly in the hands of Centurymen.

The lodgment threatened the rear of the entire enemy defense line along the Meurthe. That line quickly began to roll up like a *feldgrau*-colored carpet. A division seeing its first battle action had driven a wedge through a defensive position in the Vosges that had withstood attack since Julius Caesar's day. It had already gone far toward winning an accolade bestowed after the war, when the chief of staff of German Army Group G would refer to the Century as "a crack assault division with daring and flexible leadership."[32]

Thanks to the enemy's accelerating withdrawal, early on the afternoon of the fifteenth, the Red Raiders of the 399th were able to hasten along the road to Raon-l'Etape. Repulsing a less-than-spirited counterattack at the first road junction it encountered, Colonel Zehner's battalion burst through a strongly held roadblock, capturing a German mortar platoon. Night finally halted the Raiders' advance within striking distance of the division's next major objective, Raon-l'Etape.[33]

The 399th could not safely proceed until the 397th moved up from its position farther to the rear and secured its lower flank. At General Burress's urging, the 397th forged ahead briskly on the morning of the sixteenth—so briskly, in fact, that shortly before noon, its 1st Battalion moved too far in front of the rest of the regiment and lost contact with it. When informed of the error, Burress—who kept close to the front via a mobile headquarters consisting of a jeep and a van that contained the division's papers, maps, and communications equipment—ordered Colonel Ellis to at once locate and withdraw the exposed battalion.

By then the unit had managed to extricate itself, but Ellis did not know this. Chastened and upset, he hastily set out to obey his superior's order. Racing in a jeep toward Raon-l'Etape without consulting his situation maps, the colonel and his driver blundered inside enemy lines. Before they could turn around, burp guns riddled them. Ellis's assailants quickly fled to join in the general retreat, but not before rifling the colonel's body and making off with his watch. The following morning a patrol from the 397th located the disabled jeep and recovered the bodies inside it. Because Ellis had been a personal friend as well as a long-time subordinate, Burress was shocked and saddened by his loss but kept his composure. He immediately replaced the fallen officer with Lt. Col. John M. King, formerly commander of the regiment's 1st Battalion, while seeking an officer of sufficient rank to be Ellis's permanent successor.[34]

After vacating their defenses north of Raon-l'Etape, the enemy in front of the 397th withdrew through the town, which they did not believe they could hold, and took up prepared positions on high ground to the south as well as east, around the small village of La Trouche. While the 397th, advancing toward Raon-l'Etape, saw relatively little action during the balance of the sixteenth, the 399th saw plenty. Shortly before noon, Colonel Zehner's battalion attacked a hill mass that included Hill 539, aiming for its summit, the Tête des Reclos ("Top of the Wilderness"). The summit commanded the Plaine Valley and the highway in its midst that led southwest to Raon-l'Etape.

The steeply inclined objectives presented heavy obstacles to the attackers. They abounded in "logged-over foxholes with clear fields of fire, and the enemy had to be rooted out one by one from these miniature forts. The task would have been hard in open country, but here the dense forest was made impenetrable by heavy undergrowth." Unable to attack along the road leading to the top of the hill mass, Zehner, wearing his customary red silk scarf and dour expression, led his Raiders up a slope so steep that GIs slipped and slid on the way to the top, their uniforms soaked in mud and melted snow.[35]

When the Germans opened fire from the upper slopes and summit, several men were pinned down. One unit, the weapons platoon of D Company, was caught in a particularly vicious cross fire, but its men fought back gamely. Sgt. Richard S. Atkinson, unable to discern his assailants in the dead space before they appeared over the nearest crest, stood up, lifted his 30-caliber, water-cooled machine gun from its tripod, cradled the forty-pound weapon in his arms, and fired it from the hip, to great effect. Atkinson's superior, Sergeant Steinman, who would take down one hundred or more Germans during Operation Nordwind, targeted an enemy emplacement that had forced his men to hug the cold, slushy earth. After moving part of his platoon into position to deliver a harassing fire, Steinman, under a covering fusillade, began crawling toward the German gunners with his M1 carbine upraised. The enemy opened up as soon as they saw him. Bullets

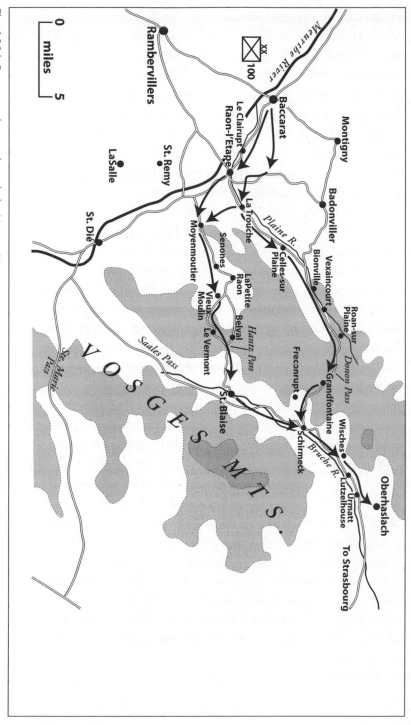

The 100th Division advance through the Vosges Mountains.

chewed up the ground around him, but Steinman kept moving. A few yards from his target, the Swiss-born noncom got to his feet and charged, his rifle spitting. He downed a gunner with a single round, and by rapid firing chased another into retreat. Stunned by the wild, one-man attack, other defenders surrendered en masse. Steinman rounded up sixteen before ending his assault, which had broken the back of the German ambush. In so doing he had freed another company of the 399th that had been forced to go to earth in a precarious position. His exceptional bravery and determination would win the unneutral Swiss a Distinguished Service Cross.

Another embattled unit of the 399th, A Company, was caught in an ambush as it worked its way up Hill 462.8 on the left flank of the 1st Battalion. The fire raining down from the summit was so heavy and accurate that one of the company's platoons broke and fled down the slope until rallied by Capt. Richard G. Young. For a time, the entire company was so dangerously exposed that it appeared to face annihilation. Thanks to Sgt. Lucian Zarlenga of St. Louis, Missouri, a noncom in the mold of Rudolph Steinman but lacking his survival skills and/or luck, this trap, too, was finally broken. Committed to safeguarding the battalion's exposed flank, Zarlenga refused to permit his men to withdraw. Instead, he led them toward a particularly deadly enemy position, which they seized through sheer determination and massed firepower.

Constantly exposing himself to the enemy's fire, the squad leader suffered multiple wounds, to which he succumbed on the summit of Hill 462.8. For his refusal to fold against nigh-overwhelming odds, Zarlenga would be awarded a posthumous Silver Star. And for their overall contribution to gaining an objective that secured the Century's grip on the approaches to Raon-l'Etape, the Red Raiders would receive not only a personal commendation from General Burress but also a Presidential Unit Citation (the collective equivalent of the Distinguished Service Cross), the first of seven to be awarded to the battalions of the Century during its combat career.[36]

The 399th's 3rd Battalion was also heavily engaged throughout the sixteenth. After turning over recently occupied positions to advance elements of the 398th that had crossed to the east bank of the Meurthe, the battalion attacked high ground north of the 1st Battalion's sector. After being pounded by mortars and 88s, the left flank of the advancing troops—mainly L Company—was struck by a German column counterattacking from the northwest. Had L Company been dislodged from its hard-won position, the entire flank might have given way. The unit not only held on but repulsed the onslaught thanks to individual heroics of the sort performed by Sergeants Steinman and Zarlenga.

By 3 p.m. the various companies of the 399th had taken the crest of the hill mass, where they hurriedly dug in against an expected counterattack. It came just before nightfall and resulted in a particularly frenetic spell of hand-to-hand fighting before the Germans broke off and withdrew, leaving behind thirty-five dead and more than eighty prisoners. The day's exertions had cost the 399th twenty-two killed and forty-two wounded—enough casualties, presumably, to satisfy General Brooks.[37]

Most of the 100th Division spent the seventeenth regrouping for a new assault on the high ground below the Plaine and east of Raon-l'Etape. By now two battalions of the 398th had come up to join the 397th and 399th in the drive toward the division's next objectives. As the fresh troops marched past them, the battle-worn GIs of the 399th regarded them much the same as the veterans of the 45th Division had greeted the Centurymen who relieved them three weeks earlier. According to Frank Gurley, "they were a beautiful sight to behold as they moved along smoothly in 'route step' at the prescribed five-yard interval in column on either side of the road. They wore clean green helmets and spotless field jackets and carried enormous horseshoe roll packs. Their rifle muzzles wore little glove-like covers to keep moisture out." Their more experienced comrades had their fun, asking if the marching men were engineers. Infantry, they were told. "If you're infantry," one of Gurley's buddies cried, "why are you carrying all that goddam junk? I thought you were going to build a bridge over the Rhine."

Gurley was tempted to contribute a comment, not to make fun of the new arrivals but to inform them "what lay in store for them up ahead. They would soon throw away all that fancy equipment except for a few essentials; what remained would quickly turn the color of mud. They were going to lose some of their best buddies, and lead a lizard's life in wet, underground, foxhole accommodations." He decided to say nothing, reasoning, "Why should I be responsible for making them shed their equipment and innocence any sooner than absolutely necessary?"[38]

On the seventeenth, the 397th's 1st Battalion, supported by the 3rd Battalion, attacked through Raon-l'Etape, where the Plaine River met the Meurthe. Gradually they forced out the few Germans who had attempted a stand in the artillery-riddled city. Much of the fighting took place around a stone and bronze memorial in the town plaza. "It struck me as ironic," Private Bonte recalled, "that it was dedicated to World War I French troops, a war that was to end all wars." By 9 p.m., the last Germans had been evicted, and the steel-nerved explosives experts of the 325th Engineer Battalion began to deactivate the dozens of mine and booby traps the Germans had planted in the town's streets, sewers, and tunnels, including two five-hundred-pound Teller mines. Other engineers got to work rebuilding bridges the enemy had destroyed and filling in shell craters.[39]

When the men of the 397th reached the high ground southeast of the city, they were halted late in the afternoon by Germans deeply entrenched in a stone quarry. These included not only members of the Century's primary opponent, the 708th Volks-Grenadiers, but also reinforcements from other organizations hastily assembled to prevent a farther advance by the Americans. Colonel King, Colonel Ellis's successor, considered crossing the Plaine River after dark to outflank the Germans, but a vehement dissent by Capt. John A. Hine Jr. of B Company derailed the risky plan. Sergeant Howsmon, who witnessed the heated confrontation, was forever grateful to his superior for canceling an operation that might well have ended in disaster. A similar movement, conducted just before nightfall on the 398th's front, was successful.

Elements of the 397th Infantry Regiment move into Raon l'Etape past a statue in the town square dedicated to the fallen of World War I, the "war to end all wars." (*National Archives*)

Spearheading the first attack ever launched by the regiment, A Company closed out the Century's accomplishments this day by forcing its way across the Plaine well to the north and east of Raon-l'Etape. Because opposition had been fierce, the unit's first attempt failed at the cost of several casualties, so Howsmon's assessment of the dangers involved seems to have been on the mark.[40]

General Brooks, for one, was impressed by the gains this day. He told General Burress so in a phone conversation more cordial than that of three days earlier. He enthusiastically advised Burress to mass his troops and make short work of the Germans defending the ground south of Raon-l'Etape. The Century must overrun those positions as quickly as possible and pursue the retreating enemy without stopping to "mop up." Brooks was in fine fettle, and he had a right to be. The Century's unexpectedly swift success in breaching the Winter Line, securing Raon-l'Etape, and crossing the Plaine ensured that the 3rd Division could go ahead with its planned crossing of the Meurthe prior to heading for the Saales Pass. With a nod to Burress's expertise, Brooks considered having the leading elements of the 3rd cross not below Baccarat as planned but via the same bridgehead on which the Century had crossed (since then the bridge had become a target for German pilots flying captured P-47 fighters, but it remained intact). The change in strategy, however, did not take place. When resistance to the Century's drive beyond Raon-l'Etape and below the Plaine intensified, Brooks returned to his original idea of having the "Rock of the Marne" cross the Meurthe in its own sector.[41]

On Sunday the nineteenth ("one of those rare days of sunshine" in the Vosges), the battalion of the 397th that had been halted at the quarry below Raon-l'Etape forced its way across the Plaine. Despite strenuous opposition, the attackers seized high ground southeast of the town. It held the position with support from the 397th's cannon company, the 374th Field Artillery, and the 83rd Chemical Battalion, which put up a smoke screen that denied the enemy a good view of the occupiers. At about the same time, the remainder of the 1st Battalion of the 398th crossed the Plaine at La Trouche to augment A Company, which had been pinned to the riverbank by better-positioned Germans holding a series of hill masses. The now-intact battalion advanced and captured two of those hills, while the regiment's 3rd Battalion crossed farther down the river over a newly discovered bridge.

Led by Chicago-born Lt. Henry Pajak of K Company, the 3rd Battalion attacked a wooded enclave from which a murderous fire had been pouring forth. According to the division history, the unit "overran the German positions, and swept through the forest like an avalanche. Whether the Germans were caught napping, or whether the speed with which the Americans struck caught them off balance is not known. Some turned to fight, others fired a few shots and either surrendered or fled." By the time the enemy in this sector had been subdued, the final one-third of the 398th, its 2nd Battalion, had crossed the Meurthe. Within hours the regiment that General Burress had selected to take the lead from the battle-weary 399th was at full strength and ready for further action.[42]

The 399th was not the only element of the division to experience fatigue and debility. Due to the Century's rapid advance on all fronts, supply problems had begun to mount. "The men were without water or food," the division's historian wrote. "Emergency K-rations had been thrown away with burdensome packs. Even blankets could not be brought up from the rear. What few blankets the Germans had left behind in their retreat, even though soggy, were needed for the wounded who could not be evacuated after nightfall." The icy rains that drenched the Vosges almost every day the Century fought in the mountains were taking an increasing toll of men suffering from frostbite, trench foot, and pneumonia. To escape the damnable weather, some GIs resorted to dangerous expedients, including sleeping beneath parked tanks. Not until midmonth was the division issued sleeping bags— zip-up woolen blankets covered by cotton windbreakers—to ward off the chill and permit a decent night's sleep.[43]

In every regiment, attempts—sometimes Herculean—were made to get rations, equipment, and ammunition to the troops. One especially dramatic effort took place after dark on the nineteenth under the supervision of Maj. Ernest Janes, executive officer of the 3rd Battalion, 398th Infantry. Janes organized a caravan of six jeeps loaded with rations, water, and various types of ammo, which he led to the front along roads that meandered here and there, some of which had not yet been secured. Surmounting a rich assortment of obstacles, including intense darkness, roadblocks, and axle-deep mud, Janes's convoy forged onward in hopes of succoring men who had suffered through a night "as eternal as the ages." When fallen trees brought the convoy to a halt short of its destination, the major helped his men carry the marmite cans full of chow to the top of the hill the battalion had occupied. They reached the summit at 8 a.m., just in time for the GIs to enjoy the rations before they were ordered up to attack a new objective. Famished and nearly frozen troops regarded the supplies, especially the food, as manna from heaven, and Janes forever after occupied a fond place in the hearts of the men of the 3rd Battalion. Much appreciated, too, were the efforts of other supply units, such as the mess section that on November 19 brought the men of the 1st Battalion, 399th Regiment, its first hot meal since arriving at the front, a gesture that fortified the Red Raiders psychologically as well as physically.[44]

Another boon to morale came in the form of the division's first replacements—the army preferred to call them "reinforcements"—who began to appear in the ranks at this time. On the nineteenth, the 397th alone received 161 new enlisted men: "Sorely needed by the rifle companies," the official historian noted, "they soon caught the spirit of our division and within a few days were Centurymen to the core." Sorely needed indeed— by this point A Company of the 399th, typical of those units that had seen heavy action over the past three weeks, had lost 125 of its original complement of 190 men. However, many of the newcomers, lacking essential survival skills, did not live long enough to catch the Century's spirit. A preponderance were not infantry material; they were cooks, jeep drivers, hospital orderlies, and bandsmen pressed into service as riflemen. Within two hours of reaching their new unit, six replacements assigned to D Company of the 399th were killed by a single incoming 88.[45]

After dark on the nineteenth, new men and old learned that elements of the 3rd Division had managed, after four failed attempts, to cross the Meurthe in boats between Raon-l'Etape and St. Dié. Subsequently, the Century's engineer battalion laid a pontoon bridge outside Raon-l'Etape to facilitate crossings on a larger scale. At dawn the leaders of the veteran division began to coordinate operations with General Burress and his subordinates. In a matter of hours, elements of the 397th were pushing southeast from Raon-l'Etape to link with the vanguard of the 3rd. The regiment's 1st Battalion moved rapidly across the high ground along a riverbank suddenly devoid of defenders.[46]

Farther to the east at this same time, elements of the 398th attacked toward St. Prayel. Shortly after noon on the twentieth, the 2nd Battalion's advance echelon came upon a farmhouse and outbuildings in a clearing north of the village. The position appeared to be occupied by the enemy, in force unknown. A raiding unit composed of light machine gunners who had volunteered for hazardous duty was sent to investigate. A few yards shy of its objective, the team was met by rifle and machine-gun fire pouring from every window of the house. Forced to take cover in the surrounding woods, the raiders tried but failed to advance in the teeth of such a withering fire.

Taking matters into his own hands, the unit leader, Lt. Edward A. Silk of Johnstown, Pennsylvania, advanced alone into the clearing under a covering fire and managed to gain the foot of a low wall that surrounded the farm. From this shelter, Silk blasted the house with his M1 carbine, shattering windows and making kindling of their woodwork. When this failed to lessen the fire coming from within, the lieutenant sprinted to the house. The occupants had a clear shot at him, but rounds of tracer bullets failed to find their mark. Crouching as low as possible, Silk inched his way around the side of the house and when under a window through which a machine gun was firing tossed in a grenade that detonated, silencing the weapon.

When guns opened on him from other windows, Silk took refuge behind a woodpile across the yard. The Germans zeroed in on his new hiding place, so Silk sprinted to a woodshed in rear of the house, which harbored another machine-gun nest. As he raced past the shed's open door, he lobbed a grenade, but wide of the mark. Again he ran past the door, tossing his last grenade inside. This time it exploded, taking out the gun crew. Because the Germans inside the farm house continued to blast the woods sheltering his team, Silk ran back to the building and again opened on it with his carbine. When his ammunition ran out, he snatched up rocks, which he hurled at the windows while calling on the inhabitants to surrender. Unnerved by the furious, multidirectional assault, a dozen Germans filed out of the house, hands held high. Silk's raiders came forth to secure the position, an accomplishment that permitted their regiment's 2nd Battalion to advance and occupy St. Prayel. The unorthodox but highly effective one-man attack would make Edward Silk a Medal of Honor winner.[47]

Although a critical breakthrough had been achieved by the Americans, portions of the Winter Line, which the men of the 399th had come to call the "Murder Factory," remained intact thanks to the fanatical resistance of imperiled but determined defenders. After crossing the Plaine, the 398th, which was to take the advance in that sector, was forced to fend off counterattacks near La Trouche and suffered heavily at the hands of snipers. Closer to the Meurthe, however, German troops abandoned long-held positions as soon as they were confronted by the 3rd Division and the 397th Regiment, advancing almost shoulder to shoulder.[48]

On the twenty-first, the two-column drive succeeded in taking Clairefontaine, southeast of Raon-l'Etape, whereupon the 397th turned sharply northeast and headed for the Hantz Pass, gateway to Strasbourg via St. Blaise-la-Roche, the regiment's next objective. At the urging of General Brooks, who believed a full-scale pursuit was in order, General Burress tried to reach St. Blaise-la-Roche more quickly than he could using a column of ducks. The division commander organized a motorized task force—truckloads of troops supported by self-propelled howitzers, tanks, and tank destroyers. None of these heavy weapons had been used to maximum effect on the treacherous slopes of the Vosges. (More than once, tank commanders had refused to support their infantry comrades if it meant exposing their men and machines. One tank lieutenant successfully disobeyed an order from Colonel Zehner, delivered at gunpoint). Placed under Colonel Fooks of the 398th, the "flying column" was sent out along Route N-424 toward St. Blaise with high hopes of cutting off the retreating enemy short of Strasbourg.[49]

Almost every mile of the way, Task Force Fooks was stymied by minefields, felled-tree abatis, and other obstructions. The most formidable obstacles were encountered outside Senones, some eight miles from St. Blaise. After much time and effort, the road was cleared and the task force lurched forward, but it got only as far as Le Vermont. Two days later, a disappointed Burress disbanded the organization. The ducks won out: on the morning of the twenty-second, the men of the 1st Battalion, 397th, originally well to the rear of the column, passed the stalled trucks via the north side of the road between Moyenmoutier and Senones and moved east in a freezing rain that turned to snow.

On the evening of the twenty-third, the third Thanksgiving Day of America's war, E Company of the 397th occupied St. Blaise-la-Roche scant hours before the 3rd Division, having cut through Saales Pass and gotten there from the south. The seizure was so sudden and unexpected that many Germans were roused at bayonet point from their barracks beds. The Century had fought its way through the mountains to the edge of the Alsatian plain, across which the disorganized enemy continued to flee, while their confused and demoralized comrades in the High Vosges surrendered in groups or prepared to make a last, futile effort to resist.

By November 24, the tired and hungry men of the 397th went into division reserve. They badly needed the break. Recalling the troops the regiment had relieved on its first day on the line, John Sheets observed that "we are starting to resemble the veteran 45th Division troopers in numbers and the dirty appearance accompanied by the hollow-eyed one thousand yard vacant stare." To speed the recovery process, the men were served a belated holiday dinner that overflowed their mess kits: turkey, cranberry sauce, sweet potatoes, peas, rolls, and a candy bar. Others had been fed the previous day, some under memorable conditions. Private Fair of the 399th ate his meal in company with members of a graves-registration detail, the tailgate of whose truck served as a table. Inside the vehicle were the bodies of about ten GIs, "their feet only inches away from where I was eating."

The grisly sight did not affect Fair's appetite, "probably because I was so hungry," but the rich meal he consumed, after weeks on dehydrated rations, wreaked havoc on his digestive system. He was not alone. Tom Bourne recalled that "almost all of us were deathly ill during the night, and up getting rid of that rich food from one end or the other, or both." He considered the bountiful meal a "well-meant but misguided inspiration."[50]

Some of those who tolerated the repast still suffered distress. Sergeant Angier, whose company of the 399th was dug in on the northern bank of the Plaine River where it could cut off the mountain passes leading to Schirmeck, found his holiday dinner "mighty tasty," but his ability to enjoy it suffered when German 88s and 105s began dropping shells in his direction. "As the night passed on the shelling became more intense," he remembered. "We lost about five dead, nine wounded, and four that had flipped their lid to the extent that they had to be held down, and taken back as Section Eights"—suffering from what was then known as battle fatigue and what later generations would label traumatic stress syndrome.

Angier knew the reason for the prevalence of this malady: "For over twenty days we had existed in freezing weather, in constant snow and rain, and inconceivable danger. In all this time we had never washed or shaven. . . . Each of us expected to die at any split second, and they were carrying the wounded back to the aid station, bringing back rations and ammo. No rest. Fighting and carrying by day, fighting and carrying by night, guarding yourself and your buddies."[51]

Fortunately for Angier and his comrades, their misery was close to an end, albeit temporarily. It could not come soon enough for the GIs, who continued to battle rain, snow, cold, and enemy bullets and shells. Private Tillett of the 398th recalled that a fortnight would pass before "we had a shower, changed underwear and really felt warm." Still, the Germans were on the run, and they did not appear intent on stopping short of their country's border. However, four months would pass before the enemy would be pursued across the Rhine.[52]

On November 25, the 3rd and 100th divisions moved in parallel columns up the Bruche River Valley to Schirmeck—the first objective with an unmistakably Germanic name, a clear sign they were nearing the German border. The somewhat rested and reorgan-

ized 399th Infantry now had the lead, occupying Schirmeck early
that evening and patrolling the highway east and west of the town.
Soon it was met by the better part of the 398th, which, supported
by the 117th Reconnaissance Squadron, had taken a more wester-
ly route to the objective: Route N-392, which ran from La Trouche
along the south bank of the Plaine River.

From Schirmeck both divisions proceeded through the valley
toward Strasbourg, just across the Rhine from Germany. The
Century had the lead for most of the march, raising hopes that the
division would be first to enter the historic city on the heels of the
retreating foe. The Century knew it had competition. On the
twenty-third, XV Corps had broken through the Saverne Gap, and
General Haislip had dispatched a fast-moving column from the
French 2nd Armored Division to take Strasbourg. Still, it
appeared that the Century would beat both the French and
General Haislip to Strasbourg—a lure in itself, made more powerful by rumors that if the division won the race, every man would
receive a rest in the rear, and the most fortunate among them a sev-
enty-two-hour pass to Paris.[53]

Spurred on, the Century advanced more than twenty miles in
two days. On the twenty-sixth, however, a motorcycle-borne
courier overtook the vanguard at Oberhaslach as the 3rd Battalion
of the 399th prepared to cover the last fifteen miles of the journey
to Strasbourg. Suddenly everything came to a dead halt. When
hours passed without renewed movement, it became obvious that
no one was going anywhere anytime soon. To the profound dismay of all concerned, visions of Parisian delights began to fade like
old colored snapshots.

FIVE

THE MAGINOT LINE

The messenger who stopped the advance element of Seventh Army on the outskirts of Oberhaslach carried an order from Supreme Headquarters Allied Expeditionary Force (SHAEF). To bolster French morale, salve French pride, and redeem French honor, the armored column from XV Corps would enter and occupy a city of great historical and cultural importance to the country and whose streets were now free of the enemy (although the liberators were greeted by fire from guns just across the Rhine). Strasbourg, like Paris, was off-limits to the disappointed and frustrated GIs of the Century Division.

Subsequent orders from SHAEF had an even more demoralizing effect on the division and the 6th Army Group as a whole. No element of General Devers's command would be permitted to attack across the river into Germany. On November 24, General Eisenhower, accompanied by General Bradley, visited 6th Army Group headquarters at Vittel, where he firmly rejected the advice of Generals Devers and Patch that they push on into the enemy's homeland. There would be no crossing of the upper Rhine until the greater part of the German forces on the west bank had been defeated or driven across the border. As per Eisenhower's broad-front strategy, the Seventh Army was to turn north rather than continue east in order to protect the right flank of Patton's Third

Army as it prepared to attack the Saar region of Germany around Saarbrucken.[1]

Frank Gurley, who in postwar life scrutinized this confounding turn of events, believed that Eisenhower, with Bradley's strong support, had acted out of embarrassment. The Seventh Army had made swift progress through the mountains to within striking distance of Germany, while the 12th and 21 Army groups had been held back from the Siegfried Line by unexpectedly strong enemy resistance. The U.S. First Army on the left flank of Bradley's command had failed to break through, as expected, to Cologne, encircling German troops inside the Ruhr Valley. Even Eisenhower admitted that Patton's Third Army had become "roadbound and nearly halted" before Metz. So did Patton himself: in a letter to his wife on the twentieth, two days before Metz finally fell to his command, Patton noted that "the Seventh Army and the French First Army seemed to have made a monkey of me." He was referring to General de Lattre's November 16 breakthrough at the Belfort Gap, separating the lower Vosges from Switzerland's Jura Mountains. During the conference at Vittel, Devers pointedly reminded Eisenhower of the disparity between the Seventh Army's and the Third Army's achievements, but Eisenhower brushed off the comparison, suggesting that Patch's accomplishments were diminished by the caliber of his opposition, which he considered inferior to what Bradley and Montgomery had faced since breaking out of Normandy.[2]

When reviewing the decision to defer moving from Strasbourg into Germany, Gurley became convinced that SHAEF had made a major miscalculation. By late November 1944, the Germans holding the upper Rhine were so few and disorganized that an assault across the river, especially with support from Patton, would almost surely have cut off thousands of overawed Germans. This was also Devers's view of the situation—that with Patton's help he could have outflanked and defeated not only the weakened German Nineteenth Army but also the more coherent First Army.

Over the years a number of historians have accepted this thinking. Even those who refuse to declare that halting at the upper

Rhine was a major blunder suggest that Eisenhower was short-sighted and hesitant. In *Decision at Strasbourg*, David P. Colley faults Eisenhower for failing to adapt to changing situations: "He was cautious and often indecisive, and these traits may have cost the army thousands of unnecessary casualties and prolonged the war." So, too, reportedly, believed General von Rundstedt, commander of Hitler's armies in the west, who during a postwar visit with General Patch inquired why the Seventh Army had not crossed the Rhine when its enemy "had nothing to defend with." When Patch replied that he had drawn up a plan to do so and had assembled enough assault boats to execute it, von Rundstedt patted his fifty-five-year-old visitor on the shoulder and declared that "for a young fellow," he was quite astute.[3]

If the chain of events that kept the Century Division on the French side of the Rhine brought disappointment to the GIs, they were buoyed by official commendations of their performance in the Vosges, received in later days. General Brooks noted in a letter made public that

> the 100th Infantry Division made a marked contribution to the success of the VI Corps attack, first, by the capture of Raon l'Etape, an operation which breached the hinge of the German defensive position and at the same time drew forces from the center, where the main attack was to be made, and second, by the prompt capture of Schirmeck, which blocked the enemy on the left and permitted the main attack to push through without delay. Your fine division has written a bright page in the military history of our armed forces.[4]

General Burress expressed his pride in his men's accomplishments in another highly publicized letter. He lauded the Century for having completed

> a series of important and difficult operations against the enemy. All objectives have been taken. It has pierced and

rolled up the enemy winter line of the Vosges and captured the towns of Raon L'Etape and St. Blaise. By its actions it has contributed materially to the success of the larger forces. It has established a reputation for its spirit and fighting qualities, no matter how rough the terrain. Every member of the Division can take justifiable pride in its achievements in the initial and prolonged operation against the enemy. Please accept my personal appreciation and congratulations for a job well done.[5]

Neither Brooks nor Burress explained why the Seventh Army had been stopped short of the German border or what it was to do next. Eventually, the men learned that Eisenhower had set major priorities for the 6th Army Group as a whole. The French First Army, with the addition of the U.S. 36th Infantry Division, would operate in southern Alsace against a German bridgehead on the west side of the Rhine near Colmar. Meanwhile, the Seventh Army would turn north in direct support of Patton's offensive toward the Siegfried Line. Because he considered the latter operation the most critical element of his broad-front strategy, Eisenhower wanted the Third Army's flank protected regardless of the effect this subsidiary role might have on the morale of Patch's troops.[6]

The redirecting of Seventh Army from east to north would place it in opposition to the First German Army of Gen. Otto von Knobelsdorff. That command was holding terrain every bit as rugged and forbidding as that found in the High Vosges. The objectives assigned to Patch's corps commanders were equally daunting: VI Corps would fight through the Haguenau Forest of northeastern Alsace while XV Corps advanced farther to the west, crossing the Low Vosges toward some of the strongest points of the Maginot Line.[7]

At Vittel, Eisenhower had ordered Devers to reinforce General Haislip's corps for the move against the Maginot forts. The 100th Division was the first force selected; it was transferred to XV Corps on November 27. Other organizations assigned to Haislip included the 44th Infantry Division, the 12th Armored Division, and the 106th Cavalry Group. The left-flank element of VI Corps, the l03rd Division, was also made available to support Haislip if needed.[8]

None of these details were made known to the men of the Century. All they were sure of was that beginning on the twenty-sixth the division was trucked through a pass in the Vosges to Sarrebourg, twenty-five miles north of its most recent position. Having survived a grueling campaign in wretched weather (though many of their buddies had not), and assured that they had achieved every objective between Baccarat and Schirmeck, the men of the Century—newly baptized veterans all—appeared to be in good spirits as they left the High Vosges behind. They "sang old training songs during the cold ride, talked about mail, the possibilities of beer ration, sleeping in houses, a few days of rest."[9]

While outwardly chipper, many GIs turned quiet and wistful. Now more than ever, their thoughts were of hearth and home, their hearts full of longing. The yule season was approaching, a realization sharpened by the recent influx of food boxes from the States that the troops pulling reserve duty were only now opening and sharing. For thousands of young soldiers, the coming Christmas was the first they would spend apart from their families. Pangs of homesickness, stifled during combat when everyone concentrated on surviving and doing his job, were given free rein.

On the afternoon of November 28, the trucks of the 399th Infantry Regiment rolled into Sarrebourg en route to an assembly area in rural Niederweiler. It was pouring, but in the city plaza, Frank Gurley spied a solitary GI sitting bareheaded at a table in front of the local movie theater, rain streaming down his face. Beside him a phonograph was playing a sentimental ballad, a great favorite with the GIs and the loved ones they had left behind:

> I'll find you in the morning sun
> And when the night is new,
> I'll be looking at the moon
> But I'll be seeing you.[10]

Through the end of November, the Century was relegated to XV Corps reserve. The 398th Infantry Regiment moved through Sarrebourg to Plaine de Walsch and Troisfontaine, where it went into training mode, "stressing the care and cleaning of equipment." The 399th moved into Niederviller and Schneckenbusch, south of Sarrebourg, where it also began to train. When not drilling, both regiments also enjoyed a welcome rest, during which they were reacquainted with amenities long denied them. Some GIs were billeted among the local populace, where they slept in beds with boots and shoepacks off for the first time since reaching France one month earlier. Hundreds of men availed themselves of hot showers, which enabled them to scrape off the grime that had accumulated during weeks of campaigning in rain, snow, and mud (portable showers, housed in tents and trucks, had been made available in the field on a limited basis, but relatively few soldiers could leave the front long enough to use them). When they stepped out of the shower, the men of the 398th and 399th donned used but freshly laundered uniforms and clean underwear—they would never again see the filthy garments they had shucked upon arrival. A private would sometimes receive a "shower promotion," being issued a noncom's uniform, the stripes still clinging to the sleeve.[11]

In the assembly areas around Sarrebourg, Centurymen were served hot chow for the first time since arriving at the front. Except when able to appropriate edibles from occupied villages, they had lived on prepackaged rations. These were generally palatable and even nutritious—at least they kept body and soul together—but they could also be bland, tasteless, and monotonous.

For the first month the division was on the line, the men subsisted on K-rations. These consisted of dehydrated foods in waterproof boxes labeled for breakfast (powdered eggs with ham or potato pieces, crackers, and packets of Nescafé, sugar, and powdered creamer), dinner (usually a slab of the ubiquitous pork product known as Spam, more crackers, a chocolate bar), and supper (perhaps cheese and bacon bits, powdered bullion, still more crackers, tins of jelly and compressed pound cake). The Thanksgiving meal fiasco interrupted the issuance of K-rations; soon afterward, C-rations began to dominate the soldier's diet. Private Bourne attributed the subsequent scarcity of K-rations to their having been "belatedly recognized by our leaders for what they were, emergency food." This was all right, for "they were not really digestible when they were a steady diet."[12]

C-rations were canned foods such as beef or vegetable stew, corned beef, franks and beans, spaghetti, biscuits, and packets of powdered coffee or lemonade. Most GIs studiously avoided the corned beef hash; Private Bonte described it as "so lousy that even French dogs wouldn't eat it, when we gave it to them." Virtually every ration included a roll of toilet paper, which the GI kept dry in the lining of his helmet, as well as a pack of five cigarettes and a book of ten matches. Lucky Strike Green had gone to war in a big way, ensuring the tobacco company thousands of postwar cus-tomers, although, as Tom Bourne recalled, most GIs were issued lesser brands such as Fatima, Chelsea, "and others equally obscure." Although nonsmokers prized cigarettes for their value as barter, Bourne much preferred Hershey and Milky Way bars: "The rear echelon boys managed to skim off the premium smokes, but maybe there weren't any sub-standard candy bars."[13]

Opinions differed as to which ration was more tasty and edible, but because their boxes, when empty, doubled as cooking pots, K-rations provided a certain versatility. Private Khoury used his bay-onet to cut a hole in each side of the box and lit the top with a match: "The holes permitted a draft of air to circulate up through the box and let the flame burn from the top all the way down to the bottom. This made it possible to heat water to a boil in a canteen cup for soup or coffee. For variety, I would cook the Spam in the broth or make some other concoction." Unlike comrades with more delicate stomachs, Khoury "never got sick, but I know I lost any excess fat on my body."[14]

Alcoholic beverages were rarely available to the soldiers in the field. They were provided more or less freely, however, in the after-math of the Vosges campaign, as were movies, operated by Special

100th Division GIs eating C rations during a break in the fighting. (*National Archives*)

Services units. It was reported that "stubby bottles of beer and cans of peanuts" were issued, in limited quantities, to the theater-goers.

Only members of the 398th and 399th were treated to these material comforts. While those outfits trained, with special emphasis on assaulting fortified positions, the officers and men of the 397th were permitted only a couple days of rest before they returned to the field, temporarily attached to the 45th Division. On November 29, the 1st Battalion took over the foxholes, command posts, and installations of the 157th Infantry Regiment, atop high ground overlooking the highway between Saarbrucken and Haguenau. The next morning, A and C companies of the 397th were attacking north along the highway, pressing the retreating enemy toward the Moder River. Despite heavy resistance—mostly mortar and artillery fire—the regiment secured a number of lightly occupied towns in northern Alsace. During its advance it was supported by the 100th Cavalry Reconnaissance Troop, operating just to the northwest of the 397th's sector near Zittersheim and Wingen-sur-Moder. The assistance provided by the lightly armored unit enabled the 397th to make slow but steady progress toward the Maginot Line.[15]

On December 1, the Germans stopped retreating and started resisting. A patrol of I Company, attempting to seize Hill 296 near Ingwiller, twenty-two miles northeast of Sarrebourg, was halted by artillery fire from the summit. Throughout the night, the 100th Division's artillery returned the favor, pounding the German positions, but not enough to force a retreat. The next morning, I Company launched an all-out attack on the hill, led by two lieutenants, one an Oklahoman with the inspiring name of Ulysses J. Grant. The attack began well but quickly unraveled when one of Grant's platoons lost contact with the other two. Forced to huddle along a lower crest, the isolated unit was cut up by a shower of machine-gun rounds and "potato masher" hand grenades.

Escaping this trap appeared unlikely. One of the platoon's privates, Henry E. Vogel, watched aghast as his sergeant, who had located a German machine gun, "grabbed a hand grenade and r[e]ared back with perfect form to throw it. At this precise point a German hand grenade landed in his lap," blowing him to bits. Tracer bullets from a machine gun riddled another of the platoon's well-respected noncoms, leaving the men temporarily leaderless. Lieutenant Grant was farther up the slope, and his newly assigned colleague appeared as uncertain about what to do as the most frightened private.

For unknown reasons, the fire from the top suddenly slackened, permitting the trapped platoon to pick itself up and continue up the hill, foot by careful foot. It turned out to be a deadly ploy. As Private Bowman recalled, "they let us get almost on top of them before they started firing with everything [they had]. I hit the ground in a shallow depression, but bullets were going through the knapsack." He managed to wriggle out of the encumbrance, but he realized he would not get off the hill alive: "It is a strange feeling to know you are dead. There is almost a restful sense of resignation about it. I remember hoping it wouldn't hurt too much, but the only real regret I felt about being dead was that there was no way to let my parents know it was all right."

Lieutenant Grant, seeing that he could not hold the summit, shouted for everyone to hightail it downhill. "It was a precipitous retreat," wrote Bowman, who lived to take part, "but not a rout except for the new lieutenant who panicked and threw away his carbine and Grant's field telephone." When Grant rallied the survivors at the bottom of the hill, the petrified officer was not among them—once on solid ground, he had had continued running. Grant later sought to have him court-martialed but had to settle for his permanent assignment to rear-echelon duties.

Emulating his namesake, Ulysses Grant refused to abandon his objective. He re-formed the shaken troops and, rather than have them dig in for the night, as everyone had expected, led them on a lengthy circuit around the base of the hill. Apparently they moved stealthily, for they were not detected and harassed. The lieutenant finally halted them beneath a rugged precipice "almost perpendicular" to the ground. Once there, Grant sent Bowman and a second runner, Pvt. Frank Hurrle, to locate L Company, which was believed to be waiting not far away, ready to lend assistance. Late in the day Bowman and Hurrle reached the reserve unit, but its commander refused to take his men up the hill in gathering darkness. He directed the runners to remain with him through the night, but both dutifully returned to Hill 296 after nightfall—and found I Company gone.

Neither learned until the next day what had transpired in their absence. Bowman explained: "Grant had indeed taken what was left of the company up that steep slope without knowing that L Company would not be coming up the other side. They hung there all night while the defenders rolled hand grenades down on them. But they took that hill on the morning of Dec. 3 standing up. The only Germans there were dead. The rest had vanished before dawn." The enemy's departure from Hill 296 enabled the 3rd Battalion of the 397th to continue its advance north of Ingwiller.[16]

While I Company was scrambling to avoid annihilation, other elements of the 397th were suffering atop neighboring hills. On December 3, elements of the 2nd Battalion moved out to take Hill 375 near Rothbach. Short of their objective they found themselves pinned down by a barrage from guns operated by what an officer of E Company called "a fanatical enemy deeply entrenched on the

forward slope of Hill 369. . . .
The soul-jarring scream of their
lighter projectiles and the deep
roar of their bigger stuff, from
150mm howitzers and up, shook
us to the roots of our beings. We
had met some Jerry artillery
before, but never like this."

The howitzers were powerful
and deadly, but this day the GIs
encountered for the first time an
even more fearsome weapon.
After several attempts to outflank
the Germans atop Hill 369 failed,
E Company, resigned to the fact
that it had encountered a force
superior in both numbers and

A 100th Division officer radioing
for artillery support during a battle.
Portable radio communications
were essential for quick response
to enemy movements and attacks.
Note the 60mm mortar in the
background. (*National Archives*)

firepower, was moved to the right of its battalion's sector. There it
came under fire from a "flak wagon"—halftrack-mounted antiaircraft guns capable of firing 20-mm explosive and tracer rounds "in
inconceivable quantities." Thanks to the enemy, however, E
Company survived the barrage by burrowing into foxholes protected by the trunks and limbs of trees German 88s had felled
hours earlier.[17]

The next day, the 3rd Battalion took Hill 369, its way cleared
by almost four hundred rounds of high explosives delivered by the
regimental cannon company and "accurately directed by the company's forward observers . . . by means of radio." On the morning
of the fourth, the 397th moved against its major objective, Hill
375. Halted by heavy artillery, the attackers pulled back en masse
so that every gun available to the regiment could respond. The
intent was to soften up the German position, which consisted of
six-by-ten-foot holes camouflaged and protected by sandbags,
logs, and batteries of 88s. But when the regiment withdrew, the
enemy followed, preventing the counterbarrage from inflicting
many casualties.

Colonel King saw an opportunity in this unexpected turn of events. Having drawn the Germans out, he had the regiment attack as soon as its artillery support slackened. Caught off guard, the enemy resisted briefly before breaking and fleeing. By late afternoon, Hill 375 was in U.S. hands. In two days of grueling combat, the 397th had overrun the German defensive line in the Rothbach area, clearing a path to the Maginot Line via Wimmeneau, Reipertswiller, Wildenguth, Melch, and Mouterhouse.[18]

The enemy's new emphasis on delaying actions—fighting, then falling back to more-defensible positions—contributed to the perception in some circles (including SHAEF) that the 6th Army Group's offensive pace was decelerating. To the south, the reinforced French were being quite deliberate in their approach to the so-called Colmar Pocket (the bridgehead would not be completely neutralized till early February 1945). To the north, XV Corps was moving almost as slowly—too slowly, General Devers feared, to fully support the Third Army's drive through the Saar Valley. On November 26, General Haislip had ordered an advance in Patton's favor west of the Low Vosges, but with the better part of the Century and other XV Corps forces resting and reorganizing, only the 44th Division had been available to cover the Third Army's flank. On the east side of the Low Vosges, a regiment of the 45th Division had taken strategic Ingwiller on November 28, but the 397th's advance north of that town had been slowed by stiffening enemy resistance.[19]

Opposition to the XV Corps's drive came mostly from the 361st Volks-Grenadier Division. Despite its brief (five-week) training period and its mixed-bag organization (many of its men were reclassified Navy and Luftwaffe ratings), the command knew how to fight, especially on the defensive, and it benefited from effective leadership. Its Austrian-born commander, General Alfred Philippi, had identified Route N-419 as the key to the defensive positions east of the Low Vosges and was determined to deny that east-west highway to his enemy.[20]

Late on December 2, the balance of the Century Division prepared to leave its assembly areas and join the Seventh Army's
drive. The 398th and 399th had been assigned some major objec-
tives. Aware that the enemy would stoutly defend N-419, General
Haislip proposed to send both regiments along the crest of the
Low Vosges against the midpoint of the enemy line between
Ingwiller and Frohmuhl. After breaking through, the outfits were
to advance to the Maginot Line in cooperation with the 44th
Division. At the end of that twelve-mile drive, the 44th would
attack the fortified heights around Siersthal, four miles west of
Bitche. The 398th and 399th would make for the Ensemble de
Bitche, a grouping of some of the most formidable works along the
Maginot Line, including Forts Simserhof, Freudenberg,
Schiesseck, Otterbiel, and Grande Hohekirkel. These intercon-
nected, mutually supporting strongholds were to be assaulted in a
sequence yet to be determined. Once they had been captured or
neutralized, the Century would join the 44th in proceeding to the
Siegfried Line, which they would examine for weak points.[21]

When the 398th and 399th returned to the line, their initial
objectives were two German-held towns along N-419, Puberg and
Wingen-sur-Moder. Both outfits were transported by motor convoy to an assembly area near Metting, northeast of Sarrebourg.
From there the men hiked north under an icy rain. The going was
slow, and not merely because of the weather. Both regiments
encountered some of the strongest roadblocks they had ever seen,
composed of tree trunks, piled earth, wooden fencing, and anything else that would stymie marching men, motor vehicles, tanks,
and tank destroyers. One of these barriers, which blocked the
entrance to Puberg, was removed by a "tankdozer," but only after
a daring reconnaissance by Sgt. Dee Crosby of B Company, 325th
Engineers, who crawled forward under rifle and machine-gun fire
to certify that the barrier contained no antitank mines. Crosby
would be awarded a Distinguished Service Cross for his daring.
Tanks accompanying the 398th moved into Puberg and neutralized the enemy positions around it, enabling the regiment's 2nd
Battalion to secure the town.[22]

Wingen-sur-Moder, a communications center on the Moder River surrounded by steep hills that provided excellent positions for German artillerists, proved a more difficult objective. When the 398th's 1st Battalion moved against it late on the third, supported by three "Hellcat" tank destroyers of the 106th Cavalry Troop, it encountered not only additional roadblocks but a raging storm of shells from above and on the floor of the Moder Valley. The volume of fire was so great that the tank destroyers could not advance and tankdozer tactics were out of the question.

The battalion commander shifted some of his forces east to try to outflank Wingen-sur-Moder's defenders. Elements of C Company briefly gained entrance but were driven out by intense machine-gun fire. The near success distracted the Germans enough that late in the day, A Company circumvented the main roadblock, hid in a woods for a time, and then entered Wingen-sur-Moder from the south. Because darkness was descending, occupying a town that had not been reconnoitered was a risky proposition, but the company commander, Capt. Charles Kierniesky, was operating under orders to push ahead at all costs. "A gutsy guy," was how Pvt. Herman E. "Ed" Rawlins described Kierniesky, who knew his unit was in a dangerous situation but believed he would be reinforced soon after taking the town.[23]

The orders that had sent A Company into Wingen-sur-Moder were based on a misreading of the tactical situation. It is not known if they were later countermanded, but if so Kierniesky never got the word. En route to the town, A Company lost telephone communication with battalion headquarters, and a battery-operated radio phone it was carrying failed to reestablish contact. Feeling isolated and lost, the unit inched along through the streets of town in darkness so deep a man could keep in touch with the fellow in front only by touch. One stumbling GI muttered aloud: "I can't understand what the hell we're doing moving into a town in the God-damned dark. This could have waited until tomorrow!"

At a certain point, Kierniesky ordered the men to spread out and clear a half-dozen houses on the southwest edge of the town. Upon entering and finding no Germans, they were directed to assemble on the lower floors of three of the houses. The prevalent belief was that come morning, they would be joined by B and C companies, which were still looking for a way into town. Most of the GIs took refuge in the cellars, which they found crowded with civilians who had been huddling there throughout the day, petrified that they might come under a rain of shells from the hills beyond the town. Private Norman recalled that "we arranged ourselves on the cellar floor. . . . No one had sleeping bags so we just stretched out in the dark to catch a few winks."

One of Norman's buddies, Pvt. Peter G. Gomben, recalled that from the time they were ordered inside, the men "felt rather critical of our leadership. There really was no reason to move two or three hundred yards into a town and then coop yourself up in a house. It would have seemed more logical to remain in the woods over night and then with the aid of patrols, move out early the next morning. However, in the house we did go, and after we were in the homes for awhile, someone wondered whether we had placed our security outside." Everyone assumed the captain had seen to it.

Perhaps an hour after they settled in, there was a commotion outside: the sounds of running feet, then shouts and cries—in German. Suddenly every occupied house came under automatic-weapons fire. Rounds from rifles and *panzerfausts* (bazookas) shattered windows and blew holes in walls. Potato mashers came tumbling down the steps from the upper floors to explode in the darkened basements, killing and wounding GIs and citizens alike.

Once the initial shock wore off, the men of A Company realized they were trapped. Instead of retreating, the 361st Volks-Grenadiers had come down from the hills to occupy the town. For some reason never explained, few or no outposts had been set up to alert the company to their coming. Some GIs rushed upstairs, determined to fight back; others resigned themselves to captivity. Pvt. John W. Goodlow heard a GI shout: "I didn't come 3,000 miles to surrender!" Norman, who had been disabled by a grenade blast, saw members of a heavy-weapons unit that had taken refuge in his cellar remove the firing pins from their machine guns. One exclaimed that "this business of dying for your country was lots of bullshit."

The Germans quickly herded the hapless GIs outside; Norman's buddies carried him up the stairs and into the yard, where he found "Krauts all around us." One of those with upraised hands, Pvt. David A. Chambers, estimated that the entire confrontation had taken no more than fifteen minutes: "I don't think we fired a shot." Most GIs had been rendered physically incapable of resisting, dazed or paralyzed by the concussive blasts of shells and grenades in a confined space; many had temporarily lost their hearing. Captain Kierniesky, who had ordered his radioman to destroy their transmitter, surrendered himself, three other officers, and 130 enlisted men, including a dozen members of a mortar team attached to the company. Except for thirteen casualties too badly wounded to be moved, all were marched off to the rear, bound for a POW camp.[24]

Some time on December 4, after holding the 398th at bay for additional hours, the Germans departed the area. The thirteen wounded were recovered on the fifth when the 1st Battalion finally broke through to Wingen-sur-Moder. A dozen other members of the company were discovered in various places throughout the town; apparently they had gone into hiding and had escaped enemy detection. Twenty-seven other members of A Company, who had not accompanied the rest of the unit into Wingen-sur-Moder, were located outside the town.[25]

In the space of a quarter-hour, the company had been reduced from 173 officers and men to thirty-nine able-bodied enlisted men. These were placed in regimental reserve at Meisenthal, where the unit was swiftly reconstituted with replacements and transferees under Lt. Philip A. Strickler, formerly of D Company. Blame for the debacle came to rest on the shoulders of the regimental leader. On December 11, Colonel Fooks was quietly relieved of command and transferred to division headquarters. He was replaced by Colonel Paul G. Daly of General Patch's staff, a decorated veteran of World War I and a hard-driving, results-oriented leader with a reputation for fearlessness. Some reports had the commander of the regiment's 1st Battalion being relieved as well and sent back to the States. Such an action would seem to be in order, but the regimental records fail to confirm it. [26]

After securing Wingen-sur-Moder and collecting the survivors of A Company, the 398th pushed toward enemy-held Lemberg. Though they passed east of the town, which was not an assigned objective, the regiment's 2nd and 3rd battalions absorbed heavy fire as they continued on toward Bitche via Meisenthal, Goetzenbruck, and Reyersviller. The clearing of Lemberg was assigned, instead, to the 399th. Marching west of the 398th, the regiment was in a better position from which to attack. En route, D Company of the 399th lay over briefly into Wingen-sur-Moder, which still bore the marks of the recent debacle, including equipment that had been discarded by the captured GIs. The lessons of Wingen-sur-Moder were firmly planted in the division's minds. "By the time we got into town, and for a long time thereafter," wrote Private Fair, "you can be sure we had enough guards out every night and all night."[27]

The next several days brought leaden skies, near-freezing temperatures, and winds that whipped a man's face and hands so sharply they nearly drew blood, but the men continued to plod northward. The Germans were again in retreat, but at virtually every crossroads they left a roadblock that had to be patiently dismantled before the march could continue. The progress of both the Century and the 44th Division, on its left flank, slowed appreciably. General Haislip began to despair of breaching the Maginot Line and confronting Hitler's supposedly impregnable West Wall before year's end.

The men of the Century did not trouble themselves with the cares and concerns of the high command, nor did they worry about the spectacle they presented to the bemused Frenchmen they passed on the road and in the fields to either side. Frank Gurley painted a rather amusing picture of his regiment's passage through Alsace into Lorraine:

> A column of Paddlefeet winding across Europe is a pretty uniform sight, but the Joes who make up the column are all different. Some wear field jackets, some raincoats, some overcoats. Every Joe has his own style for wearing grenades and bandoliers, and ammo bags. Every bedroll is slung at a unique angle. Guys carry rifles, or carbines, or bazookas, or tommyguns, or greaseguns, or BARs, or machineguns, or mortars, or .45 pistols. The only similarity among Dogfaces are big Shoepacks and two pairs of pants which made everybody look like Mr. 5 by 5.

Whenever the soldiers encountered a farmer, they tried to bargain with him for eggs or, better still, for the chickens that produced them. The Frenchman would immediately plead, *"Pas les miens, pas les miens!"* ("They are not mine!") When a farmer used that line on two of Gurley's well-armed buddies, "we said 'Bon, monsyour, Bon!' and grabbed two. Who said the bayonet was only a valuable weapon as a can opener?"[28]

Moving to within striking distance of Lemberg on the morning of the sixth, the "paddlefeet" of the 3rd Battalion, in the middle of their regiment's three-column advance, swept down from the hills to capture the twin cities of Goetzenbruck and Sarreinsberg. At neither place did the enemy put up much of a fight. After collaring a handful of Germans slow to evacuate, the battalion, closely supported by the regimental cannon company, a platoon of the 399th's Anti-Tank Company, a combat engineer platoon, and half of a mine platoon, drove two miles up the road to the outskirts of the objective. The regiment's intelligence and reconnaissance platoon, scouting ahead of these units, had alerted the battalion that Lemberg was well defended; by all indications, the enemy intended to hold the place until forced to leave.[29]

When mortars opened up from hidden positions, the better part of the 3rd Battalion scrambled for cover. L Company, on the left of the battalion, holed up in a wood across an open field south of the town; K Company, in the battalion's center, dug in along a road subject to heavy artillery fire; and I Company, farther east, took fire from an elevation known as Hill 435. The 155-mm howitzers of the 373rd Artillery Battalion went into battery and began pounding the town, setting portions of it ablaze. The enemy replied with "long whining salvoes" of 88s and the dull thud of mortars. Scouts determined that the Germans had set up a battalion of 105-mm howitzers just south of the east-west-running highway to Enchenberg, had placed 75s and 88s north of the town, and had dug entrenchments on another elevation east of Lemberg, Hill 423.

The principal fighting at Lemberg got under way on December 7, the third anniversary of Pearl Harbor. At 9:30 a.m., the 399th launched a pincers assault on the town. Following a preliminary barrage, the 1st Battalion attacked over cleared ground that crossed the Enchenberg highway while, farther to the right, the 3rd Battalion attacked from its various positions. The Germans threw everything they had at both battalions. They devoted special attention to B and C companies, advancing from the Durrenwald Woods. Once on the open ground beyond, neither unit could move farther, trapped by what Gurley described as "ceaseless machinegun, knee high 20mm fire, and SP [self-propelled, 20-mm] guns."[30]

For almost nine hours, in a near-constant rain, the companies lay exposed to this fire, which took a grievous toll. A six-man machine-gun team of B Company under Lt. Harry Flanagan (a former track star at Notre Dame) maneuvered toward the Enchenberg highway, seeking targets of opportunity and absorbing shell upon shell, bullet after bullet; at day's end, only Flanagan remained alive. Another embattled machine gunner, Sgt. Charles Adamcek of Flanagan's company, not only survived but achieved the rare feat of knocking an attacking flak wagon out of commission. Two more of these terror weapons, which moved beyond supporting range, were captured by Pvts. Frank Rubino and Donald Taylor, who crawled up on their flanks, avoiding detection until they could spray the gunners with rifle rounds.

While the 1st Battalion was fighting for its life on uncovered ground, I and K companies launched a furious assault on the right, striking toward an eminence called Suicide Hill. Three times a storm of shells and bullets from the summit drove the attackers back across the eastward-leading road to Mouterhouse. K Company managed the farthest penetration, driving a four-hundred-yard crease in the enemy lines east of the town before being forced back by "fanatical fire" from riflemen ensconced in a series of ravines. A Company, however, cleared another well-defended height, Christmas Tree Hill, by daring to cross a field ripe with Bouncing Betties and blanketed by rifle, mortar, and machine-gun fire.

At dusk a battered and bloody B Company stumbled back to the woods it had left that morning, dragging off its wounded. Even after dark the unit suffered, this time from a barrage of 20-mm shells, "small ugly black puffs, which burst over the foxholes." The regimental history records B Company's loss this day as fifty-one, I Company's as seventy. Gurley remembered that "litters were scarce and many wounded lay in the icy rain all night. Some guys were paralyzed by morning." Thanks to an unexpected level of resistance, the pincers movement, a good idea at the time, had failed in the execution.[31]

On the morning of the eighth, a change of strategy by Colonel Tychsen sent the previously uncommitted 2nd Battalion into action. The unit was ordered to cross the railroad and highway leading to Bitche while the 1st Battalion attacked from the southwest as part of a "right hook" proposed by Colonel Zehner. To exploit any gains this maneuver made, the 3rd Battalion took on a plethora of tasks: abandoning its current position southeast of Suicide Hill, passing around the left flank of the regiment, advancing up a hill, crossing a dangerously open space, gaining the railroad embankment beyond, dashing through a railroad underpass, and entering the city from the east.[32]

It may have sounded impossibly complicated, but the overall plan worked to near perfection. By midafternoon, G Company had outflanked Suicide Hill, enabling F Company to scale it and kill those defenders XV Corps artillery had not driven off with white phosphorous shells and high explosives. Only then did the

3rd Battalion go forward. With L Company in the advance, the unit drove through a "fire-sprayed woods," ascended and descended the hills in its path, raced across the open area, poured across the embankment, and gained the underpass, which provided access to the heart of the city. Advancing beyond this point was a slower process: the Germans, determined to close off this avenue of ingress, went over to the offensive. One L Company GI recalled that "a bunch of krauts came charging through the underpass and we wiped 'em out with guns and grenades." At length, a couple of mortars were advanced to the embankment and began lobbing rounds at the Germans on the other side of the tracks.[33]

L Company's attack reminded John Khoury of "a World War I movie as we all rose up and started running across the open field toward the embankment. We had not gone more than five yards when the Germans opened up with their rapid-fire machine guns, rifles, and mortar shells." Mesmerized by the frenetic drama unfolding before his eyes, the kid from Brooklyn had an out-of-body experience:

> There was booming noise and smoke and streaking bullets whizzing all around us. I had the strangest feeling that I was not really there in the middle of all this mayhem. In my mind, I was floating as I was running straight for the cover of the railroad embankment, and I did not feel any terror or exhaustion. It was not me, but someone else who was there, and I was just an observer. I didn't even seem to hear or smell the battle. It was like a dream.

Still oblivious to his surroundings, Khoury reached the embankment, behind which he crouched until a flak wagon came into view. Suddenly persuaded of the reality of his situation, he removed the bayonet from his M1, attached a grenade launcher, and sent two grenades hurtling toward the target. He ducked too quickly to confirm a hit, but "there was no more firing from there."[34]

The Germans, stunned by L Company's attack, began to pull back. Encouraged by the movement, elements of the company's

One of three American Sherman tanks of the 781st Tank Battalion disabled by mines outside of the village of Lemberg, France, in December 1944. (*National Archives*)

2nd and 3rd battalions, firing every weapon at their command, charged across the railroad to the outskirts of town, where they occupied several houses. This critical foothold was enlarged just before dark when Colonel Zehner and his Red Raiders, supported by four Shermans on loan from the 781st Tank Battalion, dashed into the southern part of town. Three of the tanks were quickly disabled by land mines, but the fourth made it into the city within supporting range of C and A companies. Gurley breezily reported: "Charlie smashed ahead in a house-to-house campaign with the Sherman whanging 75's into cellars and the doughboys taking care of the upstairs with grenades. Able swept around to enter Lemberg from the east."[35]

Before dawn on the ninth, large sections of the town had been secured, but many defenders held out. After 5 a.m., they launched the first of four counterattacks spearheaded by tanks and flak wagons and targeting an isolated section of foxholes northeast of the city occupied by F Company of the 399th. There was real power behind this assault: in the space of fifteen minutes, two of the unit's platoons had been overrun and cut to pieces. From a ravine to the rear, Sergeant Angier watched the 20-mm platform-mounted guns advance inexorably toward foxholes in which his buddies were huddling. He realized the men were goners—"what a miserable helpless feeling that must be!" The fire from the flak wagons was severe enough, but then some eighty German infantry, advancing in their wake, fired point-blank into the holes. "We were no more than fifty yards from them on our side of the ravine," Angier recalled, "but had orders not to fire, until it was too late. Several of the Krauts came on our side of the track but I got two of them and someone threw a grenade and killed two, and the rest hightailed it back to where they had come from."[36]

By the time Angier and the remainder of F Company delivered its belated fusillade, one flak wagon had been disabled by an anti-tank grenade and the others, pounded by the XV Corps guns, had withdrawn to the far side of the railroad along with the troops supporting them. They left behind a field of horror: at least fifty-five F Company GIs lay dead or dying on the frozen earth. [37]

Many of the dead had been mangled and mutilated. For Private Knight, the jeep driver, "the most horrible" effect of the day's action "were the pieces of a B Company boy who had been run over by a German tank." The grisly sight "greatly reinforced my belief in the futility of war."[38]

The same thought must have occurred—probably more than once—to Medic George Demopoulos, who that afternoon ministered to a seemingly unending line of wounded while dodging shells and small-arms fire. Some of those he treated, including John Khoury's buddy Pvt. Carroll C. Stratmann, who had been struck in the chest by shrapnel, died despite his best efforts to save them. Late in the fight, Demopoulos amputated the shattered arm of an M Company soldier struck by a shell. Over the past month the medic had patched up dozens of men under similar conditions, but this day's experience left him, as one comrade observed, "visibly upset like I had never witnessed before." The open-air amputation—through which the patient remained conscious but refused to cry out for fear of giving away their position—had "really got to him."[39]

L Company's casualties hit Khoury just as hard. In addition to Stratmann and others, Khoury had lost a comrade he considered a close friend although not a member of his platoon: Pvt. John W. Howe Jr., of Weehawken, New Jersey, mortally wounded outside Lemberg on the ninth. Known to everyone in his circle as "Redbird" for his red hair and chirpy good humor, Howe had been standing on deck next to Khoury when their troopship pulled out of New York Harbor bound for France. As they passed the Jersey Palisades, Redbird caught sight of his house on an inland hill. The discovery had prompted Khoury to wonder aloud if either of them would see home again. He never forgot Howe's laughing reply: "If I didn't think I was coming back, they would never get me on this ship!"[40]

Late in the afternoon, Zehner's raiders, accompanied by a small group of Shermans, fought through to the downtown area. Under a light snowfall, the 1st Battalion cleared the city, street by street, house by house. By evening, only dead, disabled, and captured Germans remained in Lemberg; dozens of the latter were streaming to the rear under guard. Their comrades had drawn off toward Bitche—men, tanks, flak wagons, everything.[41]

Moving north on the right flank of the 399th, late on December 6, the 397th Infantry had approached Mouterhouse, a factory and rail center that supported the fortifications around Bitche. That evening a nine-man patrol of E Company under Sgt. Herbert Harvey sneaked inside the town, set up an observation post, and gained information from helpful civilians that aided the attack the 397th launched on the seventh. By ten o'clock that morning, forty-five minutes after jumping off, the regiment's 2nd Battalion, with Companies E and G leading, had entered Mouterhouse from the south. Meanwhile, the 1st Battalion moved northwest of the town to cut off retreat routes. Though the enemy was now nearly surrounded, the attackers proceeded with caution. As the regimental historian observed, "we stepped forward with sweaty cold hands, firmly yet hesitantly, watching our leaders for signals and trying to spot the buildings in the distance for some sign of what was waiting. Step by step we came nearer and nearer to the town, and all continued quiet. . . . It is indeed an eerie or, at least, queer feeling to be attacking like that. It is more like walking through a swamp where you know that there is quick-sand. You keep going, and maybe you will hit the quick-sand and maybe you won't, depending on your luck, and to a certain extent your skill."

Luck and skill were both with the 2nd Battalion this day, and the next. As the unit entered the town, the enemy opened on it from many locations, including a church and cemetery. Artillery on the hills beyond the town added their weight to the defense; for twenty minutes the battalion absorbed fire from 88s, heavy machine guns, and 20-mm flak guns. Ten GIs were wounded, but when the barrage slackened, the better portion of three platoons rushed the church and an adjacent schoolhouse and rooted out the defenders. Other units swept through the city's industrial district, clearing factory buildings one at a time, a slow, stressful process that resulted in additional casualties. By day's end, all but five houses along Mouterhouse's southern edge had been seized and secured. Those five—"each a separate fortress which had to be destroyed and the enemy flushed from within"—were taken on the eighth along with dozens of others on the western side of town. When it again came under 88 and flak-gun fire, the battalion called in its own artillery, which eventually silenced the enemy and forced his retreat from the town. Some Germans made it out the north end, slipping between the outposts of the 1st Battalion; many others were cut down or taken prisoner before they could escape.

Although the fight for Mouterhouse was over by nightfall on the eighth, "things were yet popping in and around the town until the 19th." The 397th had learned many lessons from the two days of combat, not the least being how to fight street to street, block to block, and house to house. The experience would stand the outfit in good stead in the operations to come, including those inside the German city of Heilbronn four months hence.[42]

Combined with the capture of Lemberg, the neutralizing of Mouterhouse removed the final obstacle to the Century's drive toward the Maginot Line. The division's next objective was as formidable as they came. The chain of concrete fortifications, artillery casemates, multistory bunkers, and various other aboveground and subterranean defenses along the border with Germany had been constructed by the French government in the 1930s to deter attacks of the sort launched against it by its European neighbor at the outset of World War I. Although intended to be inherently powerful, the line—named for André Maginot, the French minister of war—was not considered impregnable, even by the engineers who had designed it. The forts had been conceived of as a way to buy time in which the French army might mobilize before an invasion could be carried out. They were also seen as a possible deterrent to assault by encouraging an attacker to proceed, instead, across neutral Belgium. As a barrier to the military forces of Germany, the Maginot Line succeeded and failed at the same time. It did persuade Hitler's troops in the summer of 1940 to bypass its works and strike at Belgium, but by outflanking the line the invaders neutralized it. They poured into France after breaking through at the point where the line connected with Belgium's fortification system.

When the fall of the French government forced the surrender of the Maginot forts, the victors occupied them, added to their armament, and reconfigured some to face south and west instead of toward Germany. The occupants were now well prepared to oppose any advance by the U.S. and Free French troops in Devers's command. They realized that of strategic necessity the Allies would be required to assault and capture most of the forts—they could not circumvent them as the Germans had. When the attack came, the strength of the Maginot Line would be fully tested for the first time under operational conditions.[43]

The test instrument would be the 398th Regimental Combat Team, a temporary grouping of the 398th Infantry plus various support units. On December 11, the 398th had leapfrogged the

399th on the road north from Lemberg. The latter was still salving the wounds it had received in that desperately defended city and had gone into division reserve. The 397th Infantry, farther east, guarded the division's right flank against a possible counterattack by the enemy who had been driven from Mouterhouse and now occupied a chain of hills between Haguenau and Bitche. On the 398th's left, the 44th Division prepared to attack Fort Simserhof, almost two miles west of the Century's objectives.

With the exception of A Company (which had been fully reconstituted), the 398th had been less involved in the general fighting over the past two weeks and thus appeared to be the freshest component of the division. Under a new commander with a reputation for doing a job quickly, energetically, and right the first time, the outfit was General Burress's choice to spearhead a critical maneuver he could not avoid or defer. Colonel Daly had already shown effective leadership when directing the 398th in its December 13 attack on Reyersviller, two miles south of Bitche, capturing that strategic town and the well-defended ridgeline above it.[44]

The 398th was assigned to tackle two major objectives: the massive pillbox that was Fort Freudenberg and, beyond it, the eleven separate units (or "blocks"), connected by underground railways, tunnels, and communication lines that made up Fort Schiesseck. Freudenberg was itself a formidable position, but Schiesseck was a beast. Showing only a "thick mushroomed head" above ground, each of its units extended for several floors inside the snow-covered earth. State-of-the-art machinery facilitated troop movements between floors and contact with Freudenberg. Three of Schiesseck's casemates were of the disappearing-turret kind. One housed twin-mounted 135-mm guns, another sported two 75s, and the third was armed with twin-mounted 30-caliber machine guns. Both Freudenberg and Schiesseck were manned by elements of the 25th Panzer-Grenadier Division, a reconstituted version of an infantry command that had been nearly destroyed on the Russian front. Although recent fighting had taken a toll on the new organization—it had been waging strenuous delaying actions for the past two weeks as XV Corps moved toward the Maginot

A typical concrete bunker along the Maginot Line. Most of the defenses were below ground with only gun emplacements and massive reinforced concrete structures above ground that were able to withstand repeated attacks. (*National Archives*)

Line—one of its commanders claimed that the morale of the 25th Panzer-Grenadiers was high, and they would wage a desperate defense of the forts in the Century's path.

Describing the tactical situation on the morning of the fourteenth, with his outfit poised to attack, the 398th's historian wrote that

> from Bitche itself our every move was observed and relayed to batteries of 88s, which sent shells screaming and crashing into our positions with frightening accuracy. We cringed in our foxholes and wished we had dug just a little deeper as the shells exploded and tore up the ground around us. As yet we had not made a direct attempt on the forts and knew, despite the intensity of the fire we were undergoing, the enemy had not yet opened up to his full capacity.[45]

Supported by tanks of the newly operational 781st Tank Battalion and the fire of the divisional artillery—General Burress favored a liberal use of firepower to soften up any objective, even those offering so few aboveground targets—the 398th Regimental Combat Team began its attack on the afternoon of the fourteenth. Demonstrating his reluctance to sacrifice men's lives, Burress informed Colonel Daly that if his drive bogged down he should halt and wait for further support before resuming the advance. Daly, however, went ahead as if the fortunes of the day depended on his regiment, and his regiment alone.

As soon as the 398th's 1st Battalion poured out of its foxholes south of Freudenberg and began crossing open ground that sloped up toward the pillbox, virtually every gun bearing on the position started in. Until this moment, XV Corps headquarters had harbored the faint hope that the Germans would decline to defend the forts and elect to retreat to the Siegfried Line. Now "there was no doubt that the Nazis intended to hold until driven out."[46]

The men of the 1st Battalion pushed forward, heads down and shoulders hunched as if leaning into a mighty wind. As screaming shells burst all around them, many fell to the earth and hugged it desperately ("more from force of habit," the regimental historian believed, "than for the protection they knew wasn't there"). After catching their breath—and steeling their nerves—most got to their feet and resumed the advance. Units of the 2nd and 3rd battalions tried to provide covering fire from the rear, but to little effect. Pvt. Roger Witt of H Company recalled that the fire from the Bitche forts was so intense that he could not move his water-cooled machine gun close enough to do any good: "It was just lie low until the attack was over." Witt's inability to assist the attack made for "a frightening time because you were in a position where you couldn't do anything" except observe and pray for success.[47]

Despite the massive convergence of enemy fire, which littered the ground in front of Freudenberg with bodies, before the afternoon ended dozens of attackers managed to reach their objective, which they attempted to silence by firing into the fort's apertures and breaches. They delivered enough firepower to drive its occupants from their guns and into the subterranean depths. Once the defenders ceased firing, the GIs searched frantically for an entrance. They found a several-foot-thick steel door, but dynamite charges brought forward by engineer teams failed to blast it open. Nor did the explosives so much as dent the concrete walls surrounding the door, which ranged from four to twelve feet thick.

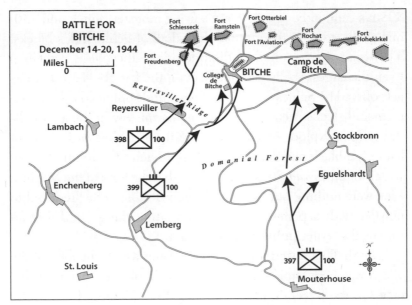

BATTLE FOR
BITCHE
December 14-20, 1944
Miles
0   1

Fort Schiesseck
Fort Ramstein
Fort Otterbiel
Fort Rochat
Fort Hohekirkel
Fort l'Aviation
Fort Freudenberg
BITCHE
Camp de Bitche
College de Bitche
Reyersviller Ridge
Reyersviller
Lambach
398 ⊠ 100
399 ⊠ 100
Domanial Forest
Stockbronn
Eguelshardt
Enchenberg
Lemberg
St. Louis
397 ⊠ 100
Mouterhouse
N

One of the key objectives of the 100th Division's advance through the Vosges
was the medieval city of Bitche, France, and its important citadel.

Stymied but not defeated, the 1st Battalion poured a continuous
fire into the observation slits of the pillbox. They did so for only a
few minutes, however, before the nearest units of Fort Schiesseck
began to concentrate fire on them. Lacking any alternative, at
Colonel Daly's order they cautiously withdrew over the ground
they had crossed hours earlier and sought refuge in the woods at
the bottom of the forward slope. They remained in that comparatively safe position through the night. The men of the 1st Battalion
could feel good about what they had accomplished this day.
Although forced to relinquish their prize, they had put it out of
commission, at least temporarily. Now Daly could concentrate on
surmounting the larger and more extensive obstacle in his path,
which posed difficulties that appeared to dwarf those of
Freudenberg.[48]

A new objective seemed to call for a new approach, so General
Burress switched tactics. For several hours on the morning of the
fifteenth, GIs attacked Fort Schiesseck at long range while corps
and division artillery, ranging from the 105-mm howitzers of the

398th's cannon company to guns firing monster 8-inch and 240-mm shells, tore up the ground around all of Schiesseck's blocks. The results were more than disappointing—they were negligible. Even the largest shells had no effect on the few aboveground targets offered by Schiesseck. Time-fuse rounds bounced off the concrete-and-steel structures to detonate harmlessly in the air. Shells designed to explode on contact struck the forts time and again but left only a black powder stain. A well-publicized opinion of a staff writer for *Stars and Stripes* had stated that the forts of the Maginot Line were nothing but "stacked up gravel" able to be "reduced to powder with a pencil." Later, after visiting the ground around Bitche, the writer published a retraction.[49]

The shelling lasted for two days, during which the men of the 398th watched, cupped their ears, and shook their heads in dismay. On the fifteenth, more than fifty P-47 Thunderbolts of the XII Tactical Air Command tried to break the stalemate, pounding both Freudenberg and Schiesseck with twenty-seven tons of bombs, many of which weighed five hundred pounds. Direct hits were scored on Schiesseck's units, including the three elevating casemates—with no visible effect.

Burress and his superiors refused to give up. On the sixteenth, their luck began to improve when direct artillery fire was applied to the forts. Several tank destroyers with their 90-mm guns, and the 155-mm howitzers of the 373rd Artillery Battalion were moved to the crest of a hill that commanded the forts and fired on them at point-blank range. At the same time, the heavier guns of the XV Corps artillery were moved into position immediately behind the hill, where they could provide closer support. "That did the trick," a division staff officer observed, "and the Germans were forced to forget their firing and withdraw to the underground portion of their casemates."[50]

This same day, the 399th Infantry, on the right flank of the 398th Regimental Combat Team, supported the operation by attacking a pillbox on the highway leading into Bitche. The assault, carried out by a squad of volunteers under Lieutenant Flanagan, secured an important foothold "right under the nose" of the city's original fortification, the symbol of its will and ability to resist any incursion: the Citadel de Bitche, first constructed in the twelfth century and rebuilt six hundred years later, attacked many times by invading armies but never conquered. The following day, the position now known as "Flanagan's Fort" having been secured, a platoon of C Company of the 399th, with machine guns and mortars attached, charged down Shoenberg Ridge, stormed the College de Bitche, south of town, and gained entrance. An observer marveled at the accuracy of the unit's mortars: "I never saw such shooting in my life!" That night the rest of C Company smashed its way inside the college and rooted out its startled occupants floor by floor. The college would furnish the regiment with a forward observation post that would remain in operation until inhospitable Germans paid a call on the 399th on New Year's Day 1945.

After the college fell to C Company, B Company seized the pillbox next to Flanagan's Fort. Meanwhile, comrades went hunting for bigger game. Elements of I and K companies, supported by tanks, infiltrated the city's eastern edge close to Camp de Bitche—an aboveground complex that housed training and weapons-storage facilities in support of the Maginot forts—killing, wounding, and capturing numerous occupants before returning to their positions overlooking the city. Frank Gurley remarked that 3rd Battalion patrols "spent their days in the woods, their nights in Bitche." By the eighteenth, Bitche had been surrounded by "a 100th Division horseshoe."[51]

On the seventeenth, when General Burress again ordered the 398th to the attack the Maginot forts, the combat team went in "with a vengeance." Its assault was preceded by a rolling barrage by the 375th Artillery Battalion that swept the ground in front of the advancing infantry. The precision bombardment did not lift until the attackers were three hundred yards from their objectives. To ensure they were reached, Colonel Daly went in at the head of the assault column. When momentum appeared to lessen, he personally relieved at least one officer whose unit had failed to keep pace with those on either side. Displaying daring but not caution, Daly exposed himself to enemy fire and went down with a severe leg wound that required his evacuation. Burress immediately replaced him with Lt. Col. Robert M. Williams, formerly of the 399th, who at twenty-eight became one of the youngest regimental commanders in the European theater.[52]

The 3rd Battalion of the 398th, in the forefront of the attack on the seventeenth, spread out to cover Freudenberg, which had resumed firing, and Schiesseck. The ground the unit crossed, infested with mines and barbed-wire entanglements, was nearly as deadly as it had been three days before, although shell craters produced by Army Air Forces bombs afforded some additional protection this day. L Company made for Unit No. 2 at Schiesseck, taking direct fire from one of the twin-mounted, disappearing-turret 135s, while I Company advanced toward No. 10 against intense 88-mm fire. Sappers of the 325th Engineers followed the riflemen, ready to plant satchel charges (twenty-five-pound, cone-shaped charges of TNT designed to cling to a vertical or horizontal surface) and other explosives as soon as they got close enough to the forts.[53]

At first, the plan appeared an exercise in futility. Engineer Lt. Samuel W. Pinnell oversaw the placement of one thousand six hundred pounds of TNT around the entrance tunnel to Unit 10 in the Schiesseck complex, but when the charge was exploded "it didn't bother it [the fort] at all—just blew down some of the lining of the tunnel wall." Even so, the blast had killed a dozen occupants. From the scene of this apparent failure, Pinnell crawled to the crest of Block No. 2, whose guns "were giving us a lot of trouble." Once he gained the crest of the ridge facing the fort, he checked for possible weak points or blind spots. Finding none, he took the incredible risk of climbing on top of the blockhouse to get "a good look-see."

Again finding no apparent weakness, Pinnell jumped down and took refuge in a shell hole just as German 88s began pouring on his position "the most concentrated barrage I've ever experienced, seen, or heard of in my life. . . . I never expected to live through it. Fifty shells landed within twenty-five feet of me. I was sprayed with rocks and dirt numerous times and two pieces of hot steel whizzed into the hole with me and buried themselves in the dirt just above my head." Only incorrect elevation kept the howitzers from zeroing in on his hiding place.

When the barrage finally lifted, Pinnell carefully retraced his steps to his battalion's position. There he organized and led a three-man team of engineers back to the fort he had scouted. Worming its way under the barbed-wire entanglements, the team spent hours planting satchel charges outside Units 2, 6, and 11. Throughout, they were exposed to a heavy shelling—Pinnell expected to die at any moment—but by some miracle everyone in the team survived, and the explosives they detonated inflicted an acceptable level of damage on their targets.[54]

Riflemen and miners worked out on the fly a routine that would prove effective against almost every unit in the Schiesseck chain. Covered by the infantry, engineers dropped a satchel charge from the top of each blockhouse or used a pole with a charge attached to bridge the moats that fronted many of the forts. When the charges detonated they not only blew in the doors of several forts but also created a ledge from which boards could be laid over the moats. Gaining entrance in this way, the engineers dropped explosives down stairways, into elevator shafts, and through ventilation ducts. When fire from other Maginot works prevented the engineers from lingering outside the forts, charges planted by their doors were detonated by bazookas fired from a safe distance.

Those Germans on the lower levels of the units not killed by the explosions found themselves trapped underground. The 398th had been ordered not to descend to the bowels of the forts to clean out their occupants. The carefully laid out lower floors were known to be stocked with machine guns and antitank weapons "for the purpose of slaughtering anyone attempting to get through. The operative strategy was to seal the pillboxes off and allow the enemy who preferred the lower levels to stay there indefinitely." Lieutenant Pinnell and his team spent portions of two days "blowing down stairs, blowing embrasures and ventilators and so forth, and then covered the turrets with a tank-dozer. We also brought up a welder and welded shut all the doors we could get to."[55]

Another rolling barrage paved the way for an attack early on the eighteenth. Artillery batteries and antitank guns, the latter firing from point-blank range, pummeled the Schiesseck units. None of these weapons, even the Long Toms of the 373rd, inflicted material damage, but the incessant pounding drove growing numbers of defenders underground, thus reducing the forts' firepower. Before a break in the shelling could allow the gunners to resume their positions, the attackers were on them, entering some of the forts through doors that had been blasted open. Those positions not taken outright were eventually surrounded and denied support from the other units.[56]

It took hours, but one fort after another was neutralized in this fashion. By late on the eighteenth, the teeth of the Maginot Line had been pulled. And yet the enemy had not lost hope of recovering what it had lost. The following day, a force of German infantry, moving through underground tunnels until able to ascend to a position thought to be hidden from American view, attempted to regain control of some of the forts. The would-be attackers, however, were detected before they could strike. Late that afternoon, Capt. Vernon C. Hines, the artillery forward observer with L Company of the 398th, was informed by a runner from another unit that a sizable force was assembling in a gully near one of the Schiesseck blockhouses, apparently ready to strike. Hines radioed for artillery fire on a position now shrouded in evening darkness. Asked to provide coordinates, the forward observer shouted into the mouthpiece: "Coordinates, hell! Just throw some in, and I'll tell you where to put them." Soon every field artillery battalion in the division as well as the 398th's cannon company was firing into the area. Fifteen minutes later, fifty Germans lay dead or dying in the gully; perhaps a dozen others were waving handkerchiefs and

Soldiers of the 100th Division inspect the massive wall of one of the forts along the Maginot Line. (*National Archives*)

strips of cloth, "unmistakably a pleading offer of surrender." The well-placed barrage effectively broke up the enemy's plans for a counterstroke.[57]

On the twentieth, the 398th's 2nd Battalion gained control of the last of the Schiesseck units. The regiment's mission then became a holding action, consolidating gains achieved at great cost. While the infantry pulled guard duty, the engineers continued their work of destruction. Many of the demolition details this day were led by Dee Crosby, already celebrated for his daring reconnaissance outside Puberg. The sergeant, up to his old heroics, constantly exposed himself to fire from the other Maginot forts while overseeing the demolition of turrets and elevators in Units 1, 2, 6, and 7. The eight hundred pounds of TNT that blew out the stairs to the last of these forts brought the total of explosives employed against Fort Schiesseck to five thousand pounds.

In the final operations around Schiesseck, a tankdozer was used to render permanently inoperable the aboveground portions of five of the units. Until this day, the fire coming from the forts had been too deadly to chance using the equipment, but on December 21, Tech. 5 Joseph Anderson of the 781st Tank Battalion volunteered for the still-risky task of burying Unit No. 9 under earth and rock, filling the moats and sealing the escape ports of Units 2 and 4, and clogging the turrets of Nos. 6 and 8. Only when the tankdozer got hung up on the apertures of No. 7 did Anderson stop. Assisted by some combat engineers, he disabled and abandoned his machine.[58]

Thanks to the exertions of the Centurymen and the effectiveness of their weapons, Freudenberg and Schiesseck no longer blocked access to a nearly defenseless Bitche. Control of these works meant that others not attacked could be outflanked and neutralized as well. Then, suddenly, with total victory in hand, everything was put on indefinite hold. At sundown on the twentieth, corps headquarters ordered the Century to relinquish its captured positions and assume a defensive posture. No explanation was forthcoming. The order stunned the men who had braved fire and fury to secure apparently impregnable objectives, in the process winning Presidential Unit Citations for the 398th's 3rd Battalion and B Company of the 325th Engineers. Every GI shook his head at the news; many cursed and swore—the same reaction the retreat from Strasbourg and the Rhine had elicited almost a month earlier.[59]

SIX

PLAN TENNESSEE

The cause of the Century division's pullback from the captured forts was von Rundstedt's counteroffensive in the Ardennes—the Battle of the Bulge—begun on December 16. Two days later, SHAEF ordered General Patton to halt his own offensive and turn north to aid the beleaguered elements of the 12th Army Group. On the nineteenth, at a conference at Verdun, the supreme commander ordered General Devers to cease all offensive operations and shift north to take over the sector Patton was evacuating. Devers was bitterly disappointed that he must curtail his nearly completed drive to the Siegfried Line. While the 44th and 100th divisions had been attacking around Bitche, the three infantry divisions and one armored division in General Brooks's VI Corps had driven north and east, crossing the Moder River, cutting through the Hagenau Forest, and reaching the German border. By December 15, Brooks's vanguard had crossed into Germany at several places within sight of the outer works of Hitler's West Wall. Now Devers had to halt the Seventh Army's forces and redeploy them farther to the rear, while postponing the French First Army's slow and difficult drive toward the Colmar Pocket.[1]

The Seventh Army's retrograde was designed not only to cover Patton's sector but to gain defensible ground in the face of an impending assault. General Patch's intelligence experts had received word of a second German counteroffensive, via the Saar River Valley. Thanks to the Third Army's enforced abandonment of the territory it had been attacking across, that valley now ran along the left flank of XV Corps. To counter the threat, General Haislip spread his forces thinly to man the twenty-three-mile line between Saarbrucken and Bitche.

As part of the change of strategy, the Century Division moved slightly north and well to the west of its most advanced positions around Bitche. It was entrusted with defending territory of varied character, from open farmland in the east to steep ridges and tree-lined draws in the center and western sectors. To reach these areas, each of the division's regiments participated in a complex sequence of position shifts. On December 21, the 397th Infantry Regiment vacated its perch on the right flank of the division, which had extended from Camp de Bitche south to Mouterhouse, and moved thirteen miles west to the country in and around Hottviller. Now on the division's far left, it assumed the position formerly held by a 44th Division regiment. Elements of the 106th Cavalry Troop took over the area the 397th had vacated. The reconnaissance unit also began to relieve the 399th in the Century's center as the latter shifted east to form the new right flank of the division on high ground just above the Lemberg-Mouterhouse road. In anticipation of an attack from the east, at first the 399th faced generally in that direction. Meanwhile, all but two companies of the 398th Infantry Regiment vacated the division's left flank and massed in woods south of Fort Schiesseck. Another portion of the 398th assembled on the hills east of Siersthal, three miles southwest of Bitche, where it covered the division's center and rear.[2]

Between the twenty-first and month's end, numerous adjustments were made to the new line, extending it even farther to the north and west while building up the division's reserve force. The reserve now included the 255th Infantry Regiment, a component of the 63rd Division, recently arrived from the States. Because the rest of the division had yet to land at Marseille due to sealift inadequacies, those units on hand had been grouped into a provisional organization under the assistant division commander, Brig. Gen. Frederick M. Harris. Pending the disembarking of the rest of the division, it was thought prudent to parcel out the new arrivals to more experienced divisions in need of reinforcement. The 253rd Infantry, another element of Task Force Harris, had been assigned to the 44th Division, on the Century's left.[3]

Even after the 255th came on line, the Century maintained its peripatetic existence. Private Miller of the 399th, upon rejoining his buddies following treatment of a wound received in the Vosges, found his outfit constantly "moving around into different locations and getting arranged in the best defensive posture possible." The principal feature of the new front line was its layered appearance. Multiple defensive lines, some running parallel to each other, some echeloned to protect the flanks, would drain the momentum of any German attack while allowing time for defenders in the rear to reinforce those up front.[4]

The effort to create a defense in depth received an impetus in the last days of the year when Plan Tennessee was put in motion. The plan, devised by General Burress and his G-3, or chief operations officer, Lt. Col. Kenneth Eckland, required each regiment to place two battalions on the main line and the third in reserve. To be effective, Plan Tennessee depended on concerted efforts to gather intelligence. Every day each outfit dispatched a patrol of platoon size or larger, both in daylight and after dark, to reconnoiter and take prisoners.

The new plan, which took its name from the division's Cumberland Mountains maneuvers, prompted still more changes of position, lasting through December. As historian Keith E. Bonn points out, the most critical moves were intended to strengthen the division's left flank around Rimling, the area through which a Saar Valley attack would come and where roads that stretched throughout the Century's sector met. The 397th's commander, Lieutenant Colonel King, had established his 3rd Battalion on the reverse slope of Schlietzen Hill northwest of Rimling. The regiment's 1st Battalion covered the east side of the little farming village, and the 2nd Battalion held the southeastern outskirts in the direction of

Bettviller and Guising. Other features of the plan included the shift of a battalion of the 398th to the village of Petit Rederching, about three miles southeast of Rimling. The balance of the 398th covered the southwest-running road from Hottviller to Enchenberg via Siersthal and Lambach. On the division's right, two battalions of the 399th had deployed across the Bitche-Lemberg highway, the third battalion being held in reserve along with the newly acquired 255th Regiment.[5]

Withers Burress took pains to guard the approaches to his new and extended front. He saw to it that hundreds of mines were planted beneath any ground an attacker seemed likely to cross, while explosives charges liable to be triggered in darkness or fog were attached to roadside trees. The roads themselves were intersected with fallen trees—payback for the enemy's penchant for creating roadblocks. Listening posts and antitank defenses were established, and telephone wire was strung all along the line, across a variety of terrain. The historian of the 925th Field Artillery Battalion recorded that "communication lines often ran as long as 5 and 6 miles, along highways, across mined fields, over rivers and streams, through swamps and ditches, along railroad tracks, over the roofs of houses, through open meadows, over treacherous enemy-observed terrain, and up heavily-wooded hillsides to the O.P.'s [observation posts] and Forward Observers."

These precautions, numerous and cleverly designed though they were, could not compensate for the fact that the Century was compelled to hold a line normally defended by three divisions. The command was stretched so thinly that in places squads of eight or ten men were trying to cover ground close to a mile in length. But there was no help for it; as Sergeant Tyson observed, "the order of the day was to keep improving our positions. In the event of a German breakthrough, we must hold this position at all costs."[6]

No one was happy about shifting from the invigorating offensive to the uncertain defensive. On his return from the hospital, Bernie Miller found among his buddies "much frustration that they had not been able to take Bitche." Sergeant Angier was down-

The Seventh Army, including the 100th Division, was ordered to stop its advance and prepare defensive positions in late December 1944 in response to the German surprise attack through the Ardennes. Here, soldiers dig holes in the frozen ground while others lay communication lines. (*National Archives*)

right angry over the change of strategy and posture. As F Company of the 399th withdrew a thousand yards or more down the Bitche-Lemberg Railroad, he "couldn't figure it out. Only a couple of days ago we were fighting our asses off to knock the Jerries off the other side of the railroad track; now we were in the same position, waiting for the bastards to come to us."[7]

Rumor had it that the division, if and when attacked, would have to repel the Germans without the support of units and weapons that had made a major contribution to the capture of Lemberg and the forts on the Maginot Line. Private Knight had heard that when other elements of Seventh Army moved north to cover Patton's withdrawal, they took "almost all of our artillery as well as all of the tanks." This was not entirely true, but when howitzers and Shermans were seen trundling north in the days following the pullback from Bitche, the Centurymen began to feel isolated and vulnerable. Over time, the men became resigned to their predicament. As Knight put it, "we could see that our hopes of spending the bitter cold days in a nice warm house in Bitche were 'kaput' so, everyone started to get as comfortable as our current conditions allowed."[8]

Comfort meant indoor living, or at least indoor sleeping. Most GIs, however, remained in foxholes and slit trenches, many of which had to be blasted out of the frozen earth by dynamite-wielding engineers. A few lucky units did not have to dig at all. George Tyson, whose L Company of the 399th had been moved well down the highway to Lemberg, found "several ancient holes already dug in our area, probably created during World War I. We examined the holes for booby traps and then moved into them." At some point Tyson's men grew concerned that their new homes might cave in, so they braced them with timber and rocks. As a senior noncom, Tyson rated a more commodious habitation. He moved into "an old French dugout which was about 8 feet square and about 6 feet deep. . . . A blanket was placed at the doorway of the dugout to black [it] out at night and also to keep out a little of the cold air. Many of us had candles that were sent to us [in gift packages], and at night we would write letters while our foxhole buddy was on guard outside."9

Even those who burrowed deeply could not escape exposure to the elements, including ever lower temperatures as the year moved to a close. According to Private Fair, the first few days after position readjustment got under way, the men suffered "especially at night, and then it snowed about six to eight inches and turned bitter cold." The only positive aspect to the plummeting thermometer was that it did away with another source of discomfort and disgust. Writing home three days before Christmas, Sergeant Edgar T. Longacre of the 397th's Cannon Company remarked that "today has been pretty cold, altho clear. It's nice to be rid of the mud at any rate."10

Surviving such weather demanded protective clothing, and lots of it. Bob Fair, like most of his buddies, adopted the layered look. Beneath everything he wore "GI underwear plus long underwear. Then I had on my wool shirt and trousers, wind-breaker trousers, a sweater, and my field jacket or overcoat. I wore regular cotton socks underneath heavy wool boot socks and boots. I had a wool stocking cap and my helmet plus a scarf and gloves." When outside his foxhole, Fair encased his feet in a sleeping bag, whether army issue or procured from a local family. Surprisingly, he "could still move around rather quickly when the situation demanded it."

A fellow machine gunner in the 399th did not feel quite as mobile; he compared himself and his buddies to "big children in cruddy overstuffed snow suits."[11]

Soldiers forced to remain outdoors attracted fire from the Maginot forts that had not been captured. Those who fell victim to enemy shells presented a removal problem. So severe was the weather that the dead froze within minutes. Graves registration personnel needed all their strength to pry the corpses from the ground and heave them into their trucks. At times the rain of shells became so intense that, as Arthur Knight wrote, "we did not feel safe to go out to answer nature's call until it would let up a little."[12]

Not everyone had to fight to remain warm, and in one piece, at the bottom of a foxhole. More fortunate—or more resourceful—GIs found shelter in farmhouses, barns, and other structures not in the direct line of German artillery. Private Miller thanked his lucky stars for the opportunity, when not out on patrol, to inhabit a barn nestled securely at the bottom of a ridge. Rank often determined who enjoyed a roof over his head. Private Knight, among many other lowly enlisted men, harbored unkind thoughts about those battalion and company officers who spent the better part of each day indoors. Knight was especially upset at a particular lieutenant, a severe disciplinarian who had made life miserable for the recruits—especially the former ASTP students—at Fort Bragg and who now inhabited a cozy house in a hamlet southwest of Lemberg. The officer was said to have taken no chances, "having [dug] a foxhole in his cellar at St. Louis. I wondered if he used a ruler to measure that hole like he used to measure our foxholes during basic training."[13]

Those literally and figuratively out in the cold faced more dangers than frigid winds and German 88s. One "freezing, windy night," Private Jelks was standing guard on his machine-gun position near Rimling "when I got a creepy feeling that I was being watched." Discerning nothing untoward in front, he whirled about: "There lying in the snow about five yards behind me was a French Moroccan soldier . . . a knife in his teeth." A member of General de Lattre's army, the man had come "all the way from our division's right flank to bum a cigarette. I had ten cigarettes, so I gave him five, and he gave me his fighting knife." Over the years Jelks wondered what might have happened had he not spotted the colonial soldier, whose unit had a reputation for sneaking into German foxholes and dispatching their occupants with a single, silent thrust: "He probably would have slit my throat and taken *all* of my cigarettes!"[14]

The stress caused by having to endure extreme weather, incoming shells, and the prospect of a major enemy assault took a physical toll, although one perhaps visible only to outside observers. Private Hancock, like Bob Fair recently returned to his outfit after recuperating from a Vosges campaign wound, was startled by once-familiar faces now scarcely recognizable:

> Everywhere I see hollow sunken eyes, dark shadow beards, and a lethargy of fatigue from the continuous night watches. . . . I recognize Staff Sergeant [Preston R.] Fitzgerald. Last summer he was a rotund first sergeant, now he looks like Mauldin's cartoon of GI Joe, his normally heavy beard accents the hollowed eyes, his paunch is replaced by the bulge of his parka, gathered into his rifle belt which sags under the weight of a full canteen and full ammo pouches. He is again, lean and hard, but now he is also a veteran of two months of combat. . . . Sgt. [James R.] Waller, always lean and supple, now seems cadaverous. His instant good humor has worn thin, but his Oklahoma accent persists. "Hancock, ain't yew got bettah sinse then tew com back heah?" The logic is inescapable, but I mimic him: "Hail no! Ah never been heah befoh an Ah jist figgered yew guys would need a lil' he'p this mawnin'!"[15]

Christmas, like Thanksgiving, brought holiday food to the men of the Century. Until the twenty-fifth, hot chow had been scarce, although occasionally made available to soldiers whose units were in a settled location beyond constant shelling distance. The rank-

and-file were happy to get any chow that was warm. Bob Fair considered the meal "excellent. . . . It tasted good even though we ate standing up or on the ground and out of our mess gear." Most units were served in shifts, half the men eating while the other half remained in their foxholes until relieved. Private Khoury received his turkey in a chow line that also provided his unit with bottles of beer and cans of peanuts. In many cases, the meal came with a special tidbit that, although not edible, was perhaps more appreciated than the chow itself: an overcoat, lined inside with fur, with a reversible cloth covering—white on one side, khaki on the other—and a parka. Khoury had fond memories of this gift: "We were warm inside the coat like never before."[16]

John Angier's platoon dined not only on turkey (a meal that he described as "long-awaited" but "overrated") but also on rabbit, courtesy of a rifleman with a good eye and a steady hand. To make the holiday more festive, another member of Angier's unit cut down an evergreen, stuck it in the ground in front of the platoon's command post, and decorated it with K-ration boxes, toilet paper, cigarette packs, and strands of the foil-like "chaff" that Army Air Forces planes dropped in hopes of disrupting enemy radar and radio communication. Angier and his fellow revelers had plenty to eat, drink, and smoke, "but not for long." There was no holiday break from sentry and patrol duty, not with rumors of an impending attack making the rounds.[17]

Not every GI was lucky enough to remain stationary long enough to enjoy his Christmas feast. Some units were kept moving across the no-man's-land between the lines. Now-Sergeant Gluesenkamp's platoon of the 397th spent the day shifting positions outside Rimling. At intervals it would halt and Gluesenkamp would try to dig a foxhole, but as soon as he got one well started the unit would move out. The newly promoted noncom calculated that he and his buddies covered more than twelve miles on the twenty-fifth. As he informed his parents in a letter three days later, "we did have a turkey dinner . . . [but] I was too tired to really appreciate the meal. I hope that 1 will never spend another Christmas like this past one."[18]

The men may have eaten under difficult conditions, but they enjoyed a feast of sorts, which was more than their leaders got. Early on Christmas Day, Col. Charles Hodge, commanding officer of the 117th Reconnaissance Squadron, then supporting the Century, was invited to General Burress's command post (which Hodge described as "a little shack") for a holiday repast, including a drink or two. Other guests of the division leader included staff officers and subordinates. Among the latter was an old colleague of Hodge's, General Murphy, Division Artillery's recently assigned commander. Hodge learned that a day or two earlier, Murphy had been involved in his first combat action of the campaign, an especially intense experience. The little group enjoyed a glass of bourbon but no turkey or cranberry sauce. In fact, the meal consisted of "some hardtack and some K-ration cheese" that everyone found something less than palatable.

The fare was hard to digest for reasons other than its age and staleness. At one point General Murphy announced, "I must have ulcers. I just can't eat anything. I can hardly get this drink down." Hodge believed he knew the reason for his colleague's difficulty, as did Burress. At the latter's urging, the colonel explained. "General Murphy, you're going through the same thing all of us have gone through. You're so scared that your stomach won't accept any food. And that's the honest truth." Murphy gave a weak smile, as if concurring in Hodge's diagnosis. As Hodge later observed, "all of us, upon our first real baptism of severe combat, didn't feel like eating much."[19]

The stress of combat, which struck especially hard at those who shouldered heavy responsibility, could do more than upset the stomach. Two days after Christmas, General Miller, the assistant division commander, was evacuated to the States to receive treatment for a worsening heart condition. Miller's temporary replacement was Brig. Gen. John S. Winn Jr., formerly chief of staff of the 36th Division. Early in January, Winn would give way to Colonel Tychsen, Burress's choice as Miller's permanent successor.

When Tychsen became acting assistant division commander, he handed the reins of the 399th Regiment to Elery Zehner.

Zehner's advancement was well received by those such as Private Gurley who appreciated the lieutenant colonel's single-minded pursuit of success and distinction. It did not find favor among those who considered Zehner too ambitious, too willing to take chances with the lives of his men. Zehner hoped, and probably expected, to gain permanent command of the regiment, but on that score he was doomed to disappointment.[20]

To raise morale the army resorted to other expedients besides a holiday feast. Around Christmastime the division got word that every nonstriper in the army had been promoted to private first class and had been awarded the Combat Infantryman Badge. The promotion brought an increase in monthly pay from fifty dollars to sixty-four dollars and eighty cents (the latter being the pay rate of those serving overseas, ten dollars more than a Stateside PFC). Most GIs were indifferent to the extra money, and they saw little honor in the award. Even so, the gestures may have had the intended effect. "We scoffed at these things," Private Bourne recalled, "and would rather have been sent home, we said. But still, they did something for morale by showing us that, though abused God knew, we were not completely ignored or forgotten."[21]

Some operational exploits during the Christmas season served to elevate morale, at least on the small-unit level. The day after Christmas, about a hundred Germans attacked the 3rd Battalion of the 397th east of Rimling. No artillery barrage preceded the assault, which gave the division's operations experts food for thought, but the 397th's cannon company was not so chary with its ammunition. With help from the 23rd Tank Battalion, it broke up the attack and propelled the enemy into retreat. Subsequent assaults—perhaps a tune-up for the anticipated offensive—struck positions held by elements of the 398th and 399th but were likewise repulsed, and the attackers pursued.[22]

On the twenty-ninth, a single GI of H Company of the 398th, Pvt. Bernard "Barney" Moeller, scored a dramatic coup by capturing a six-man enemy squad dug in east of Hottviller. The foxhole dwellers had opened fire on two of Moeller's superiors, Lt. Walter P. Smith Jr. and Sgt. Albert A. Mavreniu, who had been scouting the ground between the armies for a new position for their unit's 81-mm mortars. When the attack began, Moeller was about seventy-five yards behind the two, splicing telephone wire. Seeing that they had been pinned down, he dropped his wire cutters, picked up his M1, made a two-hundred-yard circuit around the enemy's position, and crawled to within fifteen feet of it. "Seeing the top of the head of one German soldier," Moeller fired. He knew the shot hit home, for it provoked cries of pain. "I could speak German, and I yelled for them to come out of the foxhole[s] with their hands over their heads." Two Germans, both wounded, complied, but before Moeller could corral them, a shot from another occupied foxhole clipped the side of his skull.

The shock of the near-fatal wound left Moeller in a daze that lasted several hours but did not prevent him from taking additional prisoners. Later he was told by Lieutenant Smith that "I ran into both foxholes yelling in German" and repeating one word over and over: *orsh-lochs*. Moeller was both surprised and amused: "I realized I was calling the Germans assholes. Anyway, it worked, because three more Germans came running out of the foxholes with their hands over their heads. . . . When my senses returned, I found myself in a hole with the sixth German, who was about 16 years old. He was crying for his mother. He was as scared as a baby when I pulled him out of the hole."[23]

On December 30, a platoon of C Company of the 397th, supported by four Sherman tanks and a barrage of high explosives and smoke shells, attacked enemy positions in a woods and on a hill east of Rimling. Killing a dozen Germans and capturing twenty others, the platoon removed a worrisome threat to the division's left flank. The enemy may have taken umbrage, for that afternoon, eleven captured P-47s, some showing U.S. markings, strafed and bombed elements of the 397th around Rohrbach and Petit Rederching, killing three men and wounding eight.[24]

Throughout the thirtieth, enemy patrols tried without success to penetrate the division's lines. After midnight, a squad-size force from the 398th vowed to succeed where the enemy had failed. Under Lt. Robert H. Rush, a trusted leader who had received a battlefield promotion two weeks earlier, twenty-five members of G Company left their reserve post at Hottviller on a mission grandly styled Operation Rochester. The patrol entered enemy-held Dollenbach and, at a prearranged signal, opened up with every weapon at its disposal. Explosions from thermite grenades and blasts from machine guns and Browning Automatic Rifles riddled a barracks and observation post and set several buildings on fire. The attackers also shot up a chow line in the streets of the village, making casualties of at least a dozen Germans and, according to some accounts, as many as twenty-five. Whatever the number, Rush's men returned from the successful hit-and-run action without any loss themselves.[25]

The New Year's Eve attack that forced elements of the Century to hastily decamp from its current front line could have heaped disaster and disgrace on the division; instead, it came to be regarded as one of its greatest hours. By late on January 1, both of the division's flanks were under heavy and increasing pressure, and in places they appeared to be coming apart (although some German commanders later admitted that their troops had gained "insignificant ground"). The situation was not solely the division's fault; supporting units on both ends of the line—the 44th Division on the left, the 117th Reconnaissance Squadron on the right—had given way under less pounding than the Century had withstood, leaving the latter exposed and shaky. Had the division succumbed to the forces opposing it, the collapse would have been understandable.

Instead, when the division's far right began to stagger under the weight of simultaneous blows from north and east, various units of the 399th, including its field artillery battalion, fell back, for the most part in good order. Assured that disaster was not imminent, General Burress calmly moved to shore up the flank before it disintegrated. He sent the 100th Reconnaissance Troop to reestablish contact with Task Force Hudelson, which had been isolated by the 117th's precipitate retreat to the Wingen-sur-Moder area. He also committed the better part of his available reinforcements. Though newly arrived at the front and woefully inexperienced, two battalions of the 255th Infantry of Task Force Harris blunted and delayed, though they did not halt, the German advance on the right. The 255th's 3rd Battalion solidified the U.S. hold on Lambach and Lemberg, potential rallying points for men dislodged from the front. Meanwhile, the 141st Infantry of the 36th Division, which General Patch had released from the army's reserve, took position farther to the east, strengthening as well as extending the Century's right flank. At about the same time, elements of the 398th, until now not heavily engaged, moved south and east to further reinforce the embattled 399th. The latter returned the favor when, late on January 2, a company of the 398th found itself almost surrounded. Units of the 399th attacked three times, on the third try breaking the German line and rescuing their trapped comrades.[26]

Maps prepared by the Century's plans and operations staffs in the days following the offensive suggest that by late on the second, the units stationed on the far right had withdrawn four and a half miles from just south of Bitche to the area around Goetzenbruck and Sarreinsberg. Farther west, other units forced to evacuate their positions between Bitche and Reyersviller had fallen back less than half that distance. The amount of snow-covered terrain given up is not surprising considering that elements of a single regiment, backed by portions of two others, had been under near-constant attack for almost forty-eight hours by the entire 559th Volks-Grenadier Division and portions of the 257th Volks-Grenadiers, striking with fanatical energy.[27]

A third German force was later added to the offensive in that sector, the crack 6th SS-Mountain North Division, a veteran of combat on the eastern front, described by its commanders as "unbeaten and victorious." Its unblemished record notwithstanding, the North Division failed to achieve a breakthrough. Quite the contrary, by the snowy morning of January 3, it was becoming increasingly clear to the German high command that although portions of the Century had been uprooted, the division was unwilling to relinquish enough ground to make the offensive a success—any gains along the right were insubstantial and temporary. Plan Tennessee was proving its value: holes in the division's new line were being filled as quickly as they opened, and the shouting, cursing enemy was butting his head fruitlessly against layer after layer of defenders.[28]

The defense of Lemberg, the town the 399th had taken in desperate fighting three weeks earlier, was so tenacious that even a temporary breakthrough was out of the question. The 399th's reserve battalion (with K Company of the 398th attached) had formed an L-shaped line around the town which, though at times precariously thin, resisted repeated attacks, giving those units dislodged farther north a place to rally and dig in. Elements of the enemy's Army Group Oberrhein had hoped to penetrate well beyond Lemberg, there to link with the forces of General Blaskowitz attacking from the west. Increasingly, the assumptions that underlay this strategy were being exposed as overly ambitious.

Over time, the assaults began to diverge to the east; more and more weight was committed against VI Corps's front. But success in that sector was no more achievable than along the Century's right flank. General Brooks was making inspired use of his front-line and reserve forces, shifting infantry and armored units to critical sectors at just the right time, blunting assault after assault. Here, too, the attackers were denied access to the Low Vosges, the only route to the rear of the American forces. Their inability to reach and penetrate the mountains prevented Hitler from committing two Panzer divisions being held in reserve until a breakthrough occurred.[29]

By January 7, with snow flurries in the air, combat along the Century's right flank had decreased substantially. The following day the division began to take back some of the ground lost over the previous week. The 3rd Battalion of the 399th, supported by elements of the 142nd Regiment of the 36th Division (released to XV Corps by Seventh Army headquarters) as well as by tanks and two artillery battalions, moved to attack Spitzberg and Signalberg hills, south of Reyersviller. Striking from the reverse slopes of neighboring elevations, the troops intended to take and hold the crests of both hills. Capt. Alfred E. Olsen, commanding I Company of the 399th, won a Distinguished Service Cross by leading his unit in capturing entrenchments and log fortifications on Spitzberg, thus outflanking the enemy on the summit.[30]

One of the attackers, Frank Hancock, was relieved to find that the German dugouts his platoon seized were empty except for an abandoned machine gun: "We find no booby-traps or mines, no tracks in the snow but our own. We have recaptured Spitzberg Hill." Germans, however, were still visible, snaking through woods on M Company's flanks, perhaps a half mile away. Taking over the captured weapon, Hancock tried to get a bead on the enemy but had trouble doing so. His powerfully built platoon commander had no such trouble: "Lt. [Scott J.] Witt picks up the water-cooled gun with its tripod and ammo (easily 115 pounds), moves to where he can see the Germans, and fires a half a belt while holding the gun at his hip. He sets the gun down in front of my hole, checks the field of fire, and then leisurely walks away."[31]

Early in the afternoon of the eighth, Colonel Zehner made a daring reconnaissance of the route that L Company of the 399th had earlier taken when moving southeast across a wooded draw and up Steinkopf and Signalberg hills, adjacent to Spitzberg. The operation had been a disaster from start to finish. Granted no cover behind which to form and stage an attack, L Company had been driven back to its line of departure by German 88s and machine guns. During the hasty withdrawal, the single tank accompanying the unit backed up over a wounded officer, Lt. Park B. Ashbrook, crushing his chest and pelvis. John Khoury eulogized the mortally wounded Ashbrook as "a fine officer . . . a true gentleman and a friend."[32]

Following Zehner's reconnaissance, which was made aboard a Sherman tank, then by foot, and resulted in the capture of fifteen Germans, "all with an empty Tommygun"—L Company attacked again. By nightfall it had fought its way up Signalberg to make contact with other elements of its regiment as well as E Company of the 398th, part of a reserve force in the Lambach area. Earlier that day, the reserve unit had helped I and K companies of the 399th fight off a heavy German counterattack.[33]

Zehner was not so successful when, two days later, he determined to recapture ground near Reyersviller taken from the division one week earlier. On the ninth, the acting regimental leader informed Capt. Howard D. Smith, commanding F Company of the 398th, whose combat-weary unit had been attached to the 399th, that he was to advance about a mile down a hill, through a woods, and into a draw between Spitzberg and Signalberg hills. Just beyond the gully he was to attack Reyersviller, not only regaining the town but securing both the right flank of L Company of the 399th and the left flank of K Company against enemy infiltration. Should the operation succeed, Smith was told, Zehner would follow with the entire regiment that had been entrusted to him upon Tychsen's promotion.

A member of F Company, Pvt. John P. Lonsberg, claimed that "none of us had any confidence" in Zehner's ability to keep his pledge of support. Furthermore, the mission was a heavy one, especially for an understrength unit that lacked information about the enemy's exact positions. Then, too, Smith had only a couple of hours to plan the assault and coordinate artillery assistance; and he was denied the support of tanks and tank destroyers. The laundry list of deficiencies, especially the scarcity of intelligence, prompted the captain to protest F Company's assignment, but Zehner denied the motion.

At dawn on the tenth, Smith's unit launched what Lonsberg called "the most ill-prepared attack F Co. was to make" during the war. The first shots fired by the company as it moved out were answered by artillery and mortar rounds; as Smith had feared, the Germans had his position zeroed in. Then shells from the rear began to rain down on the company; the forward observer, having been wounded, could not stop the friendly fire. Having penetrated one hundred yards without establishing a strong base of fire, the unit was forced to withdraw. Most of the men managed to crawl to safety, but those closest to the enemy line lay trapped for hours, pummeled from front and rear, until able to get off under cover of darkness. By then seven had been killed, fifteen wounded, two had been taken prisoner, and two were unaccounted for—and never seen again. It was bad enough that the causalities had to be left behind; more distressing was the news, reported by a trapped GI later rescued, that a German medic shot several of the wounded as they lay helpless in the snow.

The following evening, F Company was relieved of its assignment to the 399th and sent to the rear for reorganization. On the twelfth, Zehner was removed as acting commander of the 399th. He gave way to Col. Edward J. Maloney, whom even the hard-driving Colonel Tychsen described as "utterly ruthless" in his dealings with officers and men. No specific reason was given for Zehner's demotion, but the men of F Company always believed the disaster that befell their unit on January 10 had much to do with it.[34]

Stymied along the Century's right, the Germans put renewed energy into unhinging the division's left flank in and around Rimling. From the first hour of Nordwind, the defenders of that small but strategic farming village fought desperately against grim odds. Long after the 44th Division fell back under pounding from the 17th SS-Panzer Division, the 2nd and 3rd battalions of the 397th Infantry Regiment held their ground in the face of an equally fierce assault by the 36th Volks-Grenadiers. During the first six days of 1945, the 397th, supported closely by its cannon company and the 374th Field Artillery Battalion, repulsed wave after wave of attack. The guns cleared hundreds of *landsers* from the 397th's flanks, knocked out at least one tank advancing with infantry support, and broke up a group of fifty tanks and other vehicles assembling north of town.

Some men whose units were posted beyond the sector where the Germans concentrated their attacks had contrasting memories of their experiences. Les Gluesenkamp, whose C Company occupied foxholes around Bettviller, southeast of Rimling, recalled that "although our immediate area was not directly attacked, the chatter of machine guns, burp-guns, rifle fire, grenades, bazookas and the noise of tanks" was unnerving and occasionally deadly. Sergeant Howsmon's B Company, which held a more exposed position north of Gluesenkamp's unit, recalled the same week as "a quiet period. Aside from mortar fire which blew out our phone lines to the CPs almost daily, we had no action. Of all the places where we were [during the war], this is the one I remember most vividly and even warmly. Even though it was cold, we had good holes, hot chow, and the memory of 1 January, when we had really torn them up."[35]

The first two days of the defense of Rimling had been critical; as early as January 2, the operations officer of Blaskowitz's Army Group G conceded that his offensive—aimed at penetrating well behind the 397th's lines—had "lost its momentum." Even so, the enemy drive continued in full force. On the fourth, as part of a major effort against the now well-dug-in 44th Division, the Germans tried but failed to drive G Company of the 397th from the high ground south of Schlietzen Hill. On the fifth and sixth (the latter a "beautiful, sunshiney day without a cloud in the sky," as Private Sheets recalled), elements of the 397th switched positions to give the troops most heavily engaged thus far a break from the action. Only a single platoon of E Company had any trouble gaining its newly assigned position near Schlietzen; aided by a few light tanks, it repulsed a succession of German assaults.

After this, the enemy seemed content to shell the 2nd Battalion, which had replaced the 3rd on the outskirts of Rimling. The Germans began to suffer heavy losses; on the fifth, fifty-six infantrymen, caught trying to infiltrate U.S. lines southeast of the town, were either killed or captured. Soon stalemate, or something close to it, defined the fighting on the Century's left flank. Sheets described the situation: "The German tanks would come at us, our infantry would blast their infantry and they would withdraw. Our tanks would come back up, draw enemy artillery fire and they would withdraw. Over and over this went on."[36]

Frustrated by his inability to drive out the 397th, Blaskowitz reinforced his attack columns. In the early morning darkness of January 8, he struck in massive array, preceded by a memorable barrage. The men of the 397th had endured many a shelling, but for sheer, concentrated ferocity this one was a prize winner. A member of E Company recalled the fire as "much longer than anyone expected or had experienced before. . . . We were digging and praying like madmen." The "infernal screeching" of conventional shells and rocket-propelled *nebelwerfer* assailed the psyche as well as the ears. "They dulled us to robots as we hugged the bottoms of our holes in sheer terror," an officer recalled. "Would it *never* end?"[37]

Pvt. Jack O'Brien of the regiment's antitank company was manning a 57-mm gun emplacement south of Rimling when the shelling began. Frantic to escape the rain of fire and steel, two of his buddies "arrived at a breathless run and piled into my hole. So there we were, three of us squeezed together with shells landing every fifteen seconds. Some big stuff showered us with frozen dirt fragments. . . . Each round was preceded by a piercing whistle followed by a bone-shaking crash. We lay there fearing the always dreaded direct hit."

Before the big one could land, a messenger from platoon headquarters brought word that everyone should leave their precarious positions for the dubious safety of the farmhouse where the unit's command post was located. O'Brien's closest friend in the army, Cpl. John McCann, climbed out of an adjacent foxhole, stood up, and waved the others to the rear. As additional rounds came whistling in, McCann suddenly signaled for them to remain where they were until the shells landed, an act that saved several lives. A moment later, O'Brien "felt a tremendous concussive blast close by. There was an intense orange radiance which lasted but an instant and I could smell the stink of the explosive. Calling out for Johnny I got no answer!" Instead of making for the house, O'Brien ran to the antitank gun, which had been blown twelve feet away. He found McCann's mangled body lying between the gun trails. Though unwilling to look closely, "I knew in my heart that he was dead, no one could survive a near direct hit of that large a shell." Finally, he took off: "On reaching the safety of our house, I broke down and wept for both Johnny and myself."[38]

Nearly thirty minutes after it began, the barrage lifted. Then came the attack, spearheaded by two hundred infantry and twelve tanks sweeping down from the north. A two-pronged effort, the assault was aimed at the northwestern side of town as well as south in the direction of Guising. According to the historian of the 397th, "we sensed at once that this was it, that this was the final big push and that all possible enemy strength and weapons would eventually be used." As soon as the barrage ceased, the GIs "could hear the screeching sound of the tank treads and the screaming of the accompanying infantry all around us."[39]

The attackers overran the foxholes of E and F companies, causing chaos and consternation, but they bypassed other positions ripe for the taking. Private Drury recalled that "we all froze and they all rolled on by us passing around each end of our wooded plot. Soon after, Pete [Sgt. Peter P. Petracco, leader of E Company's 1st Platoon] had us moving in a column like Indians, fast and quiet, towards the east. . . . A German tank came back along the road looking for us as we took cover in [a] quarry until they had passed. We continued on down the hill and in the next 15 or 20 minutes dawn rose. If we had been a little later in getting to the quarry, we would have been clearly visible to the tank's machine gunner. We trudged across snow fields to the positions of our 81 mm mortars of H Company," where they found at least temporary safety.[40]

Not every member of the 2nd Battalion got off so easily. During the early hours of the attack, F Company and the 3rd Platoon of E Company were virtually destroyed, most of their men being cut off and captured. Bypassed members of E Company became "unwilling bystanders of the appalling attack." They could hear the seemingly drunken Germans, "see their fire, and at times, by the light of flares, see the men themselves as they overran Company F and circled to the 3rd Platoon's rear." Other men just beyond range of the attack watched helplessly as German troops raced through the streets of Rimling "shouting 'Heil Hitler,' and demanding American surrender."[41]

When the 17th SS entered Rimling, the Panzer unit made for the center of the rectangular village. Only two machine-gun emplacements—both near the junction of the two main roads on Rimling's northwest corner—were in a position to oppose the invasion. One gun, set up at the H Company command post about one hundred yards northeast of the junction, was quickly disabled and its crew wounded by a machine gunner on the first Panzer to enter town. The other emplacement, located in a barn closer to the crossroads, was manned by a below-strength crew consisting of Privates Ellis J. Hall (gunner), Robert L. Gorell (the company bugler, acting as assistant gunner), and an ammunition bearer whose identity remains unknown. When the first Panzer approached their position, Hall and Gorell opened on it, the former with the machine gun, the latter with a tommy gun. Infantrymen accompanying the tank returned fire; one lobbed a grenade inside the barn, mortally wounding the ammo bearer and showering Hall, Gorell, and the machine gun with debris.

While the two men scrambled to get the gun back into commission, the Panzer continued along the eastern-leading road to Epping and Urbach. Soon a second tank entered the town, occupying the position vacated by the first. Though heavily outgunned, Hall and Gorell were soon firing on the second tank. The Panzer attempted to return fire, but in the narrow street the turret could not revolve sufficiently to bring its cannon to bear on the barn. Seeing this, several Germans rushed the position, only to be cut down at point-blank range; the rest withdrew speedily.

While retreating, one tossed a potato masher inside the barn. The explosion brought a heavy door down on Hall's and Gorell's heads, rendering them temporarily unconscious. Supposing that resistance had been overcome, the second Panzer proceeded along the street to join the first tank, which had begun to back up. Suddenly men and machines were sprayed by machine-gun fire

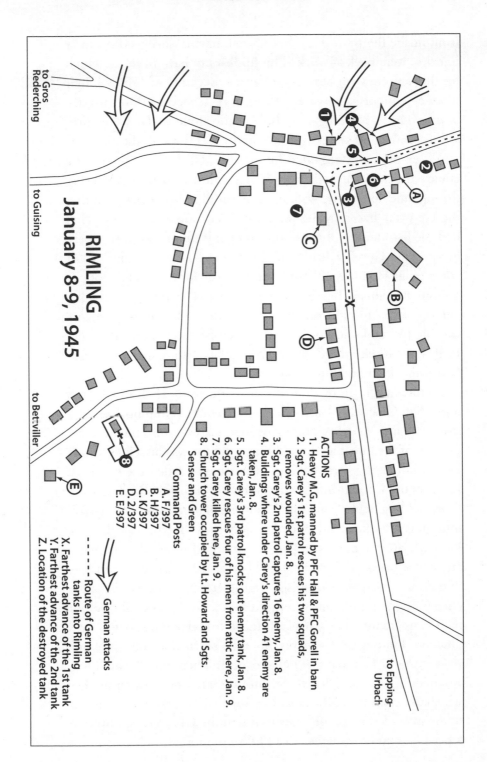

RIMLING
January 8-9, 1945

to Gros
Rederching

to Guising

to Bettviller

to Epping-
Urbach

ACTIONS

1. Heavy M.G. manned by PFC Hall & PFC Gorell in barn
2. Sgt. Carey's 1st patrol rescues his two squads, removes wounded, Jan. 8.
3. Sgt. Carey's 2nd patrol captures 16 enemy, Jan. 8.
4. Buildings where under Carey's direction 41 enemy are taken, Jan. 8.
5. Sgt. Carey's 3rd patrol knocks out enemy tank, Jan. 8.
6. Sgt. Carey rescues four of his men from attic here, Jan. 9.
7. Sgt. Carey killed here, Jan. 9.
8. Church tower occupied by Lt. Howard and Sgts. Senser and Green

Command Posts

A. F/397
B. H/397
C. K/397
D. 2/397
E. E/397

- - - - - Route of German tanks into Rimling
X. Farthest advance of the 1st tank
Y. Farthest advance of the 2nd tank
Z. Location of the destroyed tank

⟱ German attacks

from inside the barn: Hall and Gorell, having shrugged off their injuries, were back at work. This appears to have been too much for the tank crews to bear; both Panzers began to withdraw. Their infantry supports, however, were more tenacious. One used a *panzerfaust* to blow a gaping hole in the stone walls of the barn, killing Gorell and knocking Hall twenty feet through the air.

When he finally regained his senses, Hall wondered why the enemy had not finished him off or taken him prisoner. Peering through the hole in the wall, he discovered to his amazement that the Germans had retreated en masse. As soon as he could, Hall fled the barn and hobbled to the company command post, where he reported Gorell's death and the ammo bearer's wounding. At some point Hall was able to go to the rear for medical attention, though the ammo bearer died en route. For their unshakable determination to fight on against daunting odds, in the process causing two tanks and dozens of Waffen-SS to abandon Rimling, Hall and Gorell would be awarded the Distinguished Service Cross, the latter posthumously.[42]

Heroics even more dramatic than those of Hall and Gorell made Sgt. Charles F. Carey Jr., of Cheyenne, Wyoming, the division's second Medal of Honor winner. Carey's unit, the antitank platoon of the 2nd Battalion, 397th Infantry, was attached to one of the command posts that had been isolated when the southern prong of the German attack cut off the troops inside Rimling from those holding Schlietzen Hill. When one of the platoon's three 57-mm guns was knocked out of action early on the eighth by a Panzer, Carey organized a patrol composed of another noncom and three privates—members of his unit's headquarters and its 2nd Squad—and at its head set out to determine the extent of the enemy's penetration and whether the wrecked gun could be put back in operation. The patrol advanced to a spot north of the road junction. Finding no Germans, the men reached a side street just west of the H Company command post. There they located two wounded men. Carey left the group in search of German medics who had been seen in the area. Finding two, he had them minister to the wounded men, then saw to it that the GIs were removed to a safe place and the medics to a POW compound.

Carey again left the patrol when called a short distance east to F Company headquarters. There the company commander, Capt. William Stallworth, directed his attention to a building from which snipers were pinning down Stallworth's men. Carey agreed to check out the position, but first he completed his initial errand, locating and examining the knocked-out gun. Finding it damaged but still operable, Carey tended to its wounded crew members, reorganized the unit, and positioned the gun to cover Stallworth's headquarters.

It was midmorning before Carey could remove the wounded to the battalion command post, where they could receive proper medical attention. Only then did Carey start off on the errand Stallworth had assigned him. He led his small patrol to the street corner where the sniper-filled house sat. Shouting, "Cover me, I'm going in," he dashed across the street toward the front door. On the way he shot and killed two snipers posted at the house's windows, hurled a grenade through the open door, and after it detonated charged inside, firing his M1. Minutes later he emerged, sixteen prisoners in tow. After escorting his captives to the H Company command post, the sergeant returned to F Company headquarters to report having located, on the way to the snipers' position, a group of houses west of the Guising road also occupied by the enemy. His detailed report enabled patrols from F Company to clear those buildings and take forty prisoners.

Not content with his heroics thus far, that afternoon Carey, having spied a Panzer entering the west end of town, acquired a bazooka and several rounds of ammunition. Under a covering fire, he crawled to within a few yards of the rear of the tank and loosed a rocket. His first shot missed, but his second struck home, setting the tank afire. When members of the crew climbed out of the hatches to escape the blaze, he shot them down one by one, killing three and wounding and capturing one. Closing out the day's activity, Carey formed a bazooka team to oppose the entrance of other tanks into town. He stationed it in a barn near the road junction while placing a second bazooka squad near the F Company command post.

A GI firing a bazooka during the fighting in the Vosges in the winter of 1944–45. The bazooka was the chief antitank weapon for American soldiers and was their equivalent to the German *panzerfaust*. (*National Archives*)

On the morning of January 9, although pressure on the 397th had abated—at least some Germans were believed to have fallen back to regroup—a Waffen-SS unit advanced on Rimling from the northwest. It moved swiftly enough to cut off and capture F Company's command post, including the bazooka team Carey had established there. Four other members of F Company escaped to the attic of the building that housed the post. Discovering their plight, the sergeant found a ladder, propped it under an upstairs window, and led the trapped men to safety.

Early that afternoon Carey attempted to save additional comrades, members of a bazooka team surrounded in the loft of a barn just below the Epping-Urbach road. Encircling the enemy position, Carey and the four-man patrol with him eventually reached the south side of the barn, which sat adjacent to the command post recently set up by K Company of the 397th. Hoping to form an escape route for the trapped team, Carey fired a bazooka round into a building beside the barn. When the blast failed to free the surrounded team, he fitted a grenade to the carbine he was also toting. Before firing it, Carey shepherded his men across the street from the targeted building. Exposing himself to sniper fire, he ducked barely in time to avoid a round that whizzed past his head. As he strove to provide a covering fire for his men, a second round struck and killed him, ending a remarkable succession of valorous acts, any of which was deserving of a decoration.[43]

Other acts of individual heroism characterized the 397th's against-all-odds defense of Rimling. On January 7, Sgt. Robert W. Senser, a forward observer for the regimental cannon company attached to the 3rd Battalion, singlehandedly broke up an enemy patrol that had surrounded a house in which Senser and eleven other GIs lay trapped. Unwilling to risk injury to anyone but himself, Senser sent the others to the basement, then climbed to the top floor, the best place from which to defend the house. Rapid fire from his M1 carbine, delivered from various windows, appears to have made the Germans believe the upstairs was filled with defenders; after two of their number had been shot down, the rest fled.

The next day Senser, acting on a request—not an order—from his company commander, climbed to the top of a church south of Rimling, accompanied by Sgt. Daniel H. Green, the 3rd Battalion operations noncom. From the church steeple, although exposed to sniper fire from all sides, Senser used a field radio to direct a barrage of 155-mm fire on a group of Panzers that had entered the town. The "proximity fire"—shells that burst about fifty feet in the air instead of hitting the ground—was so accurate that one tank was destroyed, a second was damaged, and the others quickly retreated.

Later, a five-man German squad broke into the church and began to ascend to Senser's and Green's perch. Hearing the approach of hobnailed boots, Senser asked Green if he had any grenades. "I got two," the operations sergeant replied. "Give me one," said Senser, "and you take the other and let's pull the pin and count to two and drop them." Green recalled that the grenades killed three of the enemy and wounded the other two ("that was the only time that I know I directly contributed to killing a man during the war"). The two noncoms were not subsequently challenged. They remained in the steeple, directing fire on the enemy below, until able to descend and sneak back through the town to rejoin their units.[44]

On the morning of the ninth, while the most desperate fighting raged inside Rimling, the lower prong of the enemy pincers clamped shut on Hill 370, less than a mile south of town. The Germans advanced along the northeast slope of that elevation toward a creek bed that sheltered the 81-mm mortars of H Company. Though forced to fire their weapons at ranges so short as to endanger themselves, the mortar men broke up the attack, killing twenty-six, wounding eleven, and taking twenty-nine prisoners. Surviving Germans retreated to Hill 370, which they held until counterattacked in midmorning by a variegated force that included elements of the 1st Battalion, 398th Infantry Regiment (this day attached to the 397th) and a company of the 749th Tank Battalion. Hoping to free the high ground south of Rimling and thus prevent the town's encirclement, the GIs advanced up the slope in the teeth of a severe fire, suffering heavily. Eventually they retook Hill 370, although supporting attacks against nearby positions including Schlossberg and Schlietzen hills were beaten back by a deadly combination of infantry, tanks, and self-propelled guns.

The casualties in these fights—including almost a dozen seriously wounded GIs who had been placed inside a captured German pillbox—required immediate evacuation. Because of the ubiquitous enemy fire, the medical officer in charge refused to allow any of his people to risk carrying the wounded to the rear. They were rescued only after a litter bearer, Pvt. Marco Zagha, volunteered to remove them in an ambulance jeep. The effort took four trips, all made by Zagha alone—he refused to allow anyone else to brave the small-arms fire he received despite the Red Cross markings on his vehicle, clearly visible to the enemy. Like Hall, Gorell, and Lt. James S. Howard (an artillery observer who on the first day of Nordwind broke up a German patrol with a carbine, a pistol, and a hand grenade delivered from the same church tower that Sergeants Senser and Green occupied six days later), Zagha was awarded the Distinguished Service Cross for his heroics at Rimling—in his case, without firing a shot.[45]

Rimling had been held against tremendous pressure and at heavy cost because General Haislip had hoped that the 44th Division could counterattack, recovering the terrain lost in its sector. When this appeared unlikely, General Burress ordered the 397th and its supports to withdraw from the town after dark on the ninth. The troops fell back to higher ground across the highway north of Guising. Many evacuees left with morale intact. John Sheets and his buddies in I Company relinquished their positions west of town with "our heads high, we were not run off Le Schlietzen."[46]

For others, the withdrawal began badly but ended on a high note. Richard Drury recalled that when E Company pulled out of the town in the small hours of the tenth, "our spirits were down. Then came a sight, straight out of Hollywood. This defeated mob on the road saw over to our right on a rise—our tanks, hub to hub, 10 to 12 in a row! They were waiting for the last stragglers to clear the town. . . . It was a wonderful and reassuring sight to see and realize that a good solid MLR [main line of resistance] was already in place."

The 397th's escape had been aided by a snowfall that a member of K Company (which had been reduced to thirty officers and men during the fighting) called an "overnight blizzard" with snowflakes "the size of birds" that blanketed them from enemy view. So skillfully was the withdrawal executed that twenty minutes after the last GI departed Rimling, German infantry and tanks launched a major attack that struck nothing and captured no one. Preregistered guns south of town zeroed in on the new occupants, inflicting heavy losses. The concentration of tanks and guns within easy firing reach of the town's streets ensured that Blaskowitz's troops would penetrate no farther south except in patrol size.[47]

Its new position south of Rimling enabled the 397th to connect with the balance of the division along a more compact, and thus more defensible, line. With Nordwind having run its course in this sector, the division's left flank was again intact only a couple of miles from where it had stood on the last evening of 1944. In the center, the original line around Hottviller remained virtually undisturbed. Only on the right had the Century given up a sub-stantial amount of ground, due mainly to the almost complete lack of VI Corps support early in the fighting.

In later days the 399th had recovered ground as far north as Spitzberg Hill, between Lemberg and Reyersviller. The enemy had attempted to take back the recaptured terrain but failed. Pressure on the Century's front line had virtually ceased by January 10, although Hitler would not announce an end to Nordwind until the twenty-fifth. Even so, German forces attempt-ed to infiltrate the lines south of Reyersviller, sometimes clad in American uniforms.[48]

One night, there was an unusual amount of activity around the farmhouse used as a command post by John Angier's platoon of F Company. Visible in the glare of "artificial moonlight" generated by powerful searchlights in the division's rear, a column of twos advanced along the road toward the post. "Dressed in GI white parka snow coats," Angier wrote, "they resembled a mass of ghosts coming to haunt the garrison. We had just received from Battalion a message stating to be on the lookout for English-speaking Germans in American uniforms who were giving a considerable amount of trouble in the rear." A member of Angier's platoon, whom he identified only as Luke, got on the phone to battalion headquarters and learned that no friendly patrols had been out that night. Putting down the phone, Luke pulled back the lever of the 50-caliber machine gun whose barrel protruded through an upper window of the house. "Having waited until the very last minute," Angier recalled, "Luke let go with a full belt. You never heard such a racket in your life. Above the loud chatter of the fifty, you could hear the bloodcurdling screams and dying groans of Hitler's supermen as they would say something in German and then slump to the ground."

At dawn the next day, piles of snow-covered bodies were visible not seventy-five yards from the command post. Surveying the scene, Luke suddenly exclaimed: "Goddammit, Sarge, I must have missed a couple." Angier looked where he was pointing. A single German lay writhing about, moaning softly. Luke hoisted up a carbine, took careful aim, and squeezed the trigger: "As the bullet hit its mark, the body twitched and jerked as though someone were punching it with a stick." Luke's only comment: "How the hell [had] he lived through the night?"

Although Angier believed he was inured to a life of casual violence, something about the slaughter outside the post shook him. In a hollow voice, he remarked: "It's an awful feeling, isn't it, Luke, to be here, alive and well now, but in the next minute you may be like those bastards out there in the road." This dollop of introspection prompted Angier's habitually close-mouthed buddy to unburden himself: "As we sat there by the gun, snow blowing in our faces, he began to reminiscence of clean clothes, a shave and a bath, a warm room and a bed, steaks, highballs, cocktails, and women." Angier briefly partook of the alluring vision, though aware that "there was nothing whatsoever to do about it but to curse the bitch *war*."

Next day, the two were still emotionally raw when an unidentified colonel (Angier refers to him only as a "brass hat") showed up at the command post accompanied by a staff officer. Quite possibly the visitor was Colonel Maloney, come to familiarize himself with the forward positions of his new command. The fact that he appeared only after the fighting in this sector had died down did not endear him to Angier or Luke—neither did his brusqueness nor his evident intent to find fault.

Taking Luke, the first soldier he met, to be the senior enlisted man, the colonel snapped, "Where is your platoon?" Luke calmly detailed its position in nearby fields and houses. "What's behind you?" the officer asked. Luke stared at him and replied, "Nothing." The officer was taken aback: "There is no depth in this position." Luke responded, "You can't have depth, sir, without men, sir." The answer did not please the visitor: "Why, I could walk right through your positions at night." "Yes, sir," said Luke, patting the barrel of his machine gun, "and if you do, you will be pushing up daisies like those Krauts out there who thought they could do the same thing."[49]

The ground the Century had given up to the final enemy offensive of the war was remarkably little in comparison to that relinquished by the 44th Division on its left and those VI Corps units on its right. By the last week in January, the 100th Division's sector protruded well forward of the rest of the U.S. position between the Saar and the Rhine. Such a posture seemed worthy of official commendation. One who thought so was General Devers, who late in the month proclaimed that "the rugged American stubbornness of the combat elements of the 100th Infantry Division has played a tremendous part in stemming the tide of attack by superior enemy numbers." The general was especially impressed by the division's determination to hold Rimling until its seizure could do the Germans no strategic good, "a great accomplishment [that] forced the enemy to give up the offensive action on your front." On the right flank, "the force of a powerful enemy drive" had been met by "the prompt and effective extension of your lines to block his advance . . . a splendid example of skillful maneuver. I heartily commend all members of this division for their outstanding achievements."[50]

At war's end the 3rd Battalion of the 397th, along with H Company of the regiment—the units that had played the most conspicuous role in keeping Rimling out of the hands of an enemy who had expected to take the place in less than two days—would be awarded a Presidential Unit Citation. These were fitting tributes to an organization that, as Keith Bonn points out, despite having less than fifty days of combat experience, "stonewalled attacks by numerically superior formations of soldiers of similarly mixed background, led by veteran combat leaders. . . . Even highly seasoned, previously undefeated SS mountain troops could not defeat like numbers of similarly experienced Americans who had fought in the Ardennes and Vosges."[51]

SEVEN

"SONS OF BITCHE"

As the winter wore on, the Germans holding the line between Rimling and Reyersviller relied increasingly on cannons and mortars to carry on the war. Their daytime patrol activity dwindled to almost nothing, and no sustained attack was mounted at any point throughout the winter. Respecting the strength of the Century's lines, the German's feared to test them except gingerly and at the small-unit level.

The 100th's position could have been even stronger. A general shortage of land mines prevented the division from bolstering sectors of its main line. A jerry-rigged substitute was resorted to. Private Jelks and his comrades would string wires from tree to tree over ground an enemy patrol might cross at night. They would tie one end of the wire to a grenade "and pull the safety pin while holding down the detonator and push the grenade back into its container." When a German tripped the wire, the grenade was yanked from its container and exploded.

Unlike their opponents, the Germans did not lack for mines. "Every night we could hear the Krauts planting mines between their positions and ours," wrote Jelks. "We would wait until they had time to plant quite a few mines, then we would call for our 81-mm mortars to fire a high explosive . . . with a delay fuse." The result was an explosion that "threw large clods of heavy wet earth high into the air. When the clods of dirt came down they would hit the mines and set them off in a regular chain reaction. We could sometimes hear Krauts screaming when they got caught in the erupting minefield."[1]

The unremittingly cold weather, which threatened the health of the division's soldiers and limited their mobility, suggested that major operations would wait until spring. Although patrol activity continued on the American side and firefights were a common occurrence, increasingly the fighting was carried on by howitzer shells and mortar rounds. Lieutenant Fishpaw of the 374th Field Artillery Battalion observed that once the enemy ceased trying to extend its lines south of Rimling, "most of the fighting consisted of both sides firing artillery at each other," including harassing and interdiction fire delivered at intervals each day. The historian of the 925th Field Artillery Battalion noted that through the balance of the winter, his guns conducted "occasional fire missions, while our Forward Observers kept us busy firing on targets of opportunity."[2]

Extensive precautions were taken while they placed fire on the enemy's positions in bad weather:

Guns which had before blended somewhat with the scenery, now stood out like 'sore thumbs' against the blanket of white that covered the countryside. Tents, guns, and ammunition pits had to be camouflaged with white sheets. Jeeps used by our forward observers had to be coated with white paint, and the forward observers wore white parkas to lessen the chance of being seen. As the snow continued to fall day after day, the cannoneers beat paths from their dugouts to the guns. Transporting ammunition from the ammunition pits to the guns became a tedious job.[3]

The increasingly one-sided nature of offensive operations made it clear that the enemy had shot his bolt during Nordwind. On the U.S. side of no-man's-land, however, patrol activity remained brisk. Patrolling was always a dangerous job—whenever a patrol went out from his sector, Private Hancock felt "grateful to be a machine gunner in a snug dugout." Theoretically at least, the mission was enhanced by artificial moonlight, provided by A Company of the 355th Antiaircraft Searchlight Battalion. High-powered beacons, mounted on trucks well in the rear of the lines, beamed light from cloud banks onto the ground, illuminating enemy positions. Private Khoury noted that although the snow-covered earth reflected a great quantity of light, trees and other terrain features cast black shadows, thereby limiting the weapon's effectiveness. Pvt. Gerald Weber doubted that the illumination helped much, although enemy gunners continually tried to blind the searchlights.[4]

Some men disliked patrolling for reasons other than exposure to enemy fire. Private Fair hated to be sent on patrol to Reyersviller, which his unit regularly dosed with a harassing fire, because "we were firing into a town that we had once occupied. I worried more about the townspeople who had been so nice to us than I did about the German soldiers who were now there."[5]

Patrols could bring out the worst in some soldiers, who, once beyond the immediate control of their superiors, committed unconscionable acts. Some harassed and threatened civilians suspected of giving aid and comfort to the enemy; a few stole or destroyed private property; and a small minority committed what might be regarded as atrocities. One of Tom Jelks's sergeants was notorious for examining dead Germans and striking certain ones in the face with the butt of his Colt 45. "We thought he was being vengeful and showing his hatred of the Krauts," Jelks wrote, "until we saw what he was doing. He was examining them for gold teeth" to knock out and stash in a tobacco pouch bulging with spoils. Sergeant Gluesenkamp observed other GIs commit the same act, using rifle butts to loosen gold teeth and bayonets to pry them loose. Some cut off the fingers of enemy dead to obtain gold rings. "In a few isolated cases," Gluesenkamp commented, "this was attempted on [dead] G.I.'s, but orders were immediately given to stop this practice." John Khoury never witnessed such ghoulish behavior, but he did notice that a ring on the finger of a dead German whose body lay near his unit's position went missing—

along with the finger. "Sometime later," he wrote, "one of our soldiers was proudly showing everyone his 'gold collection,' which he kept in a glass jar. . . . We knew how he had collected them and most of us were disgusted with him." If Khoury knew that this was the man who had removed the German's ring and finger, he did not say.[6]

In most cases, patrols proved their value not only by pinpointing enemy positions but by taking prisoners from whom valuable information was gained on German units, movements, and, occasionally, intentions. Many captives appeared willing to give themselves up, if only to escape the rigors of combat. Some had been enticed to surrender by propaganda messages, stressing the inevitability of German defeat, broadcast from loudspeakers erected at several points on the division's line. Even when imperfectly applied, the psychological warfare appears to have had an effect. One prisoner, who had been able to hear only "snatches of the broadcast because of wind and rain," was nevertheless impressed by what he heard, as were many of his comrades. He informed the intelligence officers of the 398th Infantry Regiment that "fifty percent of his company would desert if a chance presented itself."[7]

Having raided enemy camps on many occasions, the men of the Century could understand why their occupants seemed so willing to be taken prisoner. As badly treated by their army as the GIs considered themselves, they had come to see that the troops of the Wehrmacht were more poorly clothed, poorly fed, and poorly armed and equipped than they themselves, while equally at the mercy of snow, rain, wind, cold, and enemy weapons. This knowledge was as helpful to GI morale as the increasingly common sight of Germans, in ones, twos, and larger groups, advancing toward them sans weapons, hands over their helmets. The Centurymen were also buoyed up by the news that their command had gained an enviable reputation among their opponents. Of late, Axis Sally had taken to referring to the division as "the underpaid butchers of Bitche" and by equally venomous epithets, but many POWs had another name for the Century, one that connoted respect and, more importantly, fear: The Terrible Hundredth.[8]

Although combat wrought terror and suffering, it sometimes diverted a soldier's attention from his less-than-desirable living conditions. Once the fighting died down after Nordwind, those conditions could no longer be ignored. Continuous service at the front bred physical ills and mental distress that over time took a toll on the division's fitness and readiness.

One of the most debilitating effects of long hours spent in the ground was trench foot, a condition that produced swelling, blisters, and occasionally disabling ulcers. The condition had long been a problem for the division's medics, but its incidence increased markedly as the winter wore on. Trench foot, which struck soldiers who could not take off their shoepacks to allow their feet to dry or who did not change their socks at proper intervals, became so prevalent that whole platoons were depleted by men on sick call.

The most serious illness to strike the division as winter wore on was infectious hepatitis—inflammation of the liver. Today classified as hepatitis A, the disease was known in the army (rather redundantly) by its most visible symptom, "yellow jaundice." Victims developed a sallow tinge to their skin and the whites of their eyes, precursors of more severe symptoms such as general debility, anorexia, malaise, and, in severe cases, physical collapse. When the disease struck H Company of the 398th, Thomas Tillett and his buddies assumed that "our diets caused this but maybe something else, the water perhaps." One of the first in Tillett's unit to contract the malady was Private Witt. "Roger came out one morning for roll call," Tillett recalled, "and it was really strange to see him standing there with yellow eyes and a pasty complexion feeling weak and ready to drop." Witt's condition was so severe that after being transported to a field hospital he was evacuated to the States along with other severe sufferers.[9]

Because hepatitis symptoms could mirror those of other diseases, the condition was often misdiagnosed. When Private Bourne was felled by the disease later in the year while on a three-day pass to the city of Nancy, he was never so ill in his life, "and it kept getting worse." Admitted to the local military hospital, he was placed in an isolation ward, where he was beset by a "raging fever alternating with terrible chills, delirium, semi-comatose periods (all this I was told later) and a series of doctors trying to find out if I had ever been anywhere that I could have contracted malaria. I had not, but a day or so later, still deathly ill and very weak, I began to turn yellow and was promptly diagnosed as another infectious hepatitis victim. The hospital was full of them, and I was moved into a large ward with some of my fellow-sufferers. The ward became my home for the next two months. At that time the treatment for hepatitis was bed rest and a low-fat diet, and that's what I got. . . . Everything got cured eventually," but he never again saw combat—nor did many another Centuryman similarly infected.[10]

Not every sufferer regretted contracting the disease, especially in its milder forms. As John Khoury wrote, "why some men got it and others did not was a mystery to me, because we all had the same 'haute cuisine.' Yet the guys with the yellow eyeballs and sallow complexions were very happy to leave" the unit for hospital care. "Some did not want to be cured and sent back to the front, so they sneaked into the regular chow line where they could eat lots of fatty foods and prolong their stay in the hospital. If the jaundice worsened, the patient was shipped to the U.S., and if he was cured, he was usually assigned to some rear echelon unit." According to Tom Bourne and others who studied the long-range effects of hepatitis, the army went to some lengths to downplay the manpower problems caused by the disease, either to prevent morale problems in the ranks or on the home front, or to avoid handing the enemy a propaganda coup.[11]

Regardless of what Khoury and others believed about the disease, the armywide outbreak of hepatitis A was not caused by poorly prepared rations or unclean hypodermic needles. It was the result of poor dietary habits, contaminated food, and water supplies, and the close proximity of infected and healthy soldiers. Pvt. Tom Block recalled that during the winter of 1945, food and drink were in short supply: "We had K-rations, . . . but the contents of soldiers' canteens were usually frozen; the only readily available

source of water was melted snow." Being a medic, Block took precautions with his health whenever possible; thus he heated snow
on his Coleman portable stove before drinking. Most GIs ingested
snow taken directly from the ground, unaware that it might be contaminated by vegetation or animal waste. Moreover, food was
rarely handled with clean hands. "Forget about washing your
hands," wrote Block. "Blood and grime covered mine for days at a
time."[12]

Conditions at the front were spectacularly unsanitary, and the
men were forced to improvise at risk to their health. "There were
no latrines," Block recalled. "We used our helmets [as toilets] and
dumped it over the side of the foxhole." Frank Hancock never
used his helmet that way, but he agreed that leaving one's foxhole
to answer nature's call was often out of the question: "To leave the
hole in the daytime, one rolls quickly over the back opening,
crouches and runs for cover in the woods."[13]

The French winter made life difficult, and at times unbearable,
even for healthy soldiers. GIs who thought they had become accli-
mated to snow, icy rain, and subzero temperatures found that
January and February were even harder on their bodies and psy-
ches than November and December. Not even the timber-lined
roofs, walls, and floors the men had added to their habitations
shielded them from the elements. Private Miller remembered
"cold clear moonlit nights and cloudy days. Too many of them."
He and his buddies longed for those few hours when the sun
would shine, followed by a cloudy night: "It meant we would gain
heat during the day and that the cloudy nights would hold the
warmth."

Frank Hancock thought he had experienced the worst weather
of his life in the Vosges, but here on the Alsatian plain even multiple layers of clothing provided insufficient protection from the
cold. Standing guard in two feet of snow, he would hear loud
cracking noises, "almost like pistol shots as the sap freezes in the

trees." One especially frigid night, "exposed to the weather in the firing pit behind the machine gun," he had a dream—and perhaps also a psychic vision:

> The wind is biting through parka and scarf, through the layers of clothes. When the next man relieves me, I crawl gratefully back into the dark dugout to sleep, but sleep is fitful—I am so cold. Suddenly I am walking into our warm living room at home. Mother is sitting, waiting for me, with a shawl lying across her lap. I fall on my knee and put my head on her lap. I can feel the shawl on my cheek. "It is so cold out there!" She says: "It will be all right soon." Her hand reaches out and instantly I am back in the dugout.

When he returned home after the war, Hancock learned that on that very occasion, his mother had sensed his touch and had reached out "from so far away" to return it.[14]

The snow and temperatures may have been hard to bear, but when, at intervals from mid-February to early March, warmer weather finally appeared, the situation became intolerable in other ways. One such day, Tom Bourne recalled, it was "stickily warm, and raining, the snow fast disappearing. Our hole got more and more uncomfortable as the day wore on. Leaks had appeared in the heretofore frozen roof, and C-Ration cans wired to the logs served but poorly to stem the tide. Then large chunks of the fast-melting earth began to fall out of the walls spasmodically."

Hopeful that the deterioration process had run its course, Bourne crawled into his hole and managed to fall asleep. After midnight he was awakened when "the whole roof of the foxhole, at least my side of it, suddenly settled on me, accompanied by a dull roar." Neither of the comrades who shared his dwelling had been struck, but Bourne was buried up to his neck in the viscid muck, unable to move. "It was at this unfortunate point," he recalled, "that the humor of the situation became manifest to my buddies," who took their sweet time digging him out, to the accompaniment of much laughter. Bourne's relations with them were "somewhat cool for the next few hours."[15]

Unsurprisingly, the farther from the front a soldier was stationed, the more comfortable his situation, the better his health, the higher his morale. Members of rear-echelon units slept indoors—on beds of straw if in a barn, in feather beds if in a house—although they usually did so fully clad, sharing bed space with several buddies. As often as once a week, portable showers enabled them to scrub off the grime of the French countryside, a therapeutic experience that could make even the grubbiest GI feel like a new man. Comforts and recreational facilities were more readily available to artillerymen, medical teams, and support personnel such as cooks and clerks, who, although not always beyond the reach of German 88s, were sufficiently distant to enjoy a settled, quiet existence.

Eventually the high command came to appreciate the morale benefits of offering down time to as many Centurymen as possible. By mid-February, with activity at the front still at low ebb, increasing numbers of soldiers were being shifted to the rear for rest and refit. Many were succored at the division rest center in Sarrebourg named for Cpl. Robert L. Ethridge, one of the Century's earliest Distinguished Service Cross recipients. Other men were trucked to the XV Corps Rest Center in Nancy. Bernie Miller, who enjoyed several days there with two of his buddies, recalled the center as nothing more than an old factory building, with "no pretense at being neat or soldierly. Just throw your bed together. I don't remember any food we may have gotten." None of that mattered—it was a godsend to get away from the front lines, even for a few days: "There were no tours [of duty] of any kind for us to take—we all were sort of on our own."

Toward the close of the winter, three-day passes to Paris and Brussels were being distributed with some frequency. Bob Fair was one of a dozen or so in his regiment who in March got the chance to visit the French capital. After cleaning up at the Ethridge Center, he took the train to Paris with five other GIs. He quickly found himself alone. The group entered the first bar they came to and ordered bottles of wine. "Within fifteen minutes," Fair recalled, "the other five had disappeared with women who had stopped by the table." The good boy from Little Rock, Arkansas, went back to the hotel alone. His mood improved when his sister, a Red Cross nurse attached to the First Army, flew into Paris. They saw the sights together, Fair had his first taste of champagne, and before leaving the city at furlough's end, brother and sister attended services at the city's American Chapel.[16]

While more-fortunate comrades enjoyed the vacations of their lives, those who remained at the front began to receive more frequent access to food, showers, and rest time. Upon returning from Nancy, Bernie Miller found that his company was finally getting warm food on a regular basis. This stunning development had come about through the solicitude of General Burress, who, alarmed by the incidence of digestive ailments in his command, decreed that members of every unit, including those in close proximity to the enemy, would receive at least one warm meal per day. Some units did even better: the men of E Company of the 397th enjoyed hot chow twice daily; only at the noon meal did they break out the K-rations. Miller noted that "the menu was usually adapted for portability, into sandwiches and the like, but always warm."

Portable showers, till now not readily available at the front, were erected in places within reach of troops confined to foxholes and dugouts. Those habitations were also becoming more livable. Late in the winter, Sergeant Angier recalled, "we made our holes more like home, and dug connecting trenches between holes . . . Each day the men would work on their holes, fixing the tops, digging them deeper, until we had a line of underground huts." He added that "we took great pride in our homes. It wasn't like having a room at the Astor but they were warm and cozy to a certain extent."[17]

Better food, more accessible bathing facilities, and sturdier dwelling places buttressed morale, but going into reserve had an even greater effect on a GI's frame of mind. To the men of C Company of the 399th, as well as to the members of many another unit, "morale was whether your foxhole leaked when the snow started melting, or whether it stayed dry; whether you stood guard from 8–10 and 2–4 or from 6–8 and 12–2. Morale was whether you got a dinner K ration with malted milk tablets or one with York caramels; whether you got socks, size 13, or socks that fit. Morale was hearing you might go to the Division rest center maybe in two months. It was having an attack on Steinkopf Hill called off. But most of the time morale was knowing that you were going to go on reserve in Siersthal or Glassenberg in 8 days, 6 days, 5, 4, 3, 2, tomorrow!"[18]

By midwinter, division headquarters was going to some lengths to ensure that the men were rotated to reserve areas where they could renew physical and mental stamina. Under a new policy, many units spent five days on the line and the next ten in the rear. Although such a routine might sound cushy, Private Drury believed that "being on line was actually easier than being in reserve . . . because the companies in reserve were given a wide range of necessary, but arduous tasks to perform." An officer in E Company of the 397th, stationed near Hottviller, noted that the battering his unit had absorbed at Rimling had left it in dire need of reorganization and training, especially for benefit of the replacements that had rejoined it after Nordwind. Even in reserve, "the company was trained as thoroughly as conditions permitted. The training was focused principally on the automatic weapons and the mortars, but there were also classes in field sanitation, military courtesy, and discipline."[19]

When not training, men on reserve status were able to relax, write letters home, attend religious services. Sergeant Tessmer believed that the famous adage "There are no atheists in foxholes" largely applied to the Century. The Christian noncom from Michigan looked forward to the appearance of the division's Jewish chaplain, "since he brought Matzos and Gefilte fish. Better than K rations." The men could also catch up on their pleasure reading. Tom Bourne habitually had a book to read, even in his foxhole. Richard Drury preferred works of history and biography such as the Pulitzer Prize-winning *Paul Revere and the World He Lived In*. Bernie Miller enjoyed the compact editions made available by the Armed Forces Library; he devoured everything from Earle Stanley Gardner and Raymond Chandler to Kathleen

Windsor's steamy bestseller *Forever Amber*. When Miller returned to the line, he brought several paperbacks to share with his buddies. Each would be passed around "until everyone had read it and then the last person would keep it for toilet paper."[20]

As winter slowly wound down, other developments combined to raise divisional morale. Dozens of noncommissioned officers who had proven their mettle in combat while displaying a capacity for greater responsibility received battlefield promotions. Most of those who accepted the higher rank appear to have done so from a sense of duty rather than from personal ambition, a craving for recognition, or a desire to enjoy the perks that went with a commission. Some were so little impressed by the trappings of rank that they carried their lieutenant's bars in their pockets instead of displaying them on their collars and helmets. The trend toward promoting worthy enlisted men found favor throughout the ranks, even among those who chose to turn down the opportunity. One of Private Sheets's buddies remarked that I Company of the 399th "turned into a pretty effective outfit when we got rid of the 90 day wonders, and the few [West] Pointers . . . were replaced by deserving Non-coms and privates."[21]

Another spur to morale was a noticeable increase in replacement personnel. The sudden influx of additional bodies—inexperienced as the newcomers were, and despite the extra time and effort required to turn them into reasonable facsimiles of soldiers— was a comforting development to the combat-weary veterans.

Thanks to the drop-off of operations, for the first time in months many GIs began to appreciate the beauty of their surroundings. One day Frank Hancock started for an aid station to have a minor ailment tended to:

> I roll out of the hole, crawl a few feet and run into the woods
> to a different world. There are no German positions in sight,
> no companions rubbing elbows, climbing over me in the

crowded dugout. The sky is a magnificent blue, the mountains stretch away, the snow contrasts with the dark green pine foliage and black tree trunks. . . The beauty of these snow covered mountains is overwhelming.

Suddenly Hancock felt impelled to give thanks to the painter of this glorious canvas: "God, you made a beautiful world!"[22]

From his foxhole, John Khoury began to notice the wonders of the night sky, "filled with billions of stars against a clear black background, not a cloud anywhere. . . . There was no moon, only shooting stars, a shower of meteors, streaking down from every direction. The Milky Way was never more brightly lit and I was like a little mole looking up from a hole in the earth. It was so magnificent that I thought heaven must be a wonderful place. Since I was alone with nobody to talk to, I wondered if the German across from me had the same feeling."[23]

For weeks on end, night had been no friend to Les Gluesenkamp, but by late February he could tell his parents that his fears had begun to dissipate: "Don't worry about me now as we have it pretty nice even if we are at the front." He assured his mother that every night before turning in he recited the Lord's Prayer that she had taught him when he was a child, as well as the Twenty-third Psalm, "and I go to sleep without a worry, except what I'm going to eat tomorrow and memories of home."[24]

Perhaps the greatest boost to GI morale was the realization that as spring neared, the war was being won in every theater. Allied forces had captured major objectives inside Germany, including Saarbrucken and Cologne, and thousands of bombers were shattering the large metropolitan centers of the Fatherland. On the Italian front, in preparation for a spring offensive, U.S. forces were driving German troops across the Apennines toward strategic Bologna. Soviet forces, continuing the offensive that had freed their soil of the enemy, were at the Oder River, thirty miles from

Berlin. They were pushing west so rapidly that Centurymen had begun to make "not very good jokes, about how the Russians would soon be meeting us."[25]

In the Pacific, Allied forces had landed on Luzon, the largest and most strategic island in the Philippines; after a horrific bloodletting, U.S. marines had captured Iwo Jima; and plans had been laid to attack the islands on the doorstep of the Japanese mainland. Air raids were already striking Tokyo, large sections of which would soon be immolated by firebombs. At Yalta, in the Crimea, the heads of the major Allied countries—Franklin Roosevelt, Winston Churchill, Joseph Stalin—met to adjudicate territorial claims to a postwar Germany.[26]

By early March, with the snow now gone from the French countryside, it became clear to all but the least observant GI that General Eisenhower would soon give the go-ahead to enter Germany in full force. On the seventh, an armored division of the U.S. First Army crossed the Rhine at Remagen on a bridge the enemy had failed to destroy. Within a week, finishing touches were being applied to plans for a Seventh Army offensive aimed at ending the war in eastern France. Telltale signs were increasingly evident—from the wholesale replacement of shoepacks with leather combat boots with sewn-in leggings for greater comfort while marching, to the repositioning and strengthening of the forces on the Century's flanks.[27]

The overall plan (to which the lowly GIs were not privy) called for XV Corps to make the main effort, breaching the Siegfried Line as well as those portions of the Maginot Line still in enemy hands. The 45th Division had moved up on the Century's left; the 3rd Division was in position farther to the west. These commands would spearhead the corps's drive by attacking northward. As they moved out, the 100th Division would drive east toward the Maginot Line, while the 71st Division, on the extreme right of the corps, secured the flank. After overrunning the defenses around Bitche, the Century was to pivot north and attack the Siegfried Line in concert with the divisions on its left. The 71st would take over the captured works in the capacity of a holding force.

By the second week in March, preparatory movements were under way. To position itself for its part in the offensive, the Century ceded much of its front line to the 44th Division, through which all other organizations would attack. On the clear and warm morning of the thirteenth, the 324th Infantry Regiment assumed the front-line positions of the 397th west of Hottviller. Two of the 397th's battalions were trucked to Bining and Rohrbach, while the 2nd Battalion remained in reserve near Petit Rederching. On the other flank, elements of the 71st Division took over the positions around Sarreinsburg long held by the 399th. This permitted the latter to move to Holbach; the following day units of the 71st relieved other elements of the 399th around Spitzberg Hill, permitting most of the regiment to go into temporary reserve.[28]

Once the regiments reached their assigned positions—the 397th (now commanded by Col. Gordon Singles) on the left of the division, the 398th in the center, the 399th on the right—the men received refresher courses in attacking fortified works. No amount of last-minute training, however, would guarantee the success of the coming endeavor. The impending assault would encounter more obstacles than the average attack force. The proscribed route to the Century's targets—the city of Bitche, its citadel, Camp de Bitche, and the fortified positions on the Maginot Line—led north and then east. This path would carry the division simultaneously across the front and rear of its objectives. Each target area had been strengthened over the past two months with mines, entrenchments, wire entanglements, and roadblocks. Furthermore, because the 45th Division on the Century's left was due to attack straight north and the 71st Division on the right had been assigned a holding mission, the 100th would find its flanks exposed soon after its assault began. Finally, the acknowledged key to cracking the German defenses was Fort Schiesseck. To capture it once again, the division would have to defeat a grouping of artillery, mortar, and *nebelwerfer* units on the high ground around Schorbach, north of the fort.

At 1 a.m. on the fifteenth, the guns of the XV Corps let loose with what Sergeant Longacre, who after months of service in a cannon company was inured to the sounds of heavy guns, called the largest and loudest barrage he had ever heard: "Again at 3 A. M. another barrage woke me up. What noise!" Richard Drury and his buddies in E Company of the 397th were awed by the cannonade: "There was never a second of darkness from the flashes of the explosions as it went on for hours on end. I felt nothing but pity for the poor souls who had to endure it."[29]

The barrage benefited only the 3rd and 45th divisions; the 100th, for whom the element of surprise was a greater priority, enjoyed no artillery preparation. General Burress was not upset; corps headquarters had given him carte blanche to maneuver as he saw fit. Thus he withheld his attack until 5 a.m., four hours after the other commands involved in the offensive went forward. The delay was occasioned by his unwillingness to assault in darkness newly bolstered works protected by land mines. His prudence was justified: a map prepared by German engineers, captured later in the fight, disclosed that almost four thousand mines had been laid in front of the forts since the Century last assaulted them.[30]

Burress had assigned the main effort to the 398th, advancing in the center of the division. The same outfit had spearheaded the December assaults, striking from the southwest out of Reyersviller. Having shifted position during the intervening period, the 399th would attack this time from the west. An advance from that direction, General Burress believed, would cut off Bitche and enable the division to enter it from the rear and flank.[31]

As befit its critical role, the 398th had been given priority for artillery support once the attack got under way. The field artillery battalion designated to provide that support, the 375th, had placed its guns farther forward than customary, on line with the 398th's reserve rifle companies, so that "the initial advance of the infantry would not put the front lines out of range." The regiment began its advance without preparation fires as per the attack plan, but as soon as the element of surprise was deemed lost, fire missions phoned in by forward observers began pouring into the battalion's fire-direction center. Within minutes, the gunners of the 375th were loading and firing as rapidly as possible.[32]

A 398th Infantry soldier guards a German prisoner taken inside a Maginot fort that had been captured by the regiment in January 1945. (*National Archives*)

At first the cannonade failed to secure sufficient progress; the 398th's advance bogged down in the minefields around Freudenberg Farms, where the outfit was lashed by small-arms and machine-gun fire. Late in the morning, however, its 1st Battalion got moving, swinging north around Fort Simserhoff, capturing a strategic position north of Schiesseck, and continuing east to take the ridge below Schorbach. En route, the battalion passed through wire entanglements that contained the ghastly remains of Germans killed in the attacks of two months earlier.[33]

Before day's end, the 2nd Battalion of the 398th had seized Freudenberg Farms as well as the fort of the same name; Fort Ramstein, farther east; and every unit in the Schiesseck complex. The gains had been made possible by the accurate fire placed on all these positions by the 375th Field Artillery, which kept enemy troops, vehicles, and gun positions "under a continuous rain of fire." In a larger sense, their capture was the result of the thorough job the 325th Engineers had done in December when disabling the guns of Freudenberg and Schiesseck—this day the attackers found that every unit remained inoperable, permitting easy entry.

Tom Tillett of H Company recalled finding in a captured head-quarters facility food cooking over a fire, suggesting how quickly its occupants had fled. Tillett never forgot the smell that permeated the enemy kitchen: cherry schnapps.[34]

From the high ground around Schiesseck, the men of G Company of the 398th got a thrilling view: "There below us lay Bitche, the focal point of our effort for almost four months! Krauts were streaming downhill from us, toward Bitche. And in Bitche itself, they were high-tailing it out of town and along whatever escape route they could find. . . . [M]ost important of all, the '88' fire, which was vainly searching us out, was hitting just below us and doing no apparent damage." Many guns were falling silent, struck by bombs delivered by the pilots of XII Tactical Air Command, which provided air support to the 6th Army Group. The planes were also strafing the retreating Germans, hastening their exodus from Bitche. "We always prayed for good weather for the Army Air Forces," an officer in the 397th Infantry recalled, for bombers almost always meant "death to the Kraut artillery. Ask a GI watching our planes strafe the enemy who were our two greatest heroes; he'll probably tell you the Wright Brothers."[35]

When the 398th's initial advance bogged down, the 397th on its left took up the slack. Advancing a short distance to the north, then pivoting sharply east along a ridge outside Hottviller, A and B companies, supported by I and L, braved heavy artillery, mortar, and rocket fire to take a critical expanse of high ground northeast of Schorbach. The operation, completed by 9 a.m., put out of commission the mortar and *nebelwerfer* positions that had threatened the left flank and center of the attacking force.

When I and L companies entered Schorbach, they discovered a comparatively large village, but no inhabitants. Exploring the ghost town, the GIs came upon a churchyard in which stood a shrinelike building twenty feet square "that might have been part of ancient Greece." In front of the shrine, flanked by imposing columns that reached the roof, was a rack that extended the length of the building. On it human bones had been neatly stacked; skulls and smaller bones filled the rest of the shrine. Well aware of the enemy's reputation for atrocities, the men suspected the remains were those of victims of Nazi evil. Later they learned that when the graveyards of French towns had been filled, the bones of later dead were often stored in this manner. Not that the men needed reminding, but the bones testified anew to "the brevity of life and certainty of death."[36]

While I and L companies occupied Schorbach, A and B resumed their attack northeast of the place, cutting the strategic road east of Schorbach near its junction with the enemy's escape route from Bitche. The combined achievements paid handsome dividends. As the Century's official historian remarked, they "removed pressure from the attack on the Maginot Forts and, by eliminating supporting fires, caused the defense of the Maginot Line to collapse."[37]

When the attack forces shifted east, the 399th Infantry found itself on the division's southern flank. The regiment's mission was to protect the right via a two-pronged advance designed to encircle the Germans on the forward slopes of Signalberg, Spitzberg, and Steinkopf hills, and cut off the defenders of Bitche from the south. Leading the regiment's advance, three companies of the 3rd Battalion, each supported by a platoon of medium tanks, moved out the highway between Lemberg and Bitche and, crossing a series of rises and wooded ravines, headed for Kirscheid Ridge. From there the units would move southeast to Reyersviller, squeezing that occupied village in a pincers, the other prong of which was to be supplied by the 2nd Battalion.[38]

As M Company advanced, Frank Hancock heard "explosions from mines, artillery fire, and small arms roar and rattle through the woods to our left." *Nebelwerfer* struck the ground well to the left and rear of his position; he likened the noise they made to "the iron wheels of a streetcar turning a curve." At first the rocketeers' position was hidden from view, but then Hancock reached a hilltop from which he saw, "half a mile away, a battery of these rockets being launched, exhausts flaming and billowing smoke." *Nebelwerfer* could not be delivered with pinpoint accuracy, but these barrages were heavy enough to do some damage. Later in the fight, the 375th Artillery Battalion knocked out several rocket launchers by concentrating fire on their wooded sanctuaries.[39]

Even with screaming-meemie support, the defenders of the Maginot Line offered minimal resistance; most appeared consumed with a passion for fleeing Kirscheid Ridge. When Hancock's unit set up its machine guns and sent a few rounds in their direction, the prevailing desire turned to surrender. Lacking a white flag, several Germans wriggled out of their tunics and waved their undershirts to make their intentions clear.[40]

An hour after gaining Kirscheid Ridge, the 3rd Battalion secured one of its objectives, Schoenberg Hill, while also encircling from the rear the enemy positions on Steinkopf, Signalberg, and Spitzberg, "where the enemy had caused so much trouble for two months." That morning E and F companies teamed up to take Spitzberg Hill by direct attack. The men advanced behind, and some atop, a platoon of Shermans whose job was to cut passageways through the barbed wire and set off the land mines beyond. John Angier, hugging the turret of a tank as it rolled up the slope of Spitzberg Hill, perceived that thousands of Schu mines barred F Company's path, making progress on foot nearly impossible. About twenty-five yards from the unit's jump-off point, Angier's tank threw a tread and ground to a halt. "What a spot," he thought. "In no-man's land behind a tank that won't run and not able to move because of the mines."[41]

Without leaving his perch, Angier got on the field telephone and called for help from the commander of a second tank, which slowly moved up to take the place of its disabled companion. Before F Company could proceed, however, a German 88 came screaming in. Exploding a few feet from the side of the tank, the shell mortally wounded two of three soldiers who had hitched a ride and hurled the third several feet through the air. The GI landed in the minefield but without triggering the infernal weapons. The crew of the second tank, which had been set afire, were not so

A German *nebelwerfer* recoilless multiple rocket launcher. The *nebelwerfer* was a powerful but inaccurate infantry weapon. (*National Archives*)

fortunate. Scrambling from their burning vehicle, two died as soon as they hit the ground—and a mine.

Again denied armored support, Angier slowly and carefully led the unhurt members of his platoon around the deadly field and then uphill toward riflemen and machine gunners dug in along Spitzberg's crest. Firing as he climbed, Angier dispatched a couple of Germans, but his efforts paled in comparison to those of Sgt. Joseph Kazer, who, wielding a light machine gun from his waist, felled six and captured fourteen. By noon, Angier related, "we had slugged our way to the tip of Spitzberg Ridge, a distance of a little over 1,000 yards," and the enemy inside Reyersviller had been pincered.[42]

Acts of extraordinary courage and determination had helped gain this result. When machine and mortar fire slowed the uphill climb of Angier's unit, Sgt. Richard Trapani, a mortar observer accompanying the leading platoon of F Company, determined to eliminate the enemy positions. Armed only with a pistol, he advanced well ahead of the platoon and was soon lost to view. Some hours later, with E Company adding its weight to an assault that was still proceeding slowly, Trapani returned from his reconnaissance, having located the most troublesome emplacements. He borrowed an M1 carbine, belts of ammunition, and four hand grenades from a tanker and launched a one-man assault on the enemy positions. He used two grenades to demolish a machine-gun nest, wrecking the gun and forcing the surrender of three of its crew. Then he advanced on a second position thirty yards behind the first. With his remaining grenades he destroyed the machine gun, killing three crew members and wounding a fourth.

The removal of these obstacles permitted E and F companies to proceed somewhat more rapidly. Unwilling to wait for them, Trapani dashed into a woodlot beyond view of his comrades, seeking yet another machine gun to silence. He failed to return from this mission, and shortly after noon, the lead platoon found his body, face down in the midst of a circle formed by three dead Germans. He would be posthumously awarded a Distinguished Service Cross. Private Gurley learned that Trapani had turned down a promotion to lead a rifle company, "not wishing to risk 40 men's lives to his complete inexperience of rifle tactics." Now he had been killed "running risks no rifle platoon leader would ever be called upon to take."[43]

The same award would go to Lt. Herbert S. Verrill, a platoon leader in E Company of the 399th who braved a field of Schu mines to reach the objective assigned his unit, three German pill-boxes defended by machine guns and shielded by barbed-wire fences. Before his unit could be pinned down by the enemy gunners, Verrill plunged into the minefield, whose charges had been exposed to view by the melted snow; he ordered the men to follow—literally—in his footsteps. A mine cunningly buried beside its visible companion exploded, tearing off Verrill's right foot and wounding his left. Fighting to remain conscious, he continued to direct his unit from where he lay, "preventing panic," issuing "clear and precise orders" for its withdrawal, and placing it in a position that outflanked the forts. He refused to be evacuated until every pillbox had been captured, ensuring that he could be removed carefully and without undue danger to his rescuers. Unlike many Centurymen who won the Distinguished Service Cross the hardest way possible, Verrill survived his wounds, severe though they were.[44]

100th Infantry soldiers moving through Camp de Bitche after a hard-fought victory to liberate the town. (*National Archives*)

Some hours after E and F companies took Spitzberg Hill, G Company of the 399th jumped off against Signalberg and Steinkopf. Advancing without artillery cover, the men of G Company worked their way up the "most precipitous part" of Signalberg in order to bypass the minefields that covered more accessible slopes. The unit gained the crest under a steady fire of rifles and machine guns, and routed the entrenched Germans. Most of the defenders were killed or wounded; twenty-five here and on neighboring Steinkopf were taken prisoner. By day's end, all regimental combat teams had gained the objectives assigned to them. That night the men secured and consolidated their positions and got a few hours' sleep before resuming their operations at 6 a.m. on the sixteenth.[45]

The second day of operations completed the division's role in the opening phase of the Seventh Army's spring offensive. The assaults this day resulted in the complete ruination of Bitche, Camp de Bitche, and the remaining operable forts on the Maginot

Line. Attacking on the upper edge of the division front, the 397th's 2nd Battalion, supported by the 1st Battalion, continued east to envelop a strategic crossroads above Bitche, thereby surrounding the city. The regiment's 3rd Battalion served as a blocking force, protecting the division's left flank at a point where the 45th Division's drive to the north had produced a dangerous gap. In the center, the 398th Infantry attacked east against the old Maginot forts, most of which had been effectively silenced but some of which were defended by newly erected works. The 398th's 1st Battalion seized a series of virtually undefended positions, including Forts Petite Otterbiel and Grand Otterbiel.

Despite intermittent resistance, by noon all of these positions had been overrun. Once cleared, they became a source of wonder and perplexity to the GIs who examined them from up close. Private Knight, the jeep driver from the 399th, examined a unit in the Schiesseck complex and came away "amazed, not only by its immensity, but by its stupidity. I can easily see why the French people in general are so poor. They have not only been hit hard by the war, but they have also lost a tremendous amount of things which we enjoy in America by such a foolish expenditure as the Maginot line. It is hard to imagine how much wealth and material the French government poured into that massive waste."[46]

At 7:30 a.m., E Company of the 398th, followed by the rest of the 2nd Battalion, entered the streets of Bitche against scattered small-arms fire, thus becoming the first soldiers in eight centuries to seize the fortress city. By midmorning, men of the 3rd Battalion were advancing cautiously through the place to capture some works north and east of it. A squad of six volunteers from C Company under Lt. Elwood H. Shemwell gained access to the citadel with the assistance of a civilian who guided them around a strategically placed minefield. The medieval fortification proved to be empty of defenders; Shemwell's party took it without firing a shot. "In fact," the Century's historian recorded, the Germans "fired only five rifle shots to defend the town after the 399th entered."[47]

The citadel of Bitche, the impressive medieval fortification that commands the countryside. The Seventh Army had anticipated a difficult struggle for this structure, but the Germans abandoned the works as they retreated. (*National Archives*)

Among the first GIs to enter Bitche was E Company's commander, Capt. Thomas H. Garahan, who went to the top floor of one of the taller buildings. Leaning out a window, he proudly displayed the first American flag to fly over the conquered city. The banner had not been supplied by the division's quartermasters but had been hand-sewn during the three months the city was under siege by Maria Oblinger, proprietress of a popular inn closed down by German occupiers. Fiercely loyal to the Allied cause, she had crafted the flag while huddling with her family in the stone-arched cellar of the inn, Auberge de Strasbourg, during the city's seemingly interminable shelling. Working by the light of safety lamps and compelled to hide the flag whenever soldiers entered in search of food and spirits, she risked arrest and deportation to a concentration camp had her handiwork been discovered.[48]

In the 399th's sector, two of the regiment's battalions remained in place to protect the division's right and rear while the 1st

Battalion joined the advance through Bitche via the highway from Lemberg. By 7 a.m., thanks to the support of A and B companies, C Company was in possession of the College de Bitche for the first time since New Year's Eve. A half hour later, C Company entered the city from the south against minimal opposition.[49]

Heavier resistance was offered by the defenders of Camp de Bitche, who opened on elements of the 398th and 399th with machine guns mounted inside pillboxes erected over the winter to augment the facility's original works. Lieutenant Flanagan—who two months to the day earlier had helped secure a lodgment out-side Bitche's citadel—maneuvered his platoon of B Company of the 399th to the rear of the pillboxes while other forces, support-ed by a couple of medium tanks, attacked frontally. The two-direc-tional assault carried the position, but only after Lt. William E. Sullivan and two volunteer enlisted men—one armed with a Browning Automatic Rifle, the other with a bazooka—destroyed a machine-gun turret on one of the concrete works. Holding a grenade, its pin drawn, Sullivan strode toward the rear door of one of the pillboxes and demanded its surrender. After some hesita-tion, every occupant filed out, hands over his head; they included the commander of a Volks-Grenadier battalion, four of his staff officers, and more than seventy enlisted men.[50]

Late in the afternoon, A Company of the 399th, accompanied by a platoon of Shermans, advanced from the west against other works in the Camp de Bitche complex. Though impeded by small-arms fire and roadblocks, the attackers pushed on until, upon reaching the camp's outskirts, they suddenly encountered four Tiger tanks and some self-propelled guns mounted on Mark VI chassis. Outgunned, the Shermans quickly backtracked, but the riflemen they had been supporting dug in and fought back. Lieutenant Plante of the weapons platoon of A Company—the officer who near St. Remy the previous November had led the division's first combat patrol—grabbed a bazooka, charged one of the Tigers, threw himself on the ground, and fired a rocket that blew off one of the tank's treads, disabling it. Plante, who would also win a Distinguished Service Cross this day, was about to hurl a grenade into the tank's open turret when its machine gunner cut him down with a deadly burst.[51]

The men of A Company were about to fall back and regroup for another assault when the operable Tigers unaccountably turned and retreated along the railroad leading southeast from the camp, apparently leaving the crew of the disabled tank behind. Further resistance in this sector was suppressed when elements of the 397th Infantry, sweeping down from the north, joined in, slowly but effectively clearing Camp de Bitche, a task that continued into the early hours of the seventeenth.

Bitche's ensemble of defenses had been overrun, and history had been made. Frank Hancock summed up:

> We have penetrated the Maginot Line and left behind us a fortress that was built by Louis the Fourteenth in 1661 to guard this fertile valley. The fortress stopped the Prussians in 1870, the Kaiser's troops in 1914, the Wehrmacht in 1941, and the 100th Division in 1944. Now, in March of 1945, we have captured this same fortress, the famous Citadel of Bitche. And we earned a new nickname: "The Centurymen, Sons of Bitche."[52]

On the morning of the seventeenth, the Century pivoted north and attacked its fast-retreating opponent. It had become evident that the Germans were unable to mount even a delaying action. Intermittent resistance came in the form of sniper fire, no barrier to the division's advance toward the Siegfried Line. The 397th, still on the division's left, occupied a series of small towns north of Bitche from which the Germans had fled hours earlier; so too did the 399th on the opposite flank. The 399th then veered east and continued to march until it crossed the German border. At 2:30 p.m. on St. Patrick's Day, K Company occupied Schweix, the first town captured by the Century on enemy soil.

While the 397th and 399th probed north and east, the 398th remained around Bitche, securing ground captured over the past two days and rooting out would-be escapees who had traded *feldgrau* for civilian attire. Meanwhile, members of the division staff moved into the city to reestablish local government. Working with trusted civilian officials and French liaison officers, division headquarters took up the tasks of succoring the almost four thousand inhabitants who had been trapped in Bitche during the fighting, tending to casualties, evacuating those whose homes had been destroyed, distributing rations and medical supplies, setting up soup kitchens and sanitary facilities, and purging Bitche's political council and police force of supporters of the pro-Nazi Vichy government.[53]

While Centurymen had been capturing or neutralizing their objectives, the troops of the 3rd and 45th divisions had been similarly successful. By the twentieth, elements of both commands had breached sections of the Siegfried Line at Homburg and just southeast of Zweibruecken, leaving the Century temporarily in their dust. While their fellow divisions roared into Germany, the conquerors of Bitche took a much-needed four-day rest. General Burress and his subordinates used this period to organize a motorized push to the Rhine River in the vicinity of Ludwigshaven.

On March 22, Centurymen boarded trucks in assembly areas north of the city to begin the pursuit of the beaten enemy to and through his homeland, an operation known by an inelegant but seemingly appropriate name: the Rat Race. From the start, it was understood that the division would drive through France and into Germany at a frenetic pace. The day before everything got under way, a jeep carrying Withers Burress pulled up at the roadside position of E Company of the 397th. As the men snapped to attention, the general alighted to share a few words with them. Richard Drury, among others, was impressed by the general's "soft spoken Virginia drawl, refined looks and florid complexion." He was impressed, too, by Burress's ability to put everyone around him at ease: "You just knew he could talk comfortably with anyone at any level." Drury would not recall everything the two-star said on this occasion, but one comment stuck in his mind: Was everyone ready, the general asked, to do twenty miles a day?[54]

In fact, the division did better than that—much better. On the twenty-second it covered an average of more than thirty miles, and fifty more the next day (a member of the 398th wrote his wife, "we're rolling now—really rolling"). Under the supervision of Headquarters XXI Army Corps, to which the division was temporarily attached along with the 71st Division on its right, the entire route was covered using "organic transportation"—no vehicles other than those long assigned to the division.

On the twenty-fourth, the 3rd Battalion of the 399th became the first unit of the division to reach the Rhine, at Altripp, south of Ludwigshaven. The remainder of the regiment occupied the latter city, much of which had been flattened by Allied bombers. The 399th took possession from the 94th Division, part of Patton's Third Army, which had attacked the sniper-filled city and captured most of it. The 399th spent the next few days mopping up the city and its environs.[55]

On the twenty-fifth, as preparations to cross the upper Rhine neared completion, the Century found that it was now under VI Corps control for the first time in four months. This association would continue through the rest of the war, the end of which appeared to be fast approaching. Signs of enemy defeat and dissolution were everywhere, from those rubble-strewn cities along the German border the Century was occupying every day to the long columns of POWs being herded to the rear of the army. The GIs also passed groups of bedraggled civilians, not only displaced persons but also Russians, Greeks, Romanians, Poles, and other peoples who for years had performed slave labor for Nazi Germany. Many cheered and clapped for the GIs; some broke ranks to offer tearful thanks for their liberation.

Another sign that the war was winding down was the ubiquitous sight of abandoned German vehicles and weapons, most of them demolished by Allied bombers and some of which continued to smolder on the roadsides. "There were burned out Tanks with German Bodies hanging over the turrets," Tom Tillett remembered. The sight of human remains had become so commonplace it had lost the ability to shock. Sergeant Longacre left his unit's truck and "walked over to look closely at one dead Jerry. He had probably been there 2 or 3 days and looked just like a wax mummy in a museum. Didn't bother me or make any impression on me, altho his head was pretty well banged up and partly mashed in." More disturbing to the senses, as Tom Tillett remembered, was "all the dead horses lying out there near the road in rigor mortis. . . . The stench was powerful."[56]

Having gone through hell in the Vosges, throughout Nordwind, and during the two offensives against the Maginot Line, the weary men of the 100th Division hoped that they had seen the last of heavy combat. They prayed that the enemy, appreciating the helplessness of his position, would halt his retreat, lay down his arms, and quietly surrender—with or without the sanction of the Fuehrer.

While the Centurymen contemplated peace, across the Rhine to the south and east, the enemy hunkered down in the blackened ruins of an ancient city. Having withstood massive attacks by Allied bombers, the defenders of Heilbronn checked their weapons and waited for the coming assault.

EIGHT

FROM THE RHINE
TO THE NECKAR

Heilbronn, with a prewar population of almost one hundred thousand, was a major industrial, transportation, and communications center of obvious interest to the advancing Allied forces. Large sections of the city, nestled in the northern corner of the Neckar River basin, had been reduced to rubble, the result of a merciless bombing campaign by the British and American air arms, including a two-week-long raid by Royal Air Force bombers a little over a year earlier. The most recent attack had taken place in early December 1944, when the city was pounded by almost three hundred British bombers. Approximately seven thousand bombs, the majority of them incendiaries, struck the nearly defenseless city, devastating not only the industrial quarter to the north but also the lower residential section as well. Later it was learned that navigational errors had resulted in the central sector of Heilbronn being hit instead of a V-2 rocket training facility reported to be operating on its outskirts.

By March 1945, more than 60 percent of the city on the east bank of the Neckar lay in ruins, and six thousand five hundred of its residents had been killed; almost four thousand others had been injured by shells, fire, or flying debris. More than five thousand of Heilbronn's buildings were no longer inhabitable, and little progress had been made in removing the rubble. While every sector of the seven-hundred-year-old Swabian city had suffered, the oldest portions had absorbed the greatest damage: most of the structures that dated to medieval times had been destroyed. Still, VI Corps headquarters suspected that some factories remained capable of producing goods and services for the Wehrmacht, while there was enough operable railroad track and rolling stock to support the transportation of enemy troops, weapons, equipment, and ammunition. Furthermore, a German officer's school was still in operation south of the city, and tanks were known to be parked in that vicinity.[1]

Beyond its supposed military capacity, Heilbronn was important as a stepping-stone to a mysterious but ominous enemy position known as the National (or Alpine, or Southern) Redoubt. The redoubt—which the 6th Army Group, given its location on the southern flank of the Allied front and the direction of its advance, would necessarily confront—was an alleged last-ditch rallying point for the Nazi cause. For months there had been speculation—fueled by propaganda broadcasts out of Berlin, intercepted communiqués, and the reports of POWs—that a potent, self-contained defensive complex had been constructed amid the Alps of southern Germany and western Austria. Supposedly the defenses comprised not only fortified works but also underground bunkers housing massive reserves of weapons, including state-of-the-art aircraft and missiles. When, at Hitler's signal, tens of thousands of troops fell back to man these defenses, the Wehrmacht—and, by extension, the Third Reich—would be able to hold out indefinitely, prolonging the war for years, perhaps decades. Even if unable to stave off defeat, the redoubt's defenders could mount a suicidal stand and produce a bloodbath the likes of which the Allies could not have imagined.

Because the rumors of a last stand in southern Germany were sketchy, garbled, and contradictory, Supreme Headquarters Allied Expeditionary Force found it difficult to give them full credence.

Even so, the possibility that these defenses existed was a source of lingering concern. If the rumors sounded fantastic, so too had the reports of futuristic weapons that had proven all too accurate, such as the jet-powered Messerschmitt 262 fighter and the V-1 and V-2 rockets (the latter a long-range ballistic missile) that had showered England and Belgium, killing hundreds of inhabitants, over the past ten months. And it was not beyond imagining that a madman like Hitler would view a final slaughter as a fitting climax to his bloodthirsty quest for world domination. There was a psychological angle to this possibility: even if not fully successful, a last stand might persuade generations of Germans that their country had never surrendered and that the twisted values that defined the Third Reich retained credibility and relevance.[2]

Due to the limited industrial and agricultural resources in the region the redoubt supposedly occupied, most Allied intelligence officers discounted the idea that the Germans had constructed, in almost total secrecy, a vast expanse of above- and below-ground defenses. Yet some intelligence specialists at SHAEF believed this to be possible, and their uncertainty influenced General Eisenhower for a time.

His skepticism resurfaced once the German forces east of the Rhine began to collapse in the last days of March. SHAEF intelligence experts reported that, having been battered mercilessly in the north by the forces of Bradley and Montgomery and in the south by Jake Devers's Americans and French, none of the three German army groups in position to oppose the thrust into the Fatherland was strong enough to mount effective delaying actions, let alone a major defensive effort. By March 31, Devers's intelligence chief was declaring that "the turn of military events is effectively destroying the 'National Redoubt' for want of both territory and personnel. Any retreat into the mountains of southeastern Germany will hardly be voluntary on the part of the German leaders."[3]

In point of fact, the Redoubt had been only a myth. It was nothing more than a cleverly conceived and well-orchestrated fiction, the brainchild of Joseph Goebbels, Hitler's minister of propaganda. Goebbels had duped not only his enemies but also the soldiers and civilians of the Third Reich, who, especially with war's end drawing near, willingly perpetuated the fantasy. In the end, Eisenhower and his generals saw through the subterfuge, but they also realized that even if the Redoubt did not exist, the German forces might fall back to the Alps, a natural fortress, for a last stand. Thus Eisenhower considered launching an attack in that region, although he was unwilling to assign it top priority.[4]

On the threshold of its final offensive of the war, the Seventh Army had been beefed up to comprise ten infantry and three armored divisions. On paper at least, its opponent was even stronger. By late March, Brig. Gen. Reuben E. Jenkins, General Devers's assistant chief of staff for operations, was reporting that the defenders of western Germany were being "rapidly revitalized" by troops who had escaped the Wehrmacht's recent disasters in the Colmar Pocket and the Saar. The German First and Nineteenth armies, opposite or near the position of the 6th Army Group, consisted of twenty divisions. Nine of these were in the front line, seeking to delay the Seventh Army; five others were in line before the French First Army. The other six divisions were, as of late March, in the rear refitting but were expected to be available soon for field service. None of these organizations was close to full strength. Their ranks teemed with inexperienced youngsters and aged conscripts hardly worthy of the term "soldier." Even so, the manpower was there, and with their backs against the proverbial wall, these would-be warriors could be expected to fight fiercely in defense of their country.[5]

The planning at SHAEF called for maximum pressure to be brought to bear on the full extent of the German defensive line east of the Rhine River. Under this strategy, in the last days of March General Patch's command was to move in three directions toward as many objectives. Haislip's XV Corps would advance northeast, in part to protect the lower flank of the 12th Army Group, then drive toward Germany's industrial base in the Ruhr Valley. Patch's newly acquired XXI Corps, under Maj. Gen. Frank W. Milburn, would thrust east through the low mountain range known as the

Odenwald. General Brooks's VI Corps, consisting of the 10th Armored Division and the men of the 63rd and 100th Infantry divisions, would drive southeast between the Odenwald and the Black Forest. The armored command would spearhead the movement, its upper flank advancing in the direction of Heidelberg, Germany's historic center of higher learning. The lower column would move toward the confluence of the Neckar and Jagst rivers. The 63rd Division had been assigned Heidelberg as its immediate objective; the major objective of the 100th Division, once across the Rhine, was Heilbronn, whose occupation would place the Seventh Army in position to cut off the continuing retreat of the enemy, whether or not he was heading for the German Alps.[6]

Following four days of much-appreciated rest in the VI Corps reserve area—which included movies, a beer ration, and a concert in Neustadt featuring the leggy actress and dusky voiced chanteuse Marlene Dietrich—on the last day of March, truckloads of Centurymen headed for the Rhine, which they would cross on pontoons. Although the Seventh Army had already torn through the Siegfried Line, the Rhine had an even stronger symbolic significance as the water barrier to the enemy's homeland. Crossing the river at Ludwigshaven had been a much-anticipated event that left some GIs feeling uneasy. In G Company of the 399th, "almost everyone had pictured fanatic German resistance at that great natural barrier." The men of F Company of the 398th worried that the crossing would be "another Normandy beachhead." A member of the unit recalled that for months newspapers in the States had devoted "three inch headlines on how the Germans would use the river as a final defense line; there was not a ten year old boy in Deutschland who could not describe, at great length, the magnificence of the mighty river."[7]

Instead, the operation came off without a hitch, leaving many soldiers surprised and relieved. The unopposed crossing bolstered the corporate hope that Germany was on the verge of surrender and that war's end might be weeks, if not days, away. The crossing still had some scary moments. Sergeant Tyson of the 399th recalled the operation as a bumpy one: "The floating pontoons that made up the bridge bobbed up and down as each truck passed over," giving rise to concerns that a sudden change in the current might dump trucks and occupants into the water. Private Hancock, who had been struck by the totality of destruction on the French side of the river, whispered a prayer as he crossed: "God help these poor people. And Thank You for protecting us on that flimsy bridge!"[8]

Some men made the crossing not in trucks but atop the tanks of the 781st Tank Battalion. The tank riders found this mode of transportation "an experience incomparable to any other." A soldier in the 397th observed that "the roar of the engine and the clatter of the tracks is terrific, and the vibration becomes painful after a few hours. The dust is ever present." Failure to hold on tight could bring even more pain: "A tank lunges when it starts or stops. They can turn on a dime and usually do. If you don't . . . pay attention to what the tank is doing, you don't stay on very long."[9]

Most held on long enough to disembark in Mannheim, Germany, where a large portion of the division spent the night and part of the next day. Like Heilbronn, Mannheim had been leveled by Allied bombers, as well as by artillery batteries firing in preparation for the river crossing. Frank Hancock called the place "the most damaged city that we have seen. Four and five stories above us, empty windows are backlit by the sky. . . . The streets are empty except for piles of rubble and the smell of death." Private Fair and his buddies spent the night on the outskirts of town in what had been a hospital. "There was a huge bomb crater in one of the two buildings," he recalled, "right through half of the big Red Cross painted on the roof."[10]

The next day was Easter, and the devout attended church. A nondenominational service was held in the open air, while one of the Catholic chaplains, possibly Capt. William J. Burke of the 397th, celebrated Mass inside a bombed-out church. (Three days earlier, several hundred Jewish soldiers of the VI Corps had gath-

A sign erected by the 325th Engineer Battalion marking the 100th Infantry Division's crossing from France into Germany. The sign proved to be prophetic: the division would face its most difficult combat in Germany. (*National Archives*)

ered at an opera house in a captured German town to share a Passover supper, an occasion one Christian GI described as "a solemn, inspiriting observance.")[11]

One of the worshippers at the Catholic service, Private Khoury, recalled that "it was kind of eerie in the sanctuary with the hole in the roof letting in hazy streams of light over the scene. We laid our rifles on the floor and removed our helmets during the service." He said the experience was "very peaceful and came like a sigh of relief."[12]

From Mannheim units were dispatched by truck to nearby Bruhl, Hochheim, and Reilingen, which had to be secured before the advance on Heilbronn could begin. "We search forests, houses, barns, everywhere," wrote Frank Hancock, "looking for German troops or armed civilians that might have been bypassed in the rapid advance." The duty could be both routine and dangerous, as well as rewarding. Hancock's company captured a German army truck loaded with fresh eggs, "a real treat after six months of powdered eggs. For two days, we have all the fresh eggs we can eat, cooked anyway we wanted them."[13]

The sweep of the countryside around Mannheim offered the Centurymen their first close-up views of the common people of Germany. Some soldiers were unprepared for their hostile reception by a populace that regarded them as invaders, as opposed to the French citizenry, most of whom had greeted the Americans as liberators. Pvt. Joe Collie of B Company of the 397th found the country east of the Rhine "a total change" from the French countryside: "You didn't get anyone happy looking at you with a smile."[14]

The only exception was the occasional appearance of liberated civilian prisoners. A group of middle-aged Romanian women in babushkas and long skirts showed up at the headquarters of Frank Hancock's company to offer thanks for their deliverance. In broken English, the women explained that they had been imprisoned inside Germany, confined to factories where they sewed uniforms for the Wehrmacht; they had been fed just enough to keep them productive. Other freed slaves included Russian men and women who expressed fear at the prospect of being repatriated to their homeland, where they might be regarded as collaborators and sent to a new round of work camps.[15]

While sympathizing with the plight of these unfortunate people, the GIs were powerless to assist then beyond satisfying some basic needs. This effort was enough, however, to inspire a sense of gratification. "War is hell, and I have never liked the army," Private Knight informed his parents, "but you cannot realize what a thrill it is to see people freed from the bonds of slavery. All these people are suffering from a lack of many things but most of all they are suffering from the lack of human kindness."[16]

Numerous GIs were struck by the appearance of the places they passed through east of the Rhine. While Germany's cities and some of its larger towns had been devastated by bombs and shells, villages and farms appeared untouched, and the life of their people uninterrupted, by the war. Amazed by the "peacefulness and lack of destruction in the little towns of the Saarland as they roared by," the men of G Company of the 399th wished that the local people "had been made to feel some of the horrors of war."[17]

One member of G Company, Private Bourne, perceived a striking contrast between the villages of France and Germany. The former usually consisted of a few houses, mostly two-story stone edi-
fices, "nestled around a water trough and a huge pile of manure . .
. awaiting Spring use for fertilizer." During the months the division
spent in France, more than one jeep driver, turning too sharply in
the streets of a town, had plowed into these piles, covering themselves from head to toe with manure.[18]

The German villages appeared more modernized than those in
France—and, some GIs added, than those found in the English
countryside. John Khoury believed that the German people—perhaps as befit the master race—applied the most advanced scientif-
ic thinking to their dwellings. Models of neatness, regularity, and
conformity, they featured modern wiring, indoor plumbing, and
other twentieth-century conveniences. German farmers relied
more on machinery than field animals, and no homes were so
primitive as to combine living quarters with stables and corrals, as
many French houses did. Pvt. Keith Winston, a medic in the
398th, informed his wife that "it's hard to believe we're in
Germany. It's more like America than any place I've seen.
Generally speaking the people are healthy looking, dress well and
certainly live well." Those who lived well also lived ostentatiously.
During their travels through France, the Americans had occasionally encountered a luxurious chateau; in Germany, it seemed as if
every mountain was crowned with a castle.[19]

Most of the towns and hamlets surrounding Mannheim had
been cleared of uniformed defenders, though a few civilians took
up arms in defense of their property. This was hardly a deterrent
to looting, which some Centurymen engaged in whenever an
opportunity presented itself. Unauthorized foraging was made
easier on the mind of the GI by the knowledge that this was the
enemy's country and by the prevailing belief that its people ought
to bear some of the cost of supporting an evil regime and a horrific war. Payback was made more acceptable, too, by the prosperous
look of the German countryside, which suggested an ability to give
up some of its abundance to the invading forces.

Few of those who took from the local people appear to have suffered pangs of conscience. Pvt. Ralph L. Reeves's unit, M Company of the 399th, occupied a rural village for several days and simply "ran off the farmers." Reeves slept in a big bed for the first time in months while helping himself to a well-stocked larder: "The cellar was full of hams, fresh eggs in water or some liquid, [sauer]kraut, and a barrel of delicious hard cider. It was paradise."[20]

But cider was not the beverage of choice for thirsty soldiers. "Much of what we found to loot," wrote Tom Bourne, "turned out to be brandy. There seemed to be a great deal of it about. Apparently there were a number of small distilleries in the region, and many of us soon got quite drunk. After a day or so we were ordered to stop drinking it—I still recall the rueful regret of pouring a bottle or two down a street sewer—but a prodigious amount was consumed, and it's a wonder . . . that no ill effects I ever saw or heard of resulted from this over-indulgence."[21]

Many of Reeves's buddies actively sought mementos of their stay in Germany, especially enemy small arms. Keith Winston described the GIs as "pistol-crazy. . . . The German Luger is the most popular and sought after—so much so, that when one is found the owner is besieged with offers of trade or sale. They'll pay as much as $100." Reeves managed to acquire a 12-gauge Browning shotgun (probably abandoned by a fellow GI rather than a German soldier), which provided peace of mind during nighttime guard duty. When he finally tired of toting it, he sent it home to Illinois via his company's mail clerk. The weapon's arrival in one piece was a pleasant surprise: "I got many a rabbit for the pot after the war with that shotgun."

Other GIs—looters rather than souvenir hunters—sought to relieve their unwilling hosts of personal articles of value: jewelry, watches, knickknacks, and the like. When he attempted to graduate from souvenir hunting, however, Reeves proved a failure: "I was a lousy looter." On one occasion, he prepared to unburden a *hausfrau* of a cache of homemade preserves when she began to cry, loudly and persistently. "Damn, I couldn't take her food, so that was the end of that foray." Some days later he broke into a swanky apartment, where he spied a gorgeously detailed pocket watch. He was slipping it into his own pocket when the owner begged him to desist, claiming that he was a priest and the watch was a gift from a relative in America. Reeves did not believe the man until he produced a Roman collar and pointed out an inscription in English engraved inside the watchcase. Again the private cursed his conscience: "Damn, so much for another foray!"[22]

When the division left Mannheim for Heilbronn by motor convoy, life for everyone speeded up exponentially. Town after town flew past as truckloads and tank loads of Centurymen barreled through southwest Germany. Private Miller remembered that "we were so far ahead of our supplies that we had orders to forage for the food we needed. We rode along with cases of white Rhine wine, drinking as we went. We passed whole streets lined with houses, sheets hanging out as flags of surrender." Entering the valley of the Neckar River, the rural Illinoisan began to feel at home: "All this flat land stretched out before us and in the distance I could see the shadowy outlines of the bluffs. It was as if I had just headed out of town on the road to Edwardsville for a nice Sunday drive. And as on a Sunday drive, we didn't stay long—into the valley, across the plain and up onto high ground south of the river. We had a war to win!"[23]

The several-mile-long column wound through the enemy countryside echeloned to the right rear. The 399th Infantry moved along the bank of the Rhine, closely followed by the 375th and 925th Field Artillery Battalions. Farther to the east was the 397th Infantry Regiment, clearing pockets of defenders from woods, ridges, and other natural defensive positions. The roadblocks the regiments encountered were of the "sixty-one minute" variety. German civilians, appalled by their army's panicky flight, derisively claimed that the Americans would spend sixty minutes laughing at the ineffective barriers and one minute tearing them apart.[24]

The 398th, well to the rear in division reserve, was halted time and again to relieve elements of the 63rd Division. Since the 63rd was also motorized, the 398th had a hard time keeping up with it. Catching up was made easier when the 398th reached sections of the Autobahn. Appreciating Hitler's efforts to improve German mobility, the 398th made up for lost time. "On down through Southern Germany," the regimental historian noted, "our convoy of tanks, trucks, tank destroyers, jeeps and weapons-carriers roared. . . . riding roughshod over a land which the Nazis said would never be invaded." On April 2–3, the regiment finally over-took the vanguard of the 63rd along the banks of the Neckar near Bad Wimpfen, nine miles north of Heilbronn.[25]

In its current position, the 100th Division guarded the south flank of the Seventh Army. From time to time, the tanks and trucks of the French First Army came into view off the division's right. The 399th was supposed to maintain contact with its allies, who had crossed the Rhine at Speyer to attack southward into the Black Forest, but this was neither easy nor, at times, possible. The French had their own objectives, which they pursued with little regard for keeping in touch with the Americans. Not surprisingly, the Centurymen came to doubt General de Lattre's ability and willingness to secure their lower flank.

They were, however, impressed by the ability of the French troops to combine hard work with play. When the 399th passed through Reilingen, Private Gurley beheld dozens of colorfully attired Moroccans carrying on their shoulders "huge ammo bags, huge packs, .50 calibre machineguns, bazookas, 81 millimeter mortars," and other weapons so heavy that most GIs would have staggered under the load. One of Gurley's buddies exclaimed: "Lucky thing we weren't drafted in Africa. Those guys don't need any trucks!" Other Centurymen, including John Khoury, were amazed, and some scandalized, when passed by trucks carrying French soldiers and female civilians.[26]

For the first three days of the Rat Race, the Germans put up sporadic and brief resistance before resuming their flight. Corps headquarters began to believe that the token opposition would continue through Heilbronn and beyond. Halting to fight and defend Heilbronn made little sense. Although sections remained operable and even habitable, most of the city was so shattered as to be not worth holding. Rumors were making the rounds that the German high command had decreed Heilbronn a "free city" as it had Heidelberg—a place that would not be defended, and therefore not attacked.[27]

The intelligence experts and the rumormongers were wrong. Had anyone bothered to consider the German psyche, he would have realized that at some point the Wehrmacht would make a stand to prevent the Fatherland from being overrun, pillaged, and defiled. The place where this would take place was a crescent-shaped stretch of land forty miles long, anchored at Heilbronn and stretching north along the Neckar and northeast along the Jagst. The Germans had already taken major steps to fortify and maintain this elongated position. As one historian observes, building it had been "no mean achievement, considering the shattered condition of their combat units and the diminished power of both artillery and Luftwaffe." The enemy still possessed guns in some abundance, though most were horse-drawn, a primitive anomaly in a war defined by great advances in motive power. The German air force, on the other hand, had been a nonfactor in the fighting for months, the result of massive combat-related shortages of planes, pilots, and fuel.[28]

The Wehrmacht's rationale for holding beaten and broken Heilbronn appears rather dubious, although the city and its surroundings did offer some tactical advantages. The swift-flowing Neckar and Jagst rivers constituted natural defensive barriers. All foot and rail bridges over both having been destroyed, any attacking force—especially the armored columns rumbling along in advance of the Century—would face formidable challenges trying to reach the east bank. The city's rubble-filled streets would impede advance while facilitating defense. Unknown to American intelligence planners, the northern and central sections of Heilbronn were honeycombed with underground tunnels, constructed for commercial purposes, that could serve as conduits for manpower, supplies, and ammunition; they would also provide access to the rear and flanks of an unsuspecting foe. The high ground east of Heilbronn offered excellent vantage points for artillery. Elevated land around Bad Wimpfen, Jagstfeld, and other northern suburbs, where streams, rivers, and woods abounded, likewise played to the strength of a defender. [29]

Apparently the Germans felt that the few surviving military facilities in Heilbronn were worth defending. These included railroads, marshalling yards, a few operable factories, and the Schlieffen Barracks, the training complex south of the city. Revenge may also have factored into the decision to make a stand. Private Sheets, among other GIs, heard that the local people had persuaded soldiers who had reached the place intent on continuing their retreat that Heilbronners had been the victims of enemy atrocities. The soldiers were told that instead of concentrating on military objectives, Allied bombers had deliberately targeted the city's residential districts, wantonly killing civilians, including hundreds of women and children. "The whole town," Sheets believed, "military and civilian, man and woman, young and old, were determined to get even."[30]

Sheets's reasoning may have had a basis in fact. On April 1, German radio broadcasters had urged every civilian of Heilbronn and surrounding towns to avenge the bombing of their homeland by rising up against the enemy. Whenever an opportunity arose, they should meet the invaders with guns and knives—pitchforks and scythes, if only those were available. Failing this, they should strike from the rear, sniping at supply columns, sabotaging ammunition caches, cutting communication lines. These broadcasts appeared to tally with information gathered by U.S. intelligence specialists about the Wehrwolf movement—fifth-columnists instructed in a wide range of guerrilla activities including not only espionage and sabotage but also intimidation of suspected defeatists and collaborationists.[31]

The oft-repeated exhortation that the German people rise up and defend their cities, homes, and families had an effect. Hundreds of Volkssturm—hastily organized militiamen, many

Heilbronn following massive Allied bomber raids that occurred in late 1944. The ruins of Kilianskirche (the church of St. Kilian) are in the foreground. (*National Archives*)

well above and below conscription age—were assigned a defensive role. So too were the would-be soldiers of the Jugend. Dozens of these prepubescent warriors, many wearing the short pants of the Hitler Youth, vowed to defend Heilbronn. Organized into units commanded by Wehrmacht veterans, including officers of the Waffen-SS, the teenagers eagerly took up rifles and grenades. A few female residents of Heilbronn were also armed, apparently at their own request. They agreed to serve as snipers, picking off Americans too inclined to view women as noncombatants.

The civilians of Heilbronn would serve alongside a motley, unwieldy conglomeration of soldiers, sailors, and former Luftwaffe personnel, all caught in the dragnet cast by VI Corps as it swept the southwest reaches of Germany. Regular army units included elements of the German First Army's only remaining battle-worthy division, the 17th SS-Panzers—basically, SS Panzer-Grenadier Regiment 38, which had led the attack on Rimling during Nordwind. The better part of two battalions of the regiment had been placed in position along the Jagst River around Jagstfeld and Odheim. In that sector, the army commander, Gen. Hermann Foertsch, had also managed "through prodigious efforts" to organize a sizable defense force consisting of two battalions of engineer school troops, several combat engineer battalions, some replacement artillery and antiaircraft units, and a few tanks and assault guns.[32]

The forces defending Heilbronn and its northern suburbs had been divided into three combat groups, named for their commanders. *Kampfgruppe* Bodendorfer had been built around what remained of a regiment in the 246th Volks-Grenadier Division as well as elements of the 337th Infantry Division. According to German POW records, Bodendorfer also included fragments of two other Volks-Grenadier regiments, veterans of the Vosges campaign and the Colmar Pocket, as well as a company-size force from the once-celebrated 2nd Mountain Division.

Two battle-worn combat groups shared the mission of defending the southern environs of Heilbronn, including the towns of Sontheim and Flein. *Kampfgruppe* Krebs had as its nucleus the 719th Volks-Grenadier Division, which had seen heavy service in the Netherlands and Belgium, and also in the Saar region against units of Patton's Third Army. A regiment of the 212th Volks-Grenadier Division provided the foundation of *Kampfgruppe* Mockros; the unit had taken part in the 1940 invasion of France before being transferred to the Russian front and, after a hasty reorganization, to the Ardennes for the December 1944 offensive.[33]

Other organizations that would help hold the Neckar-Jagst River line were composed of support personnel unused to combat but capable of firing a rifle or a *panzerfaust*. These included training detachments, barrage-balloon companies, horse-pack units, military police teams, air signals regiments, and labor details. Then there was Punishment Battalion 292, consisting of prisoners released from confinement with the promise of freedom should they comport themselves honorably in combat.[34]

VI Corps headquarters did not expect a delay while crossing either of the rivers that barred their path to Heilbronn and its northern and southern reaches. The four bridges across the Neckar may have been "blown," but the Century Division had been supplied with enough material to build three pontoon spans, each capable of bearing the weight of tanks and other heavy weapons. Both XV and XXI corps were making excellent progress through the Odenwald and across the Main River; Seventh Army headquarters expected no less of VI Corps as it neared the Neckar at Heilbronn.

It was considered unlikely that the enemy would halt and fight short of Stuttgart, sixty miles south of Heilbronn. Thus General Brooks was mildly concerned when on April 2, the left-flank column of the 10th Armored Division, now more than two-thirds of the way from Heidelberg to the confluence of the Jagst and the Neckar, began to encounter intermittent but increasing resistance from General Foertsch's Volks-Grenadiers. As the Jagst came into view, the 10th Armored's tanks attracted shells from artillery on the high ground east of the stream, and enemy delaying actions bedeviled the center column of the division as it neared the Neckar north of Heilbronn. On the third, when the left column attempted to establish a bridgehead across the Jagst, opposition intensified to the point that it became clear the Germans intended to hold their crescent-shaped defensive line until forced to give it up.[35]

The Century Division spent most of April 3 rumbling through the hilly countryside west of Heilbronn. The 399th maintained the lower flank, making intermittent contact with the II Corps of the French First Army. The French continued to lag behind, leaving the flank exposed to possible counterattacks should the enemy halt and fight. To counter this threat, the 399th, supported by a platoon of tanks, a few tank destroyers, and a company of the 325th Engineers, left their trucks and began to clear the area around Gemmingen and Schwaigern, about ten miles from Heilbronn. Meanwhile, the balance of the division motored on. The 397th, in the center, covered more than twenty miles before

night; on the left, the 398th made similar progress on a line leading to Neckargartach, on the west bank of its namesake river about
a mile and a half above Heilbronn.[36]

Division headquarters, perhaps more clearly than VI Corps,
envisioned the possibility of enemy resistance on one or both sides
of the Neckar. General Burress had carefully planned his response
to this contingency. Mindful of his mission to safeguard the south
flank of the Seventh Army, he suppressed his initial impulse to
maneuver for an opening that would allow the Century to take
Heilbronn simultaneously from north and south. Instead he determined to make the major effort north of the city, where he would
be in close contact with the rest of VI Corps.[37]

Burress formalized his strategy in 100th Division Operations
Instructions No. 59, issued to various subordinates on April 3.
Under this plan, the 397th would secure the west bank opposite
Heilbronn while seeking crossing sites south of the city. These
could be used by the 399th once it finished securing the right
flank. The 397th would not cross the river until Heilbronn had
been cleared from another direction. The latter task was assigned
to the 398th, which was to cross the Neckar near Bad Wimpfen,
move south, and, in cooperation with the 10th Armored, seize and
silence the guns on the heights beyond the city. By taking
Heilbronn from the rear, the Century would be relieved of the difficult task of establishing a bridgehead on the east side of the
Neckar.[38]

The plan appeared thorough, prudent, and tactically sound. It
made maximum use of available resources while taking measures
to ensure that the enemy did not penetrate between the division's
right flank and the left flank of the wandering French. The strategy on which it was based displayed Burress's expertise in river-
crossing operations. And it bespoke his reluctance to sacrifice lives
through direct assault when less-costly flanking movements had
an equal chance of gaining the objective.

To the deep regret of the division leader, he never got the
chance to put his thinking into action. About 5 p.m. on April 3,

with the Century still fifteen miles from the Neckar, General Brooks ordered Burress to detach an infantry battalion and have it report, as soon as possible, to the commander of the 10th Armored Division at the river above Heilbronn. Some hours earlier, the 10th Armored had reached the vicinity of Neckargartach, where it attempted to establish a bridgehead. Resistance from outlying elements of Army Group Bodendorfer had rendered that job difficult, then impossible. The tankers who had anticipated crossing the Neckar without working up a sweat suddenly needed the support of riflemen, mortar men, and machine gunners.[39]

The unexpected assignment suggested that a direct assault on Heilbronn and its northern environs, something Burress had striven to avoid, was now inevitable. Without hesitating, he directed his forward element, the 3rd Battalion of the 398th Infantry, to hasten to the Neckar. As the battalion sped off in its trucks, he instructed its leader, Lt. Col. Ernest L. Janes (the officer who had brought rations to his famished troops in the Vosges), to report to the commander of the 10th Armored at Rappenau, fifteen miles northwest of Neckargartach. Upon arriving, Janes was ordered by Maj. Gen. William H. H. Morris Jr. to move his men to Neckargartach and have them cross the river in assault boats at three the next morning. Janes was assured that as soon as a large enough bridgehead had been established, a pontoon bridge would be laid behind his unit. The tanks of the 10th Armored would cross that span to provide close support.

Janes reported his conversation with Morris to division headquarters. Concerned by the uncertainties inherent in the unfolding situation, General Burress desired confirmation that Janes's people would not lack for assistance once across the river. That evening he phoned Brooks's headquarters to inquire "whether Corps was going to put in a bridge behind them." He was assured that a pontoon bridge "is being put in . . . at 0705 just above the old bridge site"—i.e., the recently destroyed bridge at Neckargartach, a little more than a mile north of Heilbronn. Burress also got on the phone with General Morris, who pledged that his division would make the bridgehead secure with armor. The assurances he received appeared to ease Burress's mind. In a subsequent conversation with Colonel Singles, commanding the 397th, he remarked, "I don't think there is much that will intervene" to complicate the crossing. Once the 10th Armored secured the bridgehead, Janes's unit would be returned to the Century's control—then the entire operation "becomes our baby."[40]

Janes's troops reached the Neckar some hours before daylight on April 4. Leaving their trucks, they assembled at the projected crossing site, three hundred yards north of the blown bridge at Neckargartach. The darkness and a persistent drizzle prevented the men from discerning what lay on the other side of the "deep, fast running" river. They attracted scattered sniper fire from the right (east) bank, although there was some reason to believe that more than a few defenders were in place there. Days earlier, elements of the division had been alerted by liberated prisoners of the Wehrmacht that heavy reinforcements had been observed "streaming into" Heilbronn, including "SS men of the highest fighting calibre."[41]

The 3rd Battalion spent the rest of the night in the houses and fields near the broken bridge. Before dawn it marched down to the river where boats piloted by members of the 55th Combat Engineers, a unit of the 10th Armored Division, were waiting. The situation did not look reassuring to the men about to cross. A later passenger from I Company of the 397th called the boats small and flimsy-looking, "a far cry from the big assault craft pictured in the newsreels of the day." Moreover, to ensure surprise, the crossing would be made without artillery preparation. Whoever was waiting on the other bank, if well-armed and alert, could make this operation difficult, perhaps chaotic.[42]

With some trepidation, members of the first unit to reach the river, K Company, piled into fourteen assault boats that shoved off under a sodden sky. At this point the Neckar was less than two hundred yards wide; the engineers, who did the rowing, told their passengers they would be covering about ten yards a minute. Most of those in K Company probably shared the feeling of Private

Soldiers of the 397th Infantry Regiment begin to cross the Neckar River in order to establish a bridgehead on the east side of the river where they would begin a push through the city of Heilbronn. (*National Archives*)

Jelks, who was rowed over the following day: "It took us about 15 minutes to cross. It seemed to me that it was taking 15 hours."[43]

Concerns notwithstanding, shortly before 3:30 a.m., K Company made it across without incident. On the east bank, about a mile north of Heilbronn, the men spilled from the boats and, after sorting themselves out, started inland. A nine-member detachment of the battalion's raider platoon, composed of volunteers for high-risk combat patrols, led the way up the steep embankment at water's edge that gave access to a long stretch of high ground. The first building it encountered was a massive electrical plant, most of which had been put out of commission by recent bombing raids. The silent advance of the raider unit was abruptly interrupted by a rifle fired from inside the plant grounds. The raiders opened fire but drew none in return. Apparently the welcoming committee consisted of a single sniper, probably now run off.[44]

Once K Company closed up on the plant grounds, the raider detachment probed them and found them deserted. Meanwhile, the boats that had returned to the west bank began to ferry across the men of L Company, followed by those of I Company. L crossed without drawing a shot; I Company was hit by burp-gun fire from a hidden position along a railroad east of the power plant. Pvt. John E. Plamp Jr., a nineteen-year-old radioman in M Company, whose section was accompanying K Company, described the ensuing confrontation: "There were Germans behind the railroad embankment because there was some small arms fire coming from them. So our gang got up on the embankment and started shooting over and tossed a few grenades and my buddy from the machine gun section came up and placed 30 calibers next to me and sprayed it around" until the few Germans vacated the area.[45]

During the hour it took the rest of the 3rd Battalion to reach the right bank, the invaders were not molested. By then, Colonel Janes had assigned objectives to his company commanders. They knew the location of these targets only from the terrain maps supplied by division headquarters. L Company was to move northeast toward the suburb of Neckarsulm and occupy a group of lumberyards about two-thirds of a mile from the highway running north from Heilbronn. The company was to align its right flank with the road that led east from the demolished bridge at Neckargartach.

K Company was ordered to advance to the right of L along the Neckargartach Road. Its mission was to penetrate about three hundred yards south, where it would enter the factory district north of Heilbronn. Then it would turn left on the Neckargartach Road and climb a range of hills to the east. The company's 1st Platoon had been assigned to take the highest of those elevations, known as Tower Hill for the ancient, castlelike edifice at its summit, behind which loomed a one-hundred-foot-tall tower. One of the division's historians observed that "even on the map it looked formidable, and [was] an obvious enemy strongpoint and observation post. In the daylight the men who looked up at it could see that its sides were steep and that the only cover they offered were scattered shacks and houses."[46]

Despite the obvious hazards, by 7:10 a.m., the 1st Platoon's leader was reporting to battalion headquarters over Private

Plamp's SCR-300 radio that his men were already atop Tower Hill. He was instructed to hold the position as a lookout. Plamp described the bunker in front of the tower as "a trench running perpendicular to the river . . . with a slot for observation and an entrance hole at the back end of it."[47]

The platoon had reached the top against relatively light resistance, although Lt. Theodore H. Lederer, commanding the M Company machine-gun section accompanying the platoon, was killed by a bullet to the forehead. Lederer's successor, Lt. Alfred J. Rizzo, faced greater opposition. Minutes after the platoon began to dig in on the forward slope and summit, a squad of Germans appeared from the rear. They began to ascend it, blithely unaware of the hill's capture. "Our machine gunners let them come up," Plamp recalled, "and then cut them down, at least most of them."[48]

While Rizzo and his men labored to secure Tower Hill, K Company's 2nd Platoon was ordered to clear the northernmost factory in the industrial district, an extensive glassworks that formed the heart of one of the city's zones of defense. The 3rd Platoon was to cross a field north of the works, secure the railroad and highway beyond, and take the high ground north of Tower Hill known (from its shape on the division's map) as Cloverleaf Hill. A machine-gun platoon of M Company was to accompany each of these units. Meanwhile, I Company assumed a reserve position three hundred yards in front of the power plant, where it began to carve out a defensive perimeter.

By 9 a.m., the 3rd Battalion had fanned out from its crossing site in several directions. L Company, moving across open fields, was skirting a huge water-filled ditch. Then it would cross the railroad from Heilbronn to Neckarsulm and head for a crescent-shaped grove of trees bordering the lumberyards. The company's right flank rested on the trestle where the Neckargartach Road crossed the railroad. One of K Company's platoons had entered the factory district; another was moving to secure the ground in front of Cloverleaf Hill. So far, so good—in fact, very good. A few snipers had provided the only opposition, and they appeared to have hightailed it to safe ground.

A view of the glassworks factory in Heilbronn, left, with Tower Hill indicated by the arrow. (*National Archives*)

Then, without warning, German artillery on the hills around Heilbronn exploded in a frenzy, sending shells screaming into the nascent bridgehead. According to the 398th's historian, "barrage after barrage landed with almost pinpoint precision on the position used for crossing, making the use of assault boats impossible and isolating the battalion on the east bank." Under cover of this fire, masses of Germans—later estimates ranged from five hundred to more than one thousand—charged out of the rubble-filled streets in the factory quarter and attacked the entire length of the 3rd Battalion's position, from the lumberyards on the north to Tower Hill on the south. Many had been hidden from view by the debris piled high in the city's streets. Others had gained the battalion's rear and flanks by maneuvering through the tunnels that ran underneath Heilbronn. The attackers included not only the regular troops of Army Group Bodendorfer but dozens of Volkssturm and Jugend.[49]

The first wave of the German counterassault emanated from the northern edge of the factory district; it struck the rear of K

Company's 2nd Platoon. A second column, sweeping west across the highway, cut off the GIs who had ascended Tower Hill. L Company and the 3rd Platoon of K Company came under fire from a third force, charging up the highway from the center of Heilbronn; this attack forced the abandonment of the plan to attack Cloverleaf Hill. Farther north, the balance of the 3rd Battalion found itself in a cross fire from machine guns and automatic weapons delivered from the factory buildings. A fourth group of attackers struck without warning from the area of the lumberyards.[50]

The main body of the 3rd Battalion was prevented from retreating to river's edge and the minimal protection afforded by the unfinished bridgehead; its men were forced to deploy and cobble together a makeshift defense. Improving their vulnerable position proved difficult. When Lt. Almon F. Brunkow crossed to the west side of the highway in search of cover for his platoon of heavy machine guns, he was hit by fire coming from a house on the edge of an adjacent field. Pvt. Leland L. Zeiter sought to lead a machine-gun squad to Brunkow's rescue, but it was forced back by a continuous stream of tracer bullets. Zeiter and the rest of his squad withdrew to the railroad bridge on the Neckargartach Road. Brunkow was subsequently captured and survived his wounds.

Once at the bridge, Zeiter's squad joined with some displaced members of L Company to make a stand against a sizable enemy force pouring out of the lumberyards to the north and the factory buildings to the south. Attacking across open fields, the Germans made suitable targets, especially for the machine guns manned by Zeiter's squad and L Company's weapons platoon. Dozens of attackers fell in the dirt and grass, but fanatical comrades filled the gaps, forcing their opponents to withdraw in small groups to the defenses established at the power plant by I Company. As they withdrew, the Centurymen were pounded not only by small-arms, machine-gun, and *panzerfaust* fire but by shells from batteries of 88s atop two of the highest hills behind Heilbronn. Ultimately, Zeiter abandoned his machine gun. Seconds later, an 88 round hit it squarely.[51]

The multidirectional attack and the withdrawal of supporting forces meant that the 1st and 2nd platoons of K Company were cut off. The latter had been pinned down in the factory district, most of its men trapped inside a house about one thousand yards south of the company's command post at the eastern end of the demolished Neckargartach bridge. One GI somehow managed to make his way to the command post to report 2nd Platoon's situation. Informed that the unit was surrounded, that its radio had failed, and that its ammunition was almost gone, Capt. William E. Nelson—who thanks to his own defective radio had lost contact with all three of his platoons—organized a rescue party, but almost as soon as it started out it attracted intense machine-gun fire that trapped it in a ditch for an hour or more.

After he finally returned to his post, Nelson dispatched two men under Sgt. Leslie Amtower to carry ammunition and a field telephone to the trapped platoon. The three managed to reach the house without drawing fire. While the two others waited outside, Amtower entered by a rear door. He found the house empty except for a wounded German and two dozen discarded GI gas masks; evidently the 2nd Platoon had been captured en masse and taken to the rear. Before the sergeant could return to company headquarters, a party of eight or ten Germans bore down on him. Fighting and falling back, Amtower was able to hold them off until he and the other GIs could safely rejoin Nelson.[52]

Late that morning, the 1st Platoon, holding the slopes and summit of Tower Hill, was assaulted in force by Army Group Bodendorfer, which until this time had been unaware of the hill's occupation. The Germans' superiority in manpower and heavy weapons should have ensured immediate success, but several waves were thrown back by the well-dug-in GIs. The position's defense was severely hampered when the platoon suddenly drew fire from the American side of the Neckar, where a buildup of guns, tanks, and tank destroyers was under way. Fortunately, John Plamp's radio was in working condition, and he was able to halt the friendly fire.

By the middle of the afternoon, with the Germans regrouping for yet another assault, Lt. Harry W. Arbegast, the commander of M Company's heavy-mortar section who had accompanied the 1st Platoon up the hill in the role of a forward observer, decided to call in 81-mm mortar fire from across the river. At his order, Plamp got on the radio and roused a buddy in the mortar section. "We want fire right here on our position to keep the Krauts back," Plamp told him. "We want some HE [high explosives] light."

The mortar man put down his radio as if to check something; when he got back on, he replied sheepishly: "John, I'm sorry but we're all out of HE light. All we've got left is champagne." Plamp didn't know whether to laugh or weep. "The previous afternoon," the radio man recalled, "we had overrun what was apparently a German officer's PX dump," which included a cache of liquor. Blithely assuming that the war was all but over, "we offloaded about half our ammunition and loaded up with half champagne and cognac."[53]

When the Germans made a final rush to the summit, the platoon was overrun, but it did not go quietly. The officer who led the attack, later taken prisoner, informed his captors that Lieutenant Rizzo and his men "fired every weapon they had and threw hand grenades until we were within four or five yards of them. It finally took all of the 90 men of my company to subdue them."[54]

John Plamp realized that the end had come when an eighteen-year-old buddy huddling beside him in the observation bunker let out a scream, dropped his rifle, and jumped on Plamp's back. "Take it easy," Plamp told him, but when he turned he saw that the GI had been shot through the neck "and there was a German soldier throwing another round into him." Plamp managed to scramble out of the bunker but was immediately surrounded by armed Germans; along with the other survivors of 1st Platoon, he was compelled to surrender. As the Germans herded them together, Plamp noticed that his captors wore a variety of uniforms, testifying to the heterogeneous composition of Army Group Bodendorfer: there were infantrymen, Volkssturm, Luftwaffe personnel, sailors, even veterans of the famed Afrika Korps.

The prisoners of Tower Hill were not at once marched off into captivity. When some were lined up in front of a machine gun, they feared they were dead. At the last minute, an officer ordered that the GIs be treated as prisoners of war. Supposedly the man had himself been a POW for a time, perhaps taken during the attacks on the Maginot Line. His captors had placed him in their own foxhole, where he escaped the murderous artillery fire, a gesture of humanity he now reciprocated.[55]

Although several times on the verge of being cut off and surrounded, most of the men in L Company made it back to the reserve line some three hundred yards south of the electrical plant. Here everyone dug in, clinging to the makeshift defenses. The Germans who had attacked out of the rubble of the factory district assailed this perimeter but were tossed back by M1 and machine-gun fire, and also by shells from the howitzers and mortars that General Burress was stockpiling on the west bank.

To this point none of the weapons on the Neckargartach side had placed a truly effective fire on the enemy. During the early hours of the fight, the artillery observer at the power plant had been unable to call in fire due to the close proximity of attackers and defenders. The salvos from the 88s on the hills behind Heilbronn had been much more destructive: in the days leading up to the fighting, their crews had established accurate target coordinates. One example was a direct hit that had knocked out a heavy mortar on the west bank, influencing other mortar crews to withdraw to safer ground. By late in the morning, however, the observer at the electrical plant was able to place howitzer and mortar rounds on the enemy at the lumberyards, in the glassworks, and in the fields near the railroad bridge.[56]

Fortified by this support, shortly before noon, the 3rd Battalion attempted to take back some of the ground it had been compelled to relinquish. I Company led the way, supported on its left and rear by L Company and on the right by the remnant of K Company, some twenty men. The GIs advanced west across open fields toward the enemy's latest position in a bombed-out section of the factory district. The riflemen advanced under the protection of a rolling barrage generated by some light mortars that had been brought across the river and set up at the power plant.

Seven riflemen of I Company fell to Mauser, Schmeisser, and machine-gun fire during the advance, as did two aid men, shot down even though their medical corps armbands were prominently displayed. One of the medics, Tech. 5 Joseph P. Nebesney, refused to be evacuated despite having been hit three times. He continued to minister to other wounded, in the process exposing himself repeatedly to enemy fire. A fourth round finished him off.[57]

The advance achieved two purposes. It threw the battalion's opponents on the defensive while forcing them to postpone, if not cancel, additional assaults. Most importantly, it gave the Centurymen a firm grip on an advanced line that ran south along the edge of the water-filled ditch as far as the Neckargartach Road, then west to the river. This line was too long to be properly secured; as one of the Seventh Army's official historians has written, its defenders looked warily toward the hills to the east, "which could throw artillery shells down on their exposed positions, and they knew their necks were stuck out between the lumberyards on their north flank and the factories on their south flank, both of which were filling up with enemy strength." Still, they were determined to hold a position that could serve as a staging area for additional advances once the rest of the division crossed the river to their support.[58]

How long it would take for that to occur weighed heavily on the minds of the men of the 3rd Battalion of the 398th Infantry Regiment; it was also a source of concern to the Century's leaders. By early afternoon, Generals Burress and Tychsen were striving mightily to get a grasp on the tactical situation north of Heilbronn and develop a proper response. Whatever they decided could be communicated at once to the 3rd Battalion, for a phone line had already been established between the forward observation post at Neckargartach and division headquarters. Another line had been strung across the river to Colonel Janes's command post, though it constantly came under artillery fire; by midday of the fourth it had been severed and reconnected several times.[59]

Burress's initial reaction to the 3rd Battalion's plight was to rush reinforcements across the river on the pontoon bridge that the 10th Armored had pledged to lay that morning. But no bridge was in place; efforts by General Morris's engineers to construct one had been halted by the accurate fire of the German artillery. Burress's strategy—to maneuver north of Heilbronn, where he would be supported by elements of the 63rd Infantry Division, and to come in from the rear—had been checked by those same guns.

While waiting for the balance of the 397th and 398th to close up on Heilbronn, Burress suddenly had another cause for concern: he learned that General Brooks had relieved the 10th Armored from supporting the Century. Morris's tanks were being shifted to the north flank of the Seventh Army, near the confluence of the Jagst and Tauber rivers. "Presumably," the division historian wrote, the new plan was designed "to take advantage of a break there and encircle the Germans by driving back west, in the rear of Heilbronn."

In essence, corps headquarters had co-opted Burress's plan and had assigned its execution to another command. When the 10th Armored departed the river to accomplish its newly assigned objectives, the 100th Division would be left on its own to deal with the expanding crisis on its doorstep, a crisis that would not have occurred had its leader's strategy been adopted. There now appeared to be no alternative to a full-scale commitment to the fighting on the east side of the Neckar. Withdrawing the 3rd Battalion was out of the question—it would be extremely difficult as well as costly, and would encourage the enemy to resist. Moreover, the effect on divisional morale of failing to go to the aid of comrades in distress was incalculable.[60]

The result was "a staggering tactical problem" for Withers Burress and his troops: "By action of higher authority, the General had become committed to an unplanned maneuver with a battalion of Centurymen on the east side of the Neckar and being violently attacked by vastly superior forces." Forced to abandon a plan based on maneuver, indirect assault, and the minimizing of casualties, the Century's commander steeled himself to launch a sweeping frontal assault fraught with nightmarish possibilities.[61]

NINE

HEILBRONN:
THE ASSAULT CROSSINGS

When he awoke on the cold and cloudy morning of April 3, 1945, Lt. William J. Law, commander of E Company, 397th Infantry, harbored the suspicion that the next few days were going to be bad ones for his division, his company, and himself. Law, a twenty-three-year-old from the Bronx, had been leading his company for the past three weeks, his immediate superior having been evacuated from the combat zone with a severe case of pneumonia. Law quickly made a favorable impression on his men, who respected his intelligence, good judgment, and tactical acumen. They also appreciated his no-nonsense leadership and his obvious interest in their physical well-being.[1]

Upon assuming command, Law had led E Company in clearing a string of occupied and formerly occupied villages in France and across the border in Germany: North Pirmasens, Neustadt, Hochdoch, Schifferstadt, and others. Most of these places were found to be free of the enemy. "The white flag of surrender flew from every house in every town through which we roared," Law recalled, "pillowslips and sheets and nightgowns and petticoats, all converted suddenly into something more than protection from chilled air." Some had been evacuated only hours earlier; their former inhabitants left behind roadblocks that had to be laboriously removed. In other towns, Germans lingered to blast E Company with 88s and antitank guns, or to shower it with sniper fire. The retreating enemy suffered in return, mostly at the hands of the field artillery battalions and cannon companies that were struggling to keep pace with Law's unit and other fast-moving companies and battalions. Outside one village, E Company happened upon a rifleman who had been manning a roadblock until a round of high explosives found him. The man lay "scattered over a 40-foot area. There were no recognizable parts of his body; only minute fragments of flesh and a red putty-like substance."

Even when the Germans appeared disposed to hasten away, clearing town after town took a toll. No longer transported by motor convoy, E Company was forced to make one of the most grueling marches of the war on that third day of April—fourteen hours straight, "one foot in front of the other in a stupid procession. As each hour passed, it seemed that they couldn't keep us going another hour," but they did, until men began collapsing by the wayside. Law, unwilling to show fatigue, was angry at the way his men were being treated. He saw to it that those too tired to go on got a seat aboard the tanks that accompanied the regimental column. After dark and in a steady rain, the march finally ended at the farm village of Furfeld, twenty miles from where the unit had begun the day. Everyone was "terribly exhausted and wet and anxious for a place to lie down." Law billeted the company in local homes and gave permission to his men to sleep with their boots off, so as "to care for bloody, blistered feet and to rest throbbing arches."

Law and his subordinates, including his friend Lt. Pete Petracco, expected that after such a grueling trek, the company would be allowed to rest the next day. "We were therefore disbelieving," Law wrote, "when, early the next morning, we were alerted and told to be ready to make a motor march by 0800." Well in advance of that hour, the men, groaning and cursing, were roused from their cruelly brief slumber. Following a quick but warm breakfast brought up by its cooks, E Company—five officers and 147 enlisted men strong—entered upon its 154th day of combat operations by piling into two-and-a-half-ton trucks for the nine-mile drive to the Neckar.[2]

Two hours after staring out on that deceptively bright and sunny April 4, Law was flagged down by a passenger in a jeep, the operations officer of the 2nd Battalion, who told him to get in. As the convoy resumed its lumbering pace, the jeep sped toward Neckargartach, where the pervasive thump of artillery indicated a battle in progress. To Law's surprise, he was conveyed to division headquarters, where he alighted to join a constellation of stars that included Generals Burress and Morris and members of their staffs. The high-ranking party was poring over a map, but when Law approached, Burress broke away to speak to him. After receiving Law's salute, the general explained the situation and E Company's role in it. A battalion that had crossed the Neckar was fighting for its life. Its defensive perimeter north of Heilbronn was under constant attack and in danger of giving way; its flank was exposed and vulnerable. Law's unit, now only a few miles from the river and coming fast, was the logical candidate to reinforce the trapped GIs. Law never forgot the tone of concern in Burress's voice as he imparted his orders: "Get your company across the river as quick as you can and block the attack on the flank." As soon as the balance of the 2nd Battalion arrived, it would follow E Company to the east bank.

When Burress was through speaking, he sent Law to talk to Morris. Law explained to the armored commander the mission assigned to him and inquired as to support. Law realized that without a bridge in place, no tanks could accompany him across, but he hoped that enough armor could be positioned at river's edge to provide a covering fire. Morris, who was already pulling up stakes and preparing to move north, replied that he could be of no help. Law would have been excused had he suspected that the reason behind this refusal was Morris's reluctance to expose his tanks to the German guns on the hills behind the city.[3]

A chagrined Law saluted and went to the rear, where he waited for the company to arrive. When it came up, just before 2 p.m., he hastily explained the situation to Lieutenants Petracco and Craig

Davison and the senior noncoms, then hustled the unit down to the left bank of the river. Assault boats were rounded up, and the men were rowed across the river by members of the division's own 325th Engineer Battalion. Before they embarked, a smoke screen was laid upon the surface of the river by the 163rd Chemical Smoke Generator Company. While the smoke effectively hid the boats and their passengers from enemy view, it also gave the German artillery a target at which to aim. The commanding heights from which the guns fired provided a clear, broad view of the river, ensuring that no bridges would be built at or near this crossing site. Work had begun there on a treadway bridge, equipped with ramps for motor vehicles, which would be crucial to placing tanks on the far side of the river, but the engineer teams had been driven from the river time after time by the accurate fire of those cannons.[4]

Law was profoundly relieved when the crossing was completed without injury. By arrangement, the company landed in the shadow of the power plant, which was still in friendly hands but also in the sights of the German gunners. Scrambling from the boats, the men poised before a section of factory buildings to the right of the generating plant occupied by an unknown number of the enemy. The company unloaded and emplaced its sections of light machine guns and mortars (the heavier weaponry—water-cooled .30-caliber machine guns and 81-mm mortars were too bulky to be ferried across immediately). As his men spread out and began to advance inland, Law set up a command post in the right rear corner of the power plant complex. Once E Company established a perimeter that covered the southern flank of Colonel Janes's position, other elements of the 397th's 2nd Battalion reached the west side of the river and began the ferrying process. Not until about five-thirty, however, with daylight fading, was the entire battalion on the right bank.[5]

By two-thirty, Law was leading E Company into the factory district north of Heilbronn via a gap in the five-foot-high concrete wall that bordered it. Other men attempted to climb the wall. Pvt. Clarence M. Rincker of H Company, a mortar observer attached to Law's unit lugging on his back a heavy SCR-300 radio, doubted he could top the barrier. As he approached it, however, a sniper's bullet "snapped past my head with such a loud crack that I just about jerked my head off in reflex. . . . I took off immediately and had no trouble clearing the stone wall in one big jump."[6]

With the 2nd Platoon leading, E Company pushed beyond a coal pile and crossed a loading yard toward a red brick building inside a glassworks occupied by the enemy. The defenders teamed with comrades holding a building on the left of the works to catch the advancing GIs in a deadly cross fire. As the men of the 2nd Platoon hit the dirt, members of the 1st Platoon attacked across open ground toward a house just outside the power-generating complex that Law took to be the plant superintendent's home. The platoon reached the house, but artillery and automatic arms fire kept the men from entering. Working to the attackers' disadvantage was the ground that surrounded the house, which Law described as "wide open and flat, extending back to hills that dominated the area. The hills afforded the Germans excellent observation into our area of operations."

The cross fire raking the 2nd Platoon expanded until the unit was taking bullets from three directions. "We were pinned down on flat ground and suffering casualties," its commander recalled. "We were in trouble and needed artillery support. We didn't get it." All they had was a mortar section, dug in behind and on the flank of the coal pile, but its men were serving as infantry. They were helping hold a beachhead for later-arriving forces to form behind, but they could provide little assistance to their beleaguered comrades amid the glassworks.[7]

To relieve pressure on the 2nd Platoon at the superintendent's house, Law ordered the 3rd Platoon to attack on its right. The added firepower enabled both units to advance to a line of supply sheds behind the glass factory. "That was a better position," Law observed, "but we still sustained some casualties," every one of which he took personally. Sixty years later, he felt the same burden of responsibility and guilt that he began to shoulder on this sunny but dark day for his company.[8]

While the 2nd Platoon had been relieved of pressure at least temporarily, the 1st Platoon around the superintendent's house was still immobilized. Realizing that the dwelling had little tactical value, Law moved the unit back behind the coal pile and power station. As the men withdrew, several fell to artillery fire—those damned guns on the hills seemed to have every square yard of the company's operating area zeroed in. Law saw Pete Petracco pick up one of the wounded and carry him to cover, an act that would win the lieutenant the first decoration to be awarded for the fighting in and around Heilbronn.[9]

Petracco, a native of Wayne, New Jersey, and the recipient of a battlefield promotion that every member of the 1st Platoon believed he deserved, had been determined to relieve his unit, now pinned to the earth in the open area inside the glass factory. Accompanied by a bazooka man and Private Rincker with the SCR-300, Petracco had scurried from building to building in the factory district, braving small-arms and machine-gun fire every step of the way, while searching for better cover for his troops. Late in the afternoon, the three soldiers gained entrance to a sugar-factory warehouse near a German machine-gun nest that was concentrating fire on the platoon's hiding place. Hoping to get a shot at the gunner, the three cautiously ascended a ladder to a metal catwalk that ran the length of the warehouse's upper floor. From an open window at the end of the walk, they spied a one-story building about fifty feet away where the machine gunner was holed up. With a clear view of the 1st Platoon's position, the German was making life precarious for his victims, blasting chunks of steel and concrete from the buildings surrounding them. As Rincker put it, "every time some GI made a bad move the machinegun spit out a bunch of bullets in his direction."

Unable to get any closer to his target without drawing fire, Petracco ordered the bazooka man to fire through the roof of the machine gunner's building. Petracco knew it was a difficult shot; in fact, a direct hit from that awkward position appeared impossible. To everyone's surprise, the bazooka round penetrated the building's roof and just missed the gunner, who quickly swung his

HEILBRONN April 4-12, 1945

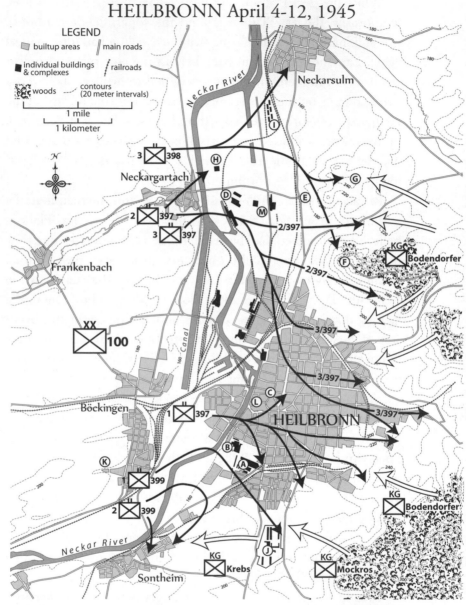

LEGEND

- ▦ builtup areas
- ▮ individual buildings & complexes
- ⬚ woods
- ‖ main roads
- ⫽ railroads
- --- contours (20 meter intervals)

1 mile
1 kilometer

Neckar River

Neckarsulm

3 ☒ 398

Neckargartach

2 ☒ 397
3 ☒ 397

Frankenbach

XX
☒ 100

Böckingen

1 ☒ 397

1 ☒ 399

2 ☒ 399

Neckar River

Sontheim

KG ☒ Krebs

HEILBRONN

Canal

2/397
2/397
3/397
3/397
3/397

KG ☒ Bodendorfer
KG ☒ Bodendorfer
KG ☒ Mockros

A: Knorr Works
B: Sugar Refinery
C: Kilianskirche

D: Glass Works
E: Railroad Bridge
F: Tower Hill

G: Cloverleaf Hill
H: Power Plant
I: Lumber Yards

J: Schlieffen Barracks
K: Tower Observation Post
L: Cluss Brewery
M: Fiat Plant

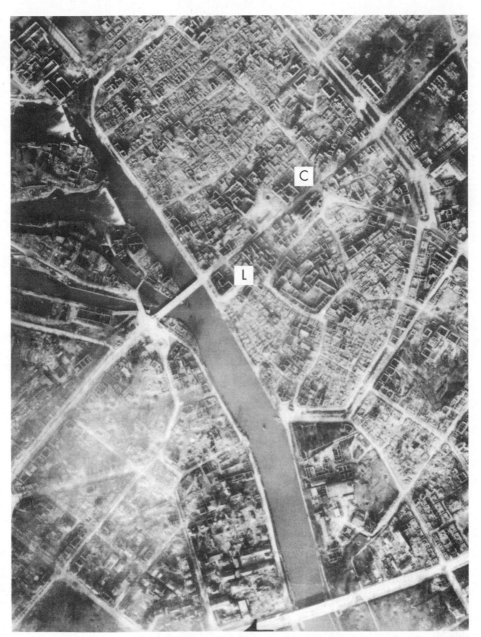

An Allied reconnaisance photograph of Heilbronn taken on March 31, 1945, showing the massive destruction left by American and British bombers. Kilianskirche (C) and the Cluss Brewery (L) are identified and can be compared to the tactical map opposite. (*National Archives*)

weapon about and loosed a clip of tracers at the catwalk. The "Fourth of July fireworks" that resulted sent sparks flying and bullets pinging off the roof girders. By some miracle, however, no one was hurt.

The failed experiment in the employment of antitank weaponry persuaded Petracco to seek a mortar barrage from across the river. Calling in fire at such a distance was risky business, but Rincker managed to contact a dependable friend in the heavy-mortar platoon of H Company, who directed round after round on the target. The first round landed two hundred feet beyond the machine-gun nest, the next one hundred feet beyond, the next fifty. Playing it safe before another round came in, the three soldiers backed down the catwalk to the far end of the warehouse, where they took cover behind a brick partition. Rincker then called for nine rounds "for effect." As he wrote, "sure enough one round did drop short right through the roof into the building where we had been." Apparently the others were more effective; no more machine-gun fire came from the targeted position.[10]

While his subordinate was freeing his men from a dangerous state of immobility, Lieutenant Law ordered the other platoons to discontinue offensive operations and assume a defensive posture. By now dusk was settling, but German artillery and mortar fire continued to shower the area around the power plant; GIs died in the gathering darkness as so many others had in broad daylight. By the time full darkness had descended, the fire had dwindled to long-range sharpshooting, although several potato mashers were tossed into E Company's "hold line" by Germans brave enough to charge the position and swift enough to escape retaliatory fire.

Now on the defensive, E Company remained the most exposed element of the Century Division. The 2nd Battalion's wire group had not yet crossed the river, so Law had no field telephone with which to maintain contact with the 1st and 2nd platoons. He had also lost radio contact, "so I didn't know how far into the glass-works they had gotten. In desperation, I sent a runner to each and neither one returned." His only consolation was word received from battalion headquarters that F Company was advancing to his support—four hours after E Company had landed on the east bank.[11]

Although Law did not know it, F Company had crossed the Neckar and taken position in a factory building just inside the concrete wall. The proximity of reinforcements was poor compensation for the situation facing the 3rd Battalion of the 398th and E Company of the 397th. Throughout the night, Clarence Rincker recalled, "we could hear the German artillery still intensely shelling the river crossing site which was preventing supplies and assistance from reaching us." The 88s also continued to stymie the efforts of the Century's engineers to lay the bridges on which to cross the heavy weapons that lent staying power to the infantry— tanks, tank destroyers, self-propelled guns, mortars—and such critical items as ammunition, rations, and medical supplies.[12]

Unwilling to wait for F Company to reach him, Law determined to reestablish contact with his scattered platoons. Believing he knew the location of Lieutenant Petracco's unit, he withdrew from his forward position and turned toward the administration building of the glass factory. His sense of direction was sound; Petracco had moved the platoon there from the power station, where Law had originally dispatched it. Accompanied by a radioman, Law crossed the open ground to the glass factory at an extended sprint, bullets whining overhead. About halfway across the lot, both men dived for cover behind a small shed. As soon as they caught their breath, they broke for the side entrance of the administration building. Rifle fire dogged their every step, but now they received a covering fire from open windows on the second floor of the building.

As Law and the radio bearer charged toward the side door, the enemy fire increased tremendously. Most of it came from a house to the right of the building; the occupants also hurled dozens of grenades. "Although intended for us," Law wrote, "the grenades hit the side of the office building and others went through the open windows. We heard calls for medics as we entered the door. We reached the second floor by taking steps two at a time. The room was dark. Walls were crumbled by the grenades. The dust was so heavy that it was difficult to breathe. We used a flashlight cautiously. There were wounded men blinded by debris and men disoriented by the concussion intensified by a small room." Among the fallen was Petracco, his uniform covered in blood from a bullet wound in the head. Within minutes, "Pete died in my arms and his men fell silent. They knew from my anguish he was dead."[13]

Every senior noncom in the platoon and several privates had been wounded or blinded by flying chunks of walls, floors, and ceilings. Others had lost their sanity under the hours-long pounding of hurled grenades; one man reportedly turned his M1 on himself. Still others moved robotically and spoke incoherently. The last sensation Sgt. William M. Ditto remembered that night was "a big flash of light, and, very dimly in my memory, an explosion." Days later he awoke in the hospital, where surgeons had removed shrapnel from his upper body. Buddies who visited Ditto informed him that after being struck, he continued to issue orders—"however, from what I was told, I didn't make sense."[14]

Unable to remain with the platoon, Law appointed a junior noncom to take command and instructed him to hold the administration building at all hazards. Later he sent a more experienced subordinate, Sgt. Thomas A. Convery Jr., to reorganize the 1st Platoon and secure the position beyond possibility of capture because "I knew if we lost it, the Germans could outflank our position and drive us into the river."[15]

Two events in quick succession defined the rest of the night for the men of E Company. Sometime between 10 p.m. and midnight, the advance element of F Company reached the glass factory grounds; the men took shelter behind the first buildings they came to. For a few hours they had little to do but secure their position. Like Law and his men, F Company expected to see no sustained fighting until after dawn, but around 3 a.m., a large force of Germans that had sneaked into the loading yard under cover of darkness assaulted the glassworks. It blasted the administration building with machine guns, burp guns, and *panzerfaust*. Several Germans stopped to hurl incendiary grenades through the windows, setting the building on fire. The quickly spreading conflagration forced Sergeant Convery and his men to abandon their post and withdraw under fire across the open yard toward the company's hold line.

In the light of the fire, the fleeing GIs made excellent targets. Several, including Convery, were wounded, burned, or temporarily blinded. When he reached the command post, Convery apologized to Law for being unable to maintain his position, and for being forced to leave behind the bodies of Petracco and five others felled in the recent fighting. Convery's superior waved off his apology as "unnecessary. He had done all he could." Instead, he commended the sergeant for holding on as long as possible.[16]

In fact, five men, not six, were cremated in the blazing inferno (when the fire died out, all that could be found were their dog tags). The sixth man identified by Convery, Pvt. Victor H. Nash of Washington, DC, survived the holocaust by a miracle of biblical proportions. Nash had been among those who had been shell-shocked by the grenade attack on the administration building. Sgt. Joseph H. Crosby, a 1st Platoon medic, recalled that during the height of the assault, the private was screaming so loudly that "I put my hand pretty forcibly over his mouth." Realizing that in his present condition Nash had no hope of escaping from the building, Crosby ordered him to hide in a coal bin in the cellar where the Germans, if they seized the place, might overlook him.

When the building caught fire and the upper stories gave way, the stairway to the basement collapsed, effectively trapping Nash. Slight of build, weighing less than one-hundred pounds, the shell-shocked private was alert enough to squeeze his small frame into the corner of the cellar where the water heater stood. The gas mask he had resisted discarding enabled him to breathe despite the inferno above, "but the heat threatened to roast me alive. It occurred to me that this was how Shadrach, Meshach, and Abednego must have felt after being thrown into King Nebuchadnezzar's burning fiery furnace!" Nash began to pray for deliverance. All at once he felt a sense of calmness and reassurance appropriately so, as it turned out. The building slowly burned down around him but for some reason the flames did not reach the cellar.

The heat robbed Nash of fluids, however, and when his canteen ran dry he feared death by dehydration. To his amazement, "the Lord had provided a slowly dripping faucet near the water heater." Sustained by the trickle, Nash remained buried in the rubble of the collapsed building for four days. On the eighth, after the fighting in that sector had died out, Sgt. Crosby returned to the building in hopes of retrieving Nash's remains. Thinking that he had heard shouts from below ground, the medic cleared away some of the rubble, peered through a shell-torn hole in a portion of wall still standing, and saw Nash lying beneath layers of debris. With the help of others, Crosby cleared a path to the trapped man and extricated him—bruised and battered but otherwise unharmed— through a coal chute. Convinced that divine guidance had directed his rescuer, for the rest of his life Victor Nash gave thanks "for the mighty protective power of our great and benevolent God."[17]

It is possible that some who died in the burning administration building perished because of the flames rather than from wounds suffered before the fire began. When the building began to burn, Pvt. William H. Wagner, a member of E Company's mortar platoon, ran to a back stairwell where he and a buddy found an open window. They jumped two stories into an alley, managed to land without breaking any bones, and began running from the screams "of wounded buddies unable to escape the inferno." Nearly captured in the alley, Wagner and his comrade broke free and made it to safety.

Another who fled the inferno, Clarence Rincker, was astounded by his escape. With the building not only aflame but under rifle and *panzerfaust* fire from all sides, the radioman saw no way out, but

> I decided I would rather die in a hail of bullets than be
> burned up so I started making my way to a doorway. When
> I got out of the door I started running with no particular

destination in mind. I could see Germans in the light of the fire but so far I hadn't felt any bullets, so I just kept on running as hard as I could. In a short while I came to a factory building and still hadn't felt any bullets. I stepped inside a doorway and paused to get my breath and to try to figure out if the building was full of Germans or what.

At first it seemed quiet inside but then there seemed to be some noise like someone was in the building. I didn't have any password for the night so just called out to see if a German or a GI might respond. I was really relieved when a GI spoke to me. I convinced him I was an American and proceeded towards his voice. It turned out that there were 8 or 9 Company E men in this building and in the next thirty minutes or so stragglers came in just as I had.

The four-story building was not a safe haven. With no one in charge, the troops huddling there put up an imperfect defense of the position. There were several doors in the building, and despite all efforts to bar them, some Germans gained entrance. The GIs retreated in a body to the next floor, where they positioned themselves to repel additional intruders. If this could not be done, they determined to hold out to the last man. A medic accompanying the detachment removed the knit cap from his head and pulled it down over his helmet, covering the red crosses painted on its four sides. Taking up a rifle that had been carried by a man now dead, he announced that if he were going to die in this building he would go down fighting.

Rincker recalled that the effort to guard the stairs "seemed to be working, but pretty soon, someone thought there were Germans on the roof." At the urging of his buddies, Rincker got on his radio and put out a distress call. He attempted to reach H Company's mortar section on the west bank of the river. (Having determined that the building was made of concrete, Rincker doubted that mortar fire would cause greater harm to the occupants than the Germans seeking to seize them.) The radio, however, had been struck by a bullet early in the fight, and its transmitter was not functioning. Unable to reach anyone on the company's own frequency, after repeated attempts Rincker put in a "clear call," asking anyone within range to respond. This effort also failed, but he picked up a faint transmission "that seemed to be someone directing artillery fire" on an unknown location.[18]

Later it was determined that the caller was F Company's commander, Lt. Carl Bradshaw, whose unit had come under the same storm of rifle, machine-gun, and *panzerfaust* fire as E Company. Someone on the west bank of the Neckar responded to Bradshaw's request. A minute or two later, Rincker recalled, "8-inch shells started landing all around us and hitting our building too. This barrage was big stuff . . . [it] did the same thing as I anticipated my mortar fire would have done except it was literally blowing our building apart."

As Rincker had hoped, the shelling succeeded in emptying the building of Germans. Yet he and the other occupants, afraid to quit their hiding place prematurely, attempted to ride out the storm. At one point there was a "big thump upstairs." One of the GIs left the room to check it out; he returned to report that a piece of heavy machinery had fallen through the upper floor to the story just above the rest of them. Another round seemed to burst just above Rincker's head, creating a "brilliant flash and deafening blast" that stunned him and knocked him to the floor. When he regained his feet, he was covered with concrete dust from head to toe. Rincker feared the next shell would finish him and his comrades off, but then the barrage ceased. All remained quiet until daylight.

At first light, Rincker took a head count and found that seventeen out of perhaps forty men who had taken refuge there were still alive. Several lay dead at the windows and on the floor now awash in masonry and glass. Was this all that remained of the almost two hundred officers and men who had crossed the river as members of E Company? Rincker's fears were unjustified, but the facts were grim enough. Of the 150 members of the company who had gone into the fight that afternoon, fifty-four had been killed or wounded, a casualty rate of 36 percent.[19]

Rincker and his buddies decided that because no one knew where the Germans had gone to, they should stay put until their situation became clearer. Their prudence was rewarded when, shortly after dawn broke, a column of GIs, darting from one piece of cover to another, advanced toward the building. The occupants signaled to them that the building was in American hands. Minutes later some of the newcomers—it proved to be Lieutenant Bradshaw and several members of his company—entered the building at a dead run.

Rincker and the others quickly informed the company commander of their recent trials and adventures. As they talked, the balance of Bradshaw's unit advanced in small groups through the open yard leading to the building. Perhaps one hundred yards from the front door, they were hit by enemy weaponry: rifles and at least one machine gun. Bradshaw rushed out of the building to direct his company's defense. Shortly afterward, Rincker and the others got word that "our liberator"—whose timely call to division artillery headquarters had saved them from being surrounded, captured, or wiped out—was dead.[20]

Lieutenant Bradshaw, a well-liked and well-respected officer, had been killed while seeking a jumping-off point for an assault on the Germans holed up in the factory district. Cpl. Henry McCorkle, a radioman of H Company of the 397th who had been assigned to Bradshaw's unit as part of an observation party, recalled that when F Company crossed the river in the footsteps of Lieutenant Law's unit, Bradshaw took the post of greatest danger, leader of the "point" platoon.[21]

Once over the river, Bradshaw led the platoon south in single file. "There was an occasional bullet going overhead," McCorkle remembered, "but it did not seem that the Germans were concentrating on us at the time." At one point Bradshaw advanced well in front of the unit, personally clearing building after building in the northern tier of the factory district. When the men caught up, he had them set up a machine gun in the window of a vacated factory and fire on a row of buildings thought to be occupied by the enemy. Hoping to flush out the inhabitants, Bradshaw dispatched one squad into an open space between two of the row buildings. Snipers picked off the first two men to break cover, killing one and wounding the other. A medic assigned to F Company made three attempts to rescue the second man, risking his life to no avail. When forced back for the third time by heavy fire, the aid man began sobbing in frustration and rage.[22]

Consulting his map, Bradshaw found possible vantage points from which to neutralize the snipers. Again he left the men to sprint from one building to another, darting inside long enough to determine if it was occupied. The sharpshooters had withdrawn, but he kept up this dangerous routine, without locating the enemy, until dark. Before daylight on the fifth, the lieutenant resumed his search, backed now by the entire company. When the assault on the administration building of the glassworks began, his position prevented him from supporting E Company. He and his troops watched helplessly as comrades fled the burning building to supposed safety. One man had just begun to run when burp-gun fire hit him, "almost cutting him in half." Soon afterward, Bradshaw called in the artillery strike that cleared the Germans from the four-story building occupied by survivors of the fire.

Soon after dawn on April 5, Bradshaw set out to execute what McCorkle called "a definite plan to take certain buildings" in the factory quarter. That plan soon embroiled F Company in a firefight with an enemy force in a loading yard north of one of the targeted buildings. The Germans were well-hidden; surrounding shacks, loading docks, and a high-banked railroad spur partially bounded by a concrete wall provided excellent cover, as did sniper fire that poured from houses on either side of the yard. Hoping to outflank the enemy, Bradshaw led four men, including McCorkle, in a race across a railroad yard about sixty feet long and into a building that appeared to offer a vantage point for gaining the rear of the loading yard. The four men covered the distance one at a

100th Infantry GIs move cautiously through the rubble of Heilbronn. One of the soldiers is carrying an M-3 "Grease Gun" .45-caliber submachine gun. (*National Archives*)

time, at every step under fire of a machine gun. McCorkle was the last to break for the shelter of the building: "The fact that he [the machine gunner] had missed everyone else in our group did not reassure me when my time came."

But McCorkle, too, made it across the yard in one piece. He leapt through the open door of the building, then lay against a wall until his heart assumed its normal beating. A buddy who had cleared the yard in advance of him broke into a grin: "That looked like a battle scene right out of the movies, you running across there with the machine gun bullets kicking up dust and concrete all around your feet!" McCorkle had to smile in spite of himself; the wry commentary "broke the tension in just the right way."[23]

His mood changed drastically a few minutes later, when Bradshaw, seeking an even better position from which to fire on the yard, stepped out the back door into an alley and crossed the street. Finding no entrance in the building opposite, he darted back again, but not quickly enough. A burst of machine-gun fire slammed him to the street, mortally wounding him. Pvt. Harold E.

"Gene" Pollard was standing just behind Bradshaw when he was hit "and witnessed him go down on the dark asphalt, lying there in a pool of his own blood." A medic ran to Bradshaw's side but could do nothing: within minutes the officer was dead. His leaderless men eventually made their way back to the factory where they had left the men of E Company. The men stayed put, awaiting the advance of G Company, the next unit in line. Upon its arrival, they would resume the sweep of the factory district.[24]

Bradshaw's death figured indirectly in the next spate of activity, initiated by the advance of G Company to the loading yard. Lt. John H. Slade, whose 2nd Platoon was in the vanguard, did not realize that the position was occupied until, only a few yards off, his men suddenly attracted machine-gun and rifle fire from the far side of the yard wall. Slade had his men take cover behind the chipped and broken wall while he and Sgt. Dalton J. Yates searched for a gate through which to attack the yard. "The first Kraut I saw," Yates recalled, "was one guy sticking a gun through a hole in the wall." He responded by tossing a grenade over the top; other GIs did the same. The enemy on the other side returned the favor, and for a few minutes "a lively game of catch" ensued. Explosions rocked both sides of the wall, and casualties mounted. Some of Yates's men began firing through other holes. One opened still another with a rifle grenade; a buddy enlarged it with the butt of his M1. Peering through, they estimated that forty or so Germans occupied foxholes across the length of the loading yard and in a woods beyond; some were only about fifteen yards from the wall.

Six of his men having been killed, Slade had his radioman request mortar fire from across the river. Teams of 81-mm mortars responded; in minutes, deafening blasts were rocking the yard and showering both sides of the wall with debris. To stay alive, Slade's men held Mother Earth in a desperate embrace.

Within minutes the fire completely blanketed the Germans' position. Not even Nazi supermen could withstand such inhumane treatment; several broke from their holes and ran for their lives—not to the rear but toward the 2nd Platoon. Slade's men pre-

A group of Jugend—teenage Germans—captured during the fighting for Heilbronn. American soldiers faced a combination of Volkssturm (civilian militia), Hitler Youth, SS, and other German soldiers during the battle. (*National Archives*)

pared to cut them down, but when they came into view and their high-pitched cries became audible, the GIs realized that these were children. Some wore pieces of Wehrmacht attire; others were clad in the caps and short pants of the Hitler Youth. Sobbing hysterically, the child warriors raced toward Slade's position, hands upraised, screaming, "*Kamarade! Kamarade!*" Not all made it to safety. Several collapsed on the shell-pocked ground, having been shot in the back by their officers.

Thirty-seven Jugend reached the American side of the yard wall and immediately surrendered. Their captors had mixed feelings about the fight. A member of another unit in the 397th wrote that he and his buddies "were not happy to have to kill kids." But these particular kids had taken six American lives; in the fighting to come, Jugend would account for many more casualties. As Lieutenant Slade later put it, "before the mortars had hit them, they had fought like demons, but now, they were only a disorganized mass of 14 to 17-year-olds."

After the teenagers broke and ran, older comrades abandoned the loading yard and adjacent houses. Slade's men then turned to clearing a path to the trapped men of F Company. Almost immediately, however, the platoon recoiled against intense fire coming from a couple of houses to the right of the factory where Bradshaw's men had taken refuge. Before the 2nd Platoon could pull back, four more of its men were cut down. Finding that he could advance no farther without sacrificing additional lives, Slade withdrew the unit from its exposed position and left the loading yard behind.[25]

The barrage that pounded the Jugend had been directed by forward observers at the command post of the 2nd Battalion, 397th Infantry. One of the spotters, Sgt. Herbert Harvey (who had distinguished himself at Mouterhouse), initially ordered a single 81-mm mortar of H Company fired on the yard "for effect." When the battalion commander, Capt. Anthony J. Maiale, observed the result, he considered it weak. Maiale had just learned of the death of Lieutenant Bradshaw, formerly his senior subordinate in F Company; Bradshaw had also been a close friend. "Quite upset" by the news, the captain ordered Harvey to "stop wasting ammunition, shoot all guns." Maiale himself recorded the upshot: "In no time at all, each of 6 guns had put 9 high explosive 81 mm shells in the air. . . . I could hear the cries of the wounded. I felt no regrets. A measure of vengeance had been taken for a friend."[26]

The unit that had initiated the fighting on the right bank of the river—the 3rd Battalion, 398th Infantry—had spent a night almost as frightful and deadly as the one the companies of the 397th had experienced. Through late afternoon and into the evening of the fourth, the battalion had been harassed by a "determined enemy force" that attacked the length of the five-hundred-yard line running from the eastern side of the water ditch down to the Neckargartach Road, then along that road to the glassworks. L Company had been posted on the left of the line, I Company held the center, and K Company was on the right. The battalion's nine-man raider platoon, which was armed with machine guns, secured the sector of the line that jutted north and east of the ditch. This position—the command post for defense of the bridgehead—had to be held at all costs. The perimeter had resisted a succession of "fierce assaults."

Some of these assaults were made by *landsers* supported by Panzers, the first time in the fighting that tanks were engaged. The division G-2 (intelligence) staff estimated that the enemy had six tanks at his disposal, most if not all of them garrisoned south of Heilbronn at the Schlieffen Barracks. They were used frequently but also carefully, being returned to the shelter of the barracks after every mission. The Panzers that attacked the 3rd Battalion might have overrun its defense line but for the support it received from its mortars (the lighter, 60-mm weapons had been set up near the power plant; the 81-mm variety, too heavy to be crossed over the river, were emplaced at and near Neckargartach). Critical support was also provided by two of the division's tanks and two tank destroyers parked on the west bank of the Neckar. With this support, the battalion held its ground for the remainder of the fighting in and around Heilbronn.[27]

Throughout April 5, persistent and accurate German artillery made it impossible to construct the pontoon bridges necessary for moving tanks, tank destroyers, and self-propelled guns to the east bank of the Neckar. Colonel Singles of the 397th, who was responsible for maintaining the bridgehead, compensated by calling in ever greater amounts of counterbattery fire. With the keen eye for terrain of a veteran artillerist, division artillery commander General Murphy and his executive officer, Col. Walter H. DeLange, secured positions for their guns that offered excellent observation. They took maximum advantage of a lofty ridge that ran for a mile and a half south of Neckargartach, covering Heilbronn from its northern to its southern extremities. Along this ridge they established three major observation points: on the highest point around Neckargartach, on a hill southwest of the town, and in an old watchtower in the rear of Bockingen.* In his after-action report, DeLange admitted that the observation posts were inferior to those of the enemy, but they were supplemented by artillery observation planes, an asset denied the Germans, and they never came under heavy fire in the battle. Early in the fighting it became clear that the Germans were intent on saving their 88 rounds for targets in and around the city, chiefly the pontoons the division's engineers continued to attempt to lay.[28]

The Century concentrated its artillery fire on buildings across the river; the coordinates were relayed by forward observers accompanying the infantry units and, less frequently, by the aerial observers. Favorite targets included tanks, the Schlieffen Barracks, Tower Hill, and convoys of troops and equipment moving into Heilbronn from south and east. The barrages greatly assisted the ground troops in Heilbronn, but neither they nor the fighter air-craft of XII Tactical Air Command silenced a single German gun. Even with the advantages of observation and terrain, it was exceed-ingly difficult to place rounds on the enemy's guns, so skillfully were they concealed. Only on occasion could a target be located by muzzle blasts.[29]

Based on direct and aerial observation, division intelligence officers estimated that Heilbronn's defenders had at their disposal at least fifteen 88-mm howitzers, nine 155s, twenty 105s, and from six to eight *nebelwerfer* launchers. Most of the guns were fired

---

*Most of the Century's big guns were positioned in the middle of the divi-sion's line near Frankenbach and Kirchhausen. Providing direct support for the assault on Heilbronn were the 105-mm howitzers of the 374th Field Artillery Battalion, the cannon company of the 397th Infantry, the 242nd Field Artillery Battalion (on loan from Seventh Army headquarters), and the 155-mm Long Toms of the 373rd Battalion. North of the city, where the 1st and 2nd battalions of the 398th Infantry would later cross the river in sup-port of the 397th, were the 105s of the 375th Field Artillery Battalion and the guns of three Seventh Army battalions attached to the division: the 876th and 938th (both firing 155s) and the 194th (8-inch howitzers). The reach of these guns was such that they could also support the fighting in Heilbronn, nine miles south of their chosen positions.

from behind and atop the elevated ground overlooking the city, where their muzzle flashes were hidden by trees. German artillery fire on the 100th Division was called in by observers from elements of a so-called "flak regiment" on the forward slopes of the hills, while other observers, deployed throughout the city, directed ground fire at the advancing GIs. Although artillery was the Germans' most destructive weapon, it would appear that the most commonly used arm—more so than rifles, burp guns, or machine guns—was the *panzerfaust*, often their only source of direct fire support. Inside Heilbronn, the Century Division attracted the heaviest amount of *panzerfaust* fire it had ever encountered.[30]

Members of the 397th had the chance to find out just what the enemy's bazooka-like "beehive on a pole" could do. On April 6, D Company found in the basement of a building several cases of the cheap, easy-to-produce, but powerful *panzerfaust*. Cpl. Eugene W. Herr examined the contents and "from the graphic instructions shown on the weapon, I felt I could fire it." He carried a *panzerfaust* outside, removed the safety wire, placed it on one shoulder, pointed it at a side of the building, and pressed the trigger. There were two results: the blast and recoil nearly broke his shoulder, and "the building wall had a big hole in it." Herr's buddies feared they were under enemy attack; the company commander rushed up from the basement to request that no more *panzerfausts* be tested around his command post ("only he said it," Herr recalled, "in more explicit terms").[31]

The American version of the weapon was just as potent. On the same day that Gene Herr scared his company half to death, Pvt. Earl W. McKisson, a mortar man from the weapons platoon of I Company, then sweeping through a portion of the factory district, supplied himself with a bazooka. His reason for doing so is not clear, for McKisson had no inkling of how to use the weapon, which consisted of a five-foot-long steel tube that fired a nineteen-inch rocket weighing three-and-a-half pounds and whose back blast could inflict almost as much damage as its forward thrust. McKisson's buddy, now-Sgt. Paul Mosher, recalled that the mortar man had occasion to fire the weapon only once. His mistake was doing so with his back to a brick wall that had been weakened by shell fire. When he pulled the trigger, the wall collapsed on him. McKisson crawled out of the debris unharmed "but spitting brick dust."[32]

Because of the distance and accuracy of the enemy's shelling, the division's engineers made no attempt to lay a bridge on April 5. Assault boats, ferry boats, and rafts continued to be the only means of sending troops and supplies across the water. They returned with growing numbers of dead and wounded as well as prisoners; the latter were made to paddle the men of A Company, 325th Engineers, to the west bank.

One prisoner, taken on the fifth by the men of G Company of the 397th, proved to be of great value: an infantry captain bearing a map that outlined in broad terms the enemy's plan for defending Heilbronn. The plan divided the city's industrial district into four zones and gave a general indication of how heavily each zone was held. Rushed to the attention of higher authority, the information helped shape the division's future tactics. Other prisoners revealed the lengths to which the enemy had gone to defend the city. Those taken in the first days of the fighting included not only teens and sixty- and seventy-year-olds, but at least two women who had fought as snipers.[33]

The POWs gave an indication of how many civilians remained inside Heilbronn and who was in charge there. According to their reports, as many as three thousand residents had been trapped in the debris-riddled city. Groups large and small—some consisting of hundreds of men, women, and children—were huddling in the cellars of houses and factory buildings as well as in the underground bunkers of the Schlieffen Barracks. Some civilians had been forced into the open, precariously sheltered by the few undamaged railroad tunnels of the city. A minority were making little or no effort to shield themselves from the fighting that swirled around them as if determined not to let it interrupt their daily lives.

A member of G Company of the 397th, himself ensconced in a basement hiding place, was astonished to see a *frau* picking flowers in front of a house across the street.[34]

Many civilians were also trapped inside buildings under fire on the Neckargartach side of the river. On April 5, a medic of the 398th, Pvt. Harry J. Perrin Jr., learned that an enemy soldier had been seen climbing through the window of a house one block from the river. Accompanied by crewmen from a Sherman tank parked nearby, Perrin entered the house and made a room-to-room search: "No people. Then we checked out the basement." Hearing noises from behind a cellar door, Perrin, who lacked a weapon, hesitated to go farther. The tankers preferred that he take the lead—one handed him a Thompson submachine gun, and Perrin broke in the door. The little room beyond turned out to be filled with women and children who, hysterical with fear, suddenly began to cry and shout. Perrin and the tankers herded them upstairs, along with the lone soldier among them, who surrendered without resistance. Over the years Perrin wondered "what kept us from shooting the machine guns" and killing everyone in the room.[35]

Heilbronn's civilian officials, some of whom had advised against making a last stand in the city at the risk of destroying it, had been replaced by Nazi adherents who answered to an SS captain named Weiss. One wounded Heilbronner, a Red Cross nurse who had escaped to the Century's lines, related how she, her family, and a group of friends had taken shelter in the cellar of a house they feared would soon be seized by the Americans. To avoid being caught in a cross fire, the girl's parents had hung a white flag out an upstairs window. Captain Weiss's hand-picked mayor saw the flag and flew into a rage. At his order, a German machine-gun squad entered the cellar and opened fire; of the fourteen occupants, only the nurse survived. Other prisoners and fugitives reported that in the days before the Century's arrival, SS troops had rounded up civilians who had expressed a desire to surrender the city. Accused of defeatism and treason, dozens had been summarily hanged as a warning to other weak-willed inhabitants.[36]

Through the course of the fighting, hundreds of civilians were able to flee to safety or were removed from their hiding places by helpful GIs. So many ended up in U.S. hands that within six days of the start of the fighting, the displaced-persons center the division had set up in the rear was filled. But many citizens were not fortunate enough to reach this shelter. Tom Jelks reported from personal experience that "most of the houses had cellars and German soldiers would take refuge in those. Half the time, there would be women and children in there and we didn't know [they were] there and we would throw in a grenade and kill everyone. We couldn't help it."[37]

Not every resident took up arms against the Americans or tried to hide from the fighting. A small minority gave aid and comfort to the Century Division, sometimes at great risk to their health. One such person went to great lengths to assist B Company of the 397th. In the midst of a vicious little firefight, one of the unit's platoon leaders, Lt. Gerald James (who days earlier had fled a rest center on the French Riviera to rejoin his men in Heilbronn), was astounded to see a ten-year-old boy race across a fire-swept street to B Company's embattled position in the center of the city. James yanked him down behind a pile of rubble, then asked him what the hell he thought he was doing. When the youngster caught his breath, he explained in perfect English that he and his family— including his father, who had been conscripted into the Wehrmacht—were ardent opponents of the Nazis. Apparently of the belief that the quickest way to get father back home was to help the Americans win the war, the boy informed James of the location of a hidden artillery piece that had been making life miserable for B Company. "You follow me, sir," he told the lieutenant, "and I will show you." He also offered to locate a field telephone line that connected the enemy gunner with a fire observation post.

James did not know whether to believe the boy, but before he could stop him the youngster ran back across the street. Some minutes later he returned with a ten-foot length of telephone wire. When James asked why he had risked his life to cut the line, the boy replied matter-of-factly, "So they can't put it back together."

A 105mm howitzer in France. The 100th Division had several artillery battalions that used this weapon. (*National Archives*)

More of a believer now, James, accompanied by a radioman, followed his informant down the block, all three crouching to avoid small-arms fire. The boy led them up the stairs of a vacant apartment building. From the window of an upper room he pointed toward a building directly across the street: "They have an artillery piece in there so they can get you when you come down the street. You need to get that out." James looked where the boy was gesturing. Sure enough, a gun was firing from a ground-floor room in that building, spraying shells at the insecure position of James's unit.

Thanking the boy for his courageous assistance, James shooed him to a safer position, then had the radioman call for fire on the building. An observer attached to an unknown unit—not the 397th's own field artillery battalion—responded. When James learned that he had reached a battery of Long Toms, he asked how far back it was located. Eight or nine miles, he was told. "My God," he exclaimed, "we're only fifty yards from the building!" How could a gun so distant from the front put a shell on such a small target without causing massive collateral damage? A nonchalant voice said: "Don't worry, Lieutenant, you just give us the coordinates."

Half expecting to be blown to atoms, James gave the information as best he could. Then he and the radioman crouched behind
some furniture—a futile gesture if there ever was one. A minute
later, a shell came screaming overhead to score a direct hit on the
building across the street. The deafening silence that followed was
broken by the observer's voice: "Now give us correction." An
overwrought James shouted into the mouthpiece: *"You got the
God-damned thing!"*[38]

Once it became clear that two battalions would not suffice to turn
the tide of battle, General Burress ordered reinforcements over the
river. At about 11 a.m. on April 5, half of the 397th's 3rd
Battalion—I and L companies—crossed south of the
Neckargartach bridge in assault boats shielded by a smoke screen.
The smoke crew did its job well; an observer reported that "visibility at some places was five yards, at others anywhere from 5 to
25. The sun was practically hidden by the man-made fog."[39]

Firing blindly, German cannoneers, mortar men, and machine
gunners on the east bank failed to inflict casualties but rattled
nerves all the way across. "We paddled like our lives depended on
it," said Sergeant Tessmer of I Company. "I have no idea how long
it took, but it seemed forever. . . . Now I know how the guys in a
beach assault felt; pretty helpless." A buddy, Sergeant Mosher,
recalled that "the water was often within about two inches of coming over the sides of the boat which was seriously overloaded but
with shells falling nearby there was no time to readjust or
rearrange, so we paddled like hell for the opposite bank." Most of
the rowing was done by the combat engineers, one of whom
groused, "I hope they build these damn things with motors on 'em
for the next war."[40]

As soon as they landed, the men of I and L companies rushed
up the inclined bank toward some of the buildings in the southern
tier of the factory district. Grim sights greeted them; Mosher
recalled that "to my immediate front, starting about 100 yards out,

were the bodies of the soldiers of the 3rd battalion of the 398th which had originally assaulted the area. Perhaps a hundred bodies were visible. I had never seen so many dead comrades."[41]

Almost immediately, the newcomers encountered the enemy. A building they entered, which some men took for a salt factory, turned out to be occupied. The first German to show his head drew an M1 round; a second later "he lay face up, dead." More men moved inland; they attracted *nebelwerfer*. As usual, the rocket blasts were inaccurate but terrifying. Wiremen raced up and down the river stringing telephone cable to connect the forward position with battalion headquarters. Stretcher bearers came up carrying casualties to be evacuated to the battalion aid station. As the again-filled boats started back, additional vessels full of 3rd Battalion troops emerged from the fog and unceremoniously dumped their passengers on the bank.

I and L companies had been brought across with the intention of joining the attack on the glassworks from a direction that might outflank the defenders. But the assault began before they could properly position themselves. Around 2 p.m., F and G companies, augmented by the survivors of E Company, rushed the works, which had been pounded for hours by the guns ordered up by Colonel Singles. G Company, leading the charge, gained a strategically located row of buildings. The unit captured nearly one hundred occupants left "dazed and groggy" by the shelling. This obstacle having been removed, F Company had a relatively easy time clearing the remaining buildings in the glassworks complex. F Company then advanced to its next objective, a grove of trees along a lagoon that jutted out from the river below the Neckargartach road. This operation was completed by four o'clock or shortly after.

Denied participation in the afternoon fighting, I Company, commanded by now-Capt. Ulysses J. Grant, headed toward a tall, square building adjacent to the southeast corner of the glassworks, which proved to be a Fiat automobile assembly plant. Machine-gun and *panzerfaust* fire came from within its walls. Grant and his men advanced cautiously toward a gate in the wall that fronted the plant, which the unit's scouting detachment struggled to open. Support on the company's right and rear was provided by the lead platoon of L Company. It would appear, however, that some of Captain Grant's troops did not know of L Company's presence in the area.[42]

The L Company platoon, under Lt. Sam Stephens and advancing toward the Fiat factory from another direction, was suddenly halted by a couple of French civilians, apparently forced laborers, who dashed across the street from the plant waving a white flag. Stephens took the Frenchmen to his company commander, who spoke their language. They reported that six co-workers, still inside the plant, wished to be escorted out. The two men were directed to bring out the others. The GIs held their fire as the men raced back to the factory, now under small-arms fire from hidden positions to the left of Stephens's platoon. One of the Frenchmen was severely wounded; Stephens and some of his men were also caught in the hail of bullets. The lieutenant shouted, "Let's get the hell out of here," and all of them ran for the safety of a drainage ditch. They remained there until the balance of the platoon came to their assistance. Later Stephens learned to his anger and disgust that they had been fired on by members of I Company, who had mistaken them for the enemy.

Once the confusion had abated, the attackers made brisk work of clearing the auto plant. Inside its main building they found a single German soldier, who promptly surrendered; every comrade had fled. But no sooner had the building been occupied than it came under a barrage of 88s. Stephens recalled that within seconds, "skylights, glass and fragments of artillery shells were flying everywhere. All of us who could, took cover in the basement. The others found any protection available, and miraculously none of us were hit."[43]

By evening the plant grounds had been secured and a phone line had been strung from the main Fiat building to L Company's command post. The auto plant would serve as a forward operating location in the fighting to come. Though an unlikely defensive position, it provided ample shelter to its uneasy occupants. One of them, Private Sheets, "did not know a Fiat from a Siat, but a grease pit is a grease pit anywhere. . . . It was a bit large for a foxhole, but it would have to suffice."[44]

The seizure of the glassworks and the auto plant marked the first significant achievement of the Century in the fighting around Heilbronn: the first of the city's four defensive zones had been overrun. The taking of these objectives not only ended the threat to the bridgehead but permitted its expansion south. An immediate benefit was the largely unopposed crossing of K Company of the 397th, an operation completed around 6 p.m. As soon as it landed, the company prepared to join the units that had preceded it in a deeper and wider penetration of the factory district.

The next objective of major importance was a large gray concrete house at a point where roads from the north met the railroad tracks that led south from the glassworks. The house, which was believed to be heavily occupied, commanded the route the division must take to enter Heilbronn proper. But reaching the enemy position entailed crossing fields that offered little or no cover. From its position at the grove near the lagoon, F Company would have to advance two hundred yards across this dangerous expanse; the distance for I Company at the Fiat plant was closer to three hundred yards.

As evening approached, F Company started toward the gray house. It was dark before the first group of GIs—four riflemen and a medic—began to descend the railroad tracks, followed by a second squad. The first group had advanced less than twenty yards when a machine gun began firing from a window of the gray house, killing all five. Giving up the idea of a frontal assault, F Company withdrew to the grove; I Company, farther to the rear, fell back in turn. A second attempt on the house, this one from another direction, would wait until morning.[45]

Late on April 5, VI Corps, which had been keeping a close eye on the Century's operations, began to worry about the division's continued inability to bridge the Neckar. That evening division headquarters received a phone call from General Brooks: "Get your armor over; that is the big thing." A frustrated Withers Burress replied that "everything depends on the bridge"—the bridge that both VI Corps and 10th Armored had promised would be laid early the previous morning.[46]

The day before, Capt. Kenneth R. Franklin's A Company of the 31st Engineer Battalion had made four attempts to place pontoon floats in the river. Each float had been destroyed by German artillery fire, possibly called in by civilian observers in Neckargartach. Each attempt had met with casualties; by the morning of the fifth, one engineer had been killed and twenty wounded.

Franklin and his engineers spent April 5 constructing a four-float pontoon ferry. After dark they carried the contraption, in segments, to a sheltered position upstream from the first crossing site, where they reassembled the craft. Early on the sixth, they caught the enemy's gunners napping and managed to ferry a Sherman tank across the river. The soft earth on the eastern bank, however, prevented the ferry from making a secure landing. Appreciating the importance of placing armor on the Heilbronn side, the tank crew nudged the tank forward. The risky effort failed; unable to gain a firm hold, the tank slid back from the bank, causing the ferry to give way, and rolled into the river. Its crew barely made it out before it sank. The engineers hastened the ferry toward the west bank, where they proposed to add extra floats to facilitate the unloading process. Before the landing craft could return, a direct hit from a German 88 sank it. The Germans shelled the crossing site the rest of the day.[47]

Throughout the sixth, assault boats continued to shuttle supplies to the troops fighting in Heilbronn. Some transported M29 "weasels," tracked vehicles equipped with litters for carrying the wounded. According to John Sheets, "that little bugger did yeo-

The Americans made several attempts to construct a treadway bridge supported by pontoons across the Neckar River, but each time the bridge was destroyed by accurate German artillery fire. (*National Archives*)

man service keeping the troops supplied with K-Rations, water and ammo, plus evacuating the wounded and the dead. That thing could be heard 24 hours a day whining up and down the streets on its errands of mercy."[48]

There continued to be no means of getting heavy weaponry to the troops in the city. On the seventh, an attempt was made to cross two amphibious tanks. One of these experimental vehicles ran into the same trouble as the quite-sinkable Sherman: unable to grip the soft ground of the east bank, it slid back into the water and foundered. Sgt. Bruce O. Larson of I Company of the 397th was the last man to scramble out of the hatch before the "amphib" sank to the bottom. The second tank negotiated the embankment, but when it reached solid ground became caught on the pilings of one of the ruined bridges and could go no farther. These failures marked the final effort to pass tanks or heavy direct-fire guns over the water opposite Neckargartach. At least for the near future, the men of the Century would have to fight with the weapons they carried.[49]

TEN

HEILBRONN:
THE PINCERS CLOSE

After Captain Franklin's ferry went to the bottom of the Neckar, division headquarters decided that tanks would never be able to cross at the bridgehead opposite Neckargartach. General Burress huddled with his chief engineer, Lt. Col. Jack Mallepell, and they determined to move the bridge tools and equipment almost two miles south. If pontoons were laid adjacent to the destroyed bridge at Bockingen, heavy weapons could be transported to the center and southern sections of Heilbronn.

It was possible that the factories and residential areas here were less heavily defended than the upper reaches of the city, but like every part of Heilbronn, the streets were clogged with rubble, which would pose problems for tanks, self-propelled guns, and other heavy weapons. On the other hand, the piles of broken concrete and bricks would impede the Panzers that were reported to be stationed at and near the Schlieffen Barracks, and they would furnish cover to attackers as well as defenders. At the west bank near the ruins of the Bockingen bridge, enough buildings remained habitable to give shelter to the bridge builders. Furthermore, this stretch of the river, which included the peninsula formed by the Neckar and the loading canal that ran south from Neckargartach, had already been cleared by the sniper hunters of B Company of the 397th Infantry and the regiment's antitank company. With these factors in mind, division headquarters ordered work to begin on a new pontoon bridge before dawn on April 7.[1]

Another advantage to shifting the pontoon bridge to the Bockingen area was the existence of a bridgehead on the opposite bank of the Neckar. On the morning of April 5, General Burress, convinced that the crossing site at Neckargartach could not funnel enough troops to the east bank to turn the tide of battle, had ordered reinforcements to cross near Bockingen. The 1st Battalion of the 397th—later augmented by C Company of the 399th—was assigned the task of securing the new bridgehead. Once this was done, the better portion of the expanded battalion was to sweep north to meet the troops advancing from the factory district. Troops left behind would labor to expand the bridgehead, permitting the laying of pontoon bridges capable of bearing the weight of heavy weapons. If supported by tanks and direct-fire weapons, the converging troops could clamp a pincers on Heilbronn, squeezing its defenders out the eastern side of the city.[2]

The southern crossing began at 6:30 p.m. on the fifth. Each assault boat took only seven minutes to reach the right bank. That was time enough, however, for the Germans to lay artillery and sniper fire on the first unit to paddle across, C Company of the 397th. Unlike the crossings to the north, the GIs took casualties, with two riflemen being wounded.[3]

Private Ken Bonte had expected a rough passage. Prior to crossing, his platoon had snatched sleep inside a slaughterhouse on the west bank. "Hooks hung from the ceiling and there was dry blood on the floors," he recalled. "It was rather ominous of what lay ahead." And as the company marched down to the river, a recent replacement, "a big strapping guy" who carried a Browning Automatic Rifle, "broke down and began crying like a baby." Bonte and his buddies stared silently as medics led the man away.[4]

Although the guns beyond the town inflicted casualties, no resistance came from the east bank, perhaps because the Germans expected the GIs, once they alighted, to continue to move east into the city where they could be ambushed. Instead, the Americans turned north along the river toward some factories including a brewery. C Company had an easy time gaining entrance and persuading the former occupants to give up. Once a few Germans had been killed, forty others—most of them young, unseasoned conscripts—surrendered. The attack had taken them by a surprise, and they lacked the steadying influence of veteran officers.[5]

Soon after C Company landed, A Company joined it in and around the Cluss Brewery (B Company would cross before daylight on the sixth). Hardly anyone on the east bank enjoyed a decent night's sleep. During the night the brewery and surrounding buildings were attacked no fewer than three times. At least one German assault included tanks; at the height of the action, Bonte was horrified to see the cannon of a Panzer protruding through the open window of a room he and several buddies occupied. A quick-thinking sergeant grabbed a bazooka, placed it against the muzzle of the cannon, and fired while dropping to the floor. A tremendous blast ensued—the bazooka round had struck the live shell in the cannon barrel, blowing it apart. The wounded tank quickly withdrew. Bonte could never fully thank that "remarkable life saver" of a sergeant.[6]

The cool, rainy morning of April 6 found the men of the 397th "tired and bleary eyed but still alert." As the men of A Company took to the streets and began moving north in hopes of linking up with the 3rd Battalion, enemy artillery fire had temporarily subsided. Slowly, cautiously, they picked their way through the rubble toward the center of the city. As they moved, large portions of B and C companies fanned out to protect their right and rear. Each advancing unit included a section of heavy machine guns from D Company. The 60-mm mortars of the weapons platoons had been set up on the brewery grounds, but the 81-mm tubes of 1st Battalion remained on the west bank of the river.[7]

At first, A Company drew scattered sniper fire, but it had advanced only a couple of blocks when it encountered what was determined to be the core of the German defensive effort inside Heilbronn. Machine-gun and *panzerfaust* rounds poured forth from side streets, alleys, and the ubiquitous piles of debris. Here, in the pocket that lay between the damaged bridge at Bockingen

GIs running quickly through the rubble in order to avoid sniper fire. (*National Archives*)

and a five-hundred-year-old Gothic church two blocks from the river, Kilianskirche (the Church of St. Kilian, patron saint of rheumatics), the men of A Company would be pinned down for two days.[8]

Other elements of 1st Battalion tried to maintain mobility. C Company advanced from the brewery as far as the road that linked Heilbronn to the southern suburb of Flein; here the unit occupied several vacant buildings. To its right, B Company also reached the Flein road, en route evicting snipers from a sugar refinery and seizing a row of workers' apartments. Squads moved a short distance southeast to take position around a group of buildings owned by the Knorr Corporation, an internationally known food-processing firm, which appeared to be heavily occupied. The squads were not large enough to secure the east-west road that ran between the sugar refinery and the Knorr plant. Late in the afternoon, the enemy took this path to infiltrate behind the GIs and to regain the refinery, requiring a patrol from B Company to attack and seize it once again.

The 1st Battalion appeared to have made pretty fair progress, but shortly after 4 p.m., at least one hundred Germans, supported by several tanks, launched a broad-front assault, driving back a platoon of A Company that had been seeking to fight its way out of the pocket to the north. Dug in along the Flein road, the men of C Company held their position even when two Tiger tanks lumbered down on them. From their perch on the top floor of a six-story building, members of Les Gluesenkamp's platoon fired "several hundred rounds" at the advancing vehicles and the infantry at their rear. The Illinois sergeant supposed that "our rifle fire in combination with others of the Battalion and our artillery, prevented this attack from continuing and driving us back."[9]

Another deterrent was Sgt. Pittman Hall, who, from the upper floor of an apartment house in the path of the tanks, fired two well-placed rounds from a bazooka. The first blew out a wall of the building, giving him a clear field of fire; the second knocked out the turret gun of the leading Tiger, which, after some hesitation, withdrew. The second tank backed out of the fight when an artillery observer attached to C Company directed 8-inch shell fire against it.

Another observer brought 155-mm fire on a house on the east side of the Flein road from which *panzerfaust* blasts had been coming. When the shells started falling, nine Germans scrambled from the collapsing dwelling, to be gunned down in the street. The bodies of seventeen comrades were found inside the smoldering ruins. The balance of the German force that had struck from the east, having "lost their eagerness for close-in combat," accompanied the battered tanks to the rear.

Despite the enemy's pullback, B Company remained under threat from a force that had advanced from the south, this also supported by a pair of tanks. Two platoons of infantry led the assault, but thirty Germans were quickly cut down by a machine gun fired by Pvt. Baxter R. Smith Jr. from an apartment building west of the Flein road. The tanks continued to advance to within 150 yards of Baker Company's position, which began to come apart under the pounding of the Tigers' cannons. The company commander, Lt.

Owen E. Kirkland, ordered his men to withdraw to the sugar refinery. Kirkland stayed behind to direct bazooka fire on the tanks, a valiant effort that ended when a sniper's round found him. But before the tanks could follow up B Company's retreat, artillery fire sent their way by an observer in a liaison plane persuaded the Tigers to return to their lair near the Schlieffen Barracks.[10]

Unfortunately, the Century's engineers were not able to complete the new bridge across the Neckar at Bockingen on April 6. Nevertheless, assault boats continued to ply the river from dawn till dark. They furnished the only means of bringing troops and supplies to the battle area; thus their security was of paramount concern to the men of A Company of the 399th Infantry, who guarded the division's right and rear along the river between Bockingen and Sontheim.

To escape the shelling of the 88s on Heilbronn's hills, on the morning of the sixth the boats were moved north some four hundred yards to the foot of the demolished Bockingen bridge. This was considered a safer place, but a German patrol that had evaded the division's dragnet gained the rear of the new site and opened fire on the boats, engineers, and riflemen of A Company. The infiltrators eventually were trapped inside a row of houses that came under the fire of tanks and tank destroyers parked along the west bank of the river. Although the attack was contained, the 88s behind Heilbronn kept pounding the area, preventing the bridge builders from doing their jobs.[11]

On the morning of the sixth, in the factory district north of Heilbronn, the 2nd and 3rd battalions of the 397th prepared to resume their offensive. Members of M Company, who had spent an uncomfortable and uneasy night in various industrial buildings, geared up for the day's fighting by checking the condition of their arms and ammunition. Elements of L and M companies, including Private Jelks's heavy-machine-gun squad, were quartered in a cannery building that Jelks believed was owned by Knorr.[12]

Having determined that a frontal attack on the gray concrete house that had barred their path the previous day would be deadly and probably futile, the commanders of the 2nd and 3rd battalions agreed to a four-pronged advance from the flank. G Company, with the remnants of E Company, would move along the river, while the other companies advanced from the factory district. I Company would spearhead the latter effort from its position in the Fiat plant, closely supported by F Company. Their job was to outflank the house by capturing two rows of enemy-held warehouses about twenty-five yards to the left of it.

The 2nd Platoon of I Company made first contact with the enemy, gaining the first row of warehouses but drawing heavy fire from one of the units. Finding his men pinned down, the platoon leader, Sgt. Harold Kavarsky, dialed up thirty minutes of shelling that not only cleared the unit but killed several of its occupants as they ran to the shelter of the gray house. Kavarsky then had his machine gunners spray the second row of warehouses. Under cover of this fire, he led a group of riflemen and light machine gunners in sprinting fifty yards across an open lot to a building in the middle of the row. Climbing the steps to a loading ramp, the machine gunners let loose with several long bursts. The fire cleared the warehouse of all but five Germans, who promptly surrendered to a four-man squad led by Sgt. John P. S. Keelan. Keelan's men had joined Kavarsky just before the latter was disabled by a leg wound inflicted by an errant round from a cannon on the west bank.

In the lower level of the captured storage building, Keelan's men discovered a tunnel leading to yet another warehouse, the one closest to the gray house. With extreme caution they entered the tunnel, followed it to the end, and came up inside an unoccupied unit. From here they could fire directly on the house as well as on the cement bunker that protected it in front. Four bazooka rounds damaged the bunker, killed two of the several Germans who had been defending it, and chased the rest inside the house.

Early that afternoon, the gray house was finally cleared. By this time elements of F Company had joined I Company amid the warehouses and had taken up good positions from which to fire on their objective. M1 rifle rounds seemed to have no effect, but two well-placed rifle grenades finally persuaded the inhabitants to wave a white flag from a window. As the GIs moved in, twenty Germans emerged, hands high. Some fifty others, holed up in a factory across the street from the captured dwelling, perceiving the futility of further resistance, gave themselves up as well. The southward advance of the 2nd and 3rd battalions could now resume, and the Century's pincers began to draw closer.[13]

For the GIs inextricably enmeshed in street-to-street, building-to-building fighting, closure could not come soon enough. Daily exposure to violent death—death that could come at any minute, from any direction—was taking a grievous toll of body and mind. Private Pollard, for one, was struggling to keep his sanity: "It was difficult for me to comprehend the killing I had seen. I was numbed by the violence. I pushed it from my mind." Some of his buddies could not deal with the carnage mounting all around them. One had gone "stark raving mad," screaming out his intention "to storm the Germans single handed. . . . We had to manhandle him and get him to the rear, as he was no good to us." Pollard's platoon commander, a sober, level-headed officer, "a man I would follow anywhere," likewise reached the end of his mental endurance in the blood-stained streets of central Heilbronn: "After subjecting himself to enemy fire with total abandon, we realized he had gone bananas and he was removed from action."[14]

With the capture of the gray house, the second major strong-point in the enemy's zone-by-zone defense of the city had fallen. Two zones remained. The next one to be assaulted by the battle-weary, nerve-wracked troops comprised the remainder of the factory district and the residential quarter adjacent to it. As the men of the Century Division could have guessed, it would not be a pushover.[15]

While the fighting raged in Heilbronn, efforts were under way to extend the Century's offensive several miles to the north and a little more than a mile to the south of the main theater of operations. On the morning of April 4, the 2nd Battalion of the 398th Infantry, accompanied by tanks, tank destroyers, engineers, and medical teams, moved by motor convoy to the west bank of the Neckar River opposite Offenau, about a mile above the resort village of Bad Wimpfen. From here, the southern edge of the sector in which the 63rd Infantry Division was operating, the battalion intended to move east across the Neckar. Then it planned to cross two of the Neckar's tributaries, the Jagst and Kocher rivers, prior to sweeping south into the rear of Heilbronn, thus belatedly executing the envelopment strategy of General Burress.

Originally a pontoon bridge was to have been laid near Offenau by the 325th Engineer Battalion, but the effort had been stymied by the same enemy guns that prevented bridges from being laid farther south. Thanks to the keen eye of a battalion staff officer and to the daring of a patrol from F Company, the 398th's advance unit, a suitable crossing site was discovered and secured. The patrol also discerned that Offenau was not occupied, though it was apparent that the territory farther east was heavily held. The defenders were members of the battered but still formidable 17th SS Panzer-Grenadier Division. The division was spread out to cover the rolling countryside between the Jagst and the Kocher, including Jagstfeld, at the confluence of the Neckar and Jagst, the key point on the German defense line.

The east bank of the Neckar having been gained, Lieutenant Pinnell—the engineer officer who had risked his life to blow up Fort Schiesseck during the initial assault on the Maginot Line— directed the construction of a footbridge that by 3 p.m. on the fifth enabled elements of E, F, and H companies to cross the river. A platoon of E Company was sent to occupy Obergriesheim, a mile and a half to the northeast; there it briefly contacted elements of the 63rd Division. The rest of the company advanced to Duttenberg, two miles northeast of Offenau. At Duttenberg, the unit met G Company of the 398th, which, along with some attached tanks, had crossed the Neckar farther upstream on a bridge laid by engineers of the 63rd.[16]

Thus far the 2nd Battalion had encountered no real opposition, but from here on it would have to move cautiously. Because

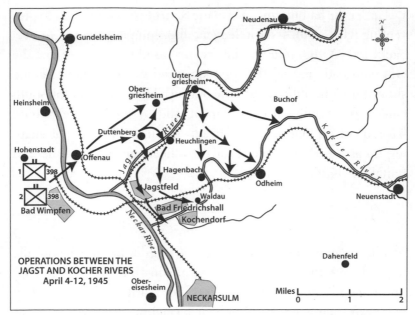

With the main body of the 100th Division having difficulty crossing the river adjacent to Heilbronn, elements of the division were ordered to cross the Neckar further north and then cross the Jagst and Kocher Rivers and advance upon Heilbronn from the north.

both the Jagst and Kocher—most of whose bridges had been destroyed—flowed into the Neckar south of the battalion's crossing site and therefore across its line of advance toward Heilbronn, they had the potential to cut the unit off from its comrades fighting in the city. The water barriers loomed up at daylight on the sixth, when G Company, under Capt. Matthew B. Einsmann, began to cross the Jagst in assault boats south of Duttenberg. Upon reaching the south bank, the company found it would have to cross two hundred yards of open ground that led toward a railroad line and, beyond the tracks, a high, thickly wooded ridge. That ridge proved to be heavily occupied by the Panzer-Grenadiers, who opened fire as soon as the GIs began crossing. Machine-gun and small-arms fire made casualties of several G Company men; it also knocked out one of H Company's heavy machine guns.

Under the hammering of "fanatic SS troops" committed to preventing Heilbronn's encirclement, the company began to reel backward. Within minutes the fire increased to the point that the GIs who had crossed the Jagst appeared on the verge of being shoved back into the water. The only available cover on the south bank was the railroad embankment, and to reach it they would have to cross a long stretch of deadly ground. The day was shaping up as a bad one indeed for the officers and men of the 2nd Battalion, 398th Regiment.[17]

While its comrades were braving a murderous fire below the Jagst, the 398th's 1st Battalion was moving into position to support the 2nd's uncovered left flank. Since April 3, the 1st Battalion had been occupying Bad Wimpfen, a celebrated prewar resort, as well as some neighboring towns neither as famous nor as salubrious. The battalion also supported some tanks that had moved into this area to fire south on the Germans in Neckarsulm. The main body of the 1st remained in position while the 2nd crossed the Neckar and the Jagst, but the countryside around Bad Wimpfen was so quiet that everyone in the 1st expected to be transferred to a more active sector.[18]

Just after midnight on April 6–7 movement orders reached battalion headquarters; within five hours, the well-rested unit was leaving Bad Wimpfen by truck for points north. In response to Division Operations Instructions No. 33, it proceeded to the 2nd Battalion's crossing site. Leaving its vehicles, B Company led the way across the Neckar on Lieutenant Pinnell's bridge. The men then began to march northeast toward a crossing site on the Jagst River above where the body of the 2nd Battalion had gotten over.

By seven o'clock, the troops of B Company approached the Jagst opposite the town of Untergriesheim. They could hear the sounds of combat two hundred yards to the south, where the 2nd Battalion was trying to make headway against the well-positioned and heavily armed enemy. By order, the newcomers moved upriver into an area thought to be less heavily defended. To some extent, this was true; by noon, the battalion had forced its way across to Untergriesheim and had begun to move cross-country toward its next objective, Odheim on the Kocher River. B and C companies now shared the advance, moving abreast of each other. For a time all appeared serene on the south side of the Jagst—only the drizzling rain marred the march—but when C Company, on the right of the column, neared the north slope of one of the many rolling hills in that vicinity, it came under oppressive fire from a variety of weapons: artillery, mortars, machine guns, and small arms. As the men dropped to the ground and tried to burrow their way to safety, their comrades in B Company scrambled into a gully farther south. It proved to be an unwise move, for in that position the unit absorbed fire not only from the front but from a second hill on the left.

For almost two hours, both companies were pinned to the earth, easy targets for the SS troops on both hills as well as on a third farther east. Not until midafternoon, by which time the enemy had been softened up by rounds from the guns of the battalion's supports—light Stuart tanks and Hellcat tank destroyers—could the companies resume their advance, albeit slowly. Yet they lurched forward only briefly before being halted again, this time by cannons and mortars firing from the hills beyond the Kocher, near Odheim.

This time battalion headquarters got on the radio. Perhaps an hour later, the fighter-bombers of XII Tactical Air Command appeared overhead and began to strafe the enemy positions. But because of the proximity of the antagonists, the planes could not fire directly on the triangular range of hills where the majority of the German forces were dug in. (Other troops and the enemy's command post were located several hundred yards farther east on Willenbach Farms.)

Early in the evening, the battalion tried to get moving again. Two platoons of C Company struggled to get into position to outflank the occupied hill to their immediate right. After gaining a few hundred yards, they were stopped in their tracks by a blizzard of bullets and shells. Artillery support was summoned, as were five light tanks. The tanks moved up smartly, intending to pass around the right side of the hill in C Company's path. Again intense fire erupted from the summit; again the advance stalled. The tank crews were reluctant to proceed without infantry support, but the men of C Company were disinclined to leave the foxholes they had scrambled to dig, especially given the volume of fire coming at them. As one GI put it, tanks could give the infantry a sense of security, but they "drew artillery fire like you wouldn't believe," making them "a blessing and a curse at the same time."[19]

Things appeared at an impasse, possibly a fatal situation for all involved in the attack. For a considerable time, neither tanks nor men moved forward. Then Pvt. Michael Colalillo climbed out of his foxhole and commenced a series of actions that would make him the division's third Medal of Honor recipient.

Nineteen-year-old Mike Colalillo hailed from Hibbing, Minnesota. The son of Italian immigrants, he grew up in a tough neighborhood that bordered the tracks of the Union Pacific Railroad. He ran with a fast crowd who made a name for them-selves—an undesirable one—with local law enforcement. "Everybody got into trouble," Colalillo recalled. He himself did so frequently enough to exasperate and worry his parents. He stole coal from passing trains, and, though less than six feet tall and only 140 pounds, he handled himself well in the rough-and-tumble environment he inhabited. He was not much of a scholar; follow-ing his mother's death, he willingly left high school in his junior year to work as a baker's assistant. "I did everything from cleaning the pans to putting jelly in the bismarcks," he recalled.

Drafted in early 1944, Colalillo was assigned to the 2nd Squad, 2nd Platoon, C Company, 398th Infantry. When his unit reached the front, he found he had to defend himself with weapons other than his fists. During his first days on the line, "there were 10 or 12 men killed in my unit. I was scared as hell. It was the first time anybody had ever been shooting at me." He learned enough survival skills to become one of the most elusive and effective scouts in his platoon. He also developed a reputation for guts and initiative. When, some weeks before the fighting at Heilbronn, his unit was pinned down by machine gunners outside Neuhutten, Germany, Colalillo and a fellow scout crawled to the rear of the enemy position and took out every gunner. Their company commander recommended each of them for a Silver Star. Colalillo's response astonished his superior: "What the hell is a Silver Star?" Like most of his comrades, decorations meant little to him; the satisfaction of doing a job well and gaining the respect of his peers and superiors counted for much more.[20]

On April 7, 1945, near Untergriesheim on the south bank of the Jagst River, Private Colalillo applied this attitude to the task of getting his platoon's stalled advance moving again. This day his unit, one of two companies spearheading the 1st Battalion's drive toward the Kocher River, had been "pinned down completely" by rifle, machine-gun, mortar, and artillery fire from atop a triangle of hills about one hundred yards west of Willenbach Farms. The majority of the fire was coming from Hill 233, opposite the left of C Company. Calls went to the rear, and a platoon of Stuart tanks slowly advanced. Their approach appeared to silence the enemy, but as soon as C Company went forward again it was stopped, as was B Company in its rear, by a heavy barrage delivered from the Odheim vicinity.

In hopes of regaining momentum, C Company's commander ordered his 1st and 2nd platoons to attack up the draw that separated Hills 233 and, farther to the right, Hill 215.8. The advancing troops were supported by the rest of their company, including its mortar and heavy-machine-gun platoons. At 7 p.m., with darkness descending, the platoons started out. They advanced several hundred yards before halting under intense small-arms fire from both hills. Again artillery support was phoned in, and five light tanks clanked forward once again to jump-start the assault. The tankers expected some support in return, but got none. The pinned-down infantrymen elected not to follow; they clung to the foxholes they had dug after the most recent shelling hit them.[21]

Concerned that the lightly armored tanks would be blasted to pieces by the enemy's cannons and mortars, Mike Colalillo climbed out of his hole and shouted for everyone within the sound of his voice to follow him. At first the men hesitated, but then the sight of a buddy racing alone toward the German lines took hold. One by one, then in groups, the platoon began to advance. Soon virtually every member of Charlie Company was on his feet, trying to keep pace with the bravest or craziest member of their unit.

Armed only with an M3A1 grease gun—a weapon scorned by most GIs as "that piece of junk"—Colalillo led the company across a long stretch of deadly ground toward a position defended by uncounted riflemen, machine gunners, and mortar men. At every step he was subjected to a withering fire; it kicked up the dirt at his feet and careened loudly off the trunks of the trees he passed. By some miracle he was not hit, but then a bullet shattered the grease gun. The defenseless private thought: "What the hell am I going to do?"[22]

The answer was to leap onto the deck of one of the Stuarts. Climbing up to the turret, he opened the hatch and politely asked the commander if he might man the tank's .30-06 Browning machine gun. Hell, yes, the officer said—and so Colalillo, who had not handled a machine gun since basic training, started firing furiously. In the growing darkness he aimed at the muzzle flashes of rifles that burst in woods ahead of him and to each side. He was assisted in his search for targets by the tank commander, who also directed cannon shells at the enemy positions. The blasts nearly knocked Colalillo from his perch, but he managed to hang on and keep firing. He now found himself "the target of every Kraut in the vicinity," but their bullets flew over and past him, pinging off the sides of the turret but missing him, sometimes by inches.

The baker's assistant proved to be a natural machine gunner. Sweeping his field of vision from right to left and back again, he took out a machine-gun nest and felled at least ten Germans. Artillery fire was now coming his way, but he kept to his post, knocking out a second machine gun hidden behind a haystack and killing an SS officer and three men holed up in an adjacent dugout.

When several enemy soldiers broke cover and charged him, he downed so many that comrades changed their minds and turned back.

Then Colalillo's gun jammed. Unable to get it working again, he shouted for help. The tank captain responded by handing up his own tommy gun: "He gave me some ammo," Colalillo recalled, "and told me to be careful getting off the tank." Taking the hint, he jumped down and advanced on foot. Creating havoc anew with the submachine gun, he destroyed another machine-gun emplacement. Then the tank he had ridden, having exhausted its ammunition, began to withdraw from the fight. After some hesitation, Colalillo decided to end his one-man offensive.[23]

He began to fall back along with other members of his company, most of whom had failed to keep pace with him. Some, however, had advanced almost as far as he had. On his way to the rear, he heard a voice from nearby: "Mike, Mike, I'm hit!" Glancing about, he spied one of C Company's squad leaders, Sgt. Jack McEvoy, lying on the ground, wounded in both legs. Discarding the tommy gun, he ran to McEvoy, lifted him, and half-carried him back to the company's original position.

The following day, Colalillo and some comrades cautiously returned to the field of the action. They found two other men, wounded but alive, whom they removed to an aid station. They also discovered the bodies of several GIs, including another squad leader, Sgt. Loma M. Hash, who, before suffering mortal wounds, had taken out several enemy positions with his M1 and hand grenades, killing "an uncounted number of Jerries." Other members of Colalillo's company had died under heroic circumstances, including Lt. Frank Reinhart. While directing a covering fire for his unit—left vulnerable by the tanks' withdrawal—Reinhart had exposed himself to enemy shelling "with utter disregard for his personal safety."[24]

For three days after the fight, Colalillo's unit went into reserve. During that period, two military policemen escorted the non-plussed soldier to regimental headquarters, where he was informed that the commander of the tank he had so ably supported had nominated him for a Medal of Honor. He would receive the award in Washington, DC, following his return from a three-day leave in Paris. For a few minutes, Colalillo was speechless. He could not understand why he was being singled out for commendation. To his mind, he had done nothing special—in the same situation, any GI would have acted as he had. Besides, he was confused: "What the hell's a Medal of Honor?"[25]

While Colalillo's unit was in reserve, Companies A and B, until then in the rear, had moved up to take over the fight for the hills approaching the Kocher River. For the next three days, despite the support of tanks and tank destroyers, the 1st Battalion was beaten back by heavy German artillery, mortar, and rifle fire. Even the fighter-bombers of XII TAC, which took out several enemy self-propelled guns, could not clear a route to the south bank of the Kocher. On the evening of April 12, the battalion was relieved by elements of the 2nd Battalion, 398th Infantry, which subsequently made contact with advance units of the 63rd Division farther east, permitting the battle-scarred 1st Battalion to go into reserve in the vicinity of its old stamping-ground, Bad Wimpfen. The SS troopers fanatically holding the line along the Kocher would abandon their positions and fall back over the next few days to fight again closer to Heilbronn.[26]

Shortly after midnight on April 5–6, the 1st and 2nd battalions of the 399th Infantry Regiment left Schwaigern for the Neckar, in the vicinity of Bockingen. The 1st Battalion occupied houses along the riverbank that looked across the water at Heilbronn and its southwestern suburb, Sontheim. The 2nd Battalion took position directly north of the 1st. For the next two days, as the battle on the east side of the water expanded, both units were reduced to the status of spectators. Their assigned mission—to guard the lower flank not only of the Century but also of the Seventh Army—took precedence over the growing need to augment the forces fighting their way, street by street, building by building, through a shattered city. (The regiment's 3rd Battalion was attached to an anti-aircraft brigade, an association that would last two weeks, ensuring that the unit would take no part in the battle along the Neckar.)[27]

When an especially urgent call for reinforcements came on the sixth, the regiment ordered C Company of the 399th to the east bank, where it would be attached for operational purposes to the 1st Battalion of the 397th. The thought of crossing a fast-moving river under the enemy's guns stirred as much dread in the hearts of the men of C Company as it had in all who preceded them. A member of a sister unit expressed the prevailing sentiment when he remarked, as he prepared to shove off, "I've seen it in the movies, but I never thought we'd have to do it!" As it happened, the crossing was only lightly opposed, and a single casualty resulted.[28]

A high observation tower behind Bockingen provided the rest of the 399th with a ringside seat. From the upper levels, artillery observers and aerial spotters had a broad, clear view of Heilbronn and the surrounding country for miles up and down the river. Private Gurley trained binoculars on the

> massive amphitheater of hills semi-circling the city. Crowding the eastern Neckar bank were tall grain elevators, fat square factories with huge surrealistic streaks of green, black, and yellow camouflage paint, gigantic cranes, railroad yards. . . . Black sponges of smoke on top of buildings [were] followed by the full-bassed crash of Corps artillery. . . . Four Shermans rattled down through Bockingen to the Canal, lined up, and started whanging away at Heilbronn. A flash of flame, a recoiling tank, a drifting black puff across the River, and two—Wham-Boom!—explosions.[29]

The view from the tower was so impressive that the high command, including now-General Tychsen and Colonel Maloney, made their way up the long, winding stairs. From the top they kept in touch by radio and phone with the troops on the ground, including C Company in the city, and suggested additional targets to the artillery observers.

They also looked for an opportunity to insert more units of the 399th into the fight. On the morning of the eighth they found one, and A and B companies were sent across the river to the southern reaches of the factory district not far from the sugar refinery and the camouflaged grain elevators of the Knorr works. There both units could safeguard the right flank of the 397th Infantry and that of C Company.

A portion of A Company made the crossing in assault boats. The remainder of the unit, as well as B Company in its entirety, had the exhilarating experience of walking across the river. Hours earlier, the division's engineers had finally succeeded in laying the pontoon bridge that would decisively influence the outcome of the fighting in and around Heilbronn.[30]

Early on April 7, the enemy gave notice that he was not ready to release Heilbronn. At about eight-thirty, more than one hundred Germans, backed by three tanks and one of those fearsome flak wagons, attacked C Company of the 399th near the sugar refinery where the unit had spent the night. The attack, which came from the south, expanded toward the lower flank of B Company of the 397th at the Knorr works, threatening to sever the connection between the companies and overwhelm each. For several nerve-wracking minutes "we were in deep trouble," Wilfred Howsmon admitted, but then the assault was turned back: "The sweet sounds of our artillery started and the tanks ran. . . . A big sigh of relief could he heard" throughout the Knorr works.[31]

On B Company's left, C Company of the 399th remained in danger of being cut off and isolated from the forces guarding the southern bridgehead. An eight-man patrol under Sgt. James Harte attacked out of the rubble between the sugar refinery and the river; it killed two Germans, took six prisoners, and forced a critical element of the attacking force in that sector to pull back. C Company was attacked two more times during the afternoon, but each effort was repulsed with the assistance of mortars and cannons well to its rear. Contact with B Company of the 397th having been regained, Lt. Vaughan Calder led the 1st and 2nd platoons of C Company of the 399th in counterattacking. Through intense effort, Calder's men recaptured the sugar refinery, which the enemy had again infiltrated, in the process winning for their battalion an oak leaf cluster—an addition to the Presidential Unit Citation it had received for the Vosges campaign.[32]

The successful counterassault enabled B Company to reestablish positions along the road to Flein that it had been forced to give up earlier in the day. When the Germans tried to regain these positions after dark, their ranks were shredded by a bank of well-positioned machine guns on the grounds of the Knorr works. The enemy's latest failure indicated that the line defending the southern bridgehead, which ran from the Knorr plant north to Kilianskirche and west to the river, had been secured. The forces holding this perimeter settled back to enjoy a mostly quiet night. B Company slept on the floors of a large building that proved to be the local office of the National Socialist Party. The next morning the men assiduously converted all manner of Nazi paraphernalia into souvenirs.[33]

Not every point on this line, however, was permanently sealed against enemy infiltration, especially given the handy routes of movement available to the city's defenders. The Centurymen were becoming increasingly aware of the tunnels that stretched beneath almost every section of the city. Before the battle these had served as air-raid shelters for the city's population; now they sheltered a variety of support facilities. Lieutenant James of Company B of the 397th discovered one tunnel under the ground floor of a bombed-out hotel in a square in the heart of the city. Curious about its usage, he followed it to the end and came up in a makeshift hospital in which German army surgeons and nurses were hard at work; no armed soldiers were present. The patients, who seemed to be enjoying good care, included a couple of wounded GIs. Discerning no threat to his unit, James decided to leave the place undisturbed and returned through the tunnel to the hotel.[34]

Not only Heilbronn was extensively undermined. Private Knight discovered tunnels beneath the streets of Bockingen, some of which had also been converted into aid stations. One had been brought to his attention by a pair of German nurses who sought his help in subduing two drunken GIs who had broken into a converted operating room and were threatening to shoot it up. Accompanied by a muscular buddy, Knight went into the tunnel and persuaded the belligerent soldiers to leave. The German doctor in charge, whom the soldiers had intended to kill, was grateful for the intervention; at his invitation, the two Americans shared a glass of medicinal wine before returning to their stations above-ground.[35]

Most tunnels were conduits of troop movement. "On several occasions," Les Gluesenkamp recalled, "there were more Germans behind us than in front. We never knew what was the score." Tom Jelks, for one, learned the score, but too late to save a buddy from grievous injury. By midday of April 6, Jelks's platoon had taken position inside buildings near a church on the northern edge of Heilbronn. Jelks set up his machine gun on the second floor of a shell-torn house that overlooked a railroad yard, certain that someone would try to attack from that direction. Late that night, a lone enemy soldier, apparently unaware that the house was occupied, entered the railroad yard, his hobnail boots scraping across the tracks. Before the man could get any closer, Jelks dropped him with a short burst.

Around noon on April 8, Jelks left his second-floor position to relieve himself in the still-functioning bathroom in the basement of the house. Afraid to leave the rail yard uncovered, he told an ammo carrier, Pvt. Herman R. Willing, to stay on the gun until he returned. When he made his way downstairs, Jelks discovered a hole in the basement floor that led to a tunnel. As he later learned, the shaft connected to another that opened through a manhole in the railroad yard. So this was how the Germans had maneuvered undetected around his company's flanks on so many recent occasions!

A series of explosions upstairs prompted Jelks to hurry back to his gun. He found that in his absence, a sniper with a *panzerfaust* had emerged from the manhole to fire several rounds at the window through which the barrel of Jelks's gun protruded. The first sight to meet his eyes was "five of our squad carrying Willing away on a door. I could see that one foot was missing and the other was just hanging on by a strip of skin." Jelks realized that "if I had not left him on the gun, it might have been me who lost both feet. I felt guilty for the longest time."[36]

In the small hours of April 7, the 2nd and 3rd battalions of the 397th—four companies moving side-by-side—departed the gray house that had taken so much effort to capture and resumed their southward advance. All made progress, but the pace was sometimes excruciatingly slow. Private Pollard described the drive as "house to house, and street to street. Every house was an enemy fort and every bombed out building became a pillbox." Each room had to be searched and armed occupants rooted out, often at bayonet point—the first time most Centurymen had used that archaic yet serviceable weapon. Throughout the day, squad leaders sent back to their commanders messages such as, "Have captured the living room and sent advanced patrols to the kitchen."[37]

One unit involved in this microcosmic warfare was Sergeant Tessmer's squad of I Company, which was assigned to clear a block of eight adjoining houses, the end unit of which, having been struck by shells, was on fire. Tessmer recalled that "we started near the flaming house and checked them out one by one until we came to the last house. Sniper fire kept us moving fast." The door to this unit was locked, so Tessmer blew it to pieces with a shell from his Browning Automatic Rifle. After a moment, he burst into the front room and was confronted by an elderly man. Unable to flee the battle because of his invalid wife, who was confined to bed in an adjoining room, Tessmer's host appeared frightened almost to death. The sergeant assured him that he meant no harm but that his squad had to check the house for soldiers. As this was taking place, "the old German went to the door and took the pieces of the lock in his hand and with a tear in his eye, said '*Ales Kaput*.'"

His mournful words appeared to fall on deaf ears, but as Tessmer left the house "the thought occurred to me that he was correct. The war raged around him, artillery shells and mortars were coming in and the fire at the end of his building would engulf his house in only a matter of hours. The war was winding down and the defense of Heilbronn was a useless exercise" in avoiding an inevitable fate. In later years, he would occasionally wonder what had become of the man and his wife. More than anything Tessmer had experienced in 187 days of combat duty, their plight had shown him war's utter futility.[38]

By day's end, F, G, I, K, and L companies had advanced six hundred yards—barely the length of a typical block in this city—against heavy to overwhelming opposition. At one point a couple of dozen Germans firing from inside some factory buildings slowed L Company's progress to a crawl. Lieutenant Stephens, a platoon leader, recalled:

> My first and second squads were pinned down by intensive rifle and machine gun fire. I was with my third squad providing covering fire when the first squad called for a medic. I dispatched one immediately, but he hadn't gone ten feet when he was hit in the leg and we had to drag him back inside the building. My company commander, who was about a block behind us, saw our desperate situation and radioed for artillery support. Before our men got their range corrected, their first shell struck the building just above the door where my third squad leader and I were standing.

Both escaped injury, although "when the air cleared, I saw the sergeant standing there with about half a stair railing draped around his neck."

Most of the fire L Company received was coming from across a railroad line perhaps one hundred yards to the east. From this same location, a small force armed mainly with *panzerfausts* sprang to the attack. A stubborn stand by Stephens's platoon and other elements of L Company prevented the bazooka wielders from gaining a foothold on the near side of the railroad. Pvt.

Tank Destroyers providing fire support from the west bank of the Neckar for 100th Division troops on the east side in Heilbronn. With the division unable to get heavy artillery across the river, armor filled the gap. (*National Archives*)

Arthur Nimrod was instrumental in this effort. From the top floor of an apartment building adjacent to the factory inside which Stephens's platoon was huddling, the Connecticut-born Nimrod "coolly provided cover for several of his buddies who were pinned down in an open lot." Stephens recommended him for the Bronze Star, which Nimrod duly received.[39]

While relieving pressure on his comrades, Nimrod was injured—not by enemy fire but by the barrage his company's commander had called in. More than any other factor, the artillery fire enabled the 2nd and 3rd battalions to hold their ground in the combined factory-residential section of Heilbronn.

Another integral element of the Century's ability to maintain itself in Heilbronn was the insertion into the fighting of tanks and tank destroyers early on April 8. The previous morning the persistent warriors of C Company of the 31st Engineers had resumed construction of a treadway bridge from a sheltered location one hundred yards south of the pontoon span that the Germans had destroyed late on the fourth and early on the fifth. As the bridge neared completion, light-weight smoke generators were ferried to the east bank and concealed in the city's littered streets as well as in the cellars of some houses on the waterfront. Although the smoke masked the labors of the engineers, it could not prevent the enemy gunners from damaging the treadway bridge before completion. However, that night a heavy overcast settled upon Heilbronn, blacking out the moonlight and thus adding to the smoke screen's effectiveness. The engineers returned to their work, and by daybreak the treadway bridge had been repaired.

Traffic began crossing before 8 a.m. on the eighth. Within a couple of hours, twenty-four tanks from the 781st Tank Battalion had crossed, as had nine Hellcats of the 824th Tank Destroyer Battalion and the antitank company of the 397th Infantry (without its 57-mm guns). Late in the morning the wind shifted sharply, breaking up the smoke screen and leaving the river and the bridge clearly visible. Before noon enemy 88s knocked out two of the bridge floats. Its traffic capacity sharply reduced, the bridge remained in operation for two more hours before sinking. By then it had placed enough armored vehicles on the east bank to ensure the security of the bridgeheads and facilitate their linkup. Two days later the engineers added to their accomplishments by building a motorized pontoon assault ferry capable of transporting a tank. During the morning of the tenth, thirteen more tanks and tank destroyers were on the east side, as were the first section of 81-mm mortars to cross. The ferrying operation would continue for as long as the Centurymen operated in Heilbronn.[40]

The movement through the factory district to the city's residential quarter—a sector that abounded in houses, apartments, parks, and groves of birch and oak—resumed on April 8, but only after a lengthy holdup. F, G, and L Companies of the 397th had to defer their advance until the better positioned I Company cleared a path through the lower tier of factory buildings. The delay was the result of rifle and machine-gun fire pouring from a brick house adjacent to an orchard in an open area of the city's midsection. Because the position blocked the advance of the 2nd and 3rd battalions toward their next objectives, artillery support was requested. Soon shells were raining down on the house and the orchard, uprooting trees and men alike.

Covered by the barrage, an I Company squad led by Sgt. Richard C. Olsen gained entrance to a strategically located factory. When Olsen's men maneuvered toward the brick house, however, their approach was detected. The volume of fire from the house increased, barely missing one of I Company's scouts, Pvt. James E. Van Damme, as he scaled a wall bordering a side yard. When attempting to follow Van Damme, a second scout, Pvt. Henry P. Perkins, was killed.

Perkins, "an amiable farmer" from Glasgow, Kentucky, married and the father of a young son, had been a favorite among the men of I Company. His death so incensed Olsen's squad that it attacked the house with a vengeance. Private Bowman, who was an eyewitness, reported that "bazooka rounds, anti-tank grenades and machinegun fire silenced the German defenders in the house, and another bazooka round forced the machine gunner in the center of the orchard to run for cover." After an extended sprint, five men reached the front door of the house. One of them bashed in the door with his rifle butt, the others rushed inside, and seven occupants quickly surrendered. Two more were seized in the basement. Private Van Damme, who had joined the attack to avenge his fellow scout, won a Silver Star for helping lead it.[41]

A major obstacle having been removed, L Company, backed by a captured 37-mm antitank gun, advanced east toward a group of factory buildings regimental headquarters had targeted. En route, the unit reached an office building at the junction of two railroads whose station was occupied by riflemen and machine gunners. This roadblock, like so many before it, was effectively removed by artillery fire called in by those forward observers who were fast becoming the unsung heroes of the battle. No longer stymied, L Company advanced and, backed by the other units in its rear,

cleared the lower tier of the factory area—one shell-scarred building, one heap of rubble, after another.

Resistance from this part of the city had begun to fade. From
midafternoon of the eighth to around noon of the ninth, the GIs
encountered increasing numbers of noncombatants. Many were
foreign nationals enslaved by the German army. On one occasion,
thirty Russian men and women were found crowded into the basement of an otherwise unoccupied factory. While fewer German
soldiers showed their faces above the rubble piles, more and more
civilians seemed to be taking shots at the Centurymen. One of
Tom Jelks's comrades took out a sniper firing from an upper floor
of a building. The assailant turned out to be twelve years old; his
rifle, said Jelks, "was taller than he was."[42]

By noon of April 9, the last row of factories had been cleared of
occupants or reduced to mounds of brick and concrete. The 2nd
and 3rd battalions were poised to cross the railroad tracks to the
heart of the city and its large residential district. The going had
been slow, and the men were nearly exhausted. The momentum
now seemed to be with the 1st Battalion, which continued to fight
its way toward its comrades to the north, a job that, theoretically at
least, was made immeasurably easier by the support of tanks and
tank destroyers.

But the 1st Battalion was having a tough time of its own.
Resistance had been especially stiff in the streets surrounding
Kilianskirche. The fighting that swirled around this shrine to the
Prince of Peace consumed the afternoon of April 6. A couple of A
Company's squads, advancing along the bank of the river, had
penetrated the enemy's defenses but only briefly before being
forced to withdraw for lack of timely reinforcement. One reason
for the lack of forward progress was the constant need to turn
around to confront Germans whose positions had been bypassed.
Heavy sniper and machine-gun fire from the rear, front, and flanks
prevented the 1st Battalion from advancing much beyond the
church that day.

American infantry advancing through one of the main streets in Heilbronn. (*National Archives*)

By the morning of the seventh, A Company had drawn up a plan for breaking through to the north bridgehead. A five-man patrol from its 1st Platoon, under Sgt. Carl Cornelius, established an outpost in a large building at the head of a triangular block northeast of Kilianskirche. The rest of the platoon took position in a building to the southeast, hoping to catch incautious snipers in a trap. The trap sprang instead on the platoon when in midafternoon, two columns of German troops approached, one from the north, the other from the east. They walked right into the carefully set ambush; converging M1 and machine-gun fire killed more than a dozen and chased off the remainder. Minutes later, however, they returned in greater force and, proceeding cautiously now, interposed between the A Company detachments as well as between the 1st Platoon and C Company, to its right and rear.

The Germans also attacked the rear of the detachment southeast of the church. To escape encirclement, the latter staged a fighting retreat to the river. There it threw together a defensive line that proved strong enough to drive the enemy from the south end of the triangular block. But the 1st Platoon failed to reestablish contact with Sergeant Cornelius's outpost northeast of the church. Fears for the squad's safety only increased.

The attacks directed at the 1st Platoon were part of a larger enemy counteroffensive from the north—apparently with Kilianskirche as its objective—that threatened to engulf all Century forces in that area. Lt. John A. Strom's 3rd Platoon of A Company had been occupying the church since the previous evening. Covered by a six-man outpost west of the church square, throughout the day Strom's men battled Germans striking from all directions. The crew of a mobile artillery piece opened on the GIs from various positions, including the grounds of the church itself. The platoon dropped grenades out stained-glass windows onto the heads of attackers trying to gain entrance to the nave of the church. Meanwhile, the men of A Company's 2nd Platoon, ensconced in the cellars of houses across the street from Kilianskirche, fired rifle rounds at enemy troops rushing through the streets.[43]

The fighting seesawed back and forth throughout the seventh, but the advantage steadily passed to the Centurymen. By early evening, the Germans were withdrawing from almost every position they had held throughout the day. Their departure enabled the widely scattered elements of A Company to reunite under growing darkness.

Though the Germans had been forced into retreat, they had accomplished much this day. Their main achievement was preventing the 1st Battalion from advancing more than a few hundred feet to the north. The attack by which the battalion had expected to break through to their comrades had been preempted; implementation would have to wait for at least one more day.[44]

Through the night the enemy kept a harassing fire on the 1st Battalion from distant positions, adding *nebelwerfer* to the arsenal of small arms, self-propelled guns, and *panzerfaust* that had confronted A Company throughout the afternoon. Numerous Germans infiltrated the battalion's lines via the underground tunnels, which most GIs knew nothing about. "Snipers would go through the lines, or rather under them," the division's historian wrote, "and fire on our guards from the rear." Before dawn, A Company made several attempts to reach the position of Cornelius's lost detachment. Each was thwarted by alert sentries and roving patrols. One patrol engaged a rescue party from the 1st Platoon in an extended and deadly duel with grenades.[45]

While A Company fought the enemy head-on during the seventh, other portions of the 1st Battalion were clearing city streets of sniper nests and roadblocks while fighting off assaults directed at their flanks. At one point attackers forced B Company to relinquish its hold on two city blocks. After a brief withdrawal, the unit halted, regrouped, turned about, counterattacked, and regained the lost ground. Meanwhile, C and D companies held their position south and east of Kilianskirche under intermittent but sometimes heavy fire. During each of these actions, the infantrymen were greatly assisted by the big guns that the divisional artillery had collected on the west side of the Neckar. By the close of April 7, the 397th's cannon company alone had fired 535 rounds of high explosives at Heilbronn's defenders. Official reports indicated that the company had played an integral role in breaking the enemy's hold on Kilianskirche.[46]

Several 1st Battalion men had memorable experiences this day. While B Company was retaking the two city blocks it had given up, Pvt. Joseph E. Fleming was ordered to check out a building thought to be a sharpshooter's nest. Finding the front entrance barricaded, Fleming, although afraid to expose himself to fire from within, worked up enough courage to scale a wooden fence leading to the rear of the building. He found no Germans in that quarter, only an abandoned machine gun whose barrel pointed through a second-story window. Had the gun been manned, he would have been a goner.

The teenager from Jasper, Alabama, moved on to an adjoining building, which he entered with extreme caution. His heart racing, he searched the open hallway, flinging open each door he came to, ready to blast any occupant, but he found none. Reaching the end of the hall, he was scared almost to death by a young woman who materialized at the foot of a stairway. In perfect English she told him to accompany her up the steps—someone wished to meet him. Fleming complied, but he warned her that he would shoot her "if anything started to look strange." At the top of the stairs, he moved cautiously down the hall to an open door the woman had indicated. Taking a deep breath, Fleming burst inside to find a German officer sitting at a table on which rested a loaded Luger. His command of English was at least as good as the woman's: "What kept you? I've been waiting to surrender for two days."[47]

While not advancing far beyond its position of the previous day, on the seventh the men of C Company also checked out occupied buildings, including some private dwellings. Pvt. Horace F. Mitchem Jr., this day serving as first scout of his platoon, was sent to explore one of the few relatively undamaged buildings in his unit's sector. Finding the front door locked, he smashed in a window with the butt of his M1. As he was about to reach through the hole for the doorknob, an elderly couple opened the door. Seeing no one else in the front room, he had the couple stand back while his buddies searched the rest of the house. In spite of himself, Mitchem felt embarrassed and a little guilty when the old lady reappeared with dust broom and pan to clean up the mess he had made.[48]

The 1st Battalion's drive to the north, which had stalled out around Kilianskirche, got moving again early on April 8 with the addition of tanks and tank destroyers that had crossed the pontoon bridge shortly after eight o'clock. The situation did not miraculously improve as soon as the heavy vehicles arrived; the first tank to go to the assistance of A Company, moving from the southwest along an enemy-infested road, was disabled by a blast from a *panzerfaust*, causing its crew to bail out and run for cover under machine-gun fire.

Another Sherman and tank destroyer had better luck, reaching the church safely by way of another route. The tank took position

Once tanks and tank destroyers entered Heilbronn they were able to take out German strong points with deadly efficiency. (*National Archives*)

at a major intersection near Kilianskirche, while the Hellcat parked northwest of the church, where it fired on German soldiers and civilians crouching behind mounds of stone and dirt in a square across the street. The Germans in the square were promptly subdued, but it took three hours for the tank, supported in turn by the riflemen it had come to assist, to silence the machine gunners around the intersection.

The tank made an especially inviting target for snipers, including several Volkssturm—men as old as seventy-five and boys as young as twelve. The machine gunner atop the turret of the Sherman returned fire, cutting down several assailants. The tankers made a point of telling their comrades in the infantry that they did not enjoy gunning down grandfathers and teenagers but felt they had no choice. Captured civilians reported that SS officers had threatened to shoot anyone who failed to snipe at the invaders.[49]

Once the Germans withdrew from the square and the intersection, two platoons of A Company advanced up the river road to gain forward positions out of which to attack next day. Lieutenant Strom's unit established a line that ran through the now-evacuated square, while the platoon of Sgt. Bennie B. Ray occupied a more advanced line thanks to the support it enjoyed from the

397th's Anti-Tank Company, which had crossed the river with the tanks and tank destroyers. The unit had come under fire from the German 88s, one of which scored a direct hit on the bridge only thirty minutes after the newcomers reached the east bank.[50]

Yet another A Company platoon, led by Lt. Walter R. Vaughan, stationed east of the intersection at Kilianskirche, was having difficulty securing the company's right flank. During the fighting around the church, two more Shermans came up to clear a street south of the triangular block, the objective of Vaughan's unit. The platoon was also supported by the 1st Platoon of C Company under the command of Sergeant Pittman Hall. Though struck by shrapnel, Hall refused to be evacuated until two of his men, also wounded, received medical care. The next morning, after pieces of metal were removed from his arm, the noncom returned to the fight. In cooperation with Vaughan's platoon, Hall had his men concentrate fire on the occupied houses in the triangular block, silencing the snipers within.

Both platoons then resumed their advance, accompanied by the Shermans. Despite attracting heavy machine-gun and *panzer-faust* fire, infantry and armor drove enemy soldiers from the triangular block. The right of A Company now secure, a squad from Vaughan's platoon made its way to the house in which Sgt. Cornelius's patrol had been isolated the previous afternoon. Inside, the would-be rescuers found only discarded equipment, indicating that the entire patrol had been captured.

During the night of April 8–9, the enemy made no direct attack on A Company's new line, although at one point a squad-size force attempted to strike from the rear. Its approach was detected by an alert lookout, Tech. 4 George F. Brazier of the 397th's anti-tank company. With his M1 carbine, Brazier killed one German, wounded two, and sent seven others scurrying away.

Given the steady resistance the 1st Battalion had encountered ever since reaching the east bank, on April 9, its men expected a new round of counterattacks. Instead, for the most part the enemy remained quietly on the defensive. Unchallenged, the battalion extended its position well to the north of Kilianskirche, thus almost clearing the entire central area of Heilbronn. At day's end the battalion, tired but encouraged by the progress it had made, halted to await the approach of troops from the north.[51]

The expected linkup did not occur the following morning, raising concerns that the forces from the upper bridgehead had been seriously delayed, perhaps even driven back. If so, the 1st Battalion might be in big trouble, especially now that the pontoon bridge was again out of commission. Sergeant Gluesenkamp noted that "an uneasy calm set in while we waited for additional tanks and reinforcements to cross the river."[52]

It appeared that higher headquarters was also concerned. Based on prisoner interrogations, the division's intelligence specialists had concluded that a major counterattack would strike both bridgeheads some time on the tenth or eleventh. Readjustments were made to the position of some units, who were told to prepare to go on the defensive. But headquarters had figured wrong. Either those questioned gave false information in hopes of confounding and frightening their captors, or they truly believed rumors of an impending offensive. In either case, no counterattack occurred, and efforts to link the bridgeheads continued.[53]

On the afternoon of the tenth, two of the Shermans attached to the 1st Battalion started north with the hope of contacting the troops who had nearly cleared the northern part of the city. The tanks met increasing resistance from Germans in factories along the river and a house a few blocks inland. Eventually they were forced to halt and direct fire at their assailants. They did such a thorough job that they used up all their ammunition, forcing them to return to their line of departure. They had failed to meet anyone from 2nd or 3rd battalions.[54]

Around noon on the ninth, the companies to the north were preparing to cross the railroad tracks six or seven blocks above Kilianskirche. One platoon each from I and K companies led the way. The infantrymen started out in good spirits, virtually assured of joining hands with the 1st Battalion and trapping between them the dwindling number of Germans able and willing to oppose the junction. But perhaps their confidence was misplaced: even before they reached the tracks, both platoons were caught in a deadly cross fire from two houses alongside the railroad. As the men dove for cover, one squad of I Company found shelter in a row of shacks to the right of an occupied house. As soon as it began to return fire, however, the squad was so heavily targeted by machine gunners that it was forced to hold its precarious position for the rest of the day. By firing from the shack, however, the squad permitted the rest of its platoon to reach the temporary safety of a factory building north of the railroad.

The platoon from K Company found itself in a similar situation, pinned down in a ditch by a fire so severe the men could not raise their heads to shoot across the embankment. Screened by smoke shells provided, via radio, by the 374th Field Artillery Battalion, the unit eventually withdrew to the same factory as its counterpart in I Company. There it would remain through the day and well into the next. As the division historian recorded, "it was now agonizingly clear that a frontal attack could not wrest the few remaining yards of the center of Heilbronn from the Germans."

On the afternoon of the tenth, after hours of careful planning and in the wake of a "blistering artillery preparation," the 3rd Battalion launched an assault against the enemy's left flank. I Company led the way under a sky darkened by the smoke of burning buildings. Its objective was a group of hardware factories along the Neckar that, if seized, might permit an envelopment of the enemy's entire position. As the unit moved out, K Company provided a covering fire from north of the railroad tracks.[55]

The men of I Company's 3rd Platoon crept down the riverbank, shielded by scattered mounds of concrete and iron and the skeletons of bombed-out buildings. At points they took cover in the more substantial-looking buildings, where they set up machine-gun emplacements. One of these, inside an old chemical-processing plant, was manned by Sgt. Joe Lize, a former professional boxer from Detroit. For several minutes, Lize poured tracer bullets out the window of his floor until a sniper fixed his position. An eyewitness, Sgt. William B. Waldecki, reported that Lize "grunted and dropped dead with a bullet in his heart. . . . [H]e put up both fists as if in defense and fell backwards."[56]

Thanks to the support of Lize and other stalwarts of the division, the main body of I Company gained entrance to the first hardware factory. Found to be empty, it was held until the 2nd Platoon, hastening along the river, reached it. Without realizing it, the 3rd Battalion was now within a few hundred yards of the tanks attached to the 1st. From behind the armored vehicles, the men of Lieutenant Strom's and Sergeant Ray's platoons of A Company were peering through the late afternoon haze for signs that their comrades were drawing near.

Having gained an important foothold, I Company decided to defer the envelopment operation until morning. In fact, it was never implemented, for next day, when the company reached the houses that had generated the deadly cross fire, they were found to be empty, as was every other former German position in the center of the city.

The event that had precipitated this wholesale withdrawal began shortly after 11 p.m. on the tenth, when a three-man party from I Company forged two hundred yards south from the hardware factories and in the stygian darkness made contact with the tanks shielding the 1st Battalion. The encounter heralded the linking of the division's bridgeheads and the closing of the pincers that General Burress had fashioned for the die-hard defenders of this shattered city. Pockets of resistance remained to be sewn up; unfinished business beckoned from the hills to the east; and heavy, well-positioned forces continued to resist above and below the city. Even so, the objective for which infantrymen, artillerymen, and tankers had struggled and suffered for nearly a week had been secured. Whatever the outcome of the fighting to the north and south, Heilbronn would be the Century's prize.[57]

ELEVEN

HEILBRONN: OUT OF THE RUINS

When General Brooks stripped the Century of its tank support on April 4, he directed the 10th Armored Division to swing wide to the northeast. The tanks were to pass in rear of the 63rd Infantry Division, which was operating against the northern flank of the German defense line along the Jagst River. The 63rd had been making slow progress toward its objectives above Heilbronn and needed support. The 10th Armored, however, was unable to supply direct and material assistance. Intent on capturing the road center of Crailsheim, forty-two miles east of Heilbronn, General Morris's command seized the place but was counterattacked by large numbers of Waffen-SS, who blocked its supply lines. After taking heavy casualties, the armored unit was forced to evacuate Crailsheim.

This unexpected resistance, the work of the 17th SS-Panzer-Grenadiers, had major repercussions for the 100th Division. When forced out of Crailsheim, General Morris changed his mind about attacking Heilbronn from the east. Instead, he headed northwest to link with the 63rd. And when General Brooks learned that a crack Panzer command had moved north to defend the Jagst River line, he ordered the 63rd Division to attack it from the north, supported by an assault from the west. The supporting effort—which had as its main objectives Jagstfeld on its namesake river and Odheim on the Kocher River—would be made by the 2nd and 3rd battalions of the 398th Regiment, detached from the Heilbronn front.[1]

Thus it was that on the cool, rainy morning of April 6, two-thirds of the 398th found themselves involved in an expanding fight along the banks of the swift-flowing Jagst and in the country to the south. The heroics of Mike Colalillo would soon free the 1st Battalion from being pinned down around Untergriesheim, enabling it to sweep toward the Kocher and confront the enemy emplacements around Odheim. The 2nd Battalion, however, had no such savior as it fought to break free of the enemy's deadly embrace along the south bank of the Jagst.

Second Battalion had got into its predicament in rather ominous fashion. Sergeant Tillett recalled that G Company had reached the north side of the river before dawn. There its men were placed in a ditch just below a generating station that supplied hydraulic power from a dam on the river. In the murky light Tillett tried to get his bearings: "As we . . . peered over [the ditch] to see what was ahead we could see the figures of the Germans along the tree line shooting down at us." The south side of the Jagst appeared to be heavily held, but "as daylight settled in and the light was brighter it was clear that we were to cross the stream" and then "a wide flat grassy area about 200 yards across." That seemed a tall order, but apparently battalion headquarters believed it could be accomplished without heavy loss.[2]

A fellow machine gunner, Sergeant Good—the lanky GI who on his first night on the line had squeezed his six-foot-six frame into an eighteen-inch-deep foxhole—did not consider the ditch a very safe position. For one thing, it was packed almost to overflowing with immobilized GIs: "We were shoulder to shoulder right along the length of the river" like fish in a barrel. Had the enemy "dropped mortars and artillery on us they'd just massacre us." The Germans, however, chose not to exploit this vulnerability. They preferred to wait until the GIs crossed to their side, where in the morning light they would make good targets.[3]

Around 6 a.m. when the assault boat crossing began—E, G, and H companies opposite Duttenberg, F Company a short distance downstream—Dick Good was perplexed. The sturdy power station afforded a more convenient means of transport: "You could have walked across on the top of that dam." Captain Einsmann of G Company had the same thought; before the crossing began, he raised the headgates of the dam, thus lowering the water level enough to permit some men to cross on it.

The preponderance of the 2nd Battalion, however, went over aboard the boats. The vessels drew so much fire that some never made it across; filled with casualties, they were forced to turn back. Those that reached the bank dumped their passengers on open ground showered by Mauser, burp-gun, and machine-gun fire. Aware that they could not survive on the edge of this two-hundred-yard stretch of earth, the men began to run for the only shelter available, the railroad embankment. Reaching it, they ducked behind it, not daring to raise their head for fear of drawing a fatal shot.

With the support of comrades to the rear, they held their position—barely. On the north bank, Captain Einsmann had established a continuous firing line that included two sections of H Company's heavy machine guns. These weapons pinned many enemy sharpshooters to their foxholes. The covering fire of greatest help, however, was provided by cannons and heavy mortars firing from a hill outside Duttenberg, directed by observers ensconced in the steeple of a village church.[4]

Eventually the guns and mortars began to drive the defenders from the high ground beyond the railroad. Most fell back several hundred yards to a prepared line sheltered by farm buildings. At that distance, Tom Tillett believed, "they could only use their rifles, not their Burp Guns."[5]

Yet shoulder arms could produce an impressive volume of fire. When the enemy pulled back, G Company tried to advance but found as many as 150 riflemen barring its path, supported by at least eight machine guns. An intense firefight ensued in which G Company lost four men killed and twenty-seven wounded. The unit inflicted fifty casualties but failed to drive the Germans from their strong position, which was braced by artillery and mortars. The position was so formidable, in fact, that when several medium tanks, which had crossed the Jagst on pontoons eighteen miles to the east near Weisbach, came up to break the stalemate, they were overmatched. A self-propelled gun knocked out one of the Shermans, and the rest beat a hasty retreat under a hail of shells.

Appreciating the futility of a further advance, Captain Einsmann ordered his company back to ground better suited to defense. Observing the withdrawal, the Germans increased their rate of fire, which they concentrated against the 3rd Platoon, on the company's right flank. Many GIs were immediately pinned down; more than a few appeared afraid to either advance or fall back. The platoon had many recent replacements who lacked the experience necessary to survive the situation they now found themselves in. They froze in place, dropped to the ground, and ignored comrades' warnings to get up and run—in any direction. Einsmann, who had made it to the south bank, shouted and waved frantically, trying to get their attention, but the fear-paralyzed rookies paid no heed.[6]

As a last resort, Einsmann broke cover and started across the bullet-pocked ground. When he reached one of the terrified replacements he would lift him to his feet and shove him toward the rear. He was joined in his rescue mission by the company's radioman, Charles E. Compton Jr. On this same field, Compton, a burly sergeant from Sylacauga, Alabama, already had made a name for himself by his courage and quick thinking. Before the crossing began, he stripped off his heavy SCR-300 radio to range up and down the river under heavy fire, realigning boats torn from their moorings by the swift current. He exposed himself even more recklessly when wading downstream to recover a few that had been washed away when abruptly abandoned by their crews. When not otherwise engaged, he used an abandoned Browning Automatic Rifle to return fire on the enemy.[7]

Now Compton dashed onto the open ground, where he not only got frightened comrades to their feet but hauled them bodily to the rear. The strapping six-footer—in postwar years a standout tackle for the University of Alabama football team—made several trips rescuing comrades disabled by wounds or fear. In the midst of one attempt he was confronted by a German determined to take him prisoner. According to the regimental historian, Compton "beat him over the head with his helmet, since he had left his M1 in order to carry his fellow soldiers." Although perhaps a bit exaggerated in the later telling, his exploits this day would make Compton a legend throughout the division. Dick Good, for one, considered him "by far the bravest person I ever saw in combat . . . a notch above" other so-called heroes of the war, many of whom received greater recognition. Put in for the Medal of Honor for his heroics this day, Compton had to settle for a Bronze Star.[8]

After breaking contact with the heavily supported enemy, G Company was ordered by battalion headquarters to move upriver to Heuchlingen. There it would join E Company under Captain Garahan, the officer who had raised the first American flag over captured Bitche. His unit had fought its way north from the crossing site by hugging the railroad. Challenged by Germans dug in atop a hill about two hundred yards from the river, E Company drove them off with mortar fire, then entered Heuchlingen, one mile northeast of Jagstfeld, where it found some tanks and the 2nd Battalion's antitank platoon.[9]

In the rain-soaked darkness of evening, an exhausted G Company, which had lost 60 percent of its strength in less than eight hours of fighting, straggled into Heuchlingen to swell its infantry and armor presence. The company's morale was at an all-time low; as its historian put it, "the loss of a good many of our buddies in such a short time while we lay there powerless to aid them in any way . . . these things are just a little too much to take and still come back for more." The men tasted "for the first time the results of defeat—defeat that lowered the head of every man and brought tears to the eyes of all."[10]

While the main body of the 2nd Battalion was moving inland, F Company of the 398th, under Lt. George H. Adams, was taking fire not only frontally from the south side of the river but also from its lower flank via Jagstfeld. The men of Fox Company, who had crossed the river about a half-mile downstream from the upper column with orders to clear Jagstfeld and then press south to the Kocher River at Waldau, were, like their comrades to the north, pinned down and suffering casualties. To one victim of this cross fire, Pvt. James C. Gibson, "it seemed as though every time I moved a Jerry would take a shot at me. Being as scared as I was was bad enough, but the rain and cold made the situation almost unbearable. . . . We laid out in the open, pinned down for nearly four hours."[11]

Finally the company gained the support of some of H Company's mortar crews. The heavy weapons near Duttenberg faced south and pounded the section of Jagstfeld from which the greatest opposition had come. Almost at once, the enemy's fire from both east and south was substantially reduced, enabling the GIs to push on for Jagstfeld. Keeping between the river and the railroad, before night they were within sight of the town, which, like Heilbronn, sported a substantial industrial district. At one point the leading squad attracted sniper fire from a pillbox, forcing the men to seek shelter in three buildings north of Jagstfeld until daybreak.[12]

Early in the morning, Lieutenant Adams received orders to proceed through the town, reach the Neckar at a destroyed bridge between the town and Bad Wimpfen, and secure the riverbank until the division's engineers could put in a prefabricated truss bridge. Adams responded by dispatching two platoons, one after another, to gain footholds on the left and right flanks of Jagstfeld. The first unit met light resistance, but the second, under Lt. Joseph Ward, encountered rifle fire from houses as well as from a pillbox that barred the platoon's path across an open field. The platoon's arsenal included a bazooka, three rounds from which sent chunks of concrete flying off the walls of the little fort. The noise of the blast and the damage it inflicted persuaded the twelve SS men inside to surrender.

Believing Jagstfeld sufficiently cleared, both platoons advanced through the streets toward the Neckar. En route they were fired on from houses off their left flank. An attached section of machine guns from H Company silenced the sudden opposition and allowed the advance to proceed toward the factories on the town's east side. When hidden adversaries opened up from this sector, the advance was again halted. One of the Sherman tanks that had crossed the Jagst at Weisbach trundled up to shell the enemy into silence. Again the movement resumed, enabling both platoons to reach a factory—a condiment-processing plant—that provided a good vantage point to the south. From this perch the men observed a railroad yard that appeared to be held in some strength. The platoons pulled back a little to discuss how to surmount this latest obstacle.[13]

F Company did not have to clear Jagstfeld by itself; late on the morning of the seventh, G Company, battered and bowed but ready to fight again, had entered a residential sector of the town on the east side of the railroad yards. While F was heading for the Neckar, G had been ordered to depart Heuchlingen and secure a bridge on the Kocher River at Waldau, one of the few the Germans had failed to destroy. As had its comrades farther west, G Company had met strong opposition since reaching Jagstfeld, its men "pinned down behind gates, walls, in buildings, and any place that would afford a little cover." The hours-long fighting around the town's railroad station had taken a new toll of the company. However, thanks partially to the "splendid" support afforded by a couple of tank destroyers, the day ended in heavier loss to the Germans—twenty casualties, including the death of the local garrison commander—as well as in their retreat.

The enemy continued to suffer after dark as they ran for their lives across bare ground. They had abandoned hiding places cleared by G Company in a block-by-block sweep of its sector. Those who survived the company's deadly fire fled northeast in the direction of Hagenbach. Their assigned mission accomplished—and their morale at least partially restored—the men of G Company "sat back to catch our breath and await the next order to

continue to the attack." Doubtless to give the unit the time it needed to recover from its battering along the Jagst, that order did not
come for four days. In the interim, its men enjoyed "quite favorable conditions . . . we had plenty of fresh eggs to eat, very little
guard to pull, and a maximum of sack time."[14]

Other elements of the 2nd Battalion were not so fortunate. On
the evening of the seventh, E Company, which had been driving
snipers from the Heuchlingen area, was ordered down to Jagstfeld
to protect the battalion's left flank. Leaving one platoon in place,
the company reached its objective at two the next morning. A few
hours later it was supporting the 2nd Platoon of F Company in
driving through the factory district, shoving back German
machine gunners and mortar men. Gaining a flanking position that
commanded the open yard south of the railroad, the water-cooled
machine guns of H Company, in the words of the division's historian, "mowed the enemy down like wheat." Meanwhile, infantrymen, holed up in buildings north of the tracks, "fired in rotation at
the Jerries retreating across the open ground."

Despite the pounding they were taking and the mounting casualties, the Germans held onto the factory district, fleeing positions
riddled by rifle rounds and bazooka rockets for more defensible
ground, which they clung to with a death grip. During the night
they even managed a counterattack, peppering a building in the
railroad yard with armor-piercing bullets that killed several F
Company men. It appeared that the enemy intended to hold
Jagstfeld to the last minute—perhaps to the last man.[15]

While the fight amid the factories went on, E Company
attempted to clear a woodlot on G Company's left flank. Three
hundred yards into the trees, the unit encountered riflemen
backed by mortars, *nebelwerfer* launchers, and a flak wagon.
Captain Garahan merely pulled back to the north end of town and
dialed up an artillery barrage, which seemed to dislodge the
enemy. Apparently, appearances were deceiving. In the middle of
the afternoon, E Company again tried to clear the woods, this time
in conjunction with a platoon from G Company on its right. A
deadly succession of mortar rounds from a hidden source broke

up this effort, forcing both units to fall back north of town. The destructive fire also succeeded in blunting the advance of an E Company patrol sent to outflank the enemy from the east.

The formidable resistance of the 17th SS Panzer-Grenadiers diminished somewhat over the next two days but did not cease. Their dogged stand paid long-range dividends: it gave German engineers the time they needed to blow up the bridge at Waldau, which occurred on the ninth. Its loss meant that the 2nd Division would have to cross the Kocher by boat in the face of an entrenched and heavily armed enemy.

The altered situation called for a major change in plans, especially after reconnaissance patrols sent out on the tenth indicated that most of Jagstfeld's defenders had departed to take up positions south of the Kocher around Kochendorf. Battalion headquarters subsequently ordered E Company, now under Lt. James A. Kiddie, northeast to Hagenbach, within striking distance of Waldau. The town appeared to be heavily defended. Unlike Jagstfeld, however, it fell as soon as several platoons penetrated it from as many directions. Once the place was declared secure, patrols were sent to the Kocher in hopes of locating crossing sites. When no suitable location was found, the patrols returned to Hagenbach to spend the night of the tenth. Meanwhile, G Company was sent along the north bank of the Neckar to Bad Friedrichshall, prior to moving downriver to Neckarsulm, there to link with the regiment's 3rd Battalion.[16]

The situation improved early on the eleventh when F Company, accompanied by tanks and tank destroyers, departed Jagstfeld for Waldau. After clearing an enemy outpost, a roadblock, and a mine field, the unit entered and secured the town. From there patrols searched the river for crossing sites. Their efforts appeared successful: a footbridge across a canal in front of the river looked to be capable of supporting a crossing if SS troops on the far bank could be neutralized.

As the reunited battalion should have guessed given its many recent difficulties, this turned out to be anything but an easy operation. When F Company began to cross the bridge after dark on

After facing stiff resistance by the 17th SS Panzer-Grenadiers, elements of the 398th Infantry Regiment were able to cross the Kocher River and begin a final push into Heilbronn from the north. (*National Archives*)

the twelfth, automatic weapons and *panzerfaust* located in Kochendorf forced its lead element to take shelter beneath a railroad underpass on the north bank. To get the advance moving, the H Company mortar men unleashed a hellish fire on Kochendorf. The enemy appeared to have been cowed; a patrol that slipped across the river in the wee hours of the thirteenth encountered no resistance. This gave the rest of the battalion the confidence to attempt a major crossing of the Kocher.

The result confounded persistent fears of heavy opposition. Most GIs passed safely over the canal bridge; some waded the river where it was knee-deep; others crossed in assault craft. On the far side they moved south and seized Kochendorf, capturing eighteen half-hearted defenders. Apparently even fanatical SS troops could appreciate the futility of resistance when the end of hostilities was clearly imminent.

The division's engineers followed the infantry to Kochendorf. Roadblocks established outside the town enabled them to construct a prefabricated bridge. While they worked, large detachments of the battalion ranged upstream and down. Some cleared Odheim; others trooped down to Neckarsulm to clasp hands with their long-lost comrades of the 3rd Battalion. The latter had recently cleared the lumberyards along the railroad north of Heilbronn, opening Neckarsulm to occupation. That town was taken "with nothing but token resistance" on the rainy morning of April 13. By noon, as surviving defenders scurried away to the east and south, contact had been established between the body of the 3rd Battalion and the vanguard of 2nd. It had been nine days since the units had served side-by-side—much sweat and blood had been shed in the interim. The long and costly separation made this reunion all the sweeter.[17]

With the notable exception of C Company, which had won plaudits for its role in the fighting that engulfed the center of Heilbronn, the 399th Infantry was the last of the Century's regiments to enter combat east of the Neckar. Its 3rd Battalion, posted well to the rear on VI Corps special duty, would not cross the river until the battle was over. After making a circuitous dash through yards and fields on the west bank, A and B companies finally crossed early on the eighth, dodging barrages from German 88s that according to Private Gurley made "guys who thought they couldn't move another step suddenly sprout wings on the bridge." The remainder of the 1st Battalion, also sprightly of step, followed shortly afterward. The 2nd Battalion, which had been assigned to division reserve, would not enter the fight until the early hours of April 12.[18]

On the eighth, portions of the 2nd Battalion assumed positions on the west bank that had been vacated by the men of the 1st. Other units of the 2nd continued to occupy Schwaigern, Grossgartach, and Schluctern, while patrolling the river below Bockingen. From these and other positions artillery observers tried to shield both bridgeheads while also assisting those indefatigable engineers striving to lay more pontoons. One of the observers, Sgt. James E. Hampton of L Company, called in a strike on a position between Cloverleaf and Tower Hills from which large-caliber shells had been menacing the upper bridgehead; the enemy fire ceased immediately and permanently. Later in the day the keen-eyed Hampton detected sniper fire coming from two houses in the same area; the fire he called in pulverized both dwellings.

Other 1st Battalion observers assisted the men of the 83rd Chemical Mortar Battalion in laying smoke on a ridgeline beyond Heilbronn being used as an observation post. When the smoke failed to drive enemy observers from Tower Hill, division artillery and mortars coordinated with the P-47 Thunderbolts of XII Tactical Air Command to strike the ancient battlement. The combined effort knocked out the tower's upper section and put its occupants to flight.[19]

When A and B companies crossed to Heilbronn, they immediately joined Charlie Company around the Knorr works. C Company had set up a strongpoint three blocks from the river along the road to Flein. Meanwhile, A and B companies—now in contact with B Company of the 397th, on their left—pushed south and east from the food-processing plant to try to expand the local bridgehead.

As the GIs advanced, the troops of *Kampfgruppe* Mockros—most of them regular Wehrmacht, augmented by Volkssturm and a smattering of Waffen–SS—hit them with everything in their arsenal. At the fork of the roads to Flein and Sontheim, the leading unit, B Company, encountered 105-mm and 150-mm artillery, self-propelled guns, and *panzerfausts*, as well as machine guns and small arms. To make affairs more interesting, two Mark IVs clanked up the Flein road to lend aid to their comrades on foot. Although the fight seemed uneven, the infantrymen of B Company battled their counterparts in *feldgrau* to a standstill while comrades with bazookas took on the tanks.

Pvt. Arthur C. Grimm would receive the Distinguished Service Cross for a particularly noteworthy encounter with one of the Mark IVs. As the tank rolled past Grimm's rubble-shielded position, heading for the main body of his unit, the bazooka man dart-ed from his hiding place and fired at the rear of the tank. The driv-er, taking offense, wheeled about and came storming back at his antagonist. Grimm stood his ground, took aim, and fired again. The second round hit the tank's turret but did not penetrate the armor. A third rocket finally brought the vehicle to a halt, where-upon Grimm set it on fire with a phosphorus rocket. It was report-ed that "as the occupants spilled out they were mowed down by fire from the entire platoon."[20]

After firing a few rounds, the other tanks turned and headed back whence they had come, ending the skirmish. By 10 p.m., all three companies had achieved their objectives for the day. Able and Baker had advanced two hundred yards through the city's southern residential district, capturing fifty prisoners. C Company, in rear of its sister units, had established a position cov-ering all three of them.[21]

The street-to-street fighting on April 9 in Heilbronn's southern reaches, intense as it seemed, paled in comparison to the work required of a raiding party from A Company, which the next morn-ing moved south of the highway to Sontheim in order to clear the approaches to the battalion's primary objective, the Schlieffen Barracks. German artillery hidden in heavy timber north and west of the training school had been pummeling the southern bridge-head; if the latter was to be secured, those gun positions had to be taken out.

The raiding party faced a Herculean task. The troops of Army Group Mockros were deeply embedded in numerous shell-torn homes north of the barracks, which they had converted into minia-ture fortresses. As their comrades in the 397th had done farther north over the past six days, the raiders cleared this area—block by block, house by house, against 88-mm, 105-mm, 150-mm, and *nebelwerfer* fire. Frank Gurley may have had this operation in mind when he described his regiment's work south of Heilbronn as "factory to factory, house to house, room to room fighting. Platoon by platoon, squad by squad, dough by dough, hit and run, run and hit, over dead krauts and under barbed wire—sweating, firing, throwing grenades, charging into blazing houses, shooting through floors."[22]

Through determination, quick maneuver, and heavy firepower, by 3 p.m. the raiders had cleared a path toward the barracks. Every fortress had been conquered; dozens of variously armed defenders lay dead or wounded, and thirteen others had given themselves up. At this point the 1st Battalion paused to reorganize, assimilate reinforcements, and plan for the final drive to the Schlieffen Barracks, to take place early on the twelfth.[23]

To support the offensive against the barracks, the 2nd Battalion had been assigned to attack downriver, capturing strategically important Sontheim and towns farther south and east. The last major component of the Century to gain the east bank of the Neckar, the battalion passed over in the early hours of April 12 at the same time as a phalanx of tanks and tank destroyers. The Shermans and Hellcats crossed on the pontoon bridge, the riflemen in assault boats and rafts. All involved were subjected to a heavy shelling. No losses occurred during the crossing, but once the men reached the far side, almost a dozen were wounded by 88-mm fire and "several vehicles" were destroyed. Shaking off the damage, the battalion and its supports moved briskly to an assembly area in the southern tip of the city.[24]

Shortly after eight o'clock that morning, as the 2nd Battalion deployed along the riverbank, the 1st Battalion began a well-orchestrated assault of the Schlieffen Barracks, which comprised perhaps a dozen four- and five-story concrete buildings with deep basements, protected in front by newly dug entrenchments. Red crosses had been painted on the buildings' exteriors in hopes of discouraging Allied bombing raids. The operation began with Baker Company crossing three hundred yards of open fields north of its objective. C Company followed in column, with A Company farther to the right. A platoon of machine gunners from D Company positioned in houses on the edge of the open field provided what Harry Flanagan, now the captain commanding B Company, called "the best machine-gun support I've ever had." The company's 1st Platoon moved down a road running along the eastern side of the field; the 3rd Platoon, accompanied by two tanks, advanced on a parallel road on the western edge.[25]

Both platoons made good progress; by ten-thirty they had drawn to within sight of the trenches, some 150 yards in advance of the barracks. Most of them were empty; some contained dead Germans—they had been cleared minutes earlier by shells called in by Captain Flanagan. After piling into the abandoned holes, the GIs peppered away at the barracks buildings, through whose windows machine guns and rifles were spitting bullets. This was not the only observed resistance; mortars emplaced on the barracks parade ground pounded the area the GIs were attacking across, while a howitzer on a hill to the east was delivering what Frank Gurley called "big bore stuff." The assault troops held their ground despite this fusillade, thanks largely to the close and constant support they received from the tanks that were blasting chunks of stone from the barracks walls and pieces of tile from their roofs.[26]

After twenty minutes of firing at middle distance, the tanks lurched forward over the stone-and-sand driveways of the barracks. At a signal, the two B Company platoons abandoned their borrowed foxholes and raced to keep up with the Shermans. The well-coordinated assault appeared to confound and intimidate the enemy. The defenders of the two corner buildings in the barracks complex stopped firing, permitting the attackers to rush inside and fill the halls with rifle fire. Many Germans were killed in the ensuing melee; many others surrendered.

Although the outcome was never in doubt, room-to-room fighting reminiscent of the prolonged struggle inside Heilbronn went on for hours. Elements of Army Group Mockros, especially the SS troopers, resisted fiercely, but they were steadily forced out of the northern tier of buildings. By early afternoon opposition in that sector had virtually ceased, many defenders having fled to the central and southern parts of the complex.

A Jagdpanther lies completely destroyed at the Schlieffen Barracks in Heilbronn. (*National Archives*)

A foothold having been gained, C Company was ordered to reinforce the first wave of attack. The newcomers moved into the middle barracks, some of which they found occupied by civilians who through miscalculation had sought refuge there. In a cellar in one of the barracks, GIs found sixty people, including many foreigners, "half starved and still terrified." They also found dozens of enemy soldiers who had been dazed and disoriented by the shelling of the tanks. When they regained their senses, all were quite willing to give themselves up.

The historian of D Company observed that from an observation post overlooking the captured garrison, the GIs "had a good view of the retreating Nazis and made their retreat a hot one." While the withdrawal continued, the balance of the 1st Battalion entered the complex to help stitch up the few remaining pockets of resistance. Within another hour or so, the "Schlieffen Red Cross Club" had changed hands. An unknown number of the enemy had fled the complex entirely, taking refuge in woods to the south and east, but in their scattered and demoralized state they posed no immediate threat. A mopping-up could wait until the morning of the fourteenth.[27]

Sontheim and its environs were defended by members of *Kampfgruppe* Krebs. Composed of troops who had spent three years on occupation and coastal defense duty along the North Sea before being committed to battle in the Low Countries, this organization was probably in better fighting shape than either of the other army groups that fought in and around Heilbronn. It would give a strong account of itself on the afternoon and evening of April 12, but it would not prevail. Its opponents this day, advancing on Sontheim with confidence and momentum, were the men of the 2nd Battalion, 399th Infantry, long-suffering dogfaces who could smell victory, if unable to taste it just yet.[28]

At 4:30 p.m., some seven and a half hours after crossing the Neckar, the battalion, augmented by a platoon each of tanks and tank destroyers, began attacking industrialized Sontheim. At first opposition was heavy, forcing Sergeant Angier and his buddies in F Company, the leading unit, to stop and drop:

> To our left front was a large white house with an orchard from which they could spot our every move. With the first crack of the rifle, we hit the sides of the road and took up the firefight. All squads deployed to the left of the road with the exception of the bazooka team and the BAR team which were hidden by the bank of the river on the right. We blasted away, and in about one and one-half hours we managed to move into town and take over an old factory building.

> Another factory had been turned into a small fortress by the Germans. From there they lashed F Company and other units coming up in its rear with weaponry that included self-propelled guns.[29]

A portion of F Company mounted an indirect assault from the west but was halted by well-constructed roadblocks. Supporting units began to hesitate and look to the rear. Sgt. Hugh Gillin of G Company heard comrades yelling "'Let's get out of here. Pull back.'" The hard-bitten noncom resisted doing so, although "the Krauts are kinda yippin' and yellin' up in the town. They're acting like they're going to run us out of town. Kind of scared everybody. So we pulled back . . . and we dug in. Couldn't get the tanks to come up with us. Finally they did, came up behind us by 30 or 40 yards. Sat there. Made you feel good, at least there was a tank there."[30]

Everyone realized they could not remain immobile. There seemed no alternative to a frontal assault, which in time was resorted to. The attack was aided not only by the covering fire of the Shermans but also by searchlights which threw a "protective mantle" over the advancing troops. The assault was successful; sometime after 10 p.m., the factory was neutralized, permitting the battalion to advance to the center of the town. Here again, however, it was stopped cold, this time by a "terrific" barrage of artillery "combined with raking machine gun fire from every road vantage point."[31]

John Angier and his buddies spent the early evening "nestled in windows and doorways . . . and between artillery bursts listened for the sound of hob-nailed shoes. That night was a frightful one." Angier was not happy that his unit had entered an unfamiliar town at night—the memory of what had happened in Wingen-sur-Moder to A Company of the 398th remained fresh. Even under artificial illumination, Angier's unit was "not properly oriented as to the exact position of the Krauts. Maybe they were around the corner, or even in the next room."[32]

By dint of strenuous and persistent effort, before dawn, Fox Company succeeded in driving through to the center of the town and securing it. At about 4 a.m. on the thirteenth, in the glow of the powerful searchlights, the drive toward the southern sector was renewed. By now artillery had softened up that sector, killing and wounding many of the estimated force of two hundred Germans. The remainder were holed up in the gymnasiums and stadiums of Sontheim's Sportplatz.[33]

The GIs moved briskly down the railroad, crossing Heilbronner Strasse to Adolf Hitler Strasse. They advanced two companies abreast—E Company had come up on F's left flank. Angier reported that the adjoining units "started moving ahead, over fences, through houses, up back alleys, over coal piles and debris." In this sometimes methodical, sometimes haphazard fashion, the Sportplatz was cleared just before daylight. By 9 a.m. the Germans, including machine gunners firing from houses south and east of the soccer fields, had been silenced.[34]

Sontheim was declared fully occupied shortly after nine-thirty. "Friday, the 13th, was a lucky day for us rather than unlucky," Angier recalled. "Many decorations were won, the SS troops and the Grenadiers were not scared troops anxious to surrender, but they were out-battled. The capture of Sontheim marked the bitter end of the nine-day struggle for Heilbronn."[35]

The sergeant's pronouncement proved somewhat premature. When the mopping-up process began, E Company, with the continuing assistance of tanks, resumed its effort to make a finish to German resistance around Sontheim. On the morning of the thirteenth, the unit, now supported on the far right by G Company, encountered opposition less than a mile south of town but overrode it and kept going. About 1 p.m., the units went their separate ways, and both enjoyed a large helping of success. Easy Company angled southeast to seize the high ground that dominated Sontheim from below, while the men of George, riding on tanks, pushed west to take neighboring Horkheim. That evening the companies pursued converging routes that enabled them to link about a mile northwest of Talheim. The junction marked the extent of the 2nd Battalion's operations during the Heilbronn campaign.[36]

On the way out of Sontheim, the men of the 2nd Battalion had received news that profoundly affected many GIs: Franklin D. Roosevelt was dead, having succumbed on April 12 to a cerebral hemorrhage at the presidential retreat in Warm Springs, Georgia. Troops to the north of Heilbronn and in the city proper had already been told of the sad event. Private Sheets, who heard the news while helping clear Heilbronn of a few die-hard defenders, summarized the reaction of his comrades: "Those GIs who were Democrats were devastated by the shocking news, the apolitical had no comment and the Republican comments are not fit to print." This was, he realized, as it should be: "The ability of citizen-soldiers, in the Army of a democratic society, to voice dissenting opinions without fear of recrimination was what this blasted war was all about."[37]

On the night of the twelfth, while the troops of the 1st Battalion secured the Schlieffen Barracks, patrols made up of men from A and C companies reconnoitered the extensive woodlands east and south of the complex. The trees crowned a long ridge that rose to an average height of more than one thousand two hundred feet; German artillerymen and mortar and *nebelwerfer* crews had buried themselves deep inside the tangled expanse. Clearing this stretch of "tortured topography" was deemed of paramount importance, for it blocked the southward advance the battalion was committed to, and its defenders were dropping shells and rockets on the captured barracks, imperiling their new occupants.

Having closely examined the western edge of the woods, the patrolmen returned important intelligence on the enemy's positions and possible strength. Armed with this information, the battalion headed southeast along the road from the barracks, A Company on the right, C Company to the left, and B Company in rear of C. Before daylight on the thirteenth, the men of Able ascended the forward slope of the ridge toward a stretch of open ground at its summit. They worked their way across that ground slowly, surely, and at first, without opposition. Then, suddenly, tracer bullets from at least five machine guns ripped into the head of the company, wounding two of its scouts.

A medic attempted to reach the scout closest to the enemy position but was driven back. Two squad leaders of the 1st Platoon,

Sgts. James Amoroso and Gilbert Moniz, risked their lives to reach the wounded man; one supplied first aid while the other covered him with M1 fire. The covering fire not only protected the wounded man but killed four Germans, persuaded five others to surrender, and knocked out one of the machine guns.

To the left of the road out of Schlieffen Barracks, A Company's 3rd Platoon, moving toward the northern slope of that part of the embattled ridge known as Hill 333.1, was also brought to a halt by machine-gun fire. Five volunteers under Sgt. John Hambric managed to crawl through the trees to the rear of the position. At a critical moment Hambric bobbed up and poured rifle fire at the gunners, killing every one. Hambric then snaked his way toward another machine-gun nest farther north. Well covered by his squad, he took out this gun as well. Among his victims was a German who charged Hambric, firing a burp gun and shouting at the top of his lungs. The sergeant coolly waited till his assailant got to within forty yards of him, then cut him down with a single M1 round. A fourth machine gun, on the far right of the occupied ridge, was put out of operation minutes later by another 3rd Platoon squad leader, Sgt. Murel Mumbower. With this, resistance at all points began to fade; by 11 a.m., the ridge was firmly in the hands of A Company.[38]

While Able Company was doing yeoman work on Hill 333.1, B and C companies were gaining ground as well. At daybreak, Charlie Company attacked through the woods several hundred yards north of the southeast-running road connecting Heilbronn with Donnbronn. It was the umpteenth time the company had conducted such an assault. "Death had become cheap by now," one of its enlisted men observed. "The attacks themselves had a certain sameness about them, a dull, grim monotony."[39]

The routine mission had an unusual ending. C Company captured twenty Germans, most of whom were literally caught napping—"so well dug in, and so sure of their positions that all were sound asleep." Then, aided by a tank brought down from the barracks that helped empty several machine-gun and sniper nests, C Company pushed east about seven hundred yards against steadily decreasing opposition until the western portion of the woods had been cleared.

With the woods secure and its left flank safe from enemy attack and artillery fire, B Company advanced on the battalion's last important objective, Flein, at about 3 p.m. The unit halted just outside the town while three of its officers, including Captain Flanagan, made a personal reconnaissance of alternate routes. The three happened upon several foxholes whose occupants—fifteen, all told—surrendered without resistance. The officers decided the company should plow ahead on the main road. The fighting lasted only minutes before a dozen or so defenders hoisted a white flag. Without further opposition, B Company entered and secured Flein.[40]

Most of the local forces had retreated out the south end of town; they were dosed with artillery fire called in by B Company's forward observer. Private Knight, who accompanied the attackers, feared that other Germans had halted their retreat and were holed up "in the nearby hills looking down our throats," but the company cleared the heights and woods south of the town without difficulty. On the edge of one woodlot the men discovered an abandoned German 88. This rare capture seemed a fitting way to end the Century's last sustained operation of the war.[41]

Even after its pincers clamped shut on the city, the division had unfinished business in the streets of central Heilbronn. Early on April 11, combined elements of the 397th's 1st and 3rd battalions attacked two buildings along the much fought-over railroad to Neckarsulm. Two days earlier their occupants had blocked the efforts of I and K companies to link with the tanks and troops coming up from the south. One of these defenses was known as the Red House, the other, perhaps whimsically, as Gestapo Headquarters.

On the previous occasion, heavy fire had poured from both, so now the GIs, expecting a difficult time securing them, mapped out attack positions and brought up two tanks from the south bridge-head. Their careful preparations went for naught: when they jumped off, they found both buildings deserted. Evidently, the enemy had abandoned the center of the city. Later in the day, the Germans were located on the eastern outskirts, where they attempted to cobble together a defense line. But the volume of fire coming from this position was so weak that the Germans must have realized that the position would not withstand even a half-hearted assault. The enemy's complete withdrawal from Heilbronn was imminent.[42]

Business also remained to be attended to on the northeast side of Heilbronn. On the morning of the eleventh, several elements of the 397th moved into this sector, each with a different objective. Fox Company drove through the eastern edge of the factory district and into the residential quarter beyond. En route to Tower Hill, its main objective, the company encountered desultory resistance. It captured twenty demoralized soldiers while rescuing more than three hundred civilians found trapped in cellars throughout the residential section.

C Company of the 397th, advancing on Fox Company's right, met greater opposition, in the form of machine-gun and burp-gun fire from two houses along the railroad tracks. While a platoon of riflemen took up flanking positions, the two tanks accompanying the unit did their best to level both buildings. When the flankers fired grenades through the windows, the twenty-some occupants decided to call it quits and surrendered. Moving on, intending to connect with F Company at the base of Tower Hill, C Company discovered two more cellars filled with terrorized civilians, including six hundred foreign-born slave laborers.[43]

Farther south, elements of the 397th's 3rd Battalion, I Company in the lead, were mopping up near the junction of the railroad and the highway that led northeast to Weinsberg. For a time the unit was held up by a roadblock made largely of girders torn from nearby buildings by artillery fire. Accompanying tanks cleared the way under a storm of sniper fire. The company commander, Captain Grant, had taken position atop one of the

Shermans and was blasting the snipers with 45-caliber rounds from its Browning machine gun. Private Jelks was riding another tank, which was hit by a *panzerfaust* round from a German who unwisely barred the path of the vehicle. The rocket struck the front of the turret, which had been heavily sandbagged, and failed to penetrate. Jelks was unhurt, "but it jarred the tank driver and shook him up pretty much. He was mad as all get out and ran the Kraut down with his tank."[44]

While the 2nd and 3rd battalions pressed eastward, so did those men of the 1st Battalion operating in the city's center. B Company, on the right flank of the battalion's column, pushed as far as the south end of a railroad tunnel underneath the road to Weinsberg. C Company, on B's left flank, advanced beyond the mouth of the tunnel, captured an enemy field hospital, then pushed northeast toward a factory where its men, after driving out some last-ditch snipers, spent the night.[45]

D Company was also involved in the action near the railroad tunnel, where some of its men were hit by artillery fire. One of these, Pvt. Ernest W. Kirchheimer, suffered shrapnel wounds in both legs. The nineteen-year-old was fighting on familiar ground: he had been born and reared in Heilbronn. Six years earlier, he had emigrated with his family to America, settling in Houston, Texas, from which he entered the army. Kirchheimer's connection with Heilbronn may have helped save his life, for when evacuated to an aid station west of the Neckar, he was treated by a captured German army doctor and nurse whose faces looked very familiar. "Imagine their astonishment," Kirchheimer recalled, "when I spoke to them not only in fluent German, but in the local dialect. The doctor looked at my dog tag and I could see his amazement when he read my name. He asked if I remembered him. Of course I did. His home and office had been in the house where we lived. Our families had been good friends." Kirchheimer never again saw or spoke to the doctor who successfully operated on his legs, but he never forgot the wartime reunion that had provided "a strange and emotional experience for both of us."[46]

A lone American soldier walks through the ruins of Heilbronn on April 12, 1945, after a 9-day struggle for the city. This was the last sustained battle by American troops against Nazi Germany before the war ended in Europe. All

subsequent movements against German cities, towns, and military units met with less resistance. Within three weeks after this photograph was taken, German forces would begin to surrender en masse. (*National Archives*)

Early on the twelfth, K and L companies advanced to the railroad in order to connect with I Company. King Company then moved northeast along the highway to Weinsberg. It covered only about three hundred yards before snipers opened fire from roadside buildings, wounding four of its men. When resistance stiffened, K Company, refusing to take additional casualties needlessly, beat a temporary retreat. Later that afternoon it advanced again, this time in the company of a tank destroyer, and cleared out the snipers.

Meanwhile, L Company attacked farther south against an enemy force that had erected barriers on top of a lofty hill below the Weinsberg highway. As the company began to climb, heavy fire from a roadblock impeded its progress. It took cover and sent back for a tank destroyer, which was soon pointing its 76-mm gun at the Germans behind the barrier. In front of the Hellcat stood a group of six Germans, recently captured in a house deceptively marked as a hospital. As L Company's commander had anticipated, the defenders were unwilling to imperil the lives of their comrades; seventeen came out from behind the roadblock, hands in the air. With the prisoners corralled and the road to Weinsberg cleared, the 3rd Battalion was soon on its way out of Heilbronn, never to return.[47]

Perhaps fittingly, the final spate of fighting in Heilbronn took place where it had begun a week earlier—a millennium in the minds of GIs forced to fight their way yard by exhausting yard through streets awash in debris and blood. On the eleventh, the Anti-Tank Company of the 397th, fighting as infantry (the unit's 57-mm gun "being practically no use" in the mopping-up operations east of Heilbronn), was assigned to take Cloverleaf Hill, an unattained objective on April 4. This day, too, it proved an elusive target. When they crossed a draw along the road that ran between Cloverleaf and Tower hills, the antitankers were pinned down by intense machine-gun fire. Minutes before, the lead platoon had flushed several Germans out of foxholes at the base of the hill and had begun to pursue. "Then everything broke loose at once," one GI recalled, "and we hit the dirt. . . . The scouts on the hill and the men up front were pinned down by fire, making like snakes."

The unit's commander dispatched a platoon to outflank the hill, but before it could get into position it was again immobilized. Having lost radio contact with supporting forces, the company could not call in artillery or mortar fire. Unable to advance or retreat, its men remained in their precarious position until darkness permitted them to crawl, one by one, to the rear. Private O'Brien, who had been left behind when the rest of the company started for the hill, watched his comrades return "with their tails dragging between their feet," frustrated and angry, and having taken casualties.[48]

Although it did not get another shot at Cloverleaf Hill, the company took great satisfaction from what transpired the next morning. For twenty minutes the artillery fire that had been lacking the previous day plastered the slopes and summit of the position. When the barrage lifted, E Company of the 397th, deployed along the western base of the heights, advanced warily to the top. Prepared for a finish fight, the attackers discovered that every defender had decamped during the night.[49]

Cloverleaf's capture left only Tower Hill—where the 1st Platoon of K Company had been overwhelmed eight days earlier— to be taken. On the afternoon of April 12, a fifteen-man patrol from F Company of the 397th, led by Sgt. James K. Russell, started up its southwestern face. The patrol encountered no trouble until nearing the shell-torn castle at the summit, when a few foxhole-dwelling Germans fired on it. Aware that they were outnumbered, they suddenly surrendered, adding to the staggering toll of 1,769 prisoners who had been taken by the Century Division.

After sending their captives to the rear, Russell had his men scour the woods around the castle for snipers. Finding none, the patrol closed in on the one-thousand-year-old battlement, rifles at the ready. To their surprise, the front gate was open—to their astonishment, a sign had been tacked to the oaken arch: "Please take note. There are only civilians in here." Sure enough, inside the GIs found only an aged caretaker and his family. Other members of the patrol, however, discovered in the basement of a cement bunker across the driveway from the castle some five hundred men, women, and children. Presumably, they had been huddling in that confined space, fearing for their lives, since the April 4 attack on the hill.

Tower Hill having been secured, the balance of F Company climbed to the summit, followed by the 2nd Battalion in its entirety. The last combat action of any consequence in and around Heilbronn was at an end. Only a few snipers with a death wish, hidden in the rubble or in the city's underground tunnels, remained to be silenced. It was on this day that division headquarters officially declared that the length and breadth of Heilbronn had been secured.

By now even those menacing German 88s, most of which had been abandoned by their crews, were in the hands of GIs who had made the grueling but satisfying climb to the top of the long-inaccessible hills behind the city. Tom Jelks's platoon took possession of one howitzer from its crew chief, an old master sergeant named Volmer: "He sure was proud of his gun and crew. We ruined his gun with thermite grenades and he was not so proud then. He was on the verge of tears."[50]

The war was not over, but the end was near. Although covered in dirt, sweat, and blood, thousands of exultant and energized Centurymen stood poised to pursue a beaten and demoralized foe in panicky flight toward a nonexistent refuge.

AFTERWORD

With the fall of Heilbronn, the war in western Germany rushed to conclusion. Yet fighting remained, and more than a few Centurymen lost their lives on the brink of victory, adding to the casualties absorbed in the streets, yards, and fields of Heilbronn: 60 killed, 250 wounded, and 112 missing and presumed captured. These figures were remarkably low considering the duration and intensity of the fighting in and around the city, and the strategic gains achieved. They testified to General Burress's defining ability to attain assigned objectives without unduly sacrificing the lives of the men he led.[1]

In a sense, the losses would be made good. Reinforcements were coming into the division from replacement depots in the rear, and the Century would soon have the support of other VI Corps components. The 63rd Infantry and the 10th Armored Divisions were advancing toward the rear of Heilbronn from north and east, respectively. They would spearhead the coming Allied effort in southwest Germany, a sweep by VI Corps up the Neckar valley toward Stuttgart and beyond, aimed at ending any chance the enemy might have of mounting a final stand in the mountains along the Austrian border. In this effort the Americans would be supported by the French First Army. General de Lattre's forces were to attack and capture Stuttgart, but only after VI Corps had bypassed that communications center to the east and south, blocking all major roads leading from the Black Forest.[2]

Not till April 16 did the army group commander, General Devers, issue formal instructions to this end. By then VI Corps, which since crossing the Rhine had been moving generally west, had completed a reorientation to the south. The Century Division, however, did not wait until the sixteenth to begin moving toward Stuttgart. Three days earlier, it had begun a multicolumn advance in that direction. The 399th Infantry held the right flank, moving from Talheim and Flein along the bank of the Neckar toward Schozach and Abstatt. Several miles to the east, the 398th was pushing south on a line from Odheim to Dahenfeld, Bitzfeld, and Buchhorn. The 397th was in the middle, striking out from Heilbronn toward Untergruppenbach and Lowenstein.[3]

Each column encountered sporadic resistance from the beaten but as-yet-unbowed enemy. Almost every day through the remainder of the month, Centurymen were killed and wounded when clearing sniper-infested towns, when ambushed from roadside woods and hills, and when removing the dozens of roadblocks the enemy had strewn across their path. The most intense fighting occurred on the eighteenth northeast of Beilstein, where the 3rd Battalion of the 399th was showered with 80- and 120-mm mortar fire from a steep, thickly wooded, almost inaccessible hill. The attempt by L and M companies to claw their way to the summit proved costly indeed. Sergeant Angier described the upshot as a chaotic melee: "Shells coming in by the hundreds, hundreds of screaming, groaning hysterical voices calling for a Medic—but there weren't enough pill-rollers to go around." By evening, when the hill was finally carried after the attackers had used "every available weapon, including pistols," the battalion had lost 17 men killed and 101 wounded—more casualties than it had suffered on any of its 170 previous days of combat.[4]

The drive and determination shown by the men of the 3rd Battalion during eleven hours of continuous fighting, which included repulsing a desperate, all-out counterattack, would win the unit its second Presidential Unit Citation (the first had been conferred for its December attack on Lemberg). It was the seventh such citation to be awarded to a component of the Century. Three

A 100th Infantry Division soldier checks a German prisoner for weapons and other contraband. (*National Archives*)

of these had celebrated the clearing of Heilbronn and its environs; they had gone to the 1st and 2nd battalions of the 397th Infantry and the 3rd Battalion of the 398th.[5]

From Beilstein and points east, the division curved southwest in a semicircular line leading back to the Neckar, on which Stuttgart sat. Over the next week there were firefights, and a few fairly substantial affairs, at such places as Obershontal, Maubach, Hertmannsweiler, Fallbach, and Stetten. But the resistance, which had a quality of last-ditch desperation, quickly dissipated. The Century stormed through one hastily evacuated Swabian town after another. Intent on bringing the enemy's retreat to a full halt, the GIs did not linger in most places long enough to post guards. The same day the 399th bled at Beilstein, two battalions of the 398th seized and cleared no fewer than twenty-two towns.

Captured soldiers and overrun civilians had begun to cooperate with the invaders, even assist them in material ways. On the twentieth, advance elements of the 399th, with the help of a German army chaplain, captured bridges across two rivers outside Winnenden before they could be blown up: their loss would have stalled indefinitely one of the division's columns.[6]

By the twenty-first, the enemy appeared to be in a state of complete collapse. Officers and men of the Wehrmacht, including many Waffen-SS, no longer committed to the concept of death before dishonor, began surrendering in droves. Even the fifth-columnists of the Wehrwolf appeared to have given up efforts to sabotage communication lines and supply depots. Having discarded their weapons, they crept back into their homes, there to stay. The Century found the roadsides lined with endless numbers of stragglers only too happy to be given the chance to surrender. On the twenty-second and twenty-third, the division captured almost two thousand Germans.

On the twenty-fourth, the division began recrossing the Neckar southeast of Stuttgart; on the west side it set to work clearing the city's suburbs. The men were mildly surprised to find Stuttgart in the hands of General de Lattre's forces. The French First Army had made more rapid progress toward its objective than General Devers had anticipated. Its gains had influenced its commander to supersede his orders to coordinate operations against Stuttgart with VI Corps. On April 18, while the Americans were still several miles above the city, de Lattre had enveloped Stuttgart from the south and east—territory that Devers had assigned to the Seventh Army.

Presented with a fait accompli, Devers acquiesced in de Lattre's unauthorized maneuver. By the twenty-second, twenty-eight thousand Germans inside Stuttgart had surrendered and the city was in French hands. Yet the army group commander was not at all pleased by his subordinate's disobedience; on the twenty-second, he ordered de Lattre to hand the city over to the Seventh Army. With the backing of Gen. Charles De Gaulle—self-appointed leader of the Free French and chief of the French provisional government—de Lattre refused. An angry Devers, who viewed the takeover of Stuttgart as a political ploy to ensure the French a seat at the peace negotiations, ordered the 100th Division to move in and take the city by force. Before an armed clash could occur, however, Devers changed his mind. Bowing to General Eisenhower's insistence that allied harmony prevail, he called off the Centurymen.[7]

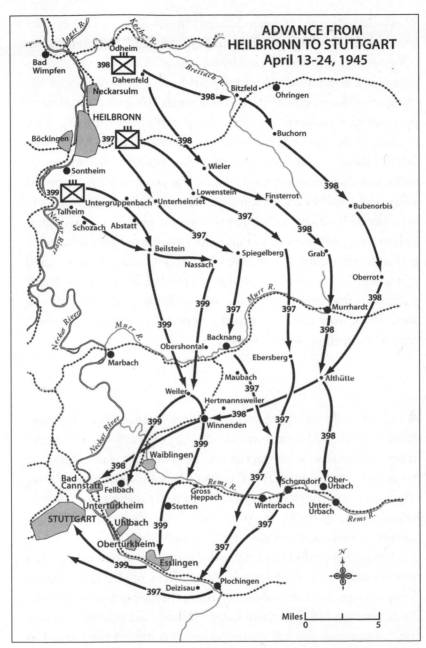

The final advance through southern Germany by the 100th Infantry Division.

A confrontation had been delayed but not averted. Two months later, SHAEF's "appeasement policy," as many GIs termed it, came to an abrupt end. Upset by reports of the city's inept governance and accusations of widespread looting and raping by the occupation force, especially by the French colonials, Eisenhower peremptorily ordered the French to withdraw. Initially, they refused. In the first week of July, a new order came down for the 397th Infantry to take over the city. The regiment, then stationed thirty miles to the south near Ulm on the Danube River, required a day and a half to reach Stuttgart. This gave the French time to consider their situation. Before his troops could be evicted at gun- or bayonet-point, the city's commander swallowed his Gallic pride and ordered a complete withdrawal. Now-Captain Law recalled that as the 397th drew within sight of the French outposts, "they pulled out that night and we occupied Stuttgart without firing a shot. Thus, what could have been a very serious rift in the embryonic western alliance was avoided."[8]

As of April 25, with all of its major components grouped around Stuttgart, the 100th Division was officially off line for the first time in six months of combat operations. Thereafter, it was assigned to Seventh Army reserve. Over the next ten days, Centurymen were relegated to guard duty around critical enemy installations such as headquarters, barracks, factories, hospitals, ammunition depots, utilities, government facilities, roads, and bridges.[9]

During this period the war in the European theater came to a quiet close. By the first week in May, forces of the 12th and 21 Army Groups had trapped enemy armies in the pocket of the Ruhr River, taking more than three hundred thousand prisoners. Their success stamped out enemy resistance in northern Germany. On May 2, Berlin fell to the Russian troops who had made contact with American forces on the River Elbe on the twenty-fifth. In the south, not enough of an organized enemy remained to man a last-ditch defense line, in the Alps or anywhere else. On May 7, with resistance on all fronts at its lowest ebb and Hitler having committed suicide in his Berlin bunker, the German high command surrendered all forces remaining in the field to Eisenhower and his lieutenants at SHAEF Headquarters in Reims, France.[10]

And so the war was over for the Century Division—its bleeding had stopped. During six and a half months of active operations, the command had suffered 4,752 casualties: 916 officers and men killed,

The announcement of the unconditional surrender of Germany is read to anxious troops on May 8, 1945. (National Archives)

3,656 wounded, and 180 missing in action. Following the trend of earlier wars, nonbattle casualties, most of them disease-related (a total of 7,425), exceeded battle losses by a considerable margin. At such cost, the division had rendered countless enemy soldiers hors de combat, including making prisoners of 13,351 of them— enough to man an average-size infantry division.[11]

The Century's reaction to Germany's surrender ran the gamut from the delirious to the subdued. In John Angier's platoon, "some of us took a last shot at a fleeing Kraut, others shook hands; Luke and I hugged each other with joy, and others got slopped-up on Schnapps." Drinking fueled the celebrating in many other units as well, as did celebratory exchanges of rifle and artillery fire. Private Sheets remembered that "it was more than a little scary for someone sober. That night all the drunks were firing their weapons including some artillery units plastering a hill with HE [high explosives]. The sounds of war were back big time and went on until perhaps 2300 hours. The only people able to sleep were the drunks who had passed out." Concerns about "incautious exuberance" prompted Bill Law to call for nonimbibing members of his company to stand guard throughout the night. A half-amused, half-disgusted Law had to put to bed a sergeant known for his abstemiousness, who had "proceeded to drink most of a newly acquired bottle of whiskey. He stepped up to the sauce like Prohibition was just around the corner."[12]

Officers were not immune from carrying on while under the influence. Captain Hine, commanding B Company of the 397th, made an appearance before his assembled unit that Private Howsmon would "remember and cherish forever." Dressed only in GI shorts, combat boots, and helmet, with a German saber strapped to his waist and a half-empty bottle of wine in one hand, Hine kept his address brief and to the point: "I want to tell you men what a helluva job you've done. Dismissed!" His words produced a flood of emotion. "We broke into cheers and tears," Howsmon recalled. "The war was over, we had made it, and the best officer in the whole army had congratulated us—in his underwear."[13]

The same news drove other men to silence and introspection. One recalled that after hearing of the surrender on the radio, he and several buddies "sat there for 2 hours and did nothing. No yelling, no throwing things in the air or getting drunk. Just sat there." While some field artillery units made the noisiest demonstration possible, one cannoneer observed that "curiously, to us it was not a day for rejoicing, but one for meditation, thinking of what had gone before and more seriously of what was to come." The artilleryman's reference was to the realization that the war in the Pacific was ongoing, and might yet engulf the Century Division. In a letter written from a hospital bed, Private Bourne, recovering from his bout with hepatitis, cautioned his parents that "the war is exactly half over. . . . I hope the Japs don't last another 5 years."[14]

In fact, within weeks of Germany's capitulation, the division was designated for shipment to the Pacific theater. By then training programs were well underway to prepare veterans and replacement troops alike for jungle fighting. The prospect of invading the Japanese mainland was worrisome, for every GI saw the typical Japanese soldier as a ferocious fighter, and as devoted to his emperor as the most fanatical SS officer had been to Hitler. The only ray of light to this gloomy prospect was the widespread belief that before shipping out to a new theater, every GI would be granted an extended leave in the States.

Neither transfer nor homecoming proved to be imminent. Early in August, the Century was alerted by Seventh Army headquarters that it would be redeployed, with a shipping date of September 10. Five days prior to the deployment alert, however, the first atomic bomb was released over Hiroshima, followed by a second over Nagasaki three days later. On August 17, General Burress could proclaim in an address to the division that "the treacherous attack of the Japanese on December 7th, 1941 has been avenged by complete defeat. For this we are grateful to our comrades in the Pacific areas."[15]

Centurymen were not grateful, however, for losing an opportunity to return to the States. Japan's surrender meant that the division would remain in Germany on occupation duty. A disappointed Edgar Longacre reported that "we had been alerted to ship home soon and lots of preparations had been made, but yesterday [August 18] everything was called off and training is to start up again tomorrow. Sure felt good while it lasted." How long their mission would continue no one could say, but, as one noncom wrote his wife from occupied Sulzbach, "it doesn't look like it is going to be such a short time."[16]

In fact, the job of subduing and controlling the German populace occupied the division until year's end, and beyond. The Century's assigned zone of occupation in southwest Germany was vast—variously estimated at between one thousand six hundred and two thousand four hundred square miles—and its duties were many and varied. Its troops guarded road intersections, bridges, and tunnels. They assisted in removing rubble and roadblocks, in defusing bombs and clearing mine fields. They assumed constabulary powers, policing every major town within their jurisdiction—questioning locals suspected of theft and other common crimes, limiting civilian travel to essential errands, and rigidly enforcing curfews. They swept the countryside for weapons and other military equipment that had not been surrendered during a publicized period of amnesty.[17]

Although the Wehrwolf had been found for the most part a toothless animal, Centurymen tracked down guerrilla leaders and stood guard over facilities and depots that might yet be the target of saboteurs and vandals. They arrested high-ranking Nazi officials and detained senior army officers for questioning. And to some degree they strove to curtail the widespread profiteering that threatened further to undermine the shattered local economy. As Private Resnick of the 399th observed, "the black market was wide open in Berlin," and its tentacles stretched to Stuttgart: "Cigarettes which cost $2 . . . in the PX [post exchange] could be sold on the black market for $200." He was incensed that many GIs—especially those military policemen charged with prohibiting it—profited from this illegal activity: "Thousands of dollars were being transferred home weekly by many of the MPs. They had had a good life in Berlin and with their loot were happy to be going home."[18]

Occupation duty also had a humanitarian aspect. Centurymen helped feed, clothe, and resettle thousands of Germans whose homes had been destroyed and livelihoods ruined. Many of the displaced persons the Centurymen cared for were foreigners, mostly ex-slaves of the German army. At times the occupation forces had to go to great lengths to prevent these people from roaming the countryside, intent on wreaking vengeance on the people whose army had abused them for so long. Officers of the division were called on to restore civil government and maintain industries and businesses disrupted by the war but considered integral to a successful occupation as well as to a reborn Germany.[19]

At first, the novelty of occupation life, especially in contrast to the hardships and dangers of combat, appealed to the GIs. Compared to the foxholes and bunkers that had been their dwelling places for the past several months, their new surroundings were sumptuous. Troops were billeted in captured barracks, private homes, and baronial estates; a few lucky enlisted men lived for weeks at a time in chalets and castles. As the historian of the 397th wrote, "the misery of 172 consecutive days on the line was rapidly dissipated in the luxury of marble stairways, plush furniture, tile baths and silk comforters. Raon-l'Etape, Mouterhouse, Rimling and Heilbronn—forgotten!—a thing of the past—as we saw our first electric lights in months and experienced the joy of hot and cold running water."[20]

The good times continued for some weeks, propped up by reviews, parades, and decoration ceremonies designed to increase esprit de corps. Morale was also enhanced by recreational sports— almost every company and battalion fielded baseball and football teams, played before bemused but fascinated locals—and by educational programs designed to facilitate the transition to civilian life and especially to give a head start to those who would attend college under the benefits of the GI Bill of Rights, passed by Congress the previous June.

The USO coordinated entertainment throughout the occupation zone; visiting actors, singers, dancers, circus acts, and comedians—including Bob Hope, Jack Benny, and Jerry Colonna—performed under its auspices. The division's chief logistics officer, Lieutenant Colonel Stegmaier, would never forget the night he took the dance floor of the local officers' club on the arm of Ingrid Bergman. And in mid-July, a deep and lasting bond was forged when hundreds of Centurymen, including General Burress and honored guests such as General Haislip, met in the Stuttgart Opera House to induct the first members of a boisterous fraternal organization known as "The Society of the Sons of Bitche." In a ceremony "as full of pomp as anything that ever graced King Arthur's Court," Pvt. Milton Trilinksy of E Company, 398th Infantry, was proclaimed "First Son." With satirical reference to the glorified titles of other fraternal societies, Sgt. David M. Swift (C Company, 399th) was anointed "Grand Exalted Biggest." The brotherhood, which would consist of several chapters and would count several thousand GIs among its members, was fated to survive as long as the veterans and their progeny kept it going.[21]

Even given these many boosts to morale and appeals to good soldiership, the early euphoria of occupation service did not endure. Many of the men had thought that once the Pacific war ended, their stay in Germany would be brief. But as their duties stretched through the summer and into the autumn, impatience and discontent mounted. Private Jelks remembered his unit's posting to the Stuttgart suburb of Bad Cannstatt as "monotonous duty" as well as inessential—much of it appeared aimed at impressing the defeated enemy: "Marching in formation every-where we went, primarily to show the Krauts what disciplined conquerors we were. Physical training, where the Krauts could see what strong, powerful brutes we were. Non-fraternization, to show the Krauts how aloof we could be."[22]

When nonfraternization rules were relaxed in mid-July, the GIs had the opportunity to get to know better their unwilling hosts. Reactions were decidedly mixed. John Sheets considered the local people "docile. Sometimes it borders on subservience." Private Khoury saw the Germans as "not the hated enemy, but rather nice, ordinary, friendly people. . . . Except for the Hitler Jugend, who scowled at us because they thought they were a superior Aryan, we found little animosity from the older civilians." Many other GIs had a much different view of the local people, the majority of whom they regarded as unrepentant for helping bring on the war. Many Germans, in fact, seemed unwilling to concede that they had been defeated. Imbued with the superman mentality, these peo-ple—lifelong civilians as well as Wehrmacht veterans—came across as arrogant and even condescending. Some employees whose places of business were now managed by American officers staged slowdowns, feigned an inability to communicate, and sabotaged equipment. Others refused to work at all, except at gunpoint.[23]

Resentful, uncooperative attitudes got under the skin of the occupiers. The people of Nurtingen, with whom Private Knight associated, universally displayed a "superior type of attitude" that kept their occupiers at a distance: "There is always going to be a barrier between the conquered and the victor." The occupation of Germany after World War I had not eradicated Germanic bellicos-ity. If the victors let their guard down, "they can still be just as dan-gerous as ever if we do not do the job right this time."[24]

Some GIs considered the Germans barbaric as well as conde-scending. That charge seemed to ring true once the horrors of the

Nazi concentration camps became widely known. That summer members of the division were sent to inspect the death camp at Dachau, which had been liberated late in April. Two men from each platoon in Bill Law's company were convoyed by truck to the camp ten miles north of Munich. Private Drury and several equally horrified comrades "toured the shower baths where they [the inmates] were gassed and the few crematory ovens. . . . Close by the crematory, we saw a small blood-soaked plot with the hanging tree, the firing squad wall, the beheading block and the pit where they were kneeling to be shot in the back of the neck."[25]

Sergeant Green, who also took the gruesome tour, expressed a typical reaction to the camp in which thousands of freed prisoners remained, awaiting deportation: "In my wildest imagination I would never have imagined man's inhumanity to man as I witnessed at Dachau that day. . . . If you can imagine a man with skin stretched tight over his skeleton—that is the way most looked." He was particularly upset to find that boxcars on the camp's railroad siding still held the bodies of hundreds of those who had gone to the showers to be gassed with Zyklon B.[26]

Within a few months, occupation had become a near-intolerable burden for most Centurymen, who desperately yearned for shipment home. Most, however, lacked the discharge points that made them eligible for redeployment. The system for determining date of discharge, widely decried as arbitrary and unfair, was based on accrued points awarded for a soldier's age, years in service, time overseas, number of children, and awards and decorations received. Most GIs had regarded medals, even those awarded for uncommon valor, of little account; now they suddenly wished they had accumulated more of them.[27]

By early fall, numbers of "high point" men were being transferred out of the division to organizations assigned an earlier discharge date. Late in September, all men with as many as sixty-five points toward discharge were ordered to prepare to ship out for home. The highest-ranking member of the division transferred out on October 13, "General Burress Day." That afternoon, on the eve of his departure for Esslingen to assume command of VI Corps, the general was honored with a commandwide review. With pomp and ceremony, the division bade their esteemed leader goodbye and wished him well as he took on the duties that went with his richly merited promotion.[28]

Except for hospitalized men, recent replacements, and those assigned military government duties, the veterans of the 100th Division received their shipment orders and sailed for home in the last weeks of the year and the early months of 1946. The great majority left Germany with a sense of having accomplished a critical mission against sometimes-dismaying odds and under living conditions too often close to unbearable. Many qualities had enabled the Centurymen to see it through: physical and mental toughness, love of country, dedication to a worthy cause, pride in doing a job well, a deep and lasting commitment to one's comrades—perhaps also a certain stubbornness and an impatience with the seemingly inessential elements of army life.

Strong leadership from the two-star down to the lowliest squad leader had gone far toward ensuring the division's operational success. So had the training the men received both in the States and overseas. Tom Bourne, for one, cited the division's extensive preparation for field service as integral to its accomplishments in France and Germany: "We did not appear on the front lines as untrained, unmotivated, and hopelessly confused victims," as certain latter-day historians have described the typical GI. "On the contrary, we were a cohesive, and in the final analysis, really superbly trained military unit. And it showed. Though we were not suddenly exposed to horrific, disastrous situations, as were the Divisions who landed in Normandy at D-Day . . . or, later, the 106th Division, one of whose early assignments was to attempt to repulse the initial German attack in the Battle of the Bulge, we were given a wartime combat assignment, and one which we carried out well."[29]

That assignment, while a lasting source of pride and satisfaction to every surviving veteran, also inflicted wounds, physical and psychological, some of which would take years to heal fully. As did thousands of comrades in other organizations, recently discharged

Centurymen faced a sometimes-uneasy transition to civilian life. For some, the period of adjustment began the minute they set foot on home ground. It began for Sam Resnick only hours after he received his discharge papers, as he walked through the streets of Brooklyn on the way to his old neighborhood. He had just emerged from the McDonald Avenue subway station, a few blocks from his family's apartment, when

> I saw two children playing with toy guns. My senses could not adjust to the fact that the guns were toys and not real and that children played with such things. . . . I stopped in my tracks, dropped my duffel bag and squatted behind it, watching the ongoing scene play out. I was in a different world—how could this transformation happen? How could this culture be so different from the one from which I just came? Don't these kids know you don't play with guns? How could they make toys and exact look-a-likes of these dangerous weapons? I picked up my duffel bag and hurriedly crossed the street to avoid the battle.

In later months, when accompanying his girlfriend to the movies, if a loud or unexpected noise on screen

> sounded like a gun going off or a shell coming in, I dropped to the floor, terrified. Any loud sound, even outdoors, caused me great fear and apprehension, even though I realized it was something other than a threat to me. . . . These reactions also caused my eyes to tear and my body to assume an almost cowering crouch, anticipating an explosion. They lasted perhaps a year or more before I could easily accept them without the physical reaction.

More than fifty years after war's end, Resnick still felt "in some small way" affected by the terrifying sights and sounds he had experienced during his career as a Centuryman: "The wounds have healed, but the scars remain."[30]

NOTES

Abbreviations

GCML	George C. Marshall Library
Intvw	Interview by the author
MSS	Letters/Manuscripts
Newsletter	*100th Infantry Division Association Newsletter*
TS	Typescript
USAHEC	U.S. Army Heritage and Education Center
100IDIS	The 100th Infantry Division Internet Site (www.100thww2.org)

Note: numbers in brackets indicate page number(s) in sources that are not paginated by the author(s).

Chapter 1: Northwind

1. Michael Bass et al., eds., *The Story of the Century* (New York, 1946), 98.

2. Bernard S. Miller Jr., *How I Took a Proficiency Exam . . . and Joined "The Greatest Generation"* (n.p., n.d.), 21-22.

3. John M. Khoury, *Love Company: L Company, 399th Infantry Regiment, of the 100th Infantry Division during World War II and Beyond* (Maywood, NJ, 2003), 73.

4. Richard E. Engler Jr., *The Final Crisis: Combat in Northern Alsace, January 1945* (Bedford, PA, 1999), 96; Operations Summary, 397th Inf. Reg., Dec. 30, 1944-Jan. 1, 1945; Operations Summary, 398th Inf. Reg., Dec. 29, 1944-Jan. 1, 1945; "Narrative History of the 399th Infantry Regiment in Combat, France, 1-31 Dec. 1944," [24]; "Narrative History of the 399th Infantry Regiment in Combat, France, 1-31 Jan. 1945," [1-3]; "Unit History of the 374th Field Artillery Battalion, 100th Infantry Division, from 1 December to 31 December 1944 Inclusive," 21; all, GCML.

5. Thomas O. Jelks, *Memoirs of a Combat Infantry Soldier* (Baltimore, n.d.), 15-16.

6. Among the better studies of the Bulge are Gerald Astor, *A Blood-Dimmed Tide: The Battle of the Bulge by the Men Who Fought It* (New York, 1993); Hugh Cole, *The Battle of the Bulge* (Old Saybrook, CT, 2001); John S. D. Eisenhower, *The Bitter Woods: The Dramatic Story . . . of the Crisis That Shook the Western Coalition. . . .* (New York, 1969); Charles McDonald, *A Time for Trumpets: The Untold Story of the Battle of the Bulge* (New York, 1997); John C. McManus, *Alamo in the Ardennes: The Untold Story of the American Soldiers Who Made the Defense of Bastogne Possible* (New York, 2007); Robert E. Merriam, *The Battle of the Bulge* (New York, 1972); Danny S. Parker, ed., *The Battle of the Bulge: The German View* (London, 1999); and John Toland, *Battle: The Story of the Bulge* (Lincoln, NE, 1999).

7. Jelks, *Combat Infantry Soldier*, 17.

8. Jeffrey J. Clarke and Robert Ross Smith, *Riviera to the Rhine (United States Army in World War II: The European Theater of Operations)* (Washington, DC, 1993), 501.

9. Miller, *How I Took a Proficiency Exam*, 22.

10. Eli Fishpaw, *The Shavetail and the Army Nurse: The Bride Wore Olive Drab* (DeLand, FL, 1998), 155.

11. Clarke and Smith, *Riviera to the Rhine*, 493-95; Charles Whiting, *The Other Battle of the Bulge: Operation Northwind* (Gloucestershire, 2007), 27-28.

12. Keith E. Bonn, *Friends and Enemies of the Century: Military Units Which Supported or Opposed the 100th Infantry Division in the European Theater of Operations, 1944-45* (Bedford, PA, 2001), 49-51; Engler, *Final Crisis*, 98-101.

13. Bass et al., eds., *Story of the Century*, 99.

14. Ibid., 101-02; Franklin Louis Gurley, ed., *399th in Action: With the 100th Infantry Division* (Stuttgart, 1945), 84.

15. Henry T. Bourne Jr., *George and Me: The Saga of an Infantryman in World War II and the Company with Whom He Fought* (Woodstock, VT, 1987), 66; Engler, *Final Crisis*, 96-98.

16. Bass et al., eds., *Story of the Century*, 100; Clarke and Smith, *Riviera to the Rhine*, 507-09; Whiting, *Other Battle of the Bulge*, 42.

17. Khoury, *Love Company*, 72.

18. Franklin Gurley, "Letter from Europe," *Newsletter* 41 (Feb. 1997): 5-7; "100th Infantry Division in World War II History," *Newsletter* 50 (July 2006): 2.

19. Gurley, ed., *399th in Action*, 79-80.

20. Ibid., 76, 80; Bass et al., eds., *Story of the Century*, 104.

21. Gurley, ed., *399th in Action*, 78; Bass et al., eds., *Story of the Century*, 103.

22. Gurley, ed., *399th in Action*, 80.

23. John D. Angier, *A 4-F Goes to War with the 100th Infantry Division* (Bennington, VT, 2008), 52.

24. Clarke and Smith, *Riviera to the Rhine*, 471-74; *Report of Operations, Seventh United States Army in France and Germany, 1944-1945*, 3 vols. (Heidelberg, 1946), 2: 482-88; Charles Whiting, *America's Forgotten Army: The Story of the U.S. Seventh* (New York, 2001), 101-02.

25. Clarke and Smith, *Riviera to the Rhine*, 505-08; Bass et al., eds., *Story of the Century*, 95, 105-06; Operations Summary, 397th Inf. Reg., Dec. 31, 1944-Jan. 1, 1945.

26. Bass et al., eds., *Story of the Century*, 106; Jelks, *Combat Infantry Soldier*, 16-17; John L. Sheets, *745 Survivor, WW-2: Combat Infantry Rifleman* (Sugarcreek, OH, 2000), 64-65.

27. Jelks, *Combat Infantry Soldier*, 17; Bass et al., eds., *Story of the Century*, 106-07; Wilfred B. Howsmon Jr., "B Company in Combat, 12 November 1944 to 8 May 1945," 20, USAHEC.

28. Bass et al., eds., *Story of the Century*, 99, 105-09; Clarke and Smith, *Riviera to the Rhine*, 505; Samuel Finkelstein et al., eds., *Regiment of the Century: The Story of the 397th Infantry Regiment* (Stuttgart, 1945), 170-73.

29. Bass et al., eds., *Story of the Century*, 107; Operations Summary, 397th Inf. Reg., Jan. 1, 1945.

30. Bass et al., eds., *Story of the Century*, 108; Jelks, *Combat Infantry Soldier*, 18-19.

31. Fishpaw, *Shavetail and the Army Nurse*, 157.

32. Sheets, *745 Survivor, WW-2*, 67.

33. Finkelstein et al., eds., *Regiment of the Century*, 170-74; Bass et al., eds., *Story of the Century*, 108-09; Allyn Vannoy, "American Stubbornness at Rimling" (online article), 1-3.

34. Finkelstein et al., eds., *Regiment of the Century*, 171.

35. Ibid., 171; Bass et al., eds., *Story of the Century*, 109.

36. Gurley, ed., *399th in Action*, 82; Arthur C. Knight, *Letters Home from a WW II 100th Division Soldier* (Missoula, MT, 1999), 93-94.

37. Bass et al., eds., *Story of the Century*, 112; Robert R. Fair, *Some Memories* (Charlottesville, VA, 1997), 52, 56.

38. Knight, *Letters Home*, 94, 226.

39. Khoury, *Love Company*, 72-73.

40. Sheets, *745 Survivor, WW-2*, 64.

41. Sam L. Resnick, "Forgotten Memories of World War II," *Newsletter* 44 (July 2000): 45.

42. Donald A. Waxman et al., *A History of Company C, 399th Infantry* (n.p., 1945), 20.

CHAPTER 2: THE 100TH INFANTRY DIVISION

1. Bass et al., eds., *Story of the Century*, 15; Finkelstein et al., eds., *Regiment of the Century*, 18.

2. Stanley Posess, ed., *Memories of a Remarkable General and Gentleman: Lieutenant General Withers A. Burress* (Beechhurst, NY, n.d.), 8, 22, 24; Keith Gibson, "Withers A. Burress—A Lifetime of Service," *Newsletter* 48 (Apr. 2001): 11; Franklin Louis Gurley, *Into the Mountains Dark: A WWII Odyssey from Harvard Crimson to Infantry Blue* (Bedford, PA, 2000), 38-39.

3. Posess, ed., *Memories of a Remarkable General*, 24; "Withers A. Burress," 1-2, Withers A. Burress MSS, USAHEC; Bernard Boston, ed., *History of the 398th Infantry Regiment in World War II* (Washington, DC, 1947), 13.

4. Posess, ed., *Memories of a Remarkable General*, 8.

5. Richard P. Drury, "The War Years—1944 to 1946," 21, GCML; "Withers A. Burress, Major General, U.S.A., Commanding General, 100th Infantry Division," 100IDIS.

6. Bass et al., eds., *Story of the Century*, 15-16; *Columbia* (SC) *Record*, Nov. 18, 1942.

7. "Maurice L. Miller, Brigadier General, U.S.A., Assistant Division Commander, 15 November 1942-27 December 1944," 100IDIS; Posess, ed., *Memories of a Remarkable General*, 2.

8. "Theodore E. Buechler, Brigadier General, U.S.A., Commanding General Division Artillery, 15 November 1942-October 1943 & August 1945-November 1945"; "John B. Murphy, Brigadier General, U.S.A., Commanding General Division Artillery, October 1943-August 1945"; both, 100IDIS.

9. "Military Biography of Andrew Christian Tychsen, Brigadier General, U.S. Army, Retired," Tychsen MSS, USAHEC; Gurley, *Into the Mountains Dark*, 46-48; "Andrew C. Tychsen, Brigadier General, U.S.A., Assistant Division Commander and, later, Commanding General, 100th Infantry Division," 100IDIS; Bass et al., eds., *Story of the Century*, 12.

10. James A. Sawicki, *Infantry Regiments of the US Army* (Dumfries, VA, 1981), 558-63; Finkelstein et al., eds., *Regiment of the Century*, 18; Boston, ed., *History of the 398th Infantry Regiment*, 8; "Military Biography of Andrew Christian Tychsen," 12, Tychsen MSS.

11. Bass et al., eds., *Story of the Century*, 15-16.

12. Angier, *A 4-F Goes to War*, 11-15, 21.

13. Ibid., 16; Bass et al., eds., *Story of the Century*, 16-18.

14. Bass et al., eds., *Story of the Century*, 18; Finkelstein et al., eds., *Regiment of the Century*, 25. According to the historian of the 397th Infantry, during the early weeks on the rifle range "scores of bandaged thumbs and swollen purple cheeks bore mute testimony to the novelty of the experience."

15. *The History of the 375th F. A. Bn.* [*Field Artillery Battalion*] (Stuttgart, 1945), 18.

16. Finkelstein et al., eds., *Regiment of the Century*, 28.

17. Intvw, J. Peter Smith (B/398), Sept. 16, 2006; Thomas J. Tillett, "Memoirs (WW II)," [1], GCML.

18. Bass et al., eds., *Story of the Century*, 22-24; Finkelstein et al., eds., *Regiment of the Century*, 28-29.

19. Bass et al., eds., *Story of the Century*, 25-30; Finkelstein et al., eds., *Regiment of the Century*, 30-33; Gurley, ed., *399th in Action*, 18; *History of the 375th F. A. Bn.*, 25-27; *Company "B," 325th Medical Battalion Combat History* (Stuttgart, 1945), 11; Catherine Cain and William Clifton Pickle, *'til Then . . . They Are Love Letters* (Olive Branch, MS, 2004), 12-32; *"And We Did": The History of the 925th Field Artillery Battalion* (Stuttgart, 1945), [20-21].

20. "Tenn. Winter Maneuvers End," *Century Sentinel*, Jan. 15, 1944; Gurley, *Into the Mountains Dark*, 37.

21. *Charlotte* (NC) *Sunday Observer*, May 14, 1944; "Pre-Deployment Training," 100IDIS; "World War II Army Specialized Training Program (ASTP)" (online article), 3; Bass et al., eds., *Story of the Century*, 30-33; Miller, *How I Took a Proficiency Exam*, 5; Hal Bingham, *Sons of Bitche* (Gainesville, FL, n.d.), [15]; Howsmon, "B Company in Combat," 4; Robert G. Tessmer, *A Soldier's Story: World War II As Seen by a Combat Veteran, December 6, 1943 through April 10, 1946* (Dearborn, MI, ca. 1994), [4]; Khoury, *Love Company*, 18-19; William C. Watson, *First-Class Privates* (Atlanta, 1994), 49; Intvw, Louis E. Lorenzo (HQ/397), Sept. 16, 2006.

22. Intvw, J. Peter Smith (B/398), Sept. 16, 2006; Miller, *How I Took a Proficiency Exam*, 3, 5-6.

23. Bourne, *George and Me*, 5; E-mail, Henry T. Bourne (G/399) to the author, Mar. 19, 2010.

24. Bass et al., eds., *Story of the Century*, 31; Finkelstein et al., eds., *Regiment of the Century*, 34; Gurley, ed., *399th in Action*, 19; Fair, *Some Memories*, 33-35; Bruno Viani, "Recollections of the Fifth War Loan Drive," *Newsletter* 47 (May 2003): 33-36; Frank E. Hancock, *An Improbable Machine Gunner* (Madison, AL, 1997), 59.

25. "Memories of the War Show," *Newsletter* 32 (Feb. 1989): 4-5; Posess, ed., *Memories of a Remarkable General*, 13; George F. Tyson Jr. and Robert V. Hamer Jr., *Company L Goes to War* (Bedford, PA, 2004), 140; Robert Kelly, "World War II Memories," 5,

GCML; Bass et al., eds., *Story of the Century*, 37; Howsmon, "B Company in Combat," 4.

26. Knight, *Letters Home*, 51; Gurley, *Into the Mountains Dark*, 37-38.

27. Knight, *Letters Home*, 46; Fair, *Some Memories*, 33. The best source on the second invasion of France is William B. Breuer, *Operation Dragoon: The Invasion of Southern France* (Novato, CA, 1987).

28. Gurley, *Into the Mountains Dark*, 55-58.

29. Fair, *Some Memories*, 35; Howsmon, "B Company in Combat," 4.

30. Bass et al., eds., *Story of the Century*, 38-40; Finkelstein et al., eds., *Regiment of the Century*, 46-49; Angier, *A 4-F Goes to War*, 23; Miller, *How I Took a Proficiency Exam*, 12; Watson, *First-Class Privates*, 57-58; Gurley, *Into the Mountains Dark*, 67-69.

31. Khoury, *Love Company*, 5-6; Bob Tessmer, "Reflections on the Atlantic Convoy," *Newsletter* 45 (Apr. 2001): 18-22; "Convoy UFG-15B—Transport Ships," *Newsletter* 45 (Apr. 2001): 18-21.

32. Khoury, *Love Company*, 7.

33. Tessmer, "Reflections on the Atlantic Convoy," 21; Caldon Norman, "European Odyssey," 3, GCML; Jack O'Brien, *Recollections of WW II* (Santa Ana, CA, 1996), 12; Rocco R. Caponigro, Memoirs, 1, GCML; Howsmon, "B Company in Combat," 5.

34. Norman, "European Odyssey," 3; Tessmer, "Reflections on the Atlantic Convoy," 19; Bill Correll, "An Infantry Soldier Temporarily Becomes a Sailor," *Newsletter* 45 (Apr. 2001): 23.

35. Bass et al., eds., *Story of the Century*, 43; A. L. Lindsey, *A Soda Jerk Goes to War* (Stanton, TX, 2001), 108-00; John F. Courter, "Remembering," 55-56, GCML.

36. Knight, *Letters Home*, 65; Gurley, *Into the Mountains Dark*, 75-76; Miller, *How I Took a Proficiency Exam*, 14; Fair, *Some Memories*, 38; Angier, *A 4-F Goes to War*, 29; Bourne, *George and Me*, 33; Jelks, *Combat Infantry Soldier*, 4; Tillett, "Memoirs (WW II)," [2]; Drury, "The War Years—1944 to 1946," 6; Tyson and Hamer, *Company L Goes to War*, 6; H. Foster Mitchem Jr., "World War II Memories," 2, GCML; Watson, *First-Class Privates*, 61; O'Brien, *Recollections of WW II*, 13; Resnick, "Forgotten Memories of World War II," 21; John Keelan, "Convoy: The Journey Itself Reveals a 'New' World," *Newsletter* 45 (Apr. 2001): 25.

37. Drury, "The War Years—1944 to 1946," 6; Fishpaw, *Shavetail and the Army Nurse*, 137; Harry J. Perrin Jr., "WW II: As I Saw It," 4, GCML.

38. Angier, *A 4-F Goes to War*, 29.

CHAPTER 3: TO THE FRONT

1. Gurley, *Into the Mountains Dark*, 77; Tyson and Hamer, *Company L Goes to War*, 7.

2. Gurley, *Into the Mountains Dark*, 75, 81.

3. Courter, "Remembering," 56; Resnick, "Forgotten Memories of World War II," 21-22.

4. Angier, *A 4-F Goes to War*, 29-33.

5. Miller, *How I Took a Proficiency Exam*, 14; Watson, *First-Class Privates*, 62; Khoury, *Love Company*, 26; Courter, "Remembering," 56.

6. Fair, *Some Memories*, 38-39; Anthony P. Altieri et al., eds., *Combat Company: U.S.*

Army, 399th Infantry Regiment, G Company (Kirchheim unter Teck, 1945), 3; Watson, *First-Class Privates*, 63; Tyson and Hamer, *Company L Goes to War*, 8.

7. Watson, *First-Class Privates*, 63-64; Hancock, *An Improbable Machine Gunner*, 70; Miller, How *I Took a Proficiency Exam*, 14.

8. Drury, "The War Years—1944 to 1946," 7; O'Brien, *Recollections of WW II*, 14.

9. Bass et al., eds., *Story of the Century*, 44-45; Khoury, *Love Company*, 26; Watson, *First-Class Privates*, 64-65; Gurley, *Into the Mountains Dark*, 86.

10. B. Lowry Bowman and Paul F. Mosher, *Company I, WW II Combat History, October 1944 through April 1945 . . . 3rd Battalion, 397th Infantry Regiment, 100th Infantry Division* (Abingdon, VA, 1996), 12.

11. Bass et al., eds., *Story of the Century*, 45; Gurley, *Into the Mountains Dark*, 79-81; Andrew C. Tychsen, "Memories of WW2," 1, Tychsen MSS.

12. Tychsen, "Memories of WW2," 1-2, Tychsen MSS.

13. Clarke and Smith, *Riviera to the Rhine*, 224-37; Russell F. Weigley, *Eisenhower's Lieutenants: The Campaigns of France and Germany, 1944-1945* (Bloomington, IN, 1981), 253-55, 260-73, 277-83, 297-301; Roland G. Ruppenthal, *Logistical Support of the Armies (United States Army in World War II: The European Theater of Operations)*, 2 vols. (Washington, DC, 1995), 2: 16-29.

14. Weigley, *Eisenhower's Lieutenants*, 301-19, 351-69.

15. Ibid., 345-46; *Report of Operations, Seventh U.S. Army*, 1: 267-86; Jacob L. Devers, "Operation Dragoon: The Invasion of Southern France," *Military Affairs* 10 (Summer 1946): 41.

16. Clarke and Smith, *Riviera to the Rhine*, 311-22, 334-45; Bowman and Mosher, *Company I, WW II Combat History*, 12-13; Frank L. Gurley, "The Vosges to Operation Northwind," *Newsletter* 29 (Feb. 1986): 1-2.

17. Keith E. Bonn, *When the Odds Were Even: The Vosges Mountains Campaign, October 1944-January 1945* (New York, 2006), 103.

18. Ibid., 1-7; "The 100th Infantry Division in World War II: What makes them so special?" 100IDIS.

19. Bonn, *Friends and Enemies of the Century*, 52-53.

20. Bourne, *George and Me*, 36, 40; Hancock, *An Improbable Machine Gunner*, 71.

21. Tychsen, "Memories of WW2," 1, Tychsen MSS; Gurley, *Into the Mountains Dark*, 89-93.

22. Khoury, *Love Company*, 31; Gurley, *Into the Mountains Dark*, 96-97.

23. Miller, *How I Took a Proficiency Exam*, 15; Roger D. Goos, Memoirs, 36-37, GCML; Bourne, *George and Me*, 40.

24. Finkelstein et al., eds., *Regiment of the Century*, 62-63.

25. Bourne, *George and Me*, 40; O'Brien, *Recollections of WW II*, 15; Hancock, *An Improbable Machine Gunner*, 72.

26. Tyson and Hamer, *Company L Goes to War*, 9-10.

27. Khoury, *Love Company*, 31; Frank L. Gurley, "First on the Front?" *Newsletter* 46 (July 2002): 12; Hancock, *An Improbable Machine Gunner*, 75; "Narrative History of the 399th Infantry Regiment [November 1944]," 1.

28. Gurley, *Into the Mountains Dark*, 99-102; Tyson and Hamer, *Company L Goes to*

War, 10; Bourne, *George and Me*, 40-43.

29. Waxman, *Company C, 399th Infantry*, 8.

30. Khoury, *Love Company*, 55; Hancock, *An Improbable Machine Gunner*, 74, 76.

31. Angier, *A 4-F Goes to War*, 36.

32. Fair, *Some Memories*, 41.

33. Gurley, ed., *399th in Action*, 175; *"And We Did,"* [41]; Bass et al., eds., *Story of the Century*, 47.

34. Clarke and Smith, *Riviera to the Rhine*, 334-36.

35. Bass et al., eds., *Story of the Century*, 48-49; Gurley, ed., *399th in Action*, 26; Tyson and Hamer, *Company L Goes to War*, 12-13.

36. Khoury, *Love Company*, 31-33.

37. Bourne, *George and Me*, 62.

38. Bass et al., eds., *Story of the Century*, 48-49; Gurley, ed., *399th in Action*, 26.

39. Angier, *A 4-F Goes to War*, 37; Bourne, *George and Me*, 41.

40. Knight, *Letters Home*, 170; "A Letter from Frank Gurley," *Newsletter* 41 (Holiday Issue, 1997): 39-41, 43; Frank L. Gurley diary, Apr. 3, 1945, USAHEC; Gurley, *Into the Mountains Dark*, 122.

41. Bass et al., eds., *Story of the Century*, 49; Gurley, *Into the Mountains Dark*, 132-39; Tyson and Hamer, *Company L Goes to War*, 12-13; Gurley, ed., *399th in Action*, 36; Fair, *Some Memories*, 42.

42. Robert M. Stegmaier, Memoir of Vosges Mountains Campaign, 1-2, GCML.

43. Finkelstein et al., eds., *Regiment of the Century*, 64; Boston, ed., *History of the 398th Infantry Regiment*, 23-24; Drury, "The War Years—1944 to 1946," 7-8; Tessmer, *A Soldier's Story*, [15]; Watson, *First-Class Privates*, 65; Norman, "European Odyssey," 7; O'Brien, *Recollections of WW II*, 14-15; Lester O. Gluesenkamp, *A Short Interval in the Life of a G. I. in World War II* (Alma, IL, ca. 1995), 21.

44. Norman, "European Odyssey," 11.

45. John Costello, "Green Arena on Top of a Ridge," *Newsletter* 47 (July 2003): 8-11; Intvw, John A. Good (H/398), Mar. 17, 2010; Intvw, Thomas Tillett (H/398), May 11, 2010.

46. Boston, ed., *History of the 398th Infantry Regiment*, 24; Operations Summary, 398th Inf. Reg., Nov. 6-8, 1944.

47. "Thad Samorajski's Recon Patrol," *Newsletter* 42 (Apr. 1998): 41-42.

48. Bass et al., eds., *Story of the Century*, 54; Clarke and Smith, *Riviera to the Rhine*, 342.

Chapter 4: The Vosges

1. Gurley, *Into the Mountains Dark*, 153.

2. Clarke and Smith, *Riviera to the Rhine*, 363-68, 387-89; Bonn, *When the Odds Were Even*, 110-24; Boston, ed., *History of the 398th Infantry Regiment*, 25.

3. Bass et al., eds., *Story of the Century*, 50-51; Gurley, ed., *399th in Action*, 27-29; Gurley, *Into the Mountains Dark*, 131-46.

4. Bass et al., eds., *Story of the Century*, 53, 203-07; *History of the 375th F. A. Bn.*, 59-60.

5. Donald Hildenbrand, "WWII Memoir of a GI from E/397," 4, GCML.

6. Khoury, *Love Company*, 34-35.

7. Bourne, *George and Me*, 37.

8. Clarke and Smith, *Riviera to the Rhine*, 388, 392; Bass et al., eds., *Story of the Century*, 55-56; Finkelstein et al., eds., *Regiment of the Century*, 78-80; Gurley, ed., *399th in Action*, 40; Bonn, *When the Odds Were Even*, 125-27.

9. Bass et al., eds., *Story of the Century*, 55; Bonn, *When the Odds Were Even*, 127-29.

10. Clarke and Smith, *Riviera to the Rhine*, 392; Jelks, *Combat Infantry Soldier*, 9.

11. Gluesenkamp, *A Short Interval in the Life of a G.I.*, 22, 26.

12. Gurley, *Into the Mountains Dark*, 165; Finkelstein et al., eds., *Regiment of the Century*, 78; Paul Mosher, "Putting on My Top Hat," *Newsletter* 46 (Apr. 2002): 38.

13. Boston, ed., *History of the 398th Infantry Regiment*, 29.

14. Gluesenkamp, *A Short Interval in the Life of a G.I.*, 26-27; Finkelstein et al., eds., *Regiment of the Century*, 79.

15. Gluesenkamp, *A Short Interval in the Life of a G.I.*, 27; Kenneth P. Bonte, *Never Too Young: A Journey with the Century* (n.p., n.d.), [33-34].

16. Boston, ed., *History of the 398th Infantry Regiment*, 25-27; *History of the 375th F. A. Bn.*, 60, 65; Operations Summary, 398th Inf. Reg., Nov. 12-17, 1944; 100th Inf. Div. S-3 Log, Nov. 12, 1944, quoted in John A. Adams, "A Division Brought Up Right," IV: 7, GCML; Finkelstein et al., eds., *Regiment of the Century*, 78-79; Gurley, ed., *399th in Action*, 33, 35.

17. Bonte, *Never Too Young*, [34].

18. Bass et al., eds., *Story of the Century*, 56-57. For a critical analysis of the fighting of the twelfth on the 397th's front by an officer who took part, see John A. Hine Jr., "The Operations of Company B, 397th Infantry (100th Infantry Division) in the Battle for Raon L'Etape, France . . . Personal Experience of a Company Commander," submitted for the Advanced Infantry Officers Course, The Infantry School (Fort Benning, GA, 1948), 37-43.

19. Bass et al., eds., *Story of the Century*, 57; Finkelstein et al., eds., *Regiment of the Century*, 79-80; Operations Summary, 397th Inf. Reg., Nov. 13, 1944; Howsmon, "B Company in Combat," 7.

20. Gurley, ed., *399th in Action*, 35; "Narrative History of the 399th Infantry Regiment [November 1944]," 7-8; Bourne, *George and Me*, 43-44.

21. Bourne, *George and Me*, 44; Bass et al., eds., *Story of the Century*, 57-58, 206; Gurley, ed., *399th in Action*, 35.

22. Posess, ed., *Memories of a Remarkable General*, 1; Recollections of 100th Inf. Div. Asst. G-2, Sept. 11, 1998, quoted in Adams, "A Division Brought Up Right," IV: 8.

23. Bass et al., eds., *Story of the Century*, 58-59; Finkelstein et al., eds., *Regiment of the Century*, 80-81.

24. Tessmer, *A Soldier's Story*, [15]; B. Lowry Bowman and Paul F. Mosher, "Company I Combat History," *Newsletter* 43 (Apr. 1999): 68-70.

25. Bowman and Mosher, "Company I Combat History," 68-69.

26. Ibid., 69; Tessmer, *A Soldier's Story*, [16].

27. Tessmer, *A Soldier's Story*, [16]; Sheets, *745 Survivor, WW-2*, 7-8.

28. Sheets, *745 Survivor, WW-2*, 8.

29. Gurley, ed., *399th in Action*, 35-36, 38; "Narrative History of the 399th Infantry

Regiment," Nov. 14, 1944; Bass et al., eds., *Story of the Century*, 59.

30. Operations Summary, 397th Inf. Reg., Nov. 15, 1944.

31. *Report of Operations, Seventh U.S. Army*, 2: 379; Gurley, ed., *399th in Action*, 38, 40-41; Gurley, *Into the Mountains Dark*, 185-92.

32. Bass et al., eds., *Story of the Century*, 59-61; Finkelstein et al., eds., *Regiment of the Century*, 80; Operations Summary, 397th Inf. Reg., Nov. 15, 1944; Bonn, *When the Odds Were Even*, 128-29.

33. Gurley, ed., *399th in Action*, 41-42; Gurley, *Into the Mountains Dark*, 193-96; "Narrative History in Combat of the 399th Infantry Regiment [November 1944]," 9-10.

34. Operations Summary, 397th Inf. Reg., Nov. 16, 1944; Bass et al., eds., *Story of the Century*, 61-62; Bowman and Mosher, "Company I Combat History," 66; Craig Davison and William J. Law, *Boxcars and Burps* (n.p., 2004), 3. The death of Col. Ellis of the 397th is covered in: Posess, ed., *Memories of a Remarkable General*, 25; Bonte, "Never Too Young," [36]; Gluesenkamp, *A Short Interval in the Life of a G.I.*, 36; Drury, "The War Years—1944 to 1946," 9, 33; William M. Marshall, "The Battle for Raon L'Etape," 4, GCML [margin comments by Sgt. O. W. Salmon, D/397].

35. "A Letter from Frank Gurley," *Newsletter* 41 (Holiday Issue, 1997): 40; Bass et al., eds., *Story of the Century*, 62.

36. Bass et al., eds., *Story of the Century*, 62-63; Gurley, ed., *399th in Action*, 41-42, 44; Gurley, *Into the Mountains Dark*, 197-214; "Century Division Quick in Adjusting to Combat: 100th Doughs Fought in Wooded Vosges With Punch That Makes Veterans," *Beachhead News* 2 (July 1, 1945): 1; Courter, "Remembering," 60; Knight, *Letters Home*, 72-73; Fair, *Some Memories*, 44.

37. Gurley, ed., *399th in Action*, 42; Tyson and Hamer, *Company L Goes to War*, 19; "Narrative History in Combat of the 399th Infantry Regiment [November 1944]," 11-12.

38. Boston, ed., *History of the 398th Infantry Regiment*, 27; Gurley, *Into the Mountains Dark*, 218-20.

39. Bass et al., eds., *Story of the Century*, 64; Finkelstein et al., eds., *Regiment of the Century*, 81; Bonte, *Never Too Young*, [37].

40. Bass et al., eds., *Story of the Century*, 64; Howsmon, "B Company in Combat," 9-10.

41. 100th Inf. Div. G-3 Journal, Nov. 18, 1944, quoted in Adams, "A Division Brought Up Right," IV: 12; Clarke and Smith, *Riviera to the Rhine*, 394-96.

42. "Narrative History in Combat of the 399th Infantry Regiment [November 1944]," 13; Bass et al., eds., *Story of the Century*, 64-66; Boston, ed., *History of the 398th Infantry Regiment*, 29-30, 34-39.

43. Bass et al., eds., *Story of the Century*, 66; Hancock, *An Improbable Machine Gunner*, 80; O'Brien, *Recollections of WW II*, 18.

44. Boston, ed., *History of the 398th Infantry Regiment*, 41; Gurley, *Into the Mountains Dark*, 236.

45. Bass et al., eds., *Story of the Century*, 65; Gurley, *Into the Mountains Dark*, 227-28.

46. Bass et al., eds., *Story of the Century*, 66; Clarke and Smith, *Riviera to the Rhine*, 396-97.

47. Bass et al., eds., *Story of the Century*, 66-67; Operations Summary, 398th Inf. Reg., Nov. 20, 1944; "Awards & Decorations, Medal of Honor [100th Infantry Division]," 1-

2, GCML.

48. Bass et al., eds., *Story of the Century*, 67-68; Boston, ed., *History of the 398th Infantry Regiment*, 43-44; Clarke and Smith, *Riviera to the Rhine*, 397-98.

49. Bass et al., eds., *Story of the Century*, 68; *Report of Operations, Seventh U.S. Army*, 2: 439-40; Clark and Smith, *Riviera to the Rhine*, 399; Gurley, *Into the Mountains Dark*, 214.

50. Finkelstein et al., eds., *Regiment of the Century*, 82; Davison and Law, *Boxcars and Burps*, 3, 5; Sheets, *745 Survivor, WW-2*, 9; Fair, *Some Memories*, 45; Bourne, *George and Me*, 59.

51. Angier, *A 4-F Goes to War*, 44-45.

52. Tillett, "Memoirs (WW II)," [2].

53. Bass et al., eds., *Story of the Century*, 69; Gurley, ed., *399th in Action*, 47-48; Clarke and Smith, *Riviera to the Rhine*, 400-01.

CHAPTER 5: THE MAGINOT LINE

1. Franklin Louis Gurley, "Policy versus Strategy: The Defense of Strasbourg in Winter 1944-1945," *Journal of Military History* 58 (1994): 481-83; David P. Colley, *Decision at Strasbourg: Ike's Strategic Mistake to Halt the Sixth Army Group at the Rhine in 1944* (Annapolis, MD, 2008), 134-38; Harry Yeide and Mark Stout, *First to the Rhine: The 6th Army Group in World War II* (Saint Paul, MN, 2007), 255-57; Clarke and Smith, *Riviera to the Rhine*, 437-40; Alfred D. Chandler Jr., et al., eds., *The Papers of Dwight David Eisenhower: The War Years*, 5 vols. (Baltimore, 1970), 3: 2320-21; Dwight D. Eisenhower, *Crusade in Europe* (Garden City, NY, 1948), 330-32.

2. Gurley, "The Vosges to Operation Northwind," 1-2.

3. Colley, *Decision at Strasbourg*, 212; Gurley, "The Vosges to Operation Northwind," 2.

4. "Strategy of Mountain Country Fighting Won Praise of Corps Commander," *Beachhead News* 2 (July 1, 1945): 1.

5. Bass et al., eds., *Story of the Century*, 70.

6. Clarke and Smith, *Riviera to the Rhine*, 440-45.

7. Ibid., 449-54; Bonn, *When the Odds Were Even*, 149-51.

8. Bass et al., eds., *Story of the Century*, 70; Bonn, *When the Odds Were Even*, 158.

9. Bass et al., eds., *Story of the Century*, 70.

10. Gluesenkamp, *A Short Interval in the Life of a G.I.*, 49; Tyson and Hamer, *Company L Goes to War*, 55; Gurley, ed., *399th in Action*, 51.

11. Bass et al., eds., *Story of the Century*, 70-71; Cain and Pickle, *'til Then*, 179-81; Gluesenkamp, *A Short Interval in the Life of a G.I.*, 47-49; Drury, "The War Years—1944 to 1946," 11; Jelks, *Combat Infantry Soldier*, 14.

12. Miller, *How I Took a Proficiency Exam*, 15-16; Jelks, *Combat Infantry Soldier*, 10; Hildenbrand, "WWII Memoir of a GI from E/397," 2; Bourne, *George and Me*, 61, 75; E-mail, Henry T. Bourne (G/399) to the author, June 22, 2010; Norman, "European Odyssey," 16; Gerald Weber, *Gerald's WW II* (Louisville, KY, 2007), 48. A steady diet of Spam could have embarrassing consequences, as Lieutenant Fishpaw of the 374th Field Artillery Battalion found out. When the men of his battery began getting sick from subsisting day after day on the food product, Fishpaw tried to convince them that "it was all

in their head, like being seasick, where one man gets sick and makes everyone else sick." At lunch the next day, however, he became violently ill upon eating a few pieces of Spam. Upon returning from a quick trip to the latrine, he was told by several of the men: "'It's all in the head, Lieutenant, it's all in the head.'" Fishpaw, *Shavetail and the Army Nurse*, 153-54.

13. Hancock, *An Improbable Machine Gunner*, 81; Bonte, *Never Too Young*, [35]; Khoury, *Love Company*, 48; Tyson and Hamer, *Company L Goes to War*, 29; Weber, *Gerald's WW II*, 48; E-Mail, Henry T. Bourne (G/399) to the author, June 22, 2010.

14. Khoury, *Love Company*, 38-39.

15. Bass et al., eds., *Story of the Century*, 71.

16. Ibid., 71-72; Finkelstein et al., eds., *Regiment of the Century*, 85.

17. Bass et al., eds., *Story of the Century*, 72-73; Bowman and Mosher, "Company I Combat History," 14-16.

18. Bass et al., eds., *Story of the Century*, 73-74; Davison and Law, *Boxcars and Burps*, 6-7; Tessmer, *A Soldier's Story*, [22].

19. Bass et al., eds., *Story of the Century*, 74; Davison and Law, *Boxcars and Burps*, 7-8; Finkelstein et al., eds., *Regiment of the Century*, 112.

20. Clarke and Smith, *Riviera to the Rhine*, 455-65.

21. Bonn, *Friends and Enemies of the Century*, 54-55.

22. Clarke and Smith, *Riviera to the Rhine*, 465-68.

23. Bass et al., eds., *Story of the Century*, 72-73.

24. Ibid., 73-74; Intvw, Herman E. Rawlings (A/398), Sept. 15, 2006; Norman, "European Odyssey," 22; Caldon R. Norman, *Whatever Happened to Company A?* (Portland, OR, 1991), 26-46; "C-Notes," *Newsletter* 43 (June 1999): 13; Boston, ed., *History of the 398th Infantry Regiment*, 48-49.

25. Boston, ed., *History of the 398th Infantry Regiment*, 49; Norman, "European Odyssey," 22-23; Norman, *Whatever Happened to Company A?*, 47-57; Operations Summary, 398th Inf. Reg., Dec. 3-4, 1944.

26. Boston, ed., *History of the 398th Infantry Regiment*, 49; Operations Summary, 398th Inf. Reg., Dec. 5, 1944.

27. Operations Summary, 398th Inf. Reg., Dec. 6-7, 11, 1944; Fair, *Some Memories*, 48.

28. Boston, ed., *History of the 398th Infantry Regiment*, 46, 49-50; Fair, *Some Memories*, 48.

29. Clarke and Smith, *Riviera to the Rhine*, 468-70; Gurley, ed., *399th in Action*, 54.

30. Gurley, ed., *399th in Action*, 54-56; Bass et al., eds., *Story of the Century*, 75.

31. Bass et al., eds., *Story of the Century*, 75; Gurley, ed., *399th in Action*, 56-59.

32. Bass et al., eds., *Story of the Century*, 75-77; Gurley, ed., *399th in Action*, 59-60; "Letter from Frank Gurley," 40; "Narrative History of the 399th Infantry Regiment, in Combat, France, 1-31 Dec. 1944," [5-7].

33. "Letter from Frank Gurley," 40.

34. Bass et al., eds., *Story of the Century*, 77-78; Gurley, ed., *399th in Action*, 60-61; "Narrative History of the 399th Infantry Regiment, in Combat, France, 1-31 Dec. 1944," [7-10]; Hancock, *An Improbable Machine Gunner*, 90; Tyson and Hamer, *Company L Goes to War*, 34-36; Altieri et al., eds., *Combat Company*, 127-28.

35. Khoury, *Love Company*, 57-58.

36. Gurley, ed., *399th in Action*, 61; "Letter from Frank Gurley," 40.

37. Bass et al., eds., *Story of the Century*, 78-79; Gurley, ed., *399th in Action*, 62; Angier, *A 4-F Goes to War*, 50-51; "Narrative History of the 399th Infantry Regiment, in Combat, France, 1-31 Dec. 1944," [10-11]; Khoury, *Love Company*, 57.

38. Gurley, ed., *399th in Action*, 62.

39. Knight, *Letters Home*, 79; Khoury, *Love Company*, 59; Tyson and Hamer, *Company L Goes to War*, 46.

40. Khoury, *Love Company*, 60.

41. Bass et al., eds., *Story of the Century*, 79; Gurley, ed., *399th in Action*, 62-63.

42. Finkelstein et al., eds., *Regiment of the Century*, 115-23; Bass et al., eds., *Story of the Century*, 76-78; Operations Summary, 397th Inf. Reg., Dec. 7-12, 1944; Davison and Law, *Boxcars and Burps*, 8-9, 11-13; Hildenbrand, "WWII Memoir of a GI from E/397," 4.

43. Clarke and Smith, *Riviera to the Rhine*, 471-75; Bonn, *When the Odds Were Even*, 8-11, 150, 156, 165, 172, 175-76, 180-86, 205-06, 250; *Report of Operations, Seventh U.S. Army*, 2: 461-62, 482-83.

44. Bass et al., eds., *Story of the Century*, 80-81; Boston, ed., *History of the 398th Infantry Regiment*, 51-52; Operations Summary, 398th Inf. Reg., Dec. 12-13, 1944; Clarke and Smith, *Riviera to the Rhine*, 470-71.

45. Bass et al., eds., *Story of the Century*, 81-82; Boston, ed., *History of the 398th Infantry Regiment*, 53.

46. Bonn, *Friends and Enemies of the Century*, 2-3; Bass et al., eds., *Story of the Century*, 81-82; Boston, ed., *History of the 398th Infantry Regiment*, 55; Operations Summary, 398th Inf. Reg., Dec. 14, 1944; *History of the 375th F. A. Bn.*, 70-71; Public Relations Office, Headquarters 100th Infantry Division, "The Fight for Bitche," [3], GCML.

47. Boston, ed., *History of the 398th Infantry Regiment*, 55; Intvw, Roger Witt (H/398), Mar. 8-9, 2010.

48. Bass et al., eds., *Story of the Century*, 81-82; Boston, ed., *History of the 398th Infantry Regiment*, 55-56.

49. Bass et al., eds., *Story of the Century*, 82-83, 92; Boston, ed., *History of the 398th Infantry Regiment*, 56-57; Operations Summary, 398th Inf. Reg., Dec. 15-16, 1944; Gurley, ed., *399th in Action*, 67, 69; *History of the 925th Field Artillery Battalion*, [53-54].

50. Bass et al., eds., *Story of the Century*, 82-83; Boston, ed., *History of the 398th Infantry Regiment*, 57; "Unit History of the 374th Field Artillery Battalion, 100th Infantry Division, from 1 December to 31 December 1944 Inclusive," 13-14; Public Relations Office, HQ 100th Inf. Div., "Fight for Bitche," [5].

51. Bass et al., eds., *Story of the Century*, 82-83, 86; Gurley, ed., *399th in Action*, 64-67, 69, 71; "Narrative History of the 399th Infantry Regiment, in Combat, France, 1-31 Dec. 1944," [16-17]; "Letter from Frank Gurley," 40-41; Knight, *Letters Home*, 81; Tyson and Hamer, *Company L Goes to War*, 57-64; Waxman, *Company C, 399th Infantry*, 16-17.

52. Bass et al., eds., *Story of the Century*, 83; Boston, ed., *History of the 398th Infantry*

Regiment, 57; Operations Summary, 398th Inf. Reg., Nov. 17, 1944; *History of the 375th F. A. Bn.*, 71-72

53. Bass et al., eds., *Story of the Century*, 83; Samuel W. Pinnell, "Diary Extract—Samuel W. Pinnell," [2], GCML; Weber, *Gerald's WW II*, 73.

54. Pinnell, "Diary Extract," [2-3].

55. Bass et al., eds., *Story of the Century*, 83-85; Pinnell, "Diary Extract," [3-4].

56. Boston, ed., *History of the 398th Infantry Regiment*, 59, 61; John Frayn Turner and Robert Jackson, *Destination Berchtesgaden: The Story of the United States Seventh Army in World War II* (London, 1975), 103-05.

57. Boston, ed., *History of the 398th Infantry Regiment*, 62; Bass et al., eds., *Story of the Century*, 93.

58. Bass et al., eds., *Story of the Century*, 93-94

59. Ibid., 94; Boston, ed., *History of the 398th Infantry Regiment*, 64-66

CHAPTER 6: PLAN TENNESSEE

1. Clarke and Smith, *Riviera to the Rhine*, 475-89; *Report of Operations, Seventh U.S. Army*, 2: 494-500.

2. Clarke and Smith, *Riviera to the Rhine*, 489-91, 499-500; *Report of Operations, Seventh U.S. Army*, 2: 563-64; Bass et al., eds., *Story of the Century*, 94-96; Finkelstein et al., eds., *Regiment of the Century*, 153-54, 165; Boston, ed., *History of the 398th Infantry Regiment*, 66-69; Gurley, ed., *399th in Action*, 71.

3. Clarke and Smith, *Riviera to the Rhine*, 500-01; Bonn, *When the Odds Were Even*, 188-89.

4. Miller, *How I Took a Proficiency Exam*, 21.

5. Bass et al., eds., *Story of the Century*, 97; Bonn, *When the Odds Were Even*, 189-90.

6. *History of the 925th Field Artillery Battalion*, [58]; Tyson and Hamer, *Company L Goes to War*, 65.

7. Miller, *How I Took a Proficiency Exam*, 21; Angier, *A 4-F Goes to War*, 53.

8. Knight, *Letters Home*, 82.

9. Weber, *Gerald's WW II*, 76; Tyson and Hamer, *Company L Goes to War*, 65-66.

10. Fair, *Some Memories*, 51; Edgar T. Longacre to Grace McCormick, Dec. 22, 1944, Longacre MSS. Sergeant Longacre is the author's late father.

11. Fair, *Some Memories*, 51-52; Hancock, *An Improbable Machine Gunner*, 97.

12. Knight, *Letters Home*, 82.

13. Ibid., Miller, *How I Took a Proficiency Exam*, 21.

14. Jelks, *Combat Infantry Soldier*, 16-17.

15. Hancock, *An Improbable Machine Gunner*, 97.

16. Fair, *Some Memories*, 50; Khoury, *Love Company*, 69.

17. Angier, *A 4-F Goes to War*, 53; Bass et al., eds., *Story of the Century*, 97.

18. Gluesenkamp, *A Short Interval in the Life of a G.I.*, 86.

19. Posess, ed., *Memories of a Remarkable General*, 14-15.

20. Tychsen, "Memories of WW2," 3, Tychsen MSS; Bass et al., eds., *Story of the Century*, 96.

21. Bourne, *George and Me*, 65-66.

22. Bass et al., eds., *Story of the Century*, 96; Finkelstein et al., eds., *Regiment of the Century*, 166.

23. "Award of Silver Star, by Cpl. Bernard (Barney) Moeller," *Newsletter* 41 (Holiday Issue, 1997): 44.

24. Bass et al., eds., *Story of the Century*, 97-98; Finkelstein et al., eds., *Regiment of the Century*, 168; Operations Summary, 397th Inf. Reg., Dec. 30, 1944.

25. Bass et al., eds., *Story of the Century*, 97-98; Jim Hazen, "The Rochester Raid," 1-2, GCML; "'Rochester Raid' Leaves Dollenbach in Bad Shape," *Stars and Stripes*, January 1945.

26. Bass et al., eds., *Story of the Century*, 102-09, 112; *Report of Operations, Seventh U.S. Army*, 2: 567-68; Clarke and Smith, *Riviera to the Rhine*, 508-09; Bonn, *When the Odds Were Even*, 221-22.

27. Bass et al., eds., *Story of the Century*, 98; Bonn, *When the Odds Were Even*, 218-20.

28. Bonn, *Friends and Enemies of the Century*, 66-67; Bonn, *When the Odds Were Even*, 219-22.

29. Clarke and Smith, *Riviera to the Rhine*, 495, 509-10.

30. Bass et al., eds., *Story of the Century*, 114-15; Gurley, ed., *399th in Action*, 87, 89-90; "Narrative History of the 399th Infantry Regiment in Combat, France, 1-31 Jan. 1945," 5-6.

31. Hancock, *An Improbable Machine Gunner*, 99.

32. Bass et al., eds., *Story of the Century*, 115; Khoury, *Love Company*, 83-84.

33. Gurley, ed., *399th in Action*, 89; Bass et al., eds., *Story of the Century*, 115.

34. John P. Lonsberg, "'F' Co., 398th Infantry, January 6 thru 11th, 1945," *Newsletter* 42 (Apr. 1998): 36-39; Tychsen, "Memories of WW2," 3, Tychsen MSS.

35. Bass et al., eds., *Story of the Century*, 109, 113-14; Gluesenkamp, *A Short Interval in the Life of a G.I.*, 95; Howsmon, "B Company in Combat," 20.

36. Bonn, *When the Odds Were Even*, 223; Sheets, *745 Survivor, WW-2*, 69, 71; Bass et al., eds., *Story of the Century*, 113.

37. Bass et al., eds., *Story of the Century*, 115; Davison and Law, *Boxcars and Burps*, 18.

38. O'Brien, *Recollections of WW II*, 33-34.

39. Bass et al., eds., *Story of the Century*, 115; Finkelstein et al., eds., *Regiment of the Century*, 180.

40. Drury, "The War Years—1944 to 1946," 13-B; Hildenbrand, "WWII Memoir of a GI from E/397," 5.

41. Davison and Law, *Boxcars and Burps*, 20.

42. Bass et al., eds., *Story of the Century*, 115-17.

43. Ibid., 117-19; "Awards & Decorations, Medal of Honor [100th Infantry Division]," 2. Although awarded for a later exploit, Sergeant Carey's posthumous Medal of Honor came through in advance of Lt. Edward A. Silk's, which was presented for valor during the Vosges campaign.

44. Bass et al., eds., *Story of the Century*, 119; Intvw, Daniel H. Green (3 Batt. HQ/397), Sept. 16, 2006.

45. Bass et al., eds., *Story of the Century*, 108, 119-20; Finkelstein et al., eds., *Regiment of the Century*, 180; Operations Summary, 397th Inf. Reg., Jan. 9, 1945; Davison and

Law, *Boxcars and Burps*, 21-25; Clarence M. Rincker, "The Battle for Rimling, France," *Newsletter* 42 (Apr. 1998): 24-25; Rufus Dalton, "The Battle for Rimling," *Newsletter* 46 (Apr. 2002): 27-28; Rufus Dalton, "Battle of Rimling—Revisited," *Newsletter* 47 (Holiday Issue, 2003): 22-23.

46. Sheets, *745 Survivor, WW-2*, 72.

47. Drury, "The War Years—1944 to 1946," 13-C; O'Brien, *Recollections of WW II*, 34; Bass et al., eds., *Story of the Century*, 107-08; Sheets, *745 Survivor, WW-2*, 71-72; "Enemy Was Forced to Abandon Push at Rimling," *Beachhead News* 2 (July 1, 1945): 2.

48. Bass et al., eds., *Story of the Century*, 120-21.

49. Angier, *A 4-F Goes to War*, 57-59.

50. Bass et al., eds., *Story of the Century*, 120; "Gen. Devers Praises 100th," *Century Sentinel* 2 (Jan. 27, 1945): 1-2.

51. Bonn, *When the Odds Were Even*, 232-34.

CHAPTER 7: "SONS OF BITCHE"

1. Tessmer, *A Soldier's Story*, [41]; Jelks, *Combat Infantry Soldier*, 25.

2. Fishpaw, *Shavetail and the Army Nurse*, 158; *History of the 925th Field Artillery Battalion*, [59].

3. *History of the 925th Field Artillery Battalion*, [56].

4. Hancock, *An Improbable Machine Gunner*, 112; Boston, ed., *History of the 398th Infantry Regiment*, 78-79; Khoury, *Love Company*, 87; Weber, *Gerald's WW II*, 58.

5. Fair, *Some Memories*, 59.

6. Jelks, *Combat Infantry Soldier*, 20; Gluesenkamp, *A Short Interval in the Life of a G.I.*, 80; Khoury, *Love Company*, 62.

7. Bass et al., eds., *Story of the Century*, 122; Gurley, ed., *399th in Action*, 104; *History of the 925th Field Artillery Battalion*, [57]; Angier, *A 4-F Goes to War*, 64-65; Operations Summary, 398th Inf. Reg., Mar. 8. 1945.

8. Bass et al., eds., *Story of the Century*, 94; Davison and Law, *Boxcars and Burps*, 28.

9. Knight, *Letters Home*, 170; Khoury, *Love Company*, 47, 76-77; Tillett, "Memoirs (WW II)," [4].

10. Bourne, *George and Me*, 70, 94-95.

11. Khoury, *Love Company*, 47; E-mail, Henry T. Bourne (G/399) to the author, June 19, 2010.

12. "C-Notes," *Newsletter* 40 (Holiday Issue, 1996): 10-11.

13. Ibid.; Hancock, *An Improbable Machine Gunner*, 103; Howsmon, "B Company in Combat," 21-22. Les Gluesenkamp (C/397) spoke of what happened to his unit's "above-ground outhouse" when spring weather came to France: "The snow disappeared and guess what was everywhere you stepped. Orders soon came for everyone to dig a hole and cover all the crap." Gluesenkamp, *A Short Interval in the Life of a G.I.*, 83.

14. Miller, *How I Took a Proficiency Exam*, 23; Hancock, *An Improbable Machine Gunner*, 112.

15. Bourne, *George and Me*, 69-70.

16. Bass et al., eds., *Story of the Century*, 123; Miller, *How I Took a Proficiency Exam*, 24-25, 28; Fair, *Some Memories*, 61-62.

17. Miller, *How I Took a Proficiency Exam*, 27; Angier, *A 4-F Goes to War*, 61.

18. Waxman, *Company C, 399th Infantry*, 20, 22.

19. Drury, "The War Years—1944 to 1946," 14; Davison and Law, *Boxcars and Burps*, 28.

20. Tessmer, *A Soldier's Story*, [42]; Drury, "The War Years—1944 to 1946," 14; Miller, *How I Took a Proficiency Exam*, 26-27.

21. Khoury, *Love Company*, 80; Bonte, "Never Too Young," [53]; Gurley, ed., *399th in Action*, 51; Sheets, *745 Survivor, WW-2*, 113.

22. Angier, *A 4-F Goes to War*, 64; Bourne, *George and Me*, 86; Hancock, *An Improbable Machine Gunner*, 113.

23. Khoury, *Love Company*, 86-87.

24. Gluesenkamp, *A Short Interval in the Life of a G.I.*, 97, 112-13.

25. Sheets, *745 Survivor, WW-2*, 100-01; Khoury, *Love Company*, 100; Bass et al., eds., *Story of the Century*, 122.

26. Basil Liddell Hart, *History of the Second World War* (New York, 1970), 629-31, 663-72, 690-93.

27. Ibid., 677-78; Charles B. MacDonald, *The Last Offensive (United States Army in World War II: The European Theater of Operations)* (Washington, DC, 1973), 208-35; Bourne, *George and Me*, 86; Posess, ed., *Memories of a Remarkable General*, 11.

28. Clarke and Smith, *Riviera to the Rhine*, 558-60; MacDonald, *Last Offensive*, 252-54; *Report of Operations, Seventh U.S. Army*, 3: 698-703; Bass et al., eds., *Story of the Century*, 123-24.

29. Bass et al., eds., *Story of the Century*, 124; Staff of the 100th Infantry Division, "Battle of Bitche," *Military Review* 26 (Oct. 1946): 36-38; Edgar T. Longacre diary, Mar. 15, 1945, in possession of the author; Drury, "The War Years—1944 to 1946," 19.

30. Bass et al., eds., *Story of the Century*, 124, 126; Hancock, *An Improbable Machine Gunner*, 121.

31. Bass et al., eds., *Story of the Century*, 124-25; Staff of 100th Inf. Div., "Battle of Bitche," 38.

32. *History of the 375th F. A. Bn.*, 82.

33. Bass et al., eds., *Story of the Century*, 125; Boston, ed., *History of the 398th Infantry Regiment*, 83-85; Operations Summary, 398th Inf. Reg., Mar. 15, 1945; Intvw, Thomas Tillett (H/398), May 11, 2010.

34. Bass et al., eds., *Story of the Century*, 125; Boston, ed., *History of the 398th Infantry Regiment*, 85-86; *History of the 375th F. A. Bn.*, 83; Intvw, Thomas Tillett (H/398), May 11, 2010.

35. Walton R. Thompson, ed., *This Is George: U.S. Army, 398th Infantry Regiment, G Company* (Stuttgart-Bad Cannstatt, 1945), 74; Davison and Law, *Boxcars and Burps*, 29.

36. Bass et al., eds., *Story of the Century*, 124-25; Finkelstein et al., eds., *Regiment of the Century*, 214-15; Staff of 100th Inf. Div., "Battle of Bitche," 38-39; Bonte, *Never Too Young*, [53]; Drury, "The War Years—1944 to 1946," 20; Weber, *Gerald's WW II*, 49.

37. Bass et al., eds., *Story of the Century*, 124-25.

38. Ibid., 125; Gurley, ed., *399th in Action*, 107; "Narrative History of the 399th Infantry Regiment, 1-31 March 1945," 12-15; Staff of 100th Inf. Div., "Battle of Bitche,"

38-39.

39. Hancock, *An Improbable Machine Gunner*, 121; *History of the 375th F. A. Bn.*, 83.

40. Hancock, *An Improbable Machine Gunner*, 121.

41. Bass et al., eds., *Story of the Century*, 125-26; Angier, *A 4-F Goes to War*, 67.

42. Angier, *A 4-F Goes to War*, 67-68; Gurley, ed., *399th in Action*, 108.

43. Bass et al., eds., *Story of the Century*, 126-27; Gurley, ed., *399th in Action*, 107.

44. Bass et al., eds., *Story of the Century*, 127; Gurley, ed., *399th in Action*, 108.

45. Bass et al., eds., *Story of the Century*, 127.

46. Ibid., 127-31; Finkelstein et al., eds., *Regiment of the Century*, 216; Operations Summary, 397th Inf. Reg., Mar. 16, 1945; Knight, *Letters Home*, 114-15.

47. Bass et al., eds., *Story of the Century*, 128; Gurley, ed., *399th in Action*, 110.

48. Boston, ed., *History of the 398th Infantry Regiment*, 86; Cain and Pickle, *'til Then*, 259; "The World's Highest Flying American Flag," *Newsletter* 43 (Apr. 1999): 24.

49. Bass et al., eds., *Story of the Century*, 128; Gurley, ed., *399th in Action*, 110; "Narrative History of the 399th Infantry Regiment, 1-31 March 1945," 15-17.

50. Bass et al., eds., *Story of the Century*, 128-29; Gurley, ed., *399th in Action*, 110, 114.

51. Bass et al., eds., *Story of the Century*, 129-30; "Narrative History of the 399th Infantry Regiment, 1-31 March 1945," 17; "Centurymen Jab to Conquer 200-Year-Old Citadel," *Beachhead News* 2 (July 1, 1945), 3.

52. Hancock, *An Improbable Machine Gunner*, 122.

53. Bass et al., eds., *Story of the Century*, 131; Gurley, ed., *399th in Action*, 115.

54. Bass et al., eds., *Story of the Century*, 130-31; *Report of Operations, Seventh U.S. Army*, 3: 726-35; Drury, "The War Years—1944 to 1946," 21.

55. Keith Winston, *V-Mail: Letters of a World War II Combat Medic*, ed. by Sarah Winston (Chapel Hill, NC, 1985), 195; Bass et al., eds., *Story of the Century*, 131-32.

56. Bass et al., eds., *Story of the Century*, 131-33; Mark A. Megna, *B Co., 399th Inf.: France [and] Germany* (Stuttgart, 1945), 29-30; Winston, *V-Mail*, 196; O'Brien, *Recollections of WW II*, 44; H. E. Pollard, *Plowboy to Doughboy* (Riggins, ID, n.d.), 27; Mitchem, "World War II Memories," 9; Edgar T. Longacre diary, Mar. 22, 1945, Longacre MSS; Davison and Law, *Boxcars and Burps*, 34; Thompson, ed., *This Is George*, 75; Tillett, "Memoirs (WW II)," [4].

CHAPTER 8: FROM THE RHINE TO THE NECKAR

1. Bass et al., eds., *Story of the Century*, 136-37; Martin H. Curtis, *Situation Tactical: Memoirs of World War II Army Combat in the European Theater of Operations* (Pittsburgh, 2004), 100; Hubert Blasi and Christhard Schrenk, *Heilbronn 1944/45: Leben und Sterben einer Stadt* (Heilbronn, 1995); Werner Gauss, *Alt-Heilbronn: Wie Wir Es Kannten und Liebten* (Heilbronn, 1952). Some of the air raids on Heilbronn are mentioned in Kit C. Carter and Robert Mueller, comps., *Combat Chronology, 1941-1945: U.S. Army Air Forces in World War II* (Washington, DC, 1991), 446-47, 552, 556.

2. *Report of Operations, Seventh U.S. Army*, 3: 807-10.

3. Ibid., 3: 761-62; MacDonald, *Last Offensive*, 407-09.

4. Reuben E. Jenkins, "The Battle of the National Redoubt," 1-4, Jenkins MSS, USA-HEC.

5. Ibid., 4-5.

6. MacDonald, *Last Offensive*, 409-15.

7. Bass et al., eds., *Story of the Century*, 131; *History of the 375th F. A. Bn.*, 75-76; Tyson and Hamer, *Company L Goes to War*, 133; Bonte, *Never Too Young*, [55]; Altieri et al., eds., *Combat Company*, 30; Bourne, *George and Me*, 92-93; *Remember When? History of Fox Company, 398th Infantry, 100th Division, 7th Army, Europe, 1944-1945* (Fellbach, 1945), 117.

8. Tyson and Hamer, *Company L Goes to War*, 133; Hancock, *An Improbable Machine Gunner*, 125; "100th Crosses Rhine and Drives East," *Century Sentinel* 3 (Apr. 7, 1945):1.

9. Miller, *How I Took a Proficiency Exam*, 32; Davison and Law, *Boxcars and Burps*, 35.

10. Hancock, *An Improbable Machine Gunner*, 126; Fair, *Some Memories*, 63.

11. Bonte, *Never Too Young*, [55]; Tyson and Hamer, *Company L Goes to War*, 134; Murray Span to "Dear Mother, Father, & Dave," Apr. 3, 1945, Span MSS, USAHEC; Winston, *V-Mail*, 201; "First Passover in 11 Years Celebrated Inside Germany," *Century Sentinel* 3 (Apr. 7, 1945): 3.

12. Khoury, *Love Company*, 96.

13. Hancock, *An Improbable Machine Gunner*, 127.

14. Intvw, Joseph H. Collie (B/397), Sept. 15, 2006.

15. Hancock, *An Improbable Machine Gunner*, 126.

16. Winston, *V-Mail*, 195; Knight, *Letters Home*, 125-26.

17. Altieri et al., eds., *Combat Company*, 30.

18. Bourne, *George and Me*, 61; Intvw, John A. Good (H/398), Mar. 17, 2010; Gluesenkamp, *A Short Interval in the Life of a G.I.*, 113; O'Brien, *Recollections of WW II*, 29.

19. E-mail, Henry T. Bourne (G/399) to the author, Mar. 18, 2010; Tessmer, *A Soldier's Story*, [21]; Courter, "Remembering," 67; Knight, *Letters Home*, 127-28; Khoury, *Love Company*, 94; Winston, *V-Mail*, 199.

20. Hancock, *An Improbable Machine Gunner*, 127-28.

21. Bourne, *George and Me*, 87-88.

22. Winston, *V-Mail*, 219; Hancock, *An Improbable Machine Gunner*, 127.

23. Miller, *How I Took a Proficiency Exam*, 33.

24. Bass et al., eds., *Story of the Century*, 133-34; MacDonald, *Last Offensive*, 410.

25. Boston, ed., *History of the 398th Infantry Regiment*, 90-91; Sheets, *745 Survivor, WW-2*, 133.

26. Miller, *How I Took a Proficiency Exam*, 33; Gurley, ed., *399th in Action*, 125; Khoury, *Love Company*, 92.

27. Knight, *Letters Home*, 116.

28. Turner and Jackson, *Destination Berchtesgaden*, 158; *Report of Operations, Seventh U.S. Army*, 3: 776; O'Brien, *Recollections of WW II*, 41; Courter, "Remembering," 66.

29. Bass et al., eds., *Story of the Century*, 136-37; MacDonald, *Last Offensive*, 413-16.

30. Sheets, *745 Survivor, WW-2*, 136-37.

31. *Report of Operations, Seventh U.S. Army*, 3: 778; Bonn, *Friends and Enemies of the Century*, 69-70.

32. Bonn, *Friends and Enemies of the Century*, 58-60, 68; MacDonald, *Last Offensive*, 412-15.

33. Bonn, *Friends and Enemies of the Century*, 68-69.

34. Ibid.; Turner and Jackson, *Destination Berchtesgaden*, 160; HQ 100th Inf. Div., Battle of Heilbronn untitled TS, 32-33, Withers A. Burress MSS, USAHEC.

35. Robert M. Stegmaier, "The 100th Infantry Division," [3-4], Stegmaier MSS, USA-HEC; MacDonald, *Last Offensive*, 409-15.

36. Bass et al., eds., *Story of the Century*, 135-36; Gurley, ed., *399th in Action*, 125; Boston, ed., *History of the 398th Infantry Regiment*, 92.

37. Bass et al., eds., *Story of the Century*, 137.

38. HQ 100th Inf. Div., Battle of Heilbronn untitled TS, 12, Burress MSS.

39. Bass et al., eds., *Story of the Century*, 137; MacDonald, *Last Offensive*, 415.

40. HQ 100th Inf. Div., Battle of Heilbronn untitled TS, 1-2, Burress MSS.

41. Stegmaier, "100th Infantry Division," [3], Stegmaier MSS; Altieri et al., eds., *Combat Company*, 31.

42. Bowman and Mosher, *Company I, WW II Combat History*, 74.

43. Bass et al., eds., *Story of the Century*, 138; Jelks, *Combat Infantry Soldier*, 30-31.

44. HQ 100th Inf. Div., Battle of Heilbronn untitled TS, 2-3, Burress MSS.

45. Intvw, John E. Plamp Jr. (M/398), Sept. 15, 2006.

46. HQ 100th Inf. Div., Battle of Heilbronn untitled TS, 3, Burress MSS.

47. Intvw, John E. Plamp Jr. (M/398), Sept. 15, 2006.

48. Ibid.; Bass et al., eds., *Story of the Century*, 138-39; HQ 100th Inf. Div., Battle of Heilbronn untitled TS, 10, Burress MSS.

49. Bass et al., eds., *Story of the Century*, 139; HQ 100th Inf. Div., Battle of Heilbronn untitled TS, 4, Burress MSS; Boston, ed., *History of the 398th Infantry Regiment*, 94-95.

50. Bass et al., eds., *Story of the Century*, 139; HQ 100th Inf. Div., Battle of Heilbronn untitled TS, 4-5, Burress MSS.

51. HQ 100th Inf. Div., Battle of Heilbronn untitled TS, 5-6, Burress MSS.

52. Ibid., 8-9; Bass et al., eds., *Story of the Century*, 141.

53. Intvw, John E. Plamp Jr. (M/398), Sept. 15, 2006.

54. HQ 100th Inf. Div., Battle of Heilbronn untitled TS, 10-11, Burress MSS; Bass et al., eds., *Story of the Century*, 141.

55. Intvw, John E. Plamp Jr. (M/398), Sept. 15, 2006; Public Relations Office, HQ 100th Inf. Div., Apr. 7, 1945 [Company K, 398th Inf. Reg. at Heilbronn], quoted in *Newsletter* 24 (Feb. 1981): 7; Weber, *Gerald's WW II*, 82; Boston, ed., *History of the 398th Infantry Regiment*, 95-96.

56. Bass et al., eds., *Story of the Century*, 140; HQ 100th Inf. Div., Battle of Heilbronn untitled TS, 6, Burress MSS.

57. HQ 100th Inf. Div., Battle of Heilbronn untitled TS, 7, Burress MSS; Bass et al., eds., *Story of the Century*, 140; Operations Summary, 398th Inf. Reg., Apr. 4, 1945.

58. HQ 100th Inf. Div., Battle of Heilbronn untitled TS, 7, Burress MSS.

59. Weber, *Gerald's WW II*, 82-83; Edward J. Williams, ed., *33 Months with the One Hundredth Signal Company, 100th Infantry Division* (Stuttgart, 1945), [15].

60. Bass et al., eds., *Story of the Century*, 141; HQ 100th Inf. Div., Battle of Heilbronn untitled TS, 12-13, Burress MSS; *Report of Operations, Seventh U.S. Army*, 3: 780.

61. Bass et al., eds., *Story of the Century*, 141.

CHAPTER 9: HEILBRONN: THE ASSAULT CROSSINGS

1. Davison and Law, *Boxcars and Burps*, 39-40; William J. Law, "Objective Heilbronn," *Newsletter* 42 (Holiday Issue, 1998): 56.

2. Davison and Law, *Boxcars and Burps*, 31-40.

3. Ibid., 43; Posess, ed., *Memories of a Remarkable General*, 11; Intvw, William J. Law (E/397), Sept. 15, 2006.

4. Ibid.; Davison and Law, *Boxcars and Burps*, 40-41; Bass et al., eds., *Story of the Century*, 142; Intvw, William J. Law (E/397), Sept. 15, 2006.

5. Davison and Law, *Boxcars and Burps*, 43-44; HQ 100th Inf. Div., Battle of Heilbronn untitled TS, 17, Burress MSS; Finkelstein et al., eds., *Regiment of the Century*, 225, 227; "Operations Summary, 397th Infantry Regiment, April 1945," 3; "397th Regimental History, April [1945]," [2], GCML.

6. Bass et al., eds., *Story of the Century*, 142; Clarence M. Rincker, "An Account of the Military Service of Clarence M. Rincker During World War II," 119-20, USAHEC.

7. Davison and Law, *Boxcars and Burps*, 44.

8. Ibid.; Intvw, William J. Law (E/397), Sept. 15, 2006.

9. Davison and Law, *Boxcars and Burps*, 44.

10. Rincker, "Account of Military Service," 120-22.

11. Davison and Law, *Boxcars and Burps*, 44; Intvw, William J. Law (E/397), Sept. 15, 2006.

12. Rincker, "Account of Military Service," 122.

13. Davison and Law, *Boxcars and Burps*, 44; Bass et al., eds., *Story of the Century*, 142-43; Rufus Dalton, "Two Days of Hell at Heilbronn," *Newsletter* 53 (July 2009): 36.

14. Davison and Law, *Boxcars and Burps*, 44; Dalton, "Two Days of Hell at Heilbronn," 36.

15. Davison and Law, *Boxcars and Burps*, 44-45.

16. Ibid., 45; Bass et al., eds., *Story of the Century*, 142-43.

17. Dalton, "Two Days of Hell at Heilbronn," 36-37; HQ 100th Inf. Div., Battle of Heilbronn untitled TS, 29, Burress MSS.

18. Ibid, 36; Rincker, "Account of Military Service," 123-24.

19. Bass et al., eds., *Story of the Century*, 143; HQ 100th Inf. Div., Battle of Heilbronn untitled TS, 21-22, Burress MSS; Rincker, "Account of Military Service," 124-25; Davison and Law, *Boxcars and Burps*, 45.

20. Rincker, "Account of Military Service," 126.

21. Dalton, "Two Days of Hell at Heilbronn," 39.

22. Ibid.; Bass et al., eds., *Story of the Century*, 144.

23. Dalton, "Two Days of Hell at Heilbronn," 39-40.

24. Ibid., 40; Rincker, "Account of Military Service," 126; Pollard, *Plowboy to Doughboy*, 30.

25. Bass et al., eds., *Story of the Century*, 145; HQ 100th Inf. Div., Battle of Heilbronn

untitled TS, 24-26, Burress MSS.

26. Dalton, "Two Days of Hell at Heilbronn," 40-41.

27. Bass et al., eds., *Story of the Century*, 143-44.

28. Ibid., 146; HQ 100th Inf. Div., Battle of Heilbronn untitled TS, 14, 27, Burress MSS.

29. HQ 100th Inf. Div., Battle of Heilbronn untitled TS, 15-16, Burress MSS.

30. Ibid., 32.

31. Gene Herr, "Recollections," *Newsletter* 46 (July 2002): 20-21.

32. Bowman and Mosher, *Company I, WW II Combat History*, 78-79.

33. HQ 100th Inf. Div., Battle of Heilbronn untitled TS, 26, 30, 33, Burress MSS.

34. Ibid., 34; Christopher Ziedler, "'Sons of Bitche' in House-to-House Combat at Heilbronn," *Newsletter* 49 (July 2005): 23.

35. Perrin, "WW II: As I Saw It," 22.

36. HQ 100th Inf. Div., Battle of Heilbronn untitled TS, 34-35, Burress MSS.

37. Ibid., 35; Intvw, Thomas O. Jelks (M/397), Sept. 16, 2006.

38. Howsmon, "B Company in Combat," 27; Intvw, Joseph H. Collie (B/397), Sept. 15, 2006. Other veterans recounted to the author this same anecdote, which had been related by Lieutenant James himself at the fiftieth reunion of the 100th Infantry Division Association. All accounts were remarkably consistent, almost to the last detail.

39. Bass et al., eds., *Story of the Century*, 147; Public Relations Office, HQ 100th Inf. Div., Apr. 6, 1945 [Company I, 397th Inf. Reg. at Heilbronn], quoted in *Newsletter* 24 (Feb. 1981): 5.

40. Public Relations Office, HQ 100th Inf. Div., Apr. 6, 1945 [Company I, 397th Inf. Reg. at Heilbronn], quoted in *Newsletter* 24 (Feb. 1981): 5; Tessmer, *A Soldier's Story*, [55]; Bowman and Mosher, *Company I, WW II Combat History*, 75-76.

41. Bowman and Mosher, *Company I, WW II Combat History*, 76.

42. HQ 100th Inf. Div., Battle of Heilbronn untitled TS, 26-28, Burress MSS; Bass et al., eds., *Story of the Century*, 147.

43. Sam Stephens, "Someone Was with Me," 1-3, GCML.

44. Sheets, *745 Survivor, WW-2*, 135.

45. Bass et al., eds., *Story of the Century*, 147; HQ 100th Inf. Div., Battle of Heilbronn untitled TS, 26-30, Burress MSS.

46. HQ 100th Inf. Div., Battle of Heilbronn untitled TS, 36, Burress MSS.

47. Ibid., 36-38; Bass et al., eds., *Story of the Century*, 147-48.

48. Sheets, *745 Survivor, WW-2*, 138-39.

49. HQ 100th Inf. Div., Battle of Heilbronn untitled TS, 38-39, Burress MSS; Bowman and Mosher, *Company I, WW II Combat History*, 80.

CHAPTER 10: HEILBRONN: THE PINCERS CLOSE

1. HQ 100th Inf. Div., Battle of Heilbronn untitled TS, 39-40, Burress MSS.

2. Ibid., 39; Bass et al., eds., *Story of the Century*, 148-49.

3. Bass et al., eds., *Story of the Century*, 148; Finkelstein et al., eds., *Regiment of the Century*, 228; Operations Summary, 397th Inf. Reg., Apr. 4; "397th Regimental History, April [1945]," [2]; HQ 397th Inf. Reg., "Citation of Unit," July 20, 1945, 1-2, GCML.

4. Bonte, *Never Too Young*, [58]; Goos memoirs, 40-41; Mitchem, "World War II Memories," 11.

5. Bass et al., eds., *Story of the Century*, 148; HQ 100th Inf. Div., Battle of Heilbronn untitled TS, 41, Burress MSS.

6. Bonte, *Never Too Young*, [58-59]; Mitchem, "World War II Memories," 11-12; Gluesenkamp, *A Short Interval in the Life of a G.I.*, 137.

7. Pollard, *Plowboy to Doughboy*, 30; Bass et al., eds., *Story of the Century*, 148-49.

8. Bass et al., eds., *Story of the Century*, 149; HQ 100th Inf. Div., Battle of Heilbronn untitled TS, 42, Burress MSS; "Heilbronn Battle Rages: Fourth of City Is Cleared by 100th Division," *Beachhead News* 2 (Apr. 7, 1945): 1, 4.

9. Bass et al., eds., *Story of the Century*, 149; Gluesenkamp, *A Short Interval in the Life of a G.I.*, 140.

10. Bass et al., eds., *Story of the Century*, 149-50; HQ 100th Inf. Div., Battle of Heilbronn untitled TS, 45, Burress MSS .

11. Bass et al., eds., *Story of the Century*, 151; HQ 100th Inf. Div., Battle of Heilbronn untitled TS, 47, Burress MSS.

12. Jelks, *Combat Infantry Soldier*, 32.

13. Bass et al., eds., *Story of the Century*, 153; HQ 100th Inf. Div., Battle of Heilbronn untitled TS, 60-62, Burress MSS.

14. Pollard, *Plowboy to Doughboy*, 31-32.

15. HQ 100th Inf. Div., Battle of Heilbronn untitled TS, 62, Burress MSS.

16. Bass et al., eds., *Story of the Century*, 162-63; Boston, ed., *History of the 398th Infantry Regiment*, 99, 103, 105; *Remember When?*, 118; Operations Summary, 398th Inf. Reg., Apr. 4-5, 1945.

17. Bass et al., eds., *Story of the Century*, 163-64; Boston, ed., *History of the 398th Infantry Regiment*, 99-101, 105-06.

18. Bass et al., eds., *Story of the Century*, 168-69.

19. Ibid., 169; Boston, ed., *History of the 398th Infantry Regiment*, 122-23, 127-29; Intvw, John A. Good (H/398), Mar. 17, 2010.

20. "Colalillo Humble About Medal of Honor," *Newsletter* 52 (Apr. 2008): 12-13.

21. Boston, ed., *History of the 398th Infantry Regiment*, 122-23, 129-30; Operations Summary, 398th Inf. Reg., Apr. 7, 1945.

22. "Colalillo Humble About Medal of Honor," 13; Sheets, *745 Survivor, WW-2*, 109.

23. "Colalillo Humble About Medal of Honor," 13; Bass et al., eds., *Story of the Century*, 169-70; Boston, ed., *History of the 398th Infantry Regiment*, 130; "Awards & Decorations, Medal of Honor [100th Infantry Division]," 2-3.

24. "Colalillo Humble About Medal of Honor," 13; Bass et al., eds., *Story of the Century*, 170; Boston, ed., *History of the 398th Infantry Regiment*, 130.

25. "Colalillo Humble About Medal of Honor," 14.

26. Boston, ed., *History of the 398th Infantry Regiment*, 122-32; Bass et al., eds., *Story of the Century*, 171.

27. Bass et al., eds., *Story of the Century*, 152-53, 183; Gurley, ed., *399th in Action*, 128-29; Knight, *Letters Home*, 116; Khoury, *Love Company*, 97; Tyson and Hamer, *Company L Goes to War*, 134.

28. *Company D, 399th Infantry* (Stuttgart, 1946), 32.

29. Gurley, ed., *399th in Action*, 130.

30. Ibid., 130-33; Bass et al., eds., *Story of the Century*, 152; HQ 100th Inf. Div., Battle of Heilbronn untitled TS, 50, Burress MSS; Operations Summary, 399th Inf. Reg.; Frank L. Gurley diary, Apr. 7-8, 1945, USAHEC.

31. Bass et al., eds., *Story of the Century*, 150; HQ 100th Inf. Div., Battle of Heilbronn untitled TS, 45-46, Burress MSS; Howsmon, "B Company in Combat," 27-28.

32. Bass et al., eds., *Story of the Century*, 150, 232; HQ 100th Inf. Div., Battle of Heilbronn untitled TS, 45-46, Burress MSS; Waxman, *Company C, 399th Infantry*, 30; Stegmaier, "100th Infantry Division," [7], Stegmaier MSS.

33. Bass et al., eds., *Story of the Century*, 150; HQ 100th Inf. Div., Battle of Heilbronn untitled TS, 46, Burress MSS; Howsmon, "B Company in Combat," 28.

34. Intvw, Joseph H. Collie (B/397), Sept. 15, 2006.

35. Knight, *Letters Home*, 117.

36. Gluesenkamp, *A Short Interval in the Life of a G.I.*, 142; Jelks, *Combat Infantry Soldier*, 32; Intvw, Thomas O. Jelks (M/397), Sept. 16, 2006.

37. Bass et al., eds., *Story of the Century*, 154; Pollard, *Plowboy to Doughboy*, 31; Stephens, "Someone Was with Me," 5; "Bitter Street Fighting in Heilbronn: Nazis Make Stand Behind River Line; Battle Fanatically," *Century Sentinel* 3 (Apr. 14, 1945): 1.

38. Tessmer, *A Soldier's Story*, [56]; E-mail, Robert G. Tessmer (I/397) to the author, Aug. 18, 2005.

39. Stephens, "Someone Was with Me," 5-6; Bass et al., eds., *Story of the Century*, 154-55; HQ 100th Inf. Div., Battle of Heilbronn untitled TS, 59-60, 62-63, Burress MSS.

40. Bass et al., eds., *Story of the Century*, 151-52; HQ 100th Inf. Div., Battle of Heilbronn untitled TS, 47-49, Burress MSS; MacDonald, *Last Offensive*, 417; "Heilbronn Fight in Fourth Day: Engineers Make Good Progress on New Bridge," *Beachhead News* 2 (April 8, 1945): 1, 4.

41. Bass et al., eds., *Story of the Century*, 155; Sheets, 745 *Survivor, WW-2*, 139-40; Bowman and Mosher, *Company I, WW II Combat History*, 81.

42. Bass et al., eds., *Story of the Century*, 155-56; Operations Summary, 397th Inf. Reg., Apr. 8-9, 1945; Intvw, Thomas O. Jelks (M/397), Sept. 16, 2006.

43. Bass et al., eds., *Story of the Century*, 156-57.

44. Ibid., 157; Gluesenkamp, *A Short Interval in the Life of a G.I.*, 142, 144.

45. Bass et al., eds., *Story of the Century*, 157.

46. Operations Summary, 397th Inf. Reg., Apr. 7, 1945; HQ 397th Inf. Reg., "Citation of Unit," July 20, 1945, 3; "397th Regimental History, April [1945]," [3]; HQ 397th Inf. Reg., "S-2 Situation Report," Apr. 7, 1945, GCML; Robert E. Kirsch and Joseph T. Mete, eds., *Mission Accomplished: Written for and by Cannon Company, 397th Infantry, 100th Infantry Division* (Stuttgart, 1945), [4].

47. Joseph E. Fleming, "Vignettes from the Vosges (and Other Places the 100th Has Been)," *Newsletter* 44 (July 2000), 44.

48. Mitchem, "World War II Memories," 13.

49. Bass et al., eds., *Story of the Century*, 157-58; HQ 100th Inf. Div., Battle of Heilbronn untitled TS, 71-72, Burress MSS; Weber, *Gerald's WW II*, 84.

50. Bass et al., eds., *Story of the Century*, 158; HQ 100th Inf. Div., Battle of Heilbronn untitled TS, 72-73, Burress MSS; O'Brien, *Recollections of WW II*, 48.

51. Bass et al., eds., *Story of the Century*, 158-59; HQ 100th Inf. Div., Battle of Heilbronn untitled TS, 74-75, Burress MSS.

52. Gluesenkamp, *A Short Interval in the Life of a G.I.*, 145. One of the most vocal critics of the lack of armored support north of the city, Pvt. Clyde T. Harkleroad (I/397), persistently blamed his battalion commander, Lt. Col. Felix Tharpe. On one occasion he did so unaware that Tharpe, wearing no insignia of rank, was standing beside him. The carping GI feared a dressing-down or worse but was spared even a mild reprimand. Afterward, however, he was known to his buddies as "Colonel Harkleroad." Bowman and Mosher, *Company I, WW II Combat History*, 82.

53. D. W. Bruner et al., *Able in Combat: Co. A, 399th Inf. Rgt., 100th Division* (n.p.: The Regiment, 1945), 40; Gurley, ed., *399th in Action*, 134.

54. Bass et al., eds., *Story of the Century*, 159; HQ 100th Inf. Div., Battle of Heilbronn untitled TS, 76, Burress MSS.

55. Bass et al., eds., *Story of the Century*, 159-60.

56. Bowman and Mosher, *Company I, WW II Combat History*, 82.

57. Bass et al., eds., *Story of the Century*, 159-60; HQ 100th Inf. Div., Battle of Heilbronn untitled TS, 77-81, Burress MSS; "100th Captures Heilbronn," *Beachhead News* 2 (Apr. 13, 1945): 1; "It Took All Means to Win the City of Heilbronn," *Beachhead News* 2 (July 1, 1945): 4.

CHAPTER 11: HEILBRONN: OUT OF THE RUINS

1. *Report of Operations, Seventh U.S. Army*, 3: 776-86; MacDonald, *Last Offensive*, 416-18.

2. Thomas Tillett, Memoir of Co. H, 398th Inf. Reg., near Jagstfeld, Apr. 6-7, 1945, [1], GCML.

3. Intvw, John A. Good (H/398), Mar. 17, 2010.

4. Ibid.; Bass et al., eds., *Story of the Century*, 164; Boston, ed., *History of the 398th Infantry Regiment*, 107-08, 118-19; Operations Summary, 398th Inf. Reg., Apr. 6, 1945; *History of the 375th F. A. Bn.*, 88.

5. Tillett, Memoir of Co. H near Jagstfeld, [1-2].

6. Ibid., [2]; Bass et al., eds., *Story of the Century*, 164-65; Boston, ed., *History of the 398th Infantry Regiment*, 108, 119.

7. Boston, ed., *History of the 398th Infantry Regiment*, 109.

8. Ibid., 119; Bass et al., eds., *Story of the Century*, 165; Tillett, Memoir of Co. H near Jagstfeld, [2]; Thompson, ed., *This Is George*, 76-77; Intvw, John A. Good (H/398), Mar. 17, 2010. The 398th's history erroneously claims that Sergeant Compton became an All-American football player for the University of Alabama. In his senior season he made Third Team All-Southeastern Conference.

9. Boston, ed., *History of the 398th Infantry Regiment*, 119-20; Bass et al., eds., *Story of the Century*, 165.

10. Thompson, ed., *This Is George*, 77.

11. Bass et al., eds., *Story of the Century*, 164; Boston, ed., *History of the 398th Infantry*

Regiment, 109-10; *Remember When?*, 120.

12. Bass et al., eds., *Story of the Century*, 165-66; Boston, ed., *History of the 398th Infantry Regiment*, 110.

13. Bass et al., eds., *Story of the Century*, 166; Boston, ed., *History of the 398th Infantry Regiment*, 110-11; *Remember When?*, 121.

14. Bass et al., eds., *Story of the Century*, 166; Boston, ed., *History of the 398th Infantry Regiment*, 111, 120; Thompson, ed., *This Is George*, 77-78.

15. Bass et al., eds., *Story of the Century*, 166-67; Boston, ed., *History of the 398th Infantry Regiment*, 115; Operations Summary, 398th Inf. Reg., Apr. 7, 1945.

16. Bass et al., eds., *Story of the Century*, 167-68; Boston, ed., *History of the 398th Infantry Regiment*, 115-18.

17. Bass et al., eds., *Story of the Century*, 171-72; Boston, ed., *History of the 398th Infantry Regiment*, 113, 118, 122; Operations Summary, 398th Inf. Reg., Apr. 11, 1945; HQ 100th Inf. Div., Battle of Heilbronn untitled TS, 83-84, Burress MSS.

18. Gurley, ed., *399th in Action*, 130, 133; Frank L. Gurley diary, Apr. 8, 1945; Fair, *Some Memories*, 65.

19. Bass et al., eds., *Story of the Century*, 152-53.

20. Ibid., 152, 160-61; HQ 100th Inf. Div., Battle of Heilbronn untitled TS, 84-85, Burress MSS; Gurley, ed., *399th in Action*, 133; Megna, *B Co., 399th Inf.*, 33-34.

21. Bass et al., eds., *Story of the Century*, 161.

22. Ibid., 161-62; Gurley, ed., *399th in Action*, 133-34.

23. Bass et al., eds., *Story of the Century*, 162.

24. Ibid., 173; Miller, *How I Took a Proficiency Exam*, 34; Bourne, *George and Me*, 96; Bingham, *Sons of Bitche*, [63]; Angier, *A 4-F Goes to War*, 72.

25. Bass et al., eds., *Story of the Century*, 173; Gurley, ed., *399th in Action*, 137; Knight, *Letters Home*, 118-19; *Company D, 399th Infantry*, 33-34; Megna, *B Co., 399th Inf.*, 34; Frank L. Gurley diary, Apr. 12-13, 1945.

26. Gurley, ed., *399th in Action*, 137.

27. Ibid., 134; Bass et al., eds., *Story of the Century*, 173-74; *Company D, 399th Infantry*, 34; HQ 100th Inf. Div., Battle of Heilbronn untitled TS, 86-87, Burress MSS; "Narrative History of the 399th Infantry Regiment, 1-30 April 1945," 11-12.

28. Bonn, *Friends and Enemies of the Century*, 69; Bass et al., eds., *Story of the Century*, 174.

29. Bass et al., eds., *Story of the Century*, 174; Angier, *A 4-F Goes to War*, 73.

30. Bass et al., eds., *Story of the Century*, 174; Bourne, *George and Me*, 97.

31. Bass et al., eds., *Story of the Century*, 174; Gurley, ed., *399th in Action*, 137-38.

32. Angier, *A 4-F Goes to War*, 73.

33. Bass et al., eds., *Story of the Century*, 174; Gurley, ed., *399th in Action*, 137-38; "Narrative History of the 399th Infantry Regiment, 1-30 April 1945," 12.

34. Bass et al., eds., *Story of the Century*, 174; Gurley, ed., *399th in Action*, 138; Angier, *A 4-F Goes to War*, 73-74.

35. Angier, *A 4-F Goes to War*, 76.

36. Bass et al., eds., *Story of the Century*, 174; Gurley, ed., *399th in Action*, 138, 140-41; Altieri et al., eds., *Combat Company*, 35.

37. Waxman, *Company C, 399th Infantry*, 34; Sheets, *745 Survivor, WW-2*, 146-47.

38. Bass et al., eds., *Story of the Century*, 174-76; HQ 100th Inf. Div., Battle of Heilbronn untitled TS, 88-89, Burress MSS; Gurley, ed., *399th in Action*, 143, 145; *Company D, 399th Infantry*, 35-36.

39. Waxman, *Company C, 399th Infantry*, 34-35.

40. Bass et al., eds., *Story of the Century*, 176; HQ 100th Inf. Div., Battle of Heilbronn untitled TS, 90-91, Burress MSS; Gurley, ed., *399th in Action*, 145.

41. Knight, *Letters Home*, 120; Bass et al., eds., *Story of the Century*, 176.

42. Bass et al., eds., *Story of the Century*, 159-60; HQ 397th Inf. Reg., "Citation of Unit," July 20, 1945, 6; Operations Summary, 397th Inf. Reg., Apr. 11, 1945.

43. Bass et al., eds., *Story of the Century*, 176-77; HQ 100th Inf. Div., Battle of Heilbronn untitled TS, 92-95, Burress MSS; Pollard, *Plowboy to Doughboy*, 32.

44. Bass et al., eds., *Story of the Century*, 177; HQ 100th Inf. Div., Battle of Heilbronn untitled TS, 93-94, Burress MSS; Jelks, *Combat Infantry Soldier*, 33; Intvw, Thomas O. Jelks (M/397), Sept. 16, 2006. Jelks added that the tank driver not only ran the German down but "backed up and ran over him again. That was one thin Kraut, about two inches thick when that tank driver got through with him."

45. Bass et al., eds., *Story of the Century*, 177; HQ 100th Inf. Div., Battle of Heilbronn untitled TS, 94-95, Burress MSS.

46. Roland Giduz, "An amazing coincidence: His childhood doctor treated his battle injuries," GCML.

47. Bass et al., eds., *Story of the Century*, 177-78.

48. John J. Noor et al., eds., *ETO History of Anti Tank Company, 397th Infantry* (Esslingen-Neckar, 1945), [35, 75]; O'Brien, *Recollections of WW II*, 50-51.

49. Noor, *Anti Tank Company, 397th Infantry* [75]; Bass et al., eds., *Story of the Century*, 178; HQ 100th Inf. Div., Battle of Heilbronn untitled TS, 96-97, Burress MSS.

50. Bass et al., eds., *Story of the Century*, 178; HQ 100th Inf. Div., Battle of Heilbronn untitled TS, 97-99, Burress MSS; Jelks, *Combat Infantry Soldier*, 34.

AFTERWORD

1. Bass et al., eds., *Story of the Century*, 178.

2. *Report of Operations, Seventh U.S. Army*, 3: 789-803; MacDonald, *Last Offensive*, 122-27.

3. MacDonald, *Last Offensive*, 427; Bass et al., eds., *Story of the Century*, 179-80.

4. Bass et al., eds., *Story of the Century*, 181-85; Knight, *Letters Home*, 121-23; Gurley, ed., *399th in Action*, 147-48; Finkelstein et al., eds., *Regiment of the Century*, 255-59; "Narrative History of the 399th Infantry Regiment, 1-30 April 1945," 22-24; Ernest L. Cole, *A Soldier's Journal* (n.p., 1995), 101-02; Tessmer, *A Soldier's Story*, [63]; Tyson and Hamer, *Company L Goes to War*, 135-37; Angier, *A 4-F Goes to War*, 77-78.

5. "Battle Honors—Citation of Unit [3rd Battalion, 397th Infantry for Beilstein, Germany, Apr. 18, 1945]," quoted in Tyson and Hamer, *Company L Goes to War*, 148-49; Bass et al., eds., *Story of the Century*, 232.

6. Bass et al., eds., *Story of the Century*, 186-87, 193-94.

7. Ibid., 187-94; MacDonald, *Last Offensive*, 428-33; *Report of Operations, Seventh U.S.*

Army, 3: 803-04; Stegmaier, "100th Infantry Division," [9], Stegmaier MSS; Hancock, *An Improbable Machine Gunner*, 135-36; Fishpaw, *Shavetail and the Army Nurse*, 174.

8. Bass et al., eds., *Story of the Century*, 199; Finkelstein et al., eds., *Regiment of the Century*, 306; Drury, "The War Years—1944 to 1946," 25; Knight, *Letters Home*, 181; Miller, *How I Took a Proficiency Exam*, 41; Jelks, *Combat Infantry Soldier*, 36; Davison and Law, *Boxcars and Burps*, 50.

9. Bass et al., eds., *Story of the Century*, 195.

10. Ibid., 195-96; Liddell Hart, *Second World War*, 677-80; Chandler et al., eds., *Papers of Dwight David Eisenhower*, 3: 2695-96.

11. Bass et al., eds., *Story of the Century*, 196. The casualty figures are from the Office of the Theater Historian, *Order of Battle: United States Army in World War II—European Theater of Operations* (December 1945), quoted in Bourne, *George and Me*, 107-08.

12. Angier, *A 4-F Goes to War*, 79; Sheets, *745 Survivor, WW-2*, 158-59; Davison and Law, *Boxcars and Burps*, 50.

13. Goos memoirs, 41; Howsmon, "B Company in Combat," 32.

14. Caponigro memoirs, 2; *Past in Review: The History of the 374th Field Artillery Battalion, 100th Infantry Division* (n.p., 1945), [26]; Bourne, *George and Me*, 95.

15. Bass et al., eds., *Story of the Century*, 200-01; Sheets, *745 Survivor, WW-2*, 170; Davison and Law, *Boxcars and Burps*, 51-52.

16. Edgar T. Longacre to Grace McCormick, Aug. 19, 1945, Longacre MSS; Cain and Pickle, *'til Then*, 309.

17. Bass et al., eds., *Story of the Century*, 198-99; Hancock, *An Improbable Machine Gunner*, 136-37; Finkelstein et al., eds., *Regiment of the Century*, 289-308; Fishpaw, *Shavetail and the Army Nurse*, 181-98; Davison and Law, *Boxcars and Burps*, 50-53; Goos memoirs, 42.

18. Bass et al., eds., *Story of the Century*, 199-200; Finkelstein et al., eds., *Regiment of the Century*, 301-02; Drury, "The War Years—1944 to 1946," 26; Miller, *How I Took a Proficiency Exam*, 41; Resnick, "Forgotten Memories of World War II," 26.

19. Bass et al., eds., *Story of the Century*, 198; Finkelstein et al., eds., *Regiment of the Century*, 299, 302-03; Knight, *Letters Home*, 157.

20. Finkelstein et al., eds., *Regiment of the Century*, 289.

21. Bass et al., eds., *Story of the Century*, 200; Finkelstein et al., eds., *Regiment of the Century*, 291-93, 305; Tyson and Hamer, *Company L Goes to War*, 142-44; Knight, *Letters Home*, 191, 195-96, 206, 221; Drury, "The War Years—1944 to 1946," 27; Miller, *How I Took a Proficiency Exam*, 40; Bourne, *George and Me*, 105; Goos memoirs, 141-42; Edgar T. Longacre to Grace McCormick, Aug. 19, 1945, Longacre MSS; Sheets, *745 Survivor, WW-2*, 172; Davison and Law, *Boxcars and Burps*, 51; "Society of the Sons of Bitche," *Beachhead News* 2 (July 13, 1945), 1; "First Son of Bitche," *Newsletter* 37 (Feb. 1994): 5; E-mail, Henry T. Bourne (G/399) to the author, Aug. 14, 2010.

22. Jelks, *Combat Infantry Soldier*, 36-37.

23. Finkelstein et al., eds., *Regiment of the Century*, 300-03, 307; Sheets, *745 Survivor, WW-2*, 154-55; Knight, *Letters Home*, 190, 223-24; Hancock, *An Improbable Machine Gunner*, 139; Khoury, *Love Company*, 117, 122.

24. Knight, *Letters Home*, 174.

25. Cain and Pickle, *'til Then*, 313; Fishpaw, *Shavetail and the Army Nurse*, 192-93; Knight, *Letters Home*, 129-30; "C-Notes," *Newsletter* 37 (Feb. 1994): 3; Roland Giduz, "Fred Lyons," *Newsletter* 46 (Holiday Issue, 2002): 21; Drury, "The War Years—1944 to 1946," 25-26.

26. Intvw, Daniel H. Green (3 Batt. HQ/397), Sept. 16, 2006.

27. Tyson and Hamer, *Company L Goes to War*, 145; Drury, "The War Years—1944 to 1946," 28; Knight, *Letters Home*, 281; Khoury, *Love Company*, 119.

28. Bass et al., eds., *Story of the Century*, 199, 201-02; Davison and Law, *Boxcars and Burps*, 52; Knight, *Letters Home*, 211, 219-22; Cain and Pickle, *'til Then*, 340, 342.

29. Bass et al., eds., *Story of the Century*, 202; Davison and Law, *Boxcars and Burps*, 52-53; Tyson and Hamer, *Company L Goes to War*, 147; Bourne, *George and Me*, 108-09.

30. Resnick, "Forgotten Memories of World War II," 27.

BIBLIOGRAPHY

UNPUBLISHED MATERIALS

100th Division Sources

Adams, John A. "A Division Brought Up Right." George C. Marshall Research Library, Lexington, VA.

"Awards & Decorations, Medal of Honor [100th Infantry Division]." George C. Marshall Research Library, Lexington, VA.

Brower, Charles F. "Address to the 100th Infantry Division Association . . . Richmond, Virginia, September 17, 2006." George C. Marshall Research Library, Lexington, VA.

Burress, Withers A. Papers. U.S. Army Heritage and Education Center, Carlisle Barracks, PA.

Caponigro, Rocco R. Memoirs. George C. Marshall Research Library, Lexington, VA.

"City of Bitche and Its Citadel: Chronology from 12th Century to the Liberation by the 100th Infantry Division in March 1945." George C. Marshall Research Library, Lexington, VA.

Courter, John F. "Remembering." George C. Marshall Research Library, Lexington, VA.

Drury, Richard P. "The War Years—1944 to 1946." George C. Marshall Research Library, Lexington, VA.

Gerhny, Bernie, Sylvester Poncik, and Jim Hazen. "Co. 'G,' 398th Infantry: The Jagst River Crossing." George C. Marshall Research Library, Lexington, VA.

Giduz, Roland. "An amazing coincidence: His childhood doctor treated his battle injuries." George C. Marshall Research Library, Lexington, VA.

Gluesenkamp, Lester O. "Addendum to Combat." George C. Marshall Research Library, Lexington, VA.

Goos, Roger D. Memoirs. George C. Marshall Research Library, Lexington, VA.

Gurley, Franklin L. Diary and Papers. U.S. Army Heritage and Education Center, Carlisle Barracks, PA.

Handy, Arch. "Reflections on Christmas 1944." George C. Marshall Research Library, Lexington, VA.

Hazen, Jim. "The Rochester Raid." George C. Marshall Research Library, Lexington, VA.

Hildenbrand, Donald. "WWII Memoir of a GI from E/397." George C. Marshall Research Library, Lexington, VA.

Hine, John A., Jr. "The Operations of Company B, 397th Infantry (100th Infantry Division) in the Battle for Raon L'Etape, France . . . Personal Experience of a Company Commander." Submitted for the Advanced Infantry Officers Course, The Infantry School. Fort Benning, GA, 1948.

"History of the Century Division." George C. Marshall Research Library, Lexington, VA.

Howsmon, Wilfred B., Jr. "B Company in Combat, 12 November 1944 to 8 May 1945." U.S. Army Heritage and Education Center, Carlisle Barracks, Pa.

Kelly, Robert. "World War II Memories." George C. Marshall Research Library, Lexington, VA.

———. "Two Incidents in the Battle for Heilbronn." George C. Marshall Research Library, Lexington, VA.

Longacre, Edgar T. Correspondence and Diary, 1944-45. In possession of the author.

Marshall, William W. "The Battle for Raon L'Etape." George C. Marshall Research Library, Lexington, VA.

Mitchem, H. Foster, Jr. "Two Incidents in the Battle for Heilbronn." George C. Marshall Research Library, Lexington, VA.

———. "World War II Memories." George C. Marshall Research Library, Lexington, VA.

Narrative Histories, Operational Summaries, and Morning Reports, 100th Infantry Division and Its Constituent Units, November 1942-December 1945. Record Group 407, Entry 427, National Archives II, College Park, MD, copies in George C. Marshall Research Library, Lexington, VA.

Norman, Caldon. "European Odyssey." George C. Marshall Research Library, Lexington, VA.

Perrin, Harry J., Jr. "WW II: As I Saw It." George C. Marshall Research Library, Lexington, VA.

Pinnell, Samuel W. "Diary Extract—Samuel W. Pinnell." George C. Marshall Research Library, Lexington, VA.

Public Relations Office, Headquarters 100th Infantry Division. "The Fight for Bitche." George C. Marshall Research Library, Lexington, VA.

Rincker, Clarence M. "An Account of the Military Service of Clarence M. Rincker During World War II." U.S. Army Heritage and Education Center, Carlisle Barracks, PA.

Smith, Robert R. "U.S. Army Service Story, 1943-1945." George C. Marshall Research Library, Lexington, VA.

Span, Murray. Papers. U.S. Army Heritage and Education Center, Carlisle Barracks, PA.

Stegmaier, Robert M. Memoir of Vosges Mountains Campaign. George C. Marshall Research Library, Lexington, VA.

———. Papers. U.S. Army Heritage and Education Center, Carlisle Barracks, PA.

Stephens, Sam. "Someone Was with Me." George C. Marshall Research Library, Lexington, VA.

Tillett, Thomas J. Memoir of Co. H, 398th Inf. Reg. near Jagstfeld, Apr. 6-7, 1945. George C. Marshall Research Library, Lexington, VA.

———. "Memoirs (WW II)." George C. Marshall Research Library, Lexington, VA.

Tychsen, Andrew C. Papers. U.S. Army Heritage and Education Center, Carlisle Barracks, PA.

OTHER

Devers, Jacob L. Papers. Historical Society of York County, York, PA.

"Enemy Operations Overview." 2 vols. George C. Marshall Research Library, Lexington, VA.

Jenkins, Reuben E. Papers. U.S. Army Heritage and Education Center, Carlisle Barracks, PA.

"War Diary of the 17th SS-Panzer-Grenadier Division, 'Gotz vom Berlichifen,' January-April 1945." George C. Marshall Research Library, Lexington, VA.

NEWSPAPERS AND NEWSLETTERS

Beachhead News (HQ, VI Army Corps)

Century Sentinel (HQ, 100th Inf. Div.)

Charlotte (NC) *Observer*

Columbia (SC) *Record*

Fort Bragg Post

Guidon (HQ, 100th Signal Co.)

On the Alert (HQ, 398th Inf. Reg.)

100th Infantry Division Association Newsletter. 53 vols. to date, September 1958- .

Powder Horn (HQ, 399th Inf. Reg.)

Red Raider (HQ, 1st Batt., 399th Inf. Reg.)

Regimental Review (HQ, 397th Inf. Reg.)

Stars and Stripes

Yank: The Army Weekly

BOOKS AND ARTICLES

100th Division Sources

Altieri, Anthony P. et al, eds. *Combat Company: U.S. Army, 399th Infantry Regiment, G Company*. Kirchheim unter Teck: Weixier, 1945.

"And We Did": The History of the 925th Field Artillery Battalion. Stuttgart: Stuttgarter Vereinsbuch Druckerei, 1945.

Angier, John D. *A 4-F Goes to War with the 100th Infantry Division*. Bennington, VT: Merriam Press, 2008.

Bass, Michael et al., eds. *The Story of the Century*. New York: Criterion Linotype & Printing, 1946.

Battery Adjust: The Story of the Fraser Fire Direction in Combat [373rd Field Artillery Battalion]. Stuttgart-Vaihlingen: Karl Scharr, Worner & Mayer, 1945.

Bingham, Hal. *Sons of Bitche*. Gainesville, FL: privately issued, n.d.

Bonn, Keith E. *Friends and Enemies of the Century: Military Units Which Supported or Opposed the 100th Infantry Division in the European Theater of Operations, 1944-45*. Bedford, PA: Aberjona Press, 2001.

Bonte, Kenneth P. *Never Too Young: A Journey with the Century*. N.p.: privately issued, n.d.

Boston, Bernard, ed. *History of the 398th Infantry Regiment in World War II*. Washington, DC: Infantry Journal, 1947.

Bourne, Henry T., Jr. *George and Me: The Saga of an Infantryman in World War II and the Company with Whom He Fought*. Woodstock, VT: privately issued, 1987.

Bowman, B. Lowry, and Paul S. Mosher. *Company I, WW II Combat History, October 1944 through April 1945 . . . 3rd Battalion, 397th Infantry Regiment, 100th Infantry Division*. Abingdon, VA: L. Bowman, 1996.

Bruner, D.W. et al. *Able in Combat: Co. A, 399th Inf. Rgt., 100th Division*. N.p.: The Regiment, 1945.

Cain, Catherine, and William Clifton Pickle. *'til Then . . . They Are Love Letters*. Olive Branch, MS: C&C, 2004.

Cannon Company, 399th Infantry. N.p.: privately issued, 1946.

Cole, Ernest L. *A Soldier's Journal*. N.p.: privately issued, 1995.

Combat Actions of Communications Platoon, 1st Bn., 397th Infantry. Stuttgart: Chr. Scheffele, 1945.

Combat History, Company "B," 325th Medical Battalion. Stuttgart: Stahle & Friedel, 1945.

Company D, 399th Infantry. Stuttgart: D Co., 399th Infantry Regiment, 1946.

Curtis, Martin H. *Situation Tactical: Memoirs of World War II Army Combat in the European Theater of Operations*. Pittsburgh: Dorrance Publishing, 2004.

Davison, Craig, and William J. Law. *Boxcars and Burps*. N.p.: privately issued, 2004.

Drewry, Fred. *100 Cav. Ren. Tr. [Cavalry Reconnaissance Troop]*. N.p.: privately issued, 1945.

Fair, Robert R. *Some Memories*. Charlottesville, VA: privately issued, 1997.

Finkelstein, Samuel et al., eds. *Regiment of the Century: The Story of the 397th Infantry Regiment*. Stuttgart: Stahle & Friedel, 1945.

Fishpaw, Eli. *The Shavetail and the Army Nurse: The Bride Wore Olive Drab*. DeLand, FL: privately issued, 1998.

Gluesenkamp, Lester O. *A Short Interval in the Life of a G.I. in World War II*. Alma, IL: privately issued, ca. 1995.

Gurley, Franklin Louis. *Into the Mountains Dark: A WWII Odyssey from Harvard Crimson to Infantry Blue*. Bedford, PA: Aberjona Press, 2000.

———, ed. *399th in Action: With the 100th Infantry Division*. Stuttgart: Stuttgarter Vereinsbuch Druckerei, 1945.

Hancock, Frank E. *An Improbable Machine Gunner*. Madison, AL: privately issued, 1997.

Headquarters Company of the 397th Infantry Regiment. Stuttgart: Stahle & Friedel, 1945.

Herbert, Paul H. *Robert Earle Herman, American Soldier*. N.p.: privately issued, n.d.

The History of the 375th F. A. Bn. [Field Artillery Battalion]. Stuttgart: privately issued, 1945.

Jelks, Thomas O. *Memoirs of a Combat Infantry Soldier*. Baltimore: privately issued, n.d.

Khoury, John M. *Love Company: L Company, 399th Infantry Regiment, of the 100th Infantry Division during World War II and Beyond*. Maywood, NJ: Chi Chi Press, 2003.

Kirsch, Robert E., and Joseph T. Mete, eds. *Mission Accomplished: Written for and by Cannon Company, 397th Infantry, 100th Infantry Division*. Stuttgart: Union Druckerei, 1945.

Knight, Arthur C. *Letters Home from a WW II 100th Division Soldier*. Missoula, MT: Big Sky Press, 1999.

Lindsey, A. L. *A Soda Jerk Goes to War*. Stanton, TX: privately issued, 2001.

Longacre, Edward G., ed. "From Slugger to Cannon Lugger." *America in WW II* 1 (June 2005): 8-13.

Megna, Mark A. *B Co., 399th Inf: France [and] Germany*. Stuttgart: B Co., 399th Inf. Regt., 1945.

Miller, Bernard S., Jr. *How I Took a Proficiency Exam . . . and Joined "The Greatest Generation"*. N.p.: privately issued, n.d.

Mosher, Paul S. *Sketches of WW II: A Personal Memoir*. Dallas, TX: privately issued, 1993.

Noor, John J. et al., eds. *ETO History of Anti Tank Company, 397th Infantry*. Esslingen-Neckar: F. & W. Mayer, 1945.

Norman, Caldon R. *Whatever Happened to Company A?* Portland, OR: privately issued, 1991.

O'Brien, Jack. *Recollections of WW II*. Santa Ana, CA: privately issued, 1996.

One Hundredth Signal Company. N.p.: privately issued, ca. 1945.

Past in Review: The History of the 374th Field Artillery Battalion, 100th Infantry Division. N.p.: privately issued, 1945.

Pollard, H. E. *Plowboy to Doughboy*. Riggins, ID: privately issued, n.d.

Posess, Stanley, ed. *Memories of a Remarkable General and Gentleman, Lieutenant General Withers A. Burress*. Beechhurst, NY: privately issued, n.d.

Program for North Carolina Industrialists . . . 100th Division, Fort Bragg, N.C. N.p.: privately issued, 1944.

Remember When? History of Fox Company, 398th Infantry, 100th Division, 7th Army, Europe, 1944-1945. Fellbach: Julius Schwertschlag, 1945.

Ross, John M., ed. *Century 100 Division Pictorial Review, 1944*. Atlanta: Albert Love Enterprises, 1944.

———. "Two Trips to Hell . . . 100th Infantry Division." *Saga* (July 1962): 40-45, 76-78.

Sheets, John L. *745 Survivor, WW-2: Combat Infantry Rifleman*. Sugarcreek, OH: Carlisle Printing, 2000.

Sperling, Philip et al. *Medics of the Century: 325th Medical Battalion, 100th Infantry Division*. Stuttgart: Stahle & Friedel, 1945.

Story of the Century: U.S. Army, 100th Infantry Division. Baton Rouge, LA: Army & Navy Publishing, 1961.

Tessmer, Robert G. *A Soldier's Story: World War II as Seen by a Combat Veteran, December 6, 1943 through April 10, 1946*. Dearborn, MI: privately issued, ca. 1994.

Thompson, Walton R., ed. *This Is George: U.S. Army, 398th Infantry Regiment, G Company*. Stuttgart-Bad Cannstatt: Dr. Cantz, 1945.

Tyson, George F., Jr., and Robert V. Hamer, Jr. *Company L Goes to War*. Bedford, PA: Aegis Consulting Group, 2004.

Vinick, Richard T. *Headquarters and Headquarters Battery, 100th Infantry Division*. Stuttgart-Vaihlingen: Karl Scharr, Worner, & Meyer, 1945.

Watson, William C. *First-Class Privates*. Atlanta: privately issued, 1994.

Waxman, Donald A. et al. *A History of Company C, 399th Infantry*. N.p.: privately issued, 1945.

Weber, Gerald C. *Gerald's WW II*. Louisville, KY: Chicago Spectrum Press, 2007.

Wiegand, Brandon T. *Index to the General Orders of the 100th Infantry Division in World War II*. Creighton, PA: D-Day Militaria, 2005.

Williams, Edward J., ed. *33 Months with the One Hundredth Signal Company, 100th Infantry Division*. Stuttgart: Stuttgarter Vereinsbuch Druckerei, 1945.

Winston, Keith. *V-Mail: Letters of a World War II Combat Medic*. Edited by Sarah Winston. Chapel Hill, NC: Algonquin Books of Chapel Hill, 1985.

OTHER

Ambrose, Stephen E. *Citizen Soldiers: The U.S. Army from the Normandy Beaches to the Bulge to the Surrender of Germany, June 7, 1944-May 7, 1945*. New York: Simon & Schuster, 1997.

———. *The Supreme Commander: The War Years of General Dwight D. Eisenhower*. Garden City, NY: Doubleday, 1970.

Astor, Gerald. *A Blood-Dimmed Tide: The Battle of the Bulge by the Men Who Fought It*. New York: Dell, 1993.

Beck, Gunther. *Die Letzten Sage des 2. Weltfrieges im Kaum Heilbronn*. N.p.: privately issued, n.d.

Blasi, Hubert, and Christhard Schrenk. *Heilbronn 1944/45: Leben und Sterben einer Stadt*. Heilbronn: Quellen and Forschungen zur Geschichte det Stadt Heilbronn, 1995.

Bonn, Keith E. *When the Odds Were Even: The Vosges Mountains Campaign, October 1944-January 1945*. New York: Ballantine Books, 2006.

Bradley, Omar N. *A Soldier's Story*. New York: Henry Holt, 1951.

Breuer, William B. *Operation Dragoon: The Invasion of Southern France*. Novato, CA: Presidio Press, 1987.

———. *Storming Hitler's Rhine: The Allied Assault, February-March 1945*. New York: St. Martin's Press, 1985.

Bryant, Arthur. *Triumph in the West, 1943-1946: Based on the Diaries and Autobiographical Notes of Field Marshal The Viscount Alanbrooke, K.G., O.M.* London: Collins, 1959.

Carter, Kit C., and Robert Mueller, comps. *Combat Chronology, 1941-1945: U.S. Army Air Forces in World War II*. Washington, DC: Center for Air Force History, 1991.

Chandler, Alfred D., Jr., et al., eds. *The Papers of Dwight David Eisenhower: The War Years*. 5 vols. Baltimore: Johns Hopkins Press, 1970.

Clarke, Jeffrey J. *Southern France, 15 August-14 September 1944 (U.S. Army*

Campaigns of World War II). Washington, DC: Center of Military History, United States Army, ca. 1994.

———, and Robert Ross Smith. *Riviera to the Rhine (United States Army in World War II: The European Theater of Operations)*. Washington, DC: Center of Military History, United States Army, 1993.

Cohn, Bernard J., comp. *Catalog of Material from the National Archives: Military Reports, After-Action Reports, Morning Reports, Signal Corps Pictures, WW II*. Glen Burnie, MD: privately issued, 2005.

Cole, Hugh. *The Battle of the Bulge*. Old Saybrook, CT: William S. Konecky Associates, 2001.

Colley, David P. *Decision at Strasbourg: Ike's Strategic Mistake to Halt the Sixth Army Group at the Rhine in 1944*. Annapolis, MD: Naval Institute Press, 2008.

Controvich, James T. *United States Army Unit Histories: A Reference and Bibliography*. Manhattan, KS: Military Affairs/Aerospace Historian Publishers, 1983.

De Lattre de Tassigny, Jean. *The History of the First French Army*. Translated by Malcolm Barnes. London: Allen & Unwin, 1952.

D'Este, Carlo. *Patton: A Genius for War*. New York: HarperCollins, 1995.

Devers, Jacob L. "Operation Dragoon: The Invasion of Southern France." *Military Affairs* 10 (Summer 1946): 2-41.

Eisenhower, Dwight D. *Crusade in Europe*. Garden City, NY: Doubleday, 1948.

———. *Report by the Supreme Commander to the Combined Chiefs of Staff on the Operations in Europe of the Allied Expeditionary Force, 8 June 1944 to 8 May 1945*. Washington, DC: U.S. Army Center of Military History, 1994.

Eisenhower, John S. D. *The Bitter Woods: The Dramatic Story . . . of the Crisis That Shook the Western Coalition. . . .* New York: G. P. Putnam's Sons, 1969.

Elstob, Peter. *Hitler's Last Offensive*. London: Secker & Warburg, 1971.

Endkampf Zwischen Mosel und Inn: XIII.SS-Armeekorps. Osnabruck: Munn Verlag GmbH, 1976.

Engler, Richard E., Jr. *The Final Crisis: Combat in Northern Alsace, January 1945*. Bedford, PA: Aberjona Press, 1999.

Gaujac, Paul. *US Field Artillery in World War II, 1941-45*. Translated by Roger Branfill-Cook. Paris: Histoire & Collections, 2009.

Gauss, Werner. *Alt-Heilbronn: Wie Wir Es Kannten und Liebten*. Heilbronn: Gauss-Verlag, 1952.

Gurley, Franklin Louis. "Policy versus Strategy: The Defense of Strasbourg in Winter 1944-1945." *Journal of Military History* 58 (1994): 481-514.

Gunther, Helmut. *Die Sturmflut und das Ende: Geschichte der 17.SS-Pz. Gren. Division, "Gotz von Berlichingen."* Munchen: Schild Verlag, 2000.

Kahn, E. J., Jr., and H. McLemore. *Fighting Divisions.* Washington, DC: Infantry Journal Press, 1945.

Liddell Hart, Basil. *History of the Second World War.* New York: G. P. Putnam's Sons, 1970.

Longacre, Edward G. "Heilbronn: One Last Place to Die." *America in WW II* 5 (March-April 2010): 26-35.

MacDonald, Charles B. *The Last Offensive (United States Army in World War II: The European Theater of Operations).* Washington, DC: Office of the Chief of Military History, 1973.

——. *The Siegfried Line Campaign (United States Army in World War II: The European Theater of Operations).* Washington, DC: Center of Military History, United States Army, 1990.

——. *A Time for Trumpets: The Untold Story of the Battle of the Bulge.* New York: Harper Perennial, 1997.

Mansoor, Peter R. *The G.I. Offensive in Europe: The Triumph of American Infantry Divisions, 1941-1945.* Lawrence: University Press of Kansas, 1999.

Markey, Michael A. *Jake: The General from West York Avenue.* York, PA: Historical Society of York County, 1998.

McManus, John C. *Alamo in the Ardennes: The Untold Story of the American Soldiers Who Made the Defense of Bastogne Possible.* New York: John Wiley & Sons, 2007.

Merriam, Robert E. *The Battle of the Bulge.* New York: Ballantine Books, 1972.

Minott, Rodney G. *The Fortress That Never Was: The Myth of Hitler's Bavarian Stronghold.* New York: Holt, Rinehart & Winston, 1964.

Mohr, G. William. *Third Infantry Division, WW II: The Victory Path Thru France and Germany.* Kokomo, IN: O & M, 1985.

Mueller, Ralph, and Jerry Turk. *Report After Action: The Story of the 103rd Infantry Division.* Innsbruck: Wagner'sche Universitas-Buchdruckerie, 1945.

Murray, G. E. Patrick. "Eisenhower as Ground-Forces Commander: The British Viewpoint." In *Beyond Combat: Essays in Military History in Honor of Russell F. Weigley,* edited by Edward G. Longacre and Theodore J. Zeman, 153–86. Philadelphia: American Philosophical Society, 2007.

——. *Eisenhower versus Montgomery: The Continuing Debate.* Westport, CT: Praeger, 1996.

Nobecourt, Jacques. *Hitler's Last Gamble: The Battle of the Bulge.* Translated by R. H. Barry. New York: Schocken Books, 1967.

Parker, Danny S., ed. *The Battle of the Bulge: The German View*. London: Greenhill Books, 1999.

Pogue, Forrest C. *George C. Marshall, Organizer of Victory, 1943-1945*. New York: Viking Press, 1973.

Pommois, Lise M. *Winter Storm: War in Northern Alsace, November 1944-March 1945*. Paducah, KY: Turner Publishing, 1991.

Report of Operations, Seventh United States Army in France and Germany, 1944-1945. 3 vols. Heidelberg: Aloys Graf, 1946.

Ruppenthal, Roland G. *Logistical Support of the Armies (United States Army in World War II: The European Theater of Operations)*. 2 vols. Washington, DC: Center of Military History, United States Army, 1995.

Sawicki, James A. *Infantry Regiments of the US Army*. Dumfries, VA: Wyvern Publications, 1981.

Sayen, John J., Jr. *US Army Infantry Divisions, 1942-43*. Oxford: Osprey Publishing, 2006.

———. *US Army Infantry Divisions, 1944-45*. Oxford: Osprey Publishing, 2007.

Staff of the 100th Infantry Division. "Battle of Bitche." *Military Review* 26 (October 1946): 36-40.

Stanton, Shelby L. *World War II Order of Battle: An Encyclopedic Reference to the Army Ground Force from Battalion through Division, 1939-1946*. rev. ed. Mechanicsburg, PA: Stackpole Books, 2006.

Stober, Hans. *Die Sturmflut und das Ende: Die Geschichte der 17.SS-Panzerdivision, "Gotz von Berlichingen": Band II. Die Deiche Brechen*. Munchen: Schild Verlag, 2000.

Toland, John. *Battle: The Story of the Bulge*. Lincoln, NE: University of Nebraska Press, 1999.

———. *The Last 100 Days*. New York: Random House, 1965.

Tucker-Jones, Anthony. *Operation Dragoon: The Liberation of Southern France, 1944*. South Yorkshire: Pen and Sword, 2010.

Turner, John Frayn, and Robert Jackson. *Destination Berchtesgaden: The Story of the United States Seventh Army in World War II*. London: Ian Allan, 1975.

Vannoy, Allyn. "American Stubbornness at Rimling." www.militaryhistoryonline.com/wwII/articles/rimling.aspx.

———. "House to House in the German Heartland." *Military Heritage* 7 (April 2006): 42-51.

Weigley, Russell F. *Eisenhower's Lieutenants: The Campaigns of France and Germany, 1944-1945*. Bloomington: Indiana University Press, 1981.

Whiting, Charles. *America's Forgotten Army: The Story of the U.S. Seventh*.

New York: St. Martin's Press, 2001.

———. *The Other Battle of the Bulge: Operation Northwind.* Gloucestershire: Spellmount Publishers, 2007.

———. *Siegfried: The Nazis' Last Stand.* New York: Cooper Square Press, 2001.

Wilmot, Chester. *The Struggle for Europe.* New York: Harper & Row, 1963.

Wyant, William K. *Sandy Patch: A Biography of Lt. Gen. Alexander M. Patch.* Westport, CT: Praeger, 1991.

Yeide, Harry, and Mark Stout. *First to the Rhine: The 6th Army Group in World War II.* Saint Paul, MN: Zenith Press, 2007.

Zaloga, Steven. *Operation* Dragoon *1944: France's Other D-Day.* Oxford: Osprey Publishing, 2009.

———. *US Field Artillery of World War II.* Oxford: Osprey Publishing, 2007.

Zoepf, Wolf T. *Seven Days in January with the 6th SS-Mountain Division in Operation NORDWIND.* Bedford, PA: Aberjona Press, 2001.

INTERVIEWS

Bourne, Henry T., Jr. (Pvt., G Co., 399th Inf.)

Cleveland, Earl L. (Pvt., D Co., 399th Inf.)

Collie, Joseph H. (Pvt., B Co., 397th Inf.)

Dobkowski, Peter C. (Pvt., M Co., 399th Inf.)

Fair, Robert R. (Cpl., D Co., 399th Inf.)

Good, John A. (T.Sgt., H Co., 398th Inf.)

Green, Daniel H. (1st Sgt., 3rd Batt., 397th Inf.)

Jelks, Thomas O. (Pvt., M Co., 397th Inf.)

Law, William J. (Maj., 2nd Batt., 397th Inf.)

Lorenzo, Louis E. (Tech. 5, HQ Co., 397th Inf.)

Miller, Bernard S., Jr. (Pvt., G Co., 399th Inf.)

Plamp, John E., Jr., (Pvt., M Co., 398th Inf.)

Rawlins, Herman E. (Pvt., A Co., 398th Inf.)

Resnick, Samuel L. (Pvt., D Co., 399th Inf.)

Smith, J. Peter (Pvt., B Co., 398th Inf.)

Smith, Robert R. (Pvt., B Co., 398th Inf.)

Stamp, Robert J. (Pvt., HQ Co., 397th Inf.)

Tessmer, Robert G. (S.Sgt., I Co., 397th Inf.)

Tillett, Thomas J. (Sgt., H Co., 398th Inf.)

Witt, Roger F. (Pvt., H Co., 398th Inf.)

MAPS

100th Division Maps. George C. Marshall Research Library, Lexington, VA.

Operations of the 100th Infantry Division in the European Theater of
  Operations (five maps). George C. Marshall Research Library, Lexington,
  VA.

WEB SITES

"The 100th Infantry Division in WW II." www.100thww2.org.

"World War II Army Specialized Training Program (ASTP)."
  www.astpww2.org.

INDEX

ACKNOWLEDGMENTS

My first debt is to my father, Edgar T. Longacre, who served in the 397th Infantry Regiment's cannon company with the rank of technical sergeant. (Dad deliberately failed his qualifying exam for Officer Candidate School, but that's another story.) My interest in his war career—heightened when I discovered some years ago the diary he kept of the last weeks of the war in France and Germany—prompted me to write this book. I only wish I had embarked on the project before his death in 1998.

I am equally indebted to those Centurymen who shared their wartime experiences in the form of written memoirs or personal interviews. I am also grateful to the widows of two veterans. Mrs. Yvonne Chany of Palmyra, Pennsylvania, wife of Sgt. Kalman J. Chany of the Headquarters Battery, 374th Field Artillery Battalion, supplied many helpful sources, including articles from back issues of the *100th Infantry Division Association Newsletter*. Mrs. Louise Lieber of Dallas, Texas, gave permission to quote from the memoirs of her husband, Sgt. Paul S. Mosher of I Company, 397th Infantry Regiment.

My research was facilitated by the excellent support of the staff of the George C. Marshall Research Library, Lexington, Virginia, which houses the most complete collection of source materials relating to the Century Division, including written and oral memoirs; division, regimental, battalion, and company reports; and all manner of unit memorabilia. Special thanks go to Paul B. Barron, director of library and archives, and Jeffrey Kozak, assistant librarian.

The U.S. Army Heritage and Education Center, Carlisle Barracks, Pennsylvania, is another major repository of research material relating to the division. Holdings include the papers of the Century's commander, Maj. Gen. Withers A. Burress; the assistant commander, Brig. Gen. Andrew C. Tychsen; and Pvt. Franklin L. Gurley (A Company, 399th Infantry), the chief historian of his regiment and later of the division itself. Here I was ably assisted by the late Dr. Art Bergeron as well as by Michael Lynch, Rich Baker, Steve Bye, Clif Hyatt, Rodney Foytik, and David Pearson.

Thanks are also due to the officers and members of the 100th Infantry Division Association, especially its vice president for systems, Henry B. "Hank" Williams; Patti Bonn, managing editor; and Tom Bourne, who edits the monthly *100th Infantry Division Association E-News*. Patti's late husband, Keith E. Bonn, author of *When the Odds Were Even* and other seminal studies of Seventh Army and Century Division operations, was instrumental in helping this project get started.

Several friends and acquaintances assisted with research. Prof. G. E. Patrick Murray of Valley Forge Military College, Wayne, Pennsylvania, gave me a deeper understanding of Allied strategy, 1944–45. Dr. Adrian Wheat (Colonel, U.S. Army, Retired), of Yorktown, Virginia, advised on health and medical topics relevant to World War II soldiers. Bob Toguchi (Colonel, U.S. Army, Retired), of Grafton, Virginia, provided from personal experience information on the Schlieffen Barracks in Heilbronn, Germany (later the U.S. Army's Wharton Barracks).

An article I wrote on the fighting at Heilbronn appeared in *America in WW II*. For various favors I thank the magazine's editor, Jim Kushlan, as well as David Deis, who drew a map to accompany the article that formed the basis for the more detailed map of the battle that appears in this book. That map and the other excellent terrain and operational maps are the work of Paul Dangel of Berwyn, Pennsylvania. Bill Godfrey of Hampton, Virginia, handled copy photography most efficiently.

For editorial support and encouragement, I thank my publisher, Bruce H. Franklin, himself a World War II historian, and Ron Silverman, my thoroughgoing editor.

Several family members assisted in one way or another. My cousin Barbara McCormick shared the V-Mail that my father sent her mother during the war. My brother, Lawrence T. Longacre, was a source of information on World War II-era artillery. My wife, Melody Ann Longacre, served throughout as my research assistant. My daughter, Kathryn R. Hamilton, helped interview those veterans whose reminiscences are critical to a thorough telling of the Century's story. Last but not least, my thirteen-year-old granddaughter, LeAnn Hamilton, taught a technologically challenged author the ins and outs of a new word-processing program.